J. Michael Straczynsk

RISING STARS®

Voices of the Dead / BRIGHT

This is the story of
how we came to be.
Of what happened to us,
and to those we knew,
and loved, and fought.
Where it went right...
And where it went wrong.

Sixty years.

One hundred and thirteen people,
born with the power.

The story of the
world we touched.
And all the places where
the world touched us.

And the terror
and the beauty
and the death
that happened in
the spaces in-between.

Our kind has never been seen before.
And when the last of us are gone,
will never be seen again.
Because there is a secret behind our creation,
and secrets like this only come around once.

J. Michael Straczynski's

RISING STARS®

Voices of the Dead / BRIGHT

Rising Stars created by
J. Michael Straczynski

Rising Stars:
Voices of the Dead
and
Bright
written by
Fiona Avery

for Top Cow Productions
Marc Silvestri_chief executive officer
Matt Hawkins_president / chief operating officer
Renae Geerlings_editor in chief
Chaz Riggs_production manager
Rob Levin_editor
Annie Pham_marketing director
Peter Lam_webmaster
Phil Smith_trades and submissions
Scott Newman_intern

for this edition
Book Design and Layout by:
Phil Smith

for Image Comics
publisher Erik Larsen

ISBN # 1-58240-613-8
Published by Image Comics®
Rising Stars volume 4 trade paperback 2006 First Printing.

Table of Contents

Voices of the Dead

BRIGHT

Cover Gallery

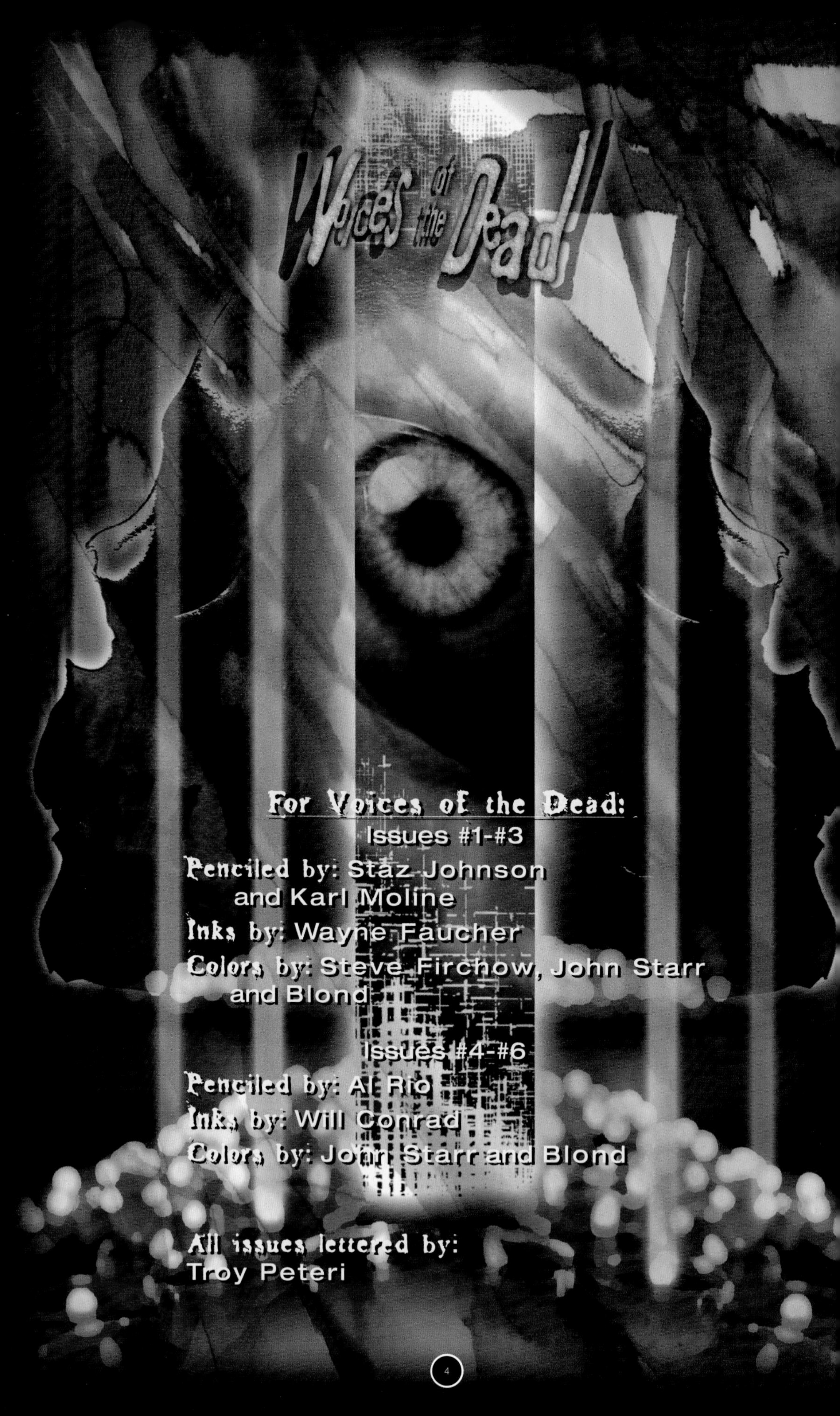
Voices of the Dead

For Voices of the Dead:

Issues #1-#3

Penciled by: Staz Johnson and Karl Moline

Inks by: Wayne Faucher

Colors by: Steve Firchow, John Starr and Blond

Issues #4-#6

Penciled by: Al Rio

Inks by: Will Conrad

Colors by: John Starr and Blond

All issues lettered by: Troy Peteri

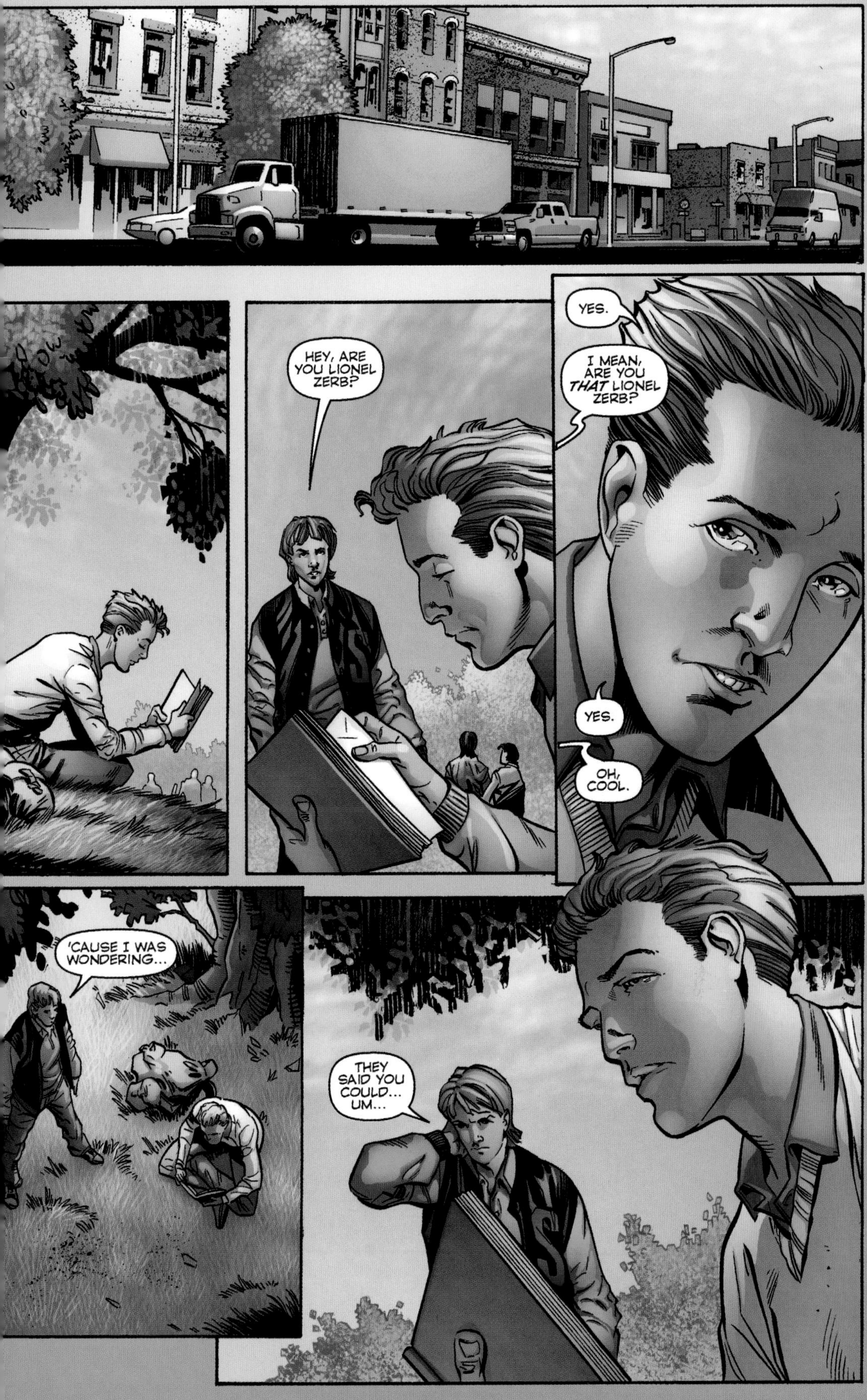

HEY, ARE YOU LIONEL ZERB?
YES.
I MEAN, ARE YOU *THAT* LIONEL ZERB?
YES.
OH, COOL.
'CAUSE I WAS WONDERING...
THEY SAID YOU COULD... UM...

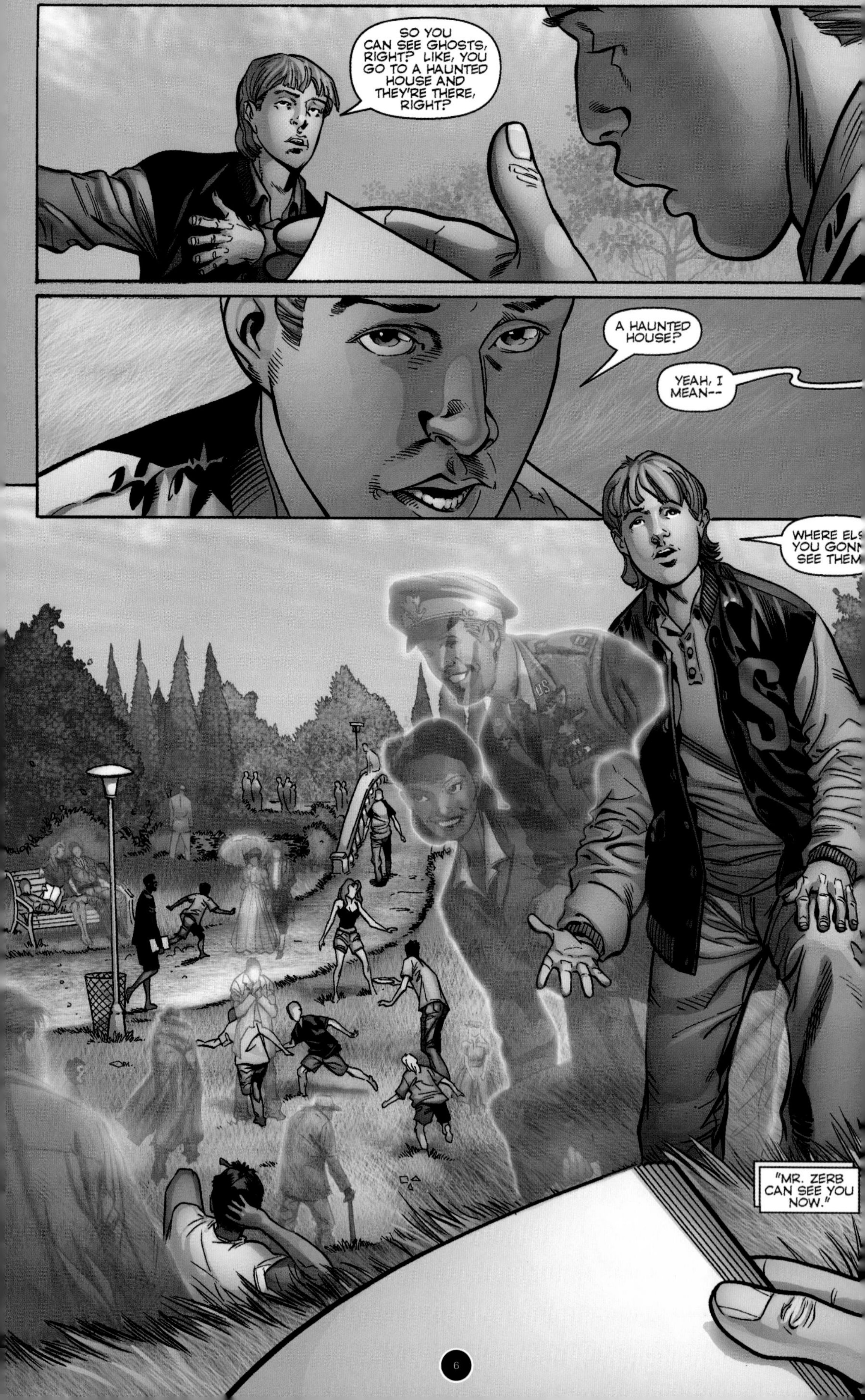

SO YOU CAN SEE GHOSTS, RIGHT? LIKE, YOU GO TO A HAUNTED HOUSE AND THEY'RE THERE, RIGHT?
A HAUNTED HOUSE?
YEAH, I MEAN--
WHERE ELS YOU GONN SEE THEM
"MR. ZERB CAN SEE YOU NOW."

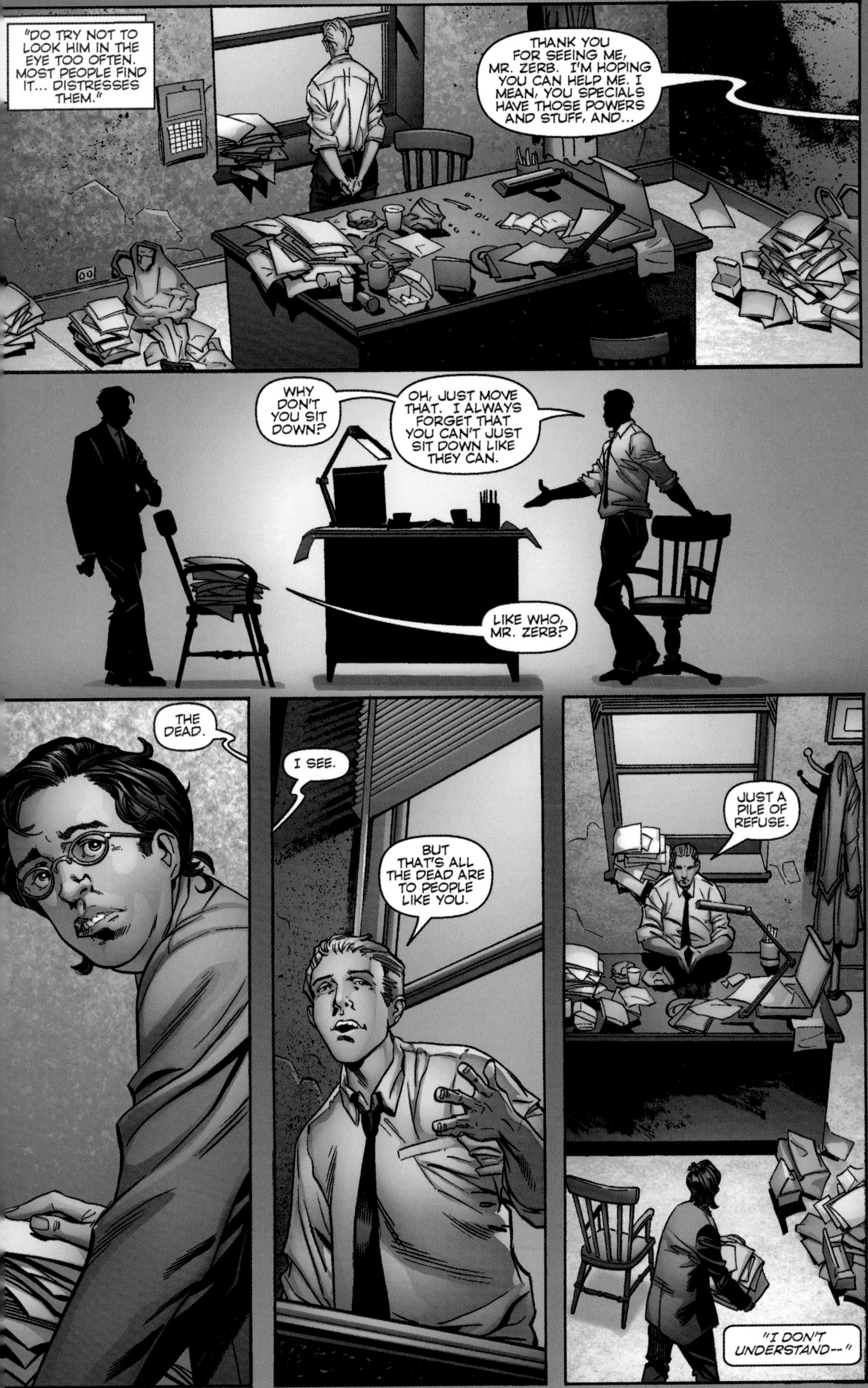
"DO TRY NOT TO LOOK HIM IN THE EYE TOO OFTEN. MOST PEOPLE FIND IT... DISTRESSES THEM."
THANK YOU FOR SEEING ME, MR. ZERB. I'M HOPING YOU CAN HELP ME. I MEAN, YOU SPECIALS HAVE THOSE POWERS AND STUFF, AND...
WHY DON'T YOU SIT DOWN?
OH, JUST MOVE THAT. I ALWAYS FORGET THAT YOU CAN'T JUST SIT DOWN LIKE THEY CAN.
LIKE WHO, MR. ZERB?
THE DEAD.
I SEE.
BUT THAT'S ALL THE DEAD ARE TO PEOPLE LIKE YOU.
JUST A PILE OF REFUSE.
"I DON'T UNDERSTAND--"

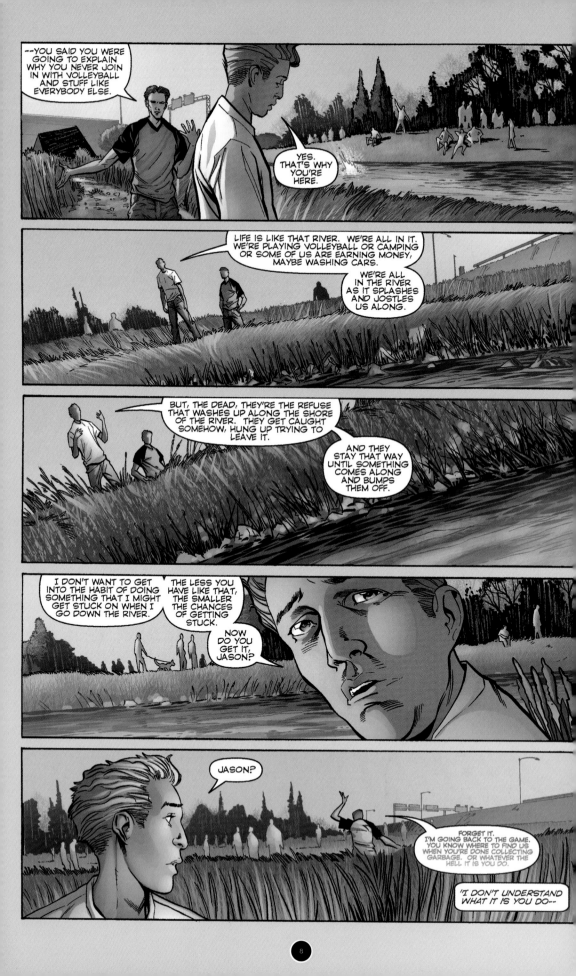

--YOU SAID YOU WERE GOING TO EXPLAIN WHY YOU NEVER JOIN IN WITH VOLLEYBALL AND STUFF LIKE EVERYBODY ELSE.

YES. THAT'S WHY YOU'RE HERE.

LIFE IS LIKE THAT RIVER. WE'RE ALL IN IT. WE'RE PLAYING VOLLEYBALL OR CAMPING OR SOME OF US ARE EARNING MONEY, MAYBE WASHING CARS.

WE'RE ALL IN THE RIVER AS IT SPLASHES AND JOSTLES US ALONG.

BUT, THE DEAD, THEY'RE THE REFUSE THAT WASHES UP ALONG THE SHORE OF THE RIVER. THEY GET CAUGHT SOMEHOW, HUNG UP TRYING TO LEAVE IT.

AND THEY STAY THAT WAY UNTIL SOMETHING COMES ALONG AND BUMPS THEM OFF.

I DON'T WANT TO GET INTO THE HABIT OF DOING SOMETHING THAT I MIGHT GET STUCK ON WHEN I GO DOWN THE RIVER.

THE LESS YOU HAVE LIKE THAT, THE SMALLER THE CHANCES OF GETTING STUCK.

NOW DO YOU GET IT, JASON?

JASON?

FORGET IT. I'M GOING BACK TO THE GAME. YOU KNOW WHERE TO FIND US WHEN YOU'RE DONE COLLECTING GARBAGE. OR WHATEVER THE HELL IT IS YOU DO.

"I DON'T UNDERSTAND WHAT IT IS YOU DO--

8

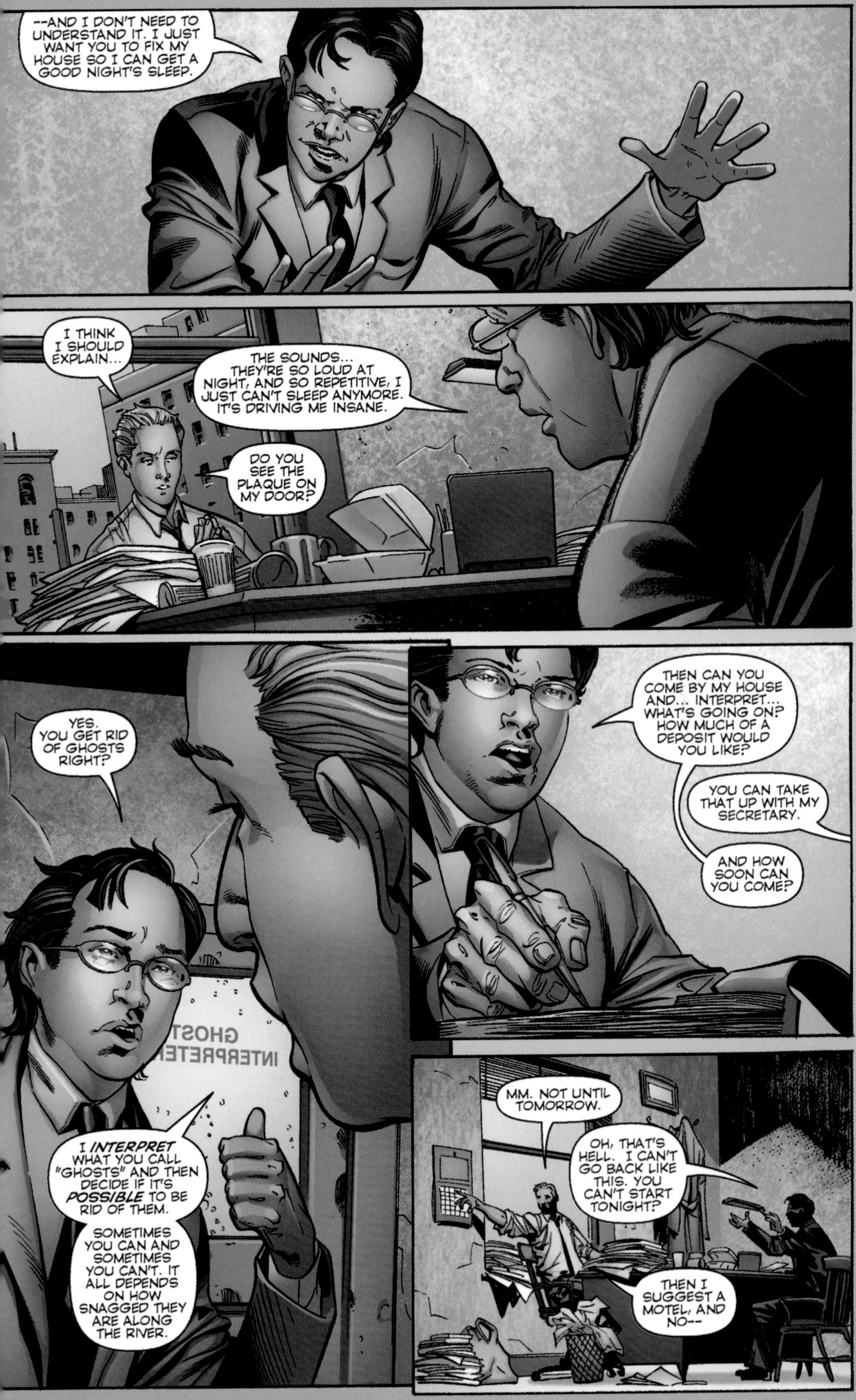

--AND I DON'T NEED TO UNDERSTAND IT. I JUST WANT YOU TO FIX MY HOUSE SO I CAN GET A GOOD NIGHT'S SLEEP.
I THINK I SHOULD EXPLAIN...
THE SOUNDS... THEY'RE SO LOUD AT NIGHT, AND SO REPETITIVE, I JUST CAN'T SLEEP ANYMORE. IT'S DRIVING ME INSANE.
DO YOU SEE THE PLAQUE ON MY DOOR?
YES. YOU GET RID OF GHOSTS RIGHT?
GHOST
INTERPRETER
I *INTERPRET* WHAT YOU CALL "GHOSTS" AND THEN DECIDE IF IT'S *POSSIBLE* TO BE RID OF THEM.
SOMETIMES YOU CAN AND SOMETIMES YOU CAN'T. IT ALL DEPENDS ON HOW SNAGGED THEY ARE ALONG THE RIVER.
THEN CAN YOU COME BY MY HOUSE AND... INTERPRET... WHAT'S GOING ON? HOW MUCH OF A DEPOSIT WOULD YOU LIKE?
YOU CAN TAKE THAT UP WITH MY SECRETARY.
AND HOW SOON CAN YOU COME?
MM. NOT UNTIL TOMORROW.
OH, THAT'S HELL. I CAN'T GO BACK LIKE THIS. YOU CAN'T START TONIGHT?
THEN I SUGGEST A MOTEL, AND NO--

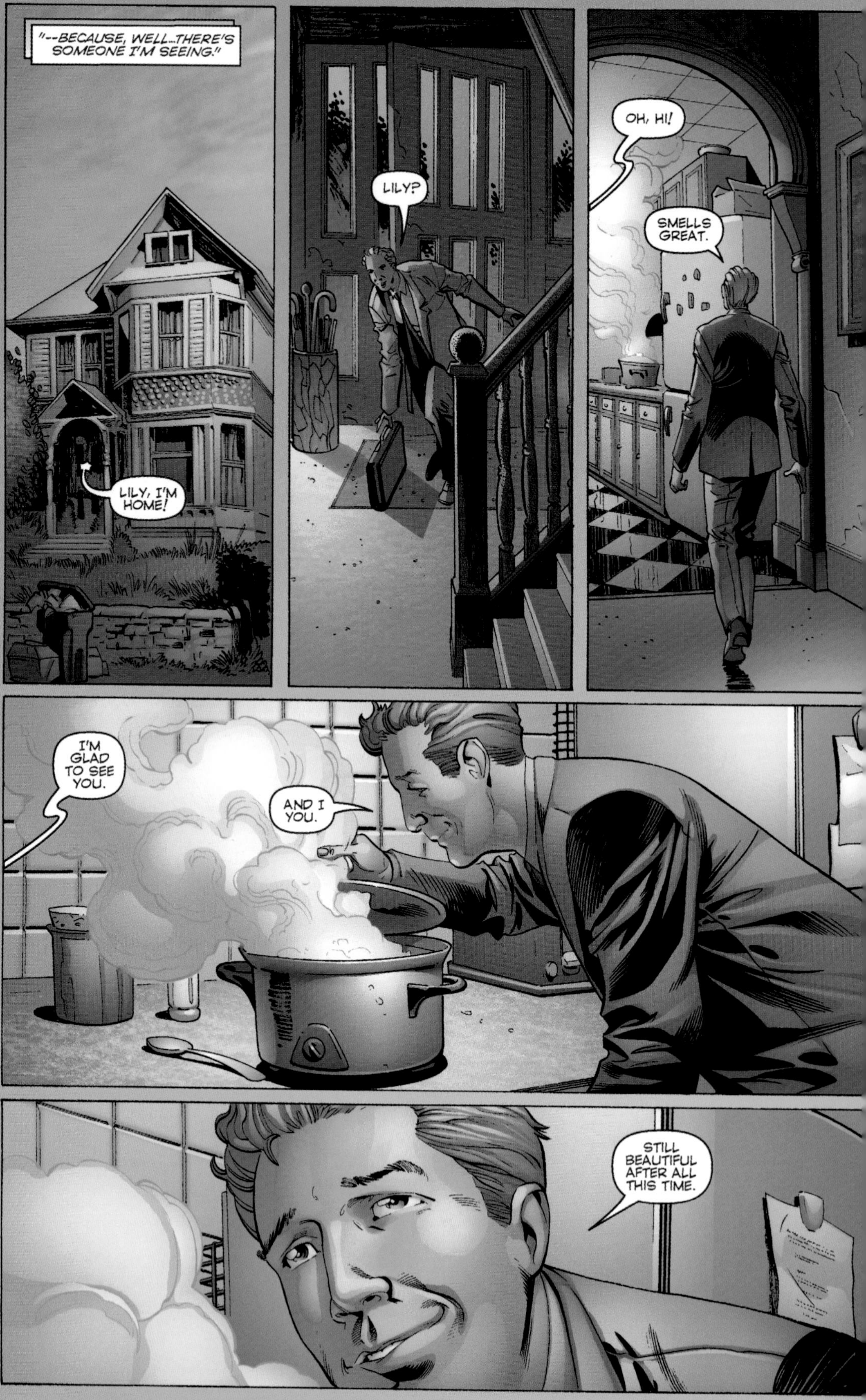
"--BECAUSE, WELL...THERE'S SOMEONE I'M SEEING."
LILY, I'M HOME!
LILY?
OH, HI!
SMELLS GREAT.
I'M GLAD TO SEE YOU.
AND I YOU.
STILL BEAUTIFUL AFTER ALL THIS TIME.

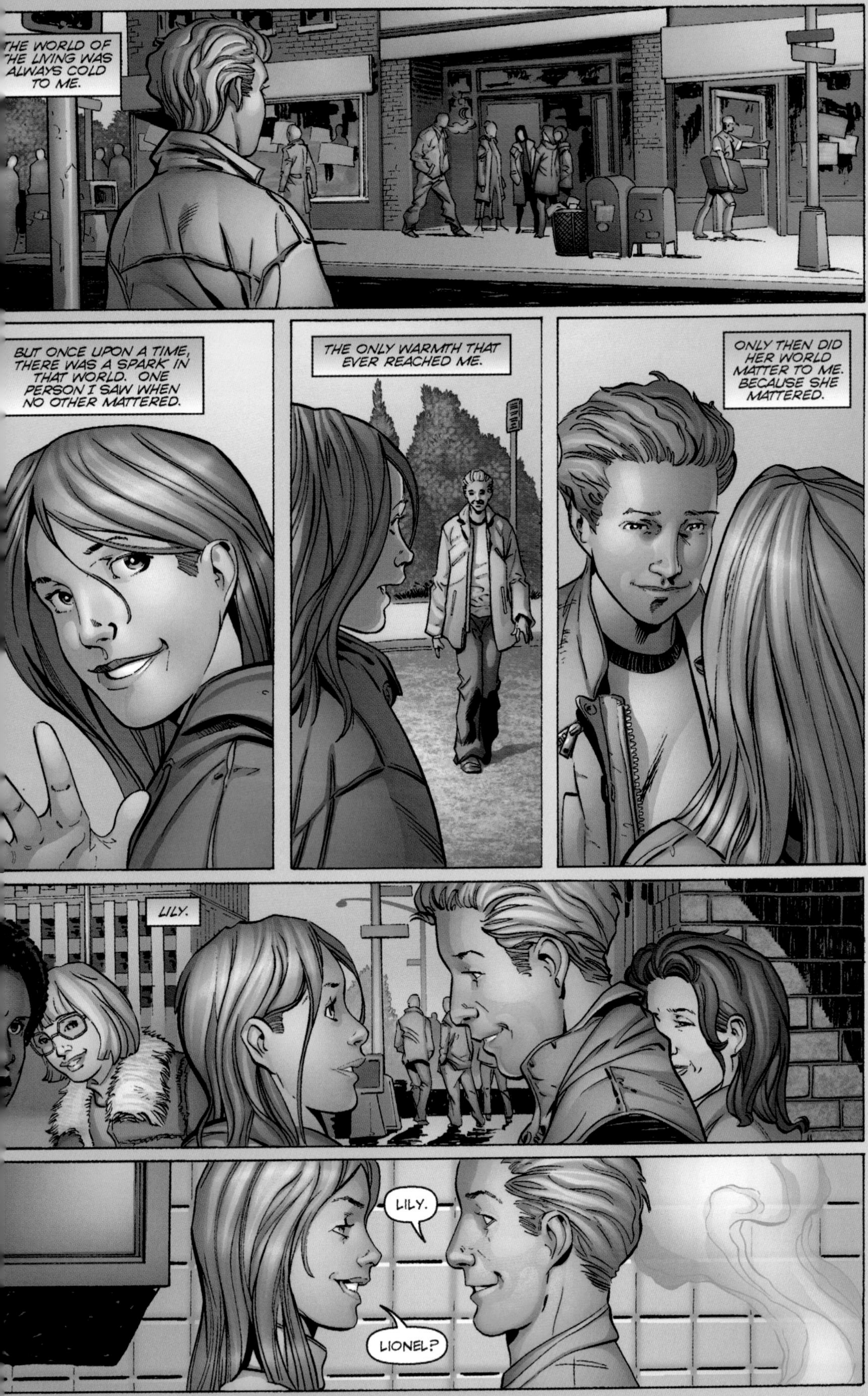

THE WORLD OF THE LIVING WAS ALWAYS COLD TO ME.
BUT ONCE UPON A TIME, THERE WAS A SPARK IN THAT WORLD. ONE PERSON I SAW WHEN NO OTHER MATTERED.
THE ONLY WARMTH THAT EVER REACHED ME.
ONLY THEN DID HER WORLD MATTER TO ME. BECAUSE SHE MATTERED.
LILY.
LILY.
LIONEL?

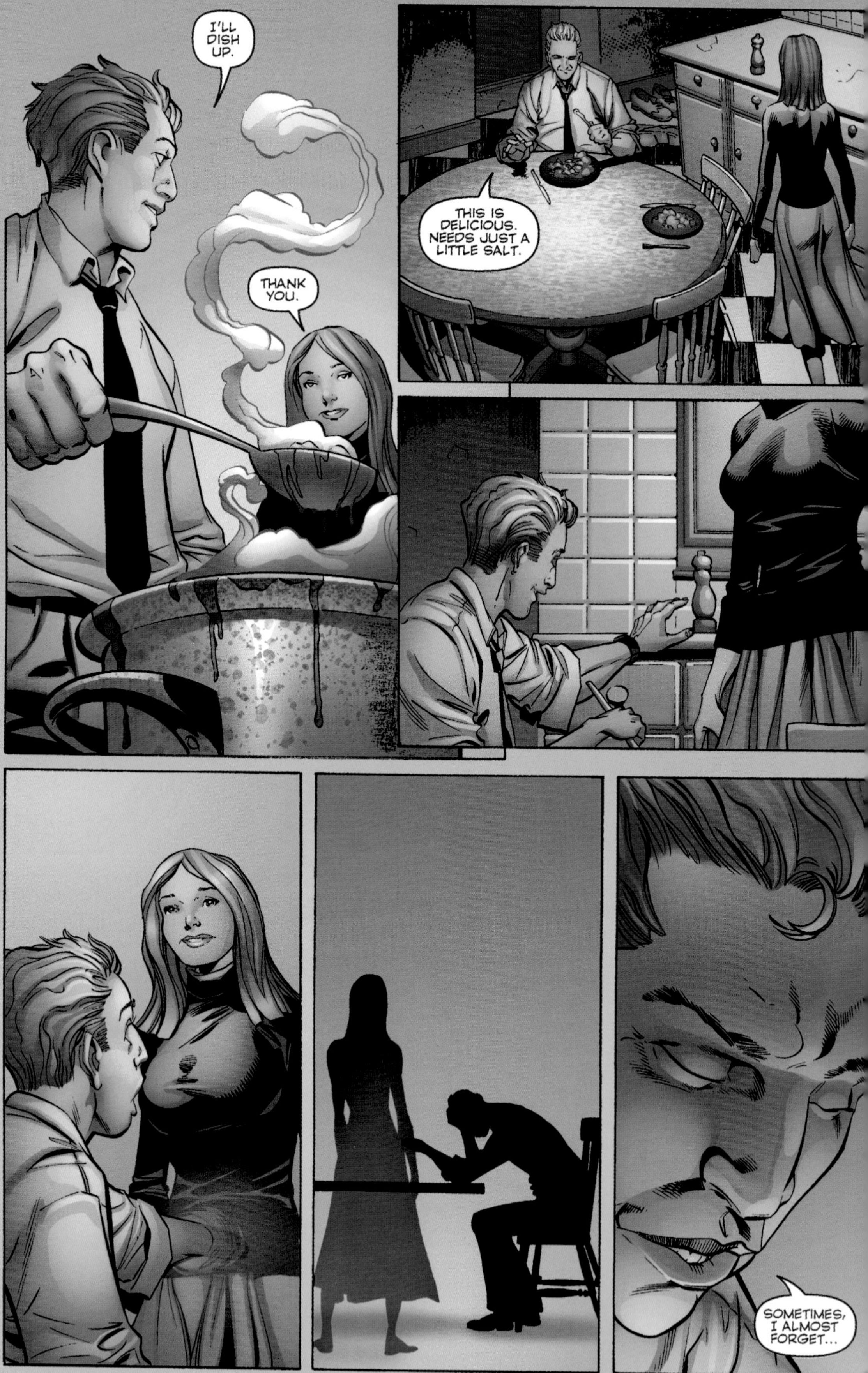
I'LL DISH UP.
THANK YOU.
THIS IS DELICIOUS. NEEDS JUST A LITTLE SALT.
SOMETIMES, I ALMOST FORGET...

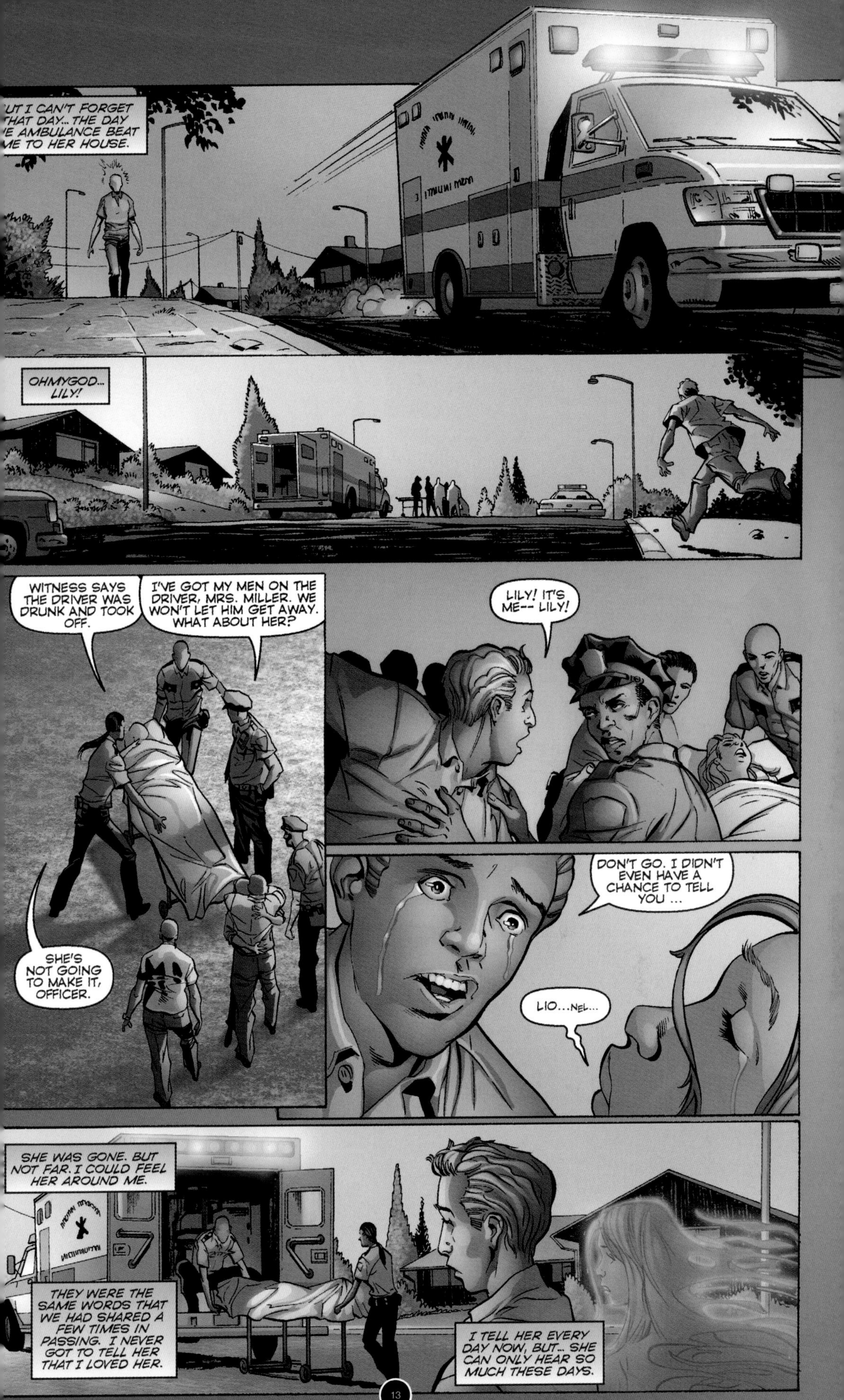
UT I CAN'T FORGET THAT DAY... THE DAY E AMBULANCE BEAT ME TO HER HOUSE.
OHMYGOD... LILY!
WITNESS SAYS THE DRIVER WAS DRUNK AND TOOK OFF.
I'VE GOT MY MEN ON THE DRIVER, MRS. MILLER. WE WON'T LET HIM GET AWAY. WHAT ABOUT HER?
SHE'S NOT GOING TO MAKE IT, OFFICER.
LILY! IT'S ME-- LILY!
DON'T GO. I DIDN'T EVEN HAVE A CHANCE TO TELL YOU ...
LIO...NEL...
SHE WAS GONE. BUT NOT FAR. I COULD FEEL HER AROUND ME.
THEY WERE THE SAME WORDS THAT WE HAD SHARED A FEW TIMES IN PASSING. I NEVER GOT TO TELL HER THAT I LOVED HER.
I TELL HER EVERY DAY NOW, BUT... SHE CAN ONLY HEAR SO MUCH THESE DAYS.

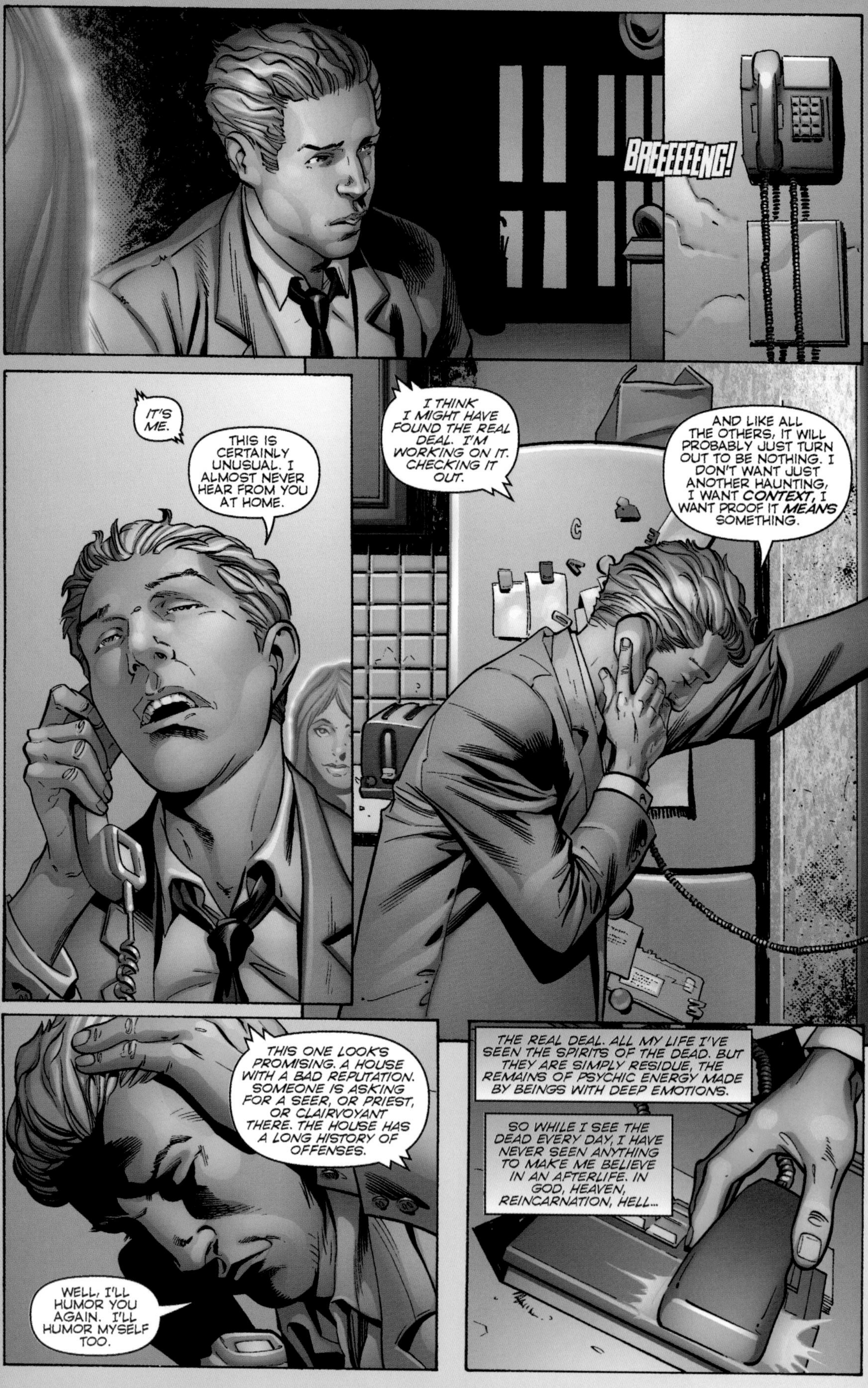
BREEEEEENG!
IT'S ME.
THIS IS CERTAINLY UNUSUAL. I ALMOST NEVER HEAR FROM YOU AT HOME.
I THINK I MIGHT HAVE FOUND THE REAL DEAL. I'M WORKING ON IT. CHECKING IT OUT.
AND LIKE ALL THE OTHERS, IT WILL PROBABLY JUST TURN OUT TO BE NOTHING. I DON'T WANT JUST ANOTHER HAUNTING, I WANT CONTEXT, I WANT PROOF IT MEANS SOMETHING.
THIS ONE LOOKS PROMISING. A HOUSE WITH A BAD REPUTATION. SOMEONE IS ASKING FOR A SEER, OR PRIEST, OR CLAIRVOYANT THERE. THE HOUSE HAS A LONG HISTORY OF OFFENSES.
WELL, I'LL HUMOR YOU AGAIN. I'LL HUMOR MYSELF TOO.
THE REAL DEAL. ALL MY LIFE I'VE SEEN THE SPIRITS OF THE DEAD. BUT THEY ARE SIMPLY RESIDUE, THE REMAINS OF PSYCHIC ENERGY MADE BY BEINGS WITH DEEP EMOTIONS.
SO WHILE I SEE THE DEAD EVERY DAY, I HAVE NEVER SEEN ANYTHING TO MAKE ME BELIEVE IN AN AFTERLIFE. IN GOD, HEAVEN, REINCARNATION, HELL...

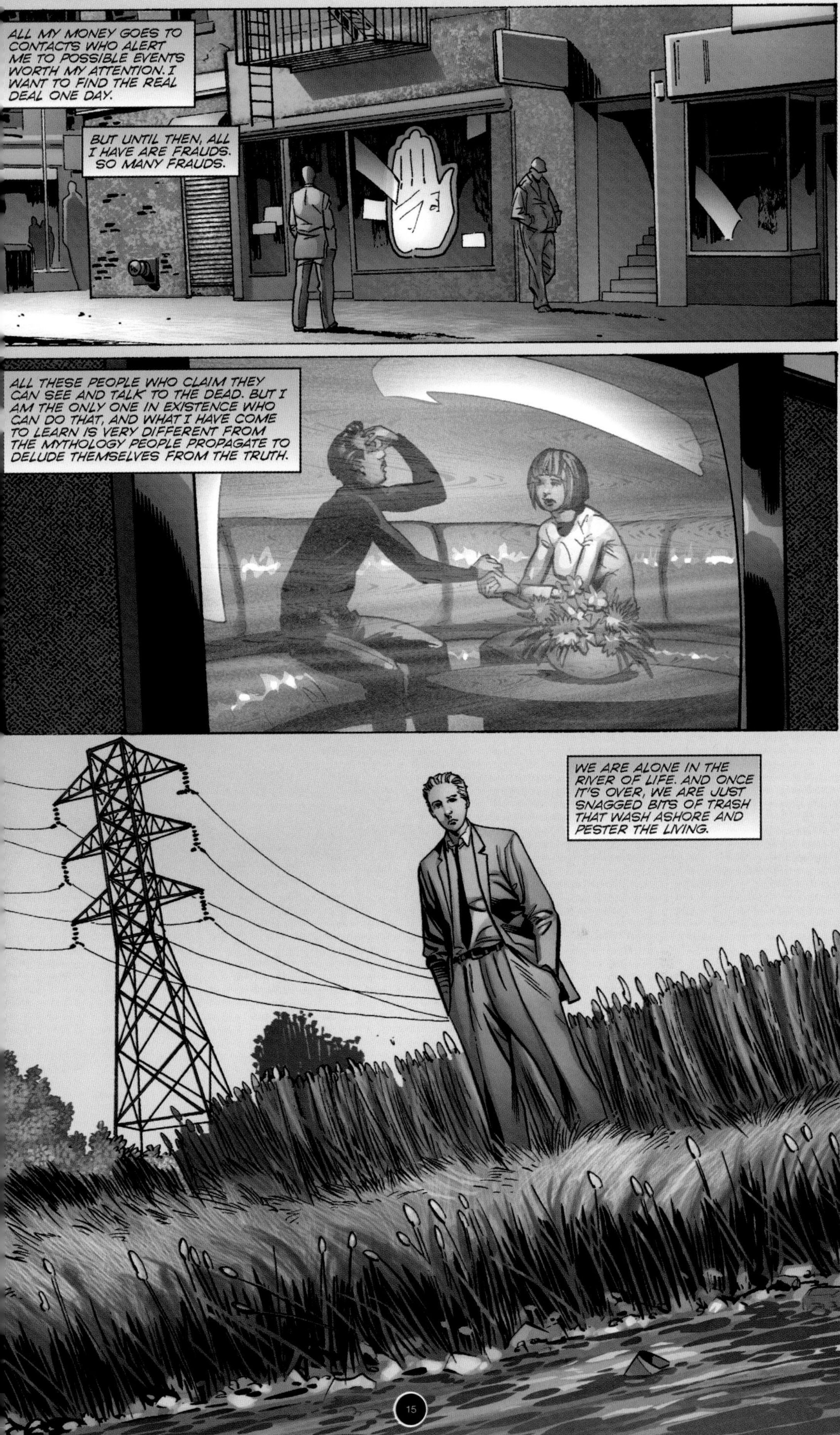
ALL MY MONEY GOES TO CONTACTS WHO ALERT ME TO POSSIBLE EVENTS WORTH MY ATTENTION. I WANT TO FIND THE REAL DEAL ONE DAY.
BUT UNTIL THEN, ALL I HAVE ARE FRAUDS. SO MANY FRAUDS.
ALL THESE PEOPLE WHO CLAIM THEY CAN SEE AND TALK TO THE DEAD. BUT I AM THE ONLY ONE IN EXISTENCE WHO CAN DO THAT, AND WHAT I HAVE COME TO LEARN IS VERY DIFFERENT FROM THE MYTHOLOGY PEOPLE PROPAGATE TO DELUDE THEMSELVES FROM THE TRUTH.
WE ARE ALONE IN THE RIVER OF LIFE. AND ONCE IT'S OVER, WE ARE JUST SNAGGED BITS OF TRASH THAT WASH ASHORE AND PESTER THE LIVING.

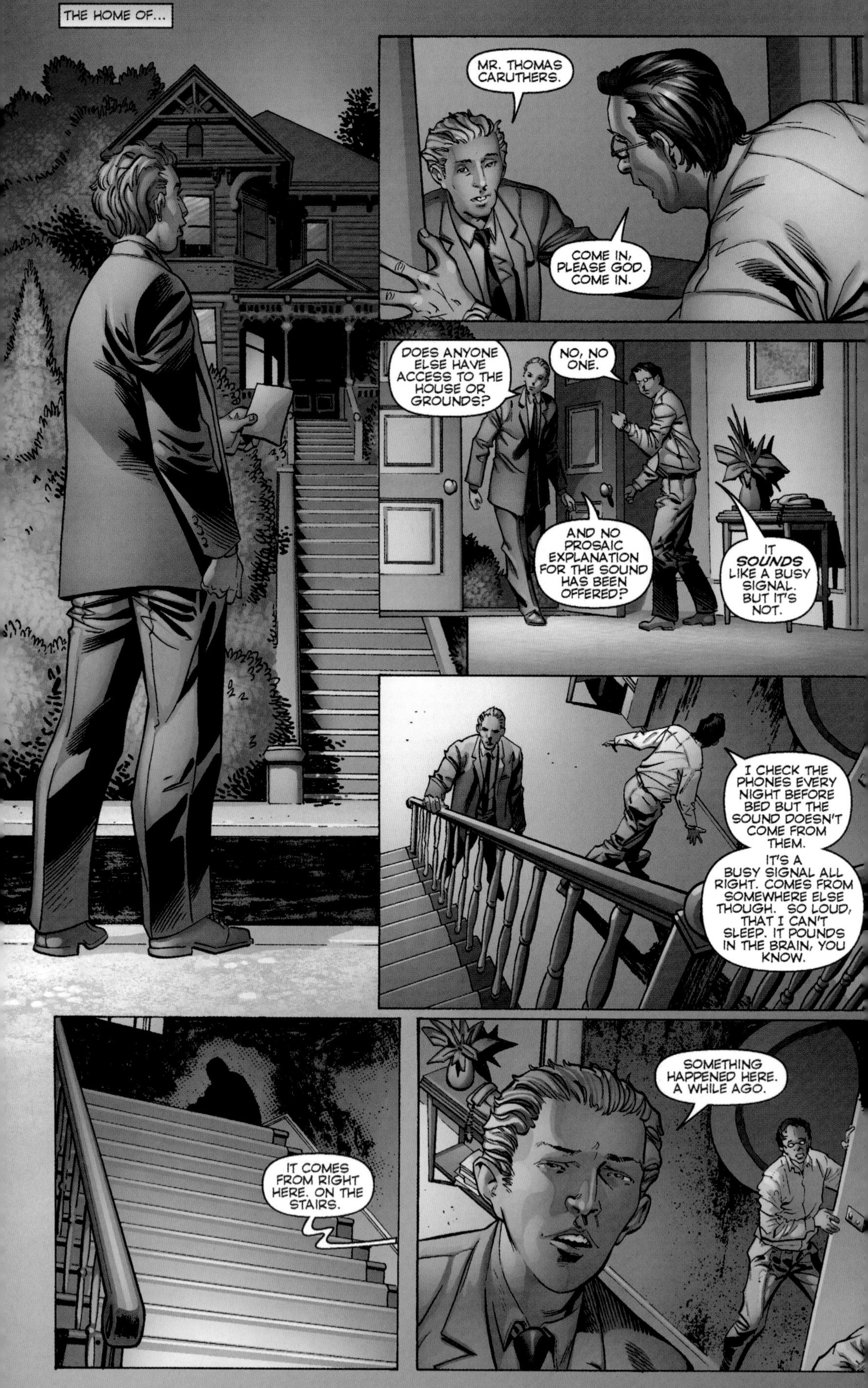

THE HOME OF...
MR. THOMAS CARUTHERS.
COME IN, PLEASE GOD. COME IN.
DOES ANYONE ELSE HAVE ACCESS TO THE HOUSE OR GROUNDS?
NO, NO ONE.
AND NO PROSAIC EXPLANATION FOR THE SOUND HAS BEEN OFFERED?
IT *SOUNDS* LIKE A BUSY SIGNAL. BUT IT'S NOT.
I CHECK THE PHONES EVERY NIGHT BEFORE BED BUT THE SOUND DOESN'T COME FROM THEM.
IT'S A BUSY SIGNAL ALL RIGHT. COMES FROM SOMEWHERE ELSE THOUGH. SO LOUD, THAT I CAN'T SLEEP. IT POUNDS IN THE BRAIN, YOU KNOW.
IT COMES FROM RIGHT HERE. ON THE STAIRS.
SOMETHING HAPPENED HERE. A WHILE AGO.

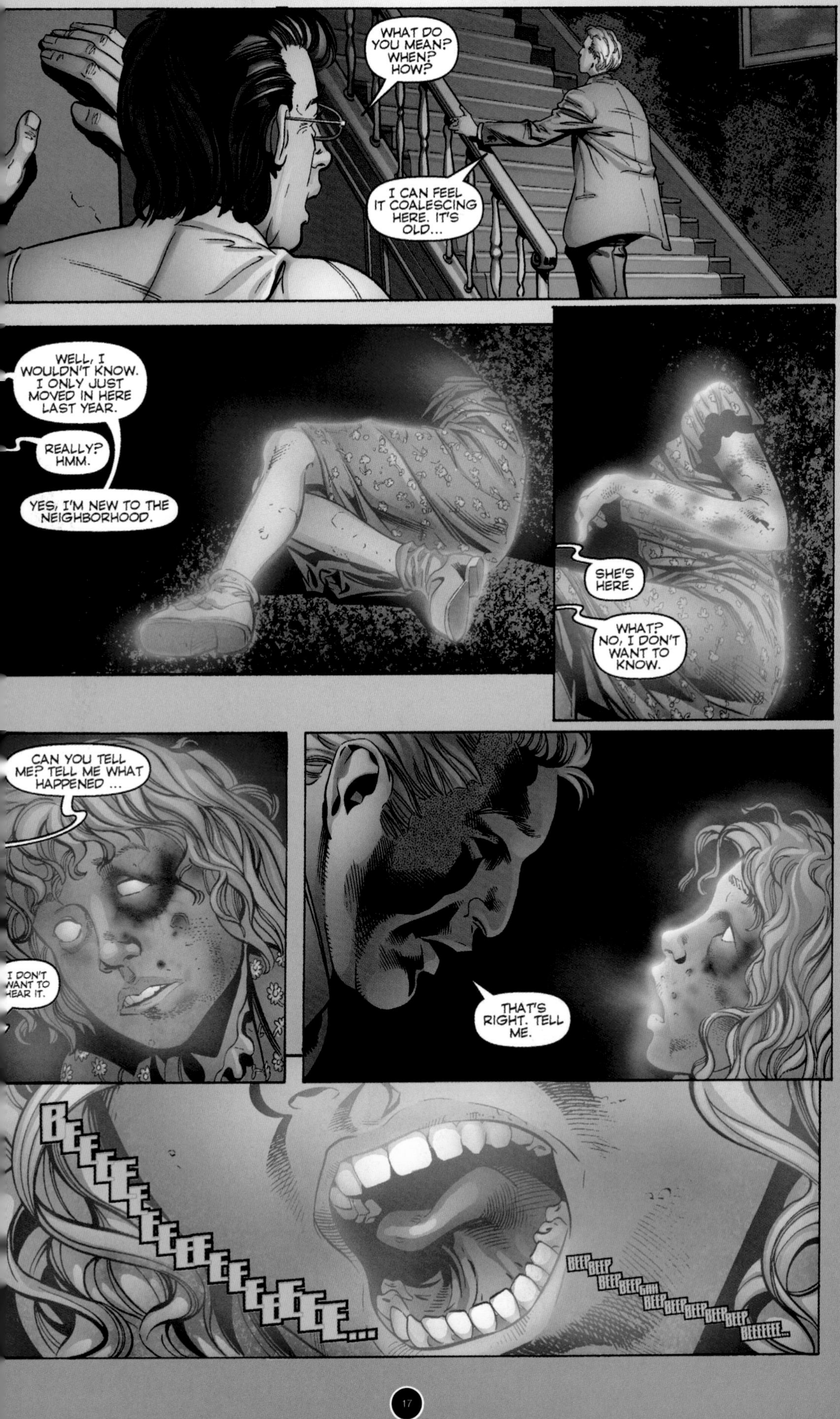

WHAT DO YOU MEAN? WHEN? HOW?
I CAN FEEL IT COALESCING HERE. IT'S OLD...
WELL, I WOULDN'T KNOW. I ONLY JUST MOVED IN HERE LAST YEAR.
REALLY? HMM.
YES, I'M NEW TO THE NEIGHBORHOOD.
SHE'S HERE.
WHAT? NO, I DON'T WANT TO KNOW.
CAN YOU TELL ME? TELL ME WHAT HAPPENED ...
I DON'T WANT TO HEAR IT.
THAT'S RIGHT. TELL ME.
BEEEEEEEEEEEEEEEE...
BEEP BEEP BEEP BEEP GAH BEEP BEEP BEEP BEEP BEEP BEEEEEEE...

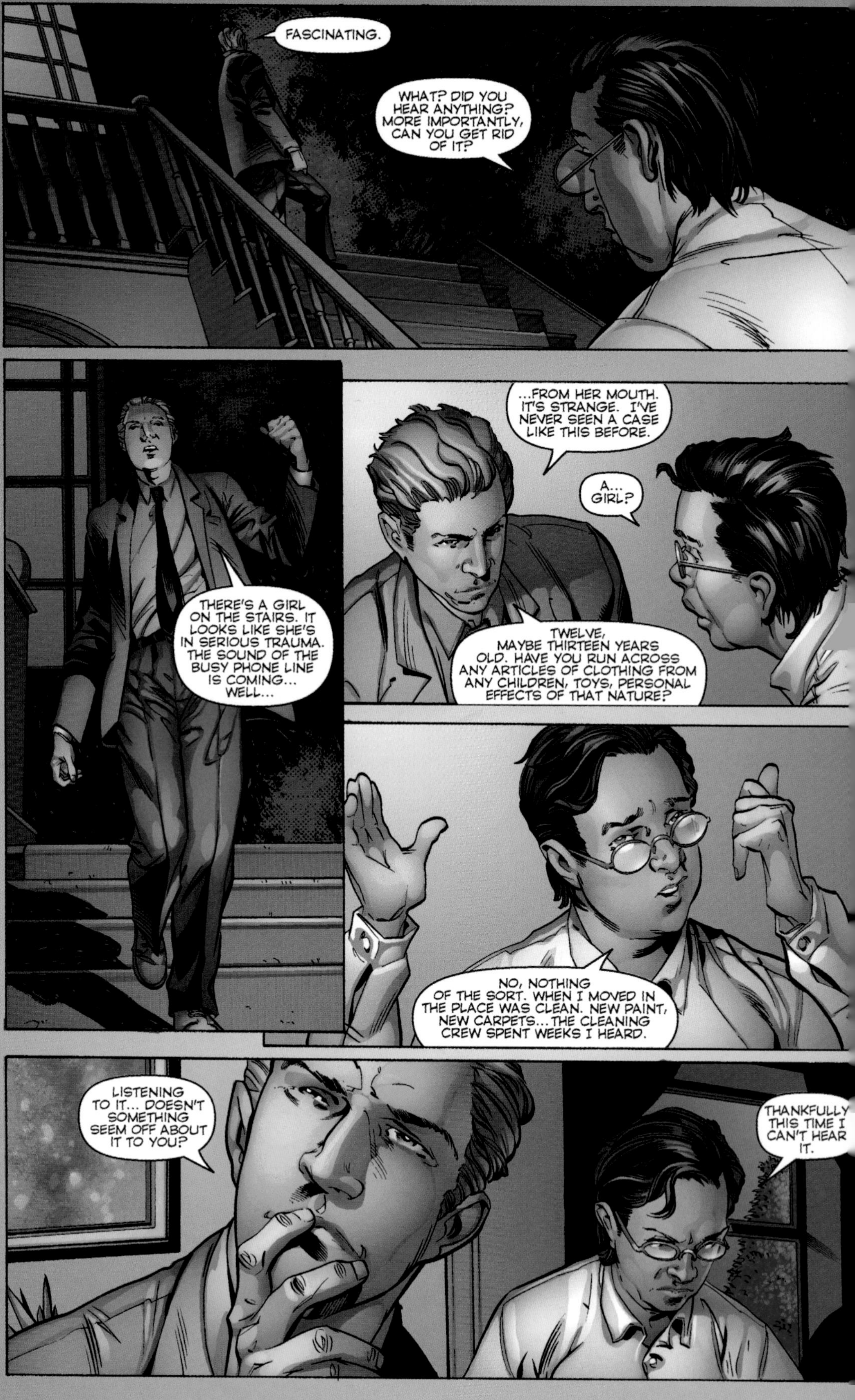
FASCINATING.
WHAT? DID YOU HEAR ANYTHING? MORE IMPORTANTLY, CAN YOU GET RID OF IT?
THERE'S A GIRL ON THE STAIRS. IT LOOKS LIKE SHE'S IN SERIOUS TRAUMA. THE SOUND OF THE BUSY PHONE LINE IS COMING... WELL...
...FROM HER MOUTH. IT'S STRANGE. I'VE NEVER SEEN A CASE LIKE THIS BEFORE.
A... GIRL?
TWELVE, MAYBE THIRTEEN YEARS OLD. HAVE YOU RUN ACROSS ANY ARTICLES OF CLOTHING FROM ANY CHILDREN, TOYS, PERSONAL EFFECTS OF THAT NATURE?
NO, NOTHING OF THE SORT. WHEN I MOVED IN THE PLACE WAS CLEAN. NEW PAINT, NEW CARPETS... THE CLEANING CREW SPENT WEEKS I HEARD.
LISTENING TO IT... DOESN'T SOMETHING SEEM OFF ABOUT IT TO YOU?
THANKFULLY THIS TIME I CAN'T HEAR IT.

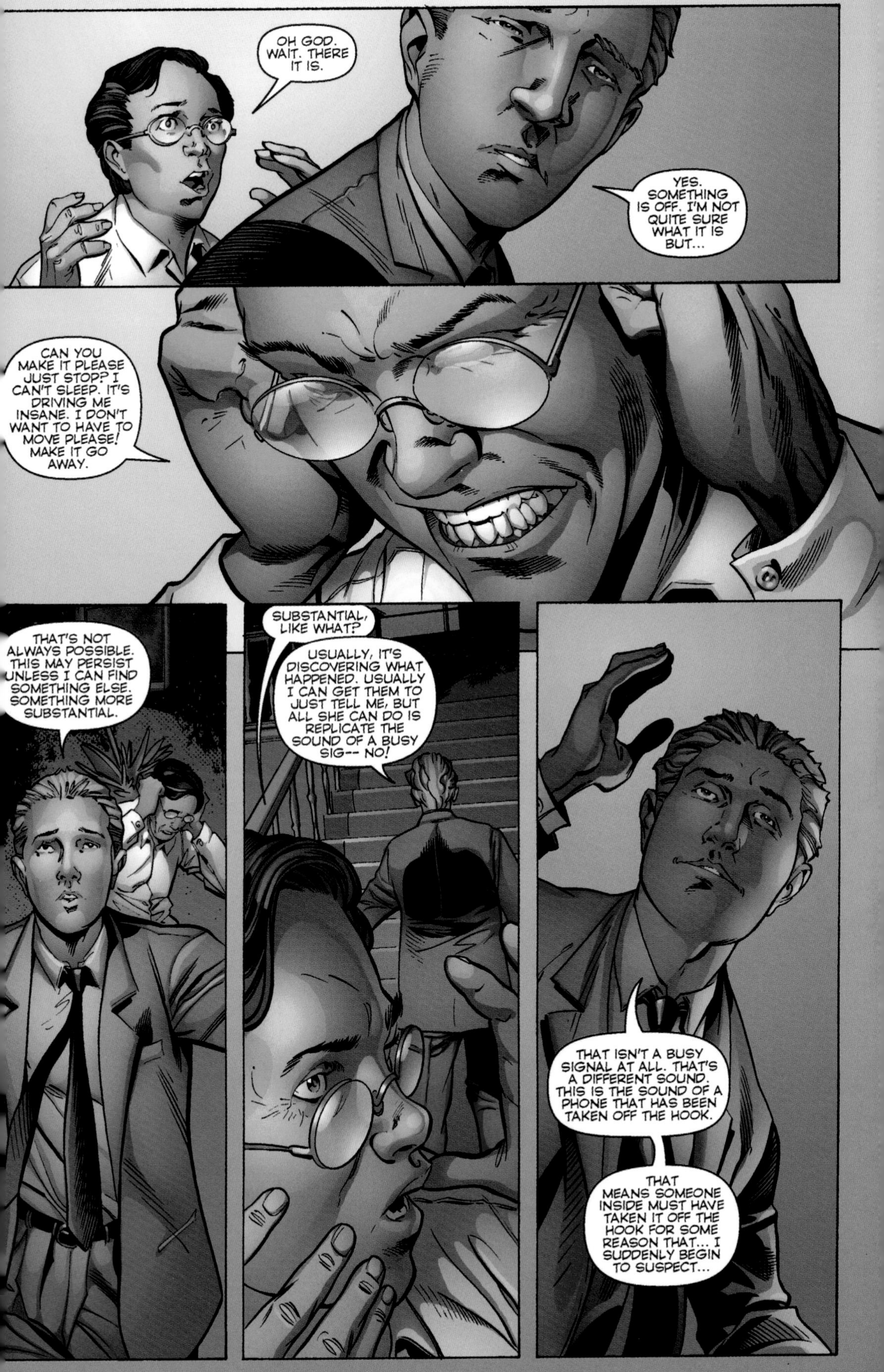

OH GOD. WAIT. THERE IT IS.
YES. SOMETHING IS OFF. I'M NOT QUITE SURE WHAT IT IS BUT...
CAN YOU MAKE IT PLEASE JUST STOP? I CAN'T SLEEP. IT'S DRIVING ME INSANE. I DON'T WANT TO HAVE TO MOVE PLEASE! MAKE IT GO AWAY.
THAT'S NOT ALWAYS POSSIBLE. THIS MAY PERSIST UNLESS I CAN FIND SOMETHING ELSE. SOMETHING MORE SUBSTANTIAL.
SUBSTANTIAL, LIKE WHAT?
USUALLY, IT'S DISCOVERING WHAT HAPPENED. USUALLY I CAN GET THEM TO JUST TELL ME, BUT ALL SHE CAN DO IS REPLICATE THE SOUND OF A BUSY SIG-- NO!
THAT ISN'T A BUSY SIGNAL AT ALL. THAT'S A DIFFERENT SOUND. THIS IS THE SOUND OF A PHONE THAT HAS BEEN TAKEN OFF THE HOOK.
THAT MEANS SOMEONE INSIDE MUST HAVE TAKEN IT OFF THE HOOK FOR SOME REASON THAT... I SUDDENLY BEGIN TO SUSPECT...

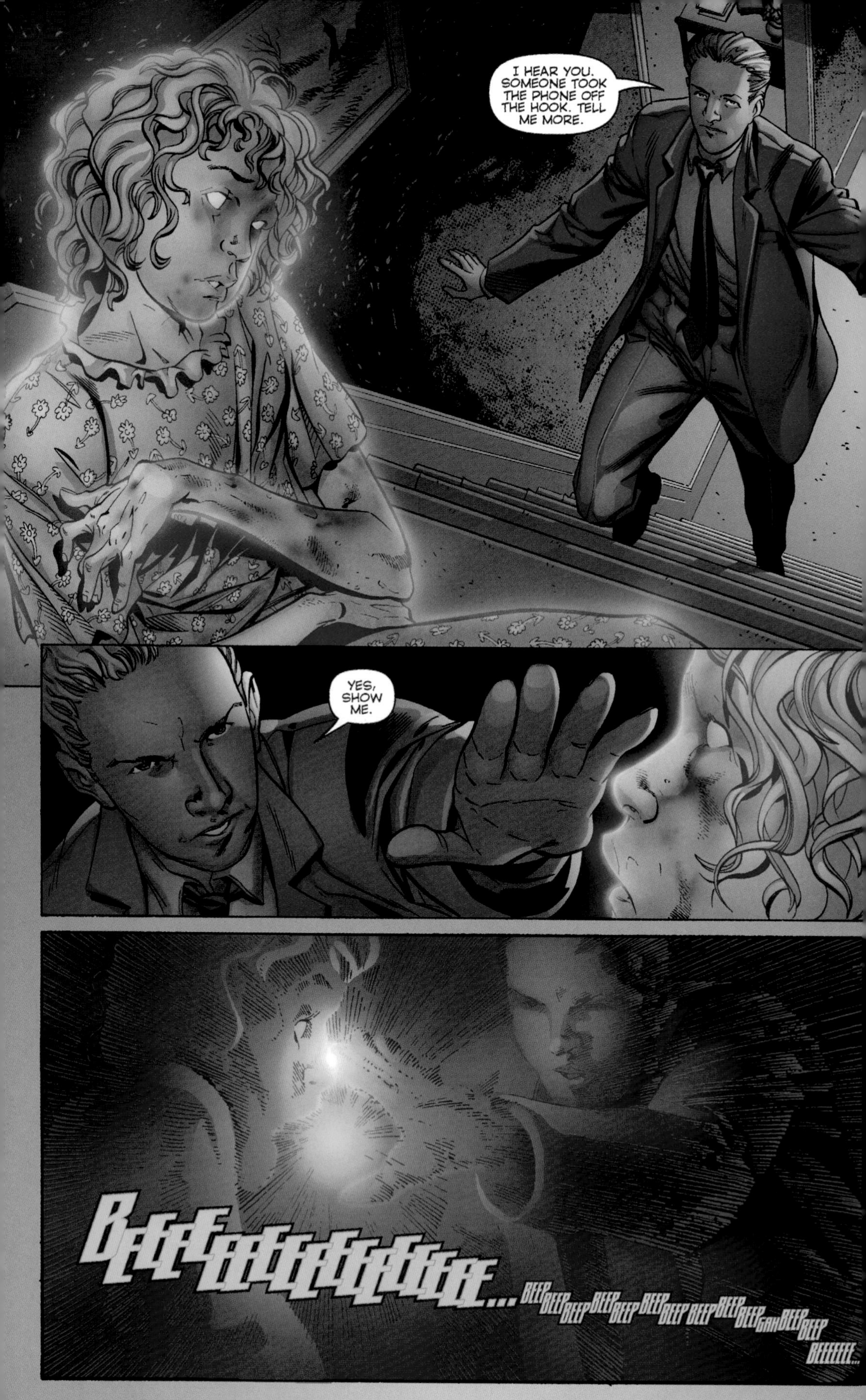
I HEAR YOU. SOMEONE TOOK THE PHONE OFF THE HOOK. TELL ME MORE.
YES, SHOW ME.
BEEEEEEEEEEEEEEEEE...
BEEP BEEP BEEP BEEP BEEP BEEP BEEP BEEP BEEP BEEP GAH BEEP BEEP
BEEEEEEE...

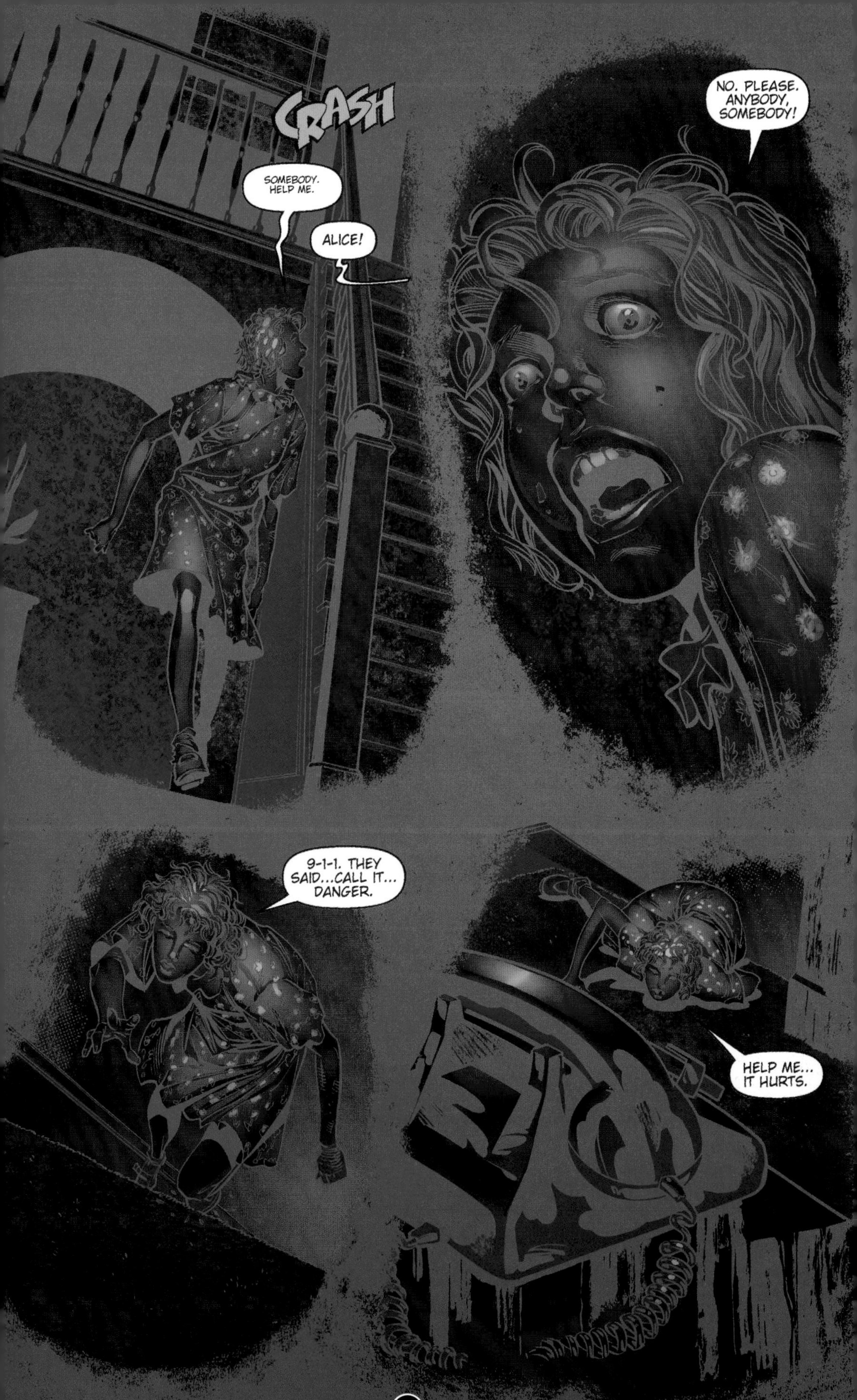
CRASH
SOMEBODY. HELP ME.
ALICE!
NO. PLEASE. ANYBODY, SOMEBODY!
9-1-1. THEY SAID...CALL IT... DANGER.
HELP ME... IT HURTS.

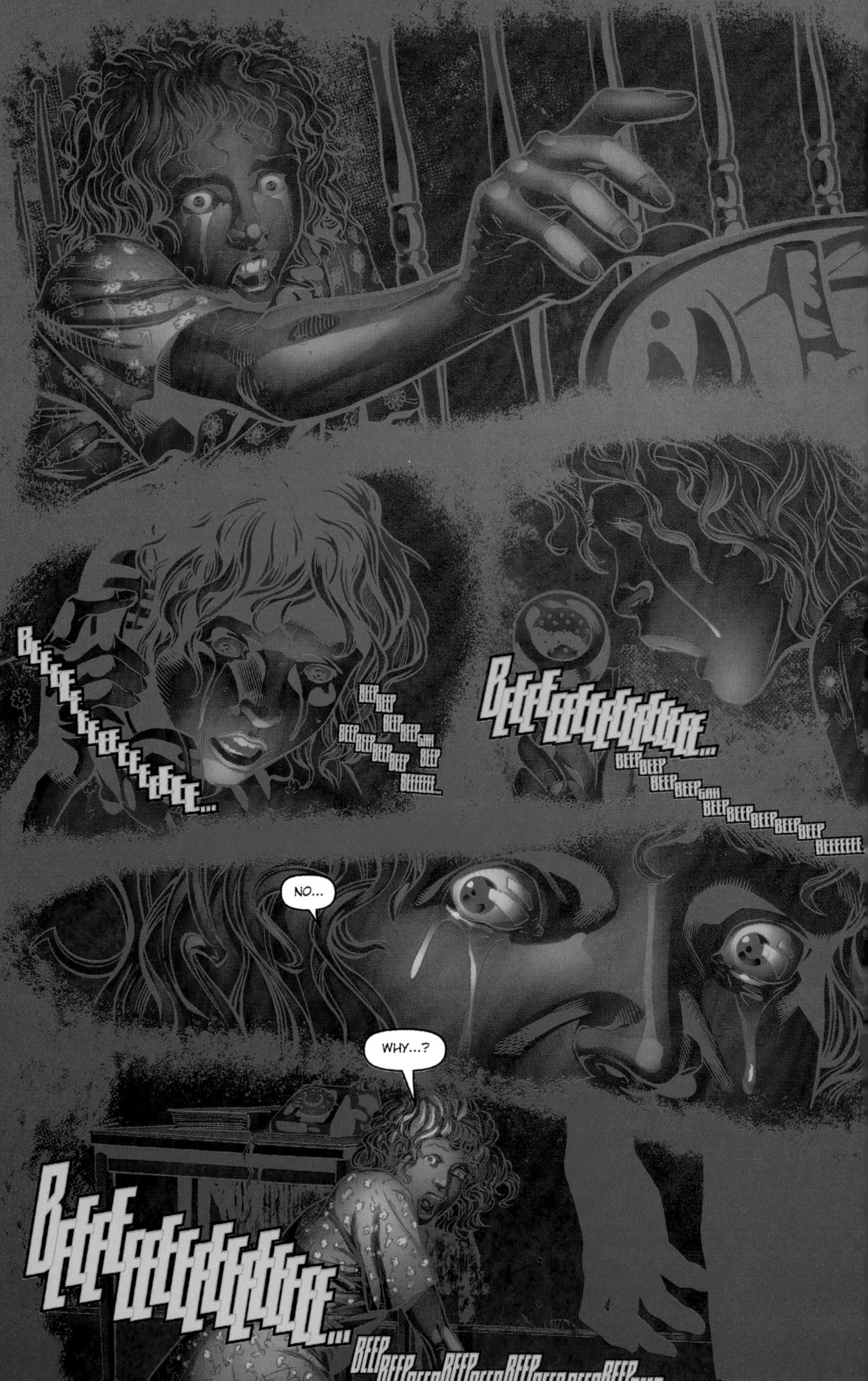
BEEEEEEEEEEEEEE...
BEEP BEEP BEEP BEEP GAH BEEP BEEP BEEP BEEP BEEP BEEEEEEE...
BEEEEEEEEEEEEEE...
BEEP BEEP BEEP BEEP GAH BEEP BEEP BEEP BEEP BEEP BEEEEEEE...
NO...
WHY...?
BEEEEEEEEEEEEEE...
BEEP BEEP BEEP BEEP BEEP BEEP BEEP BEEP BEEP BEEP GAH BEEP BEEP BEEEEEEE...

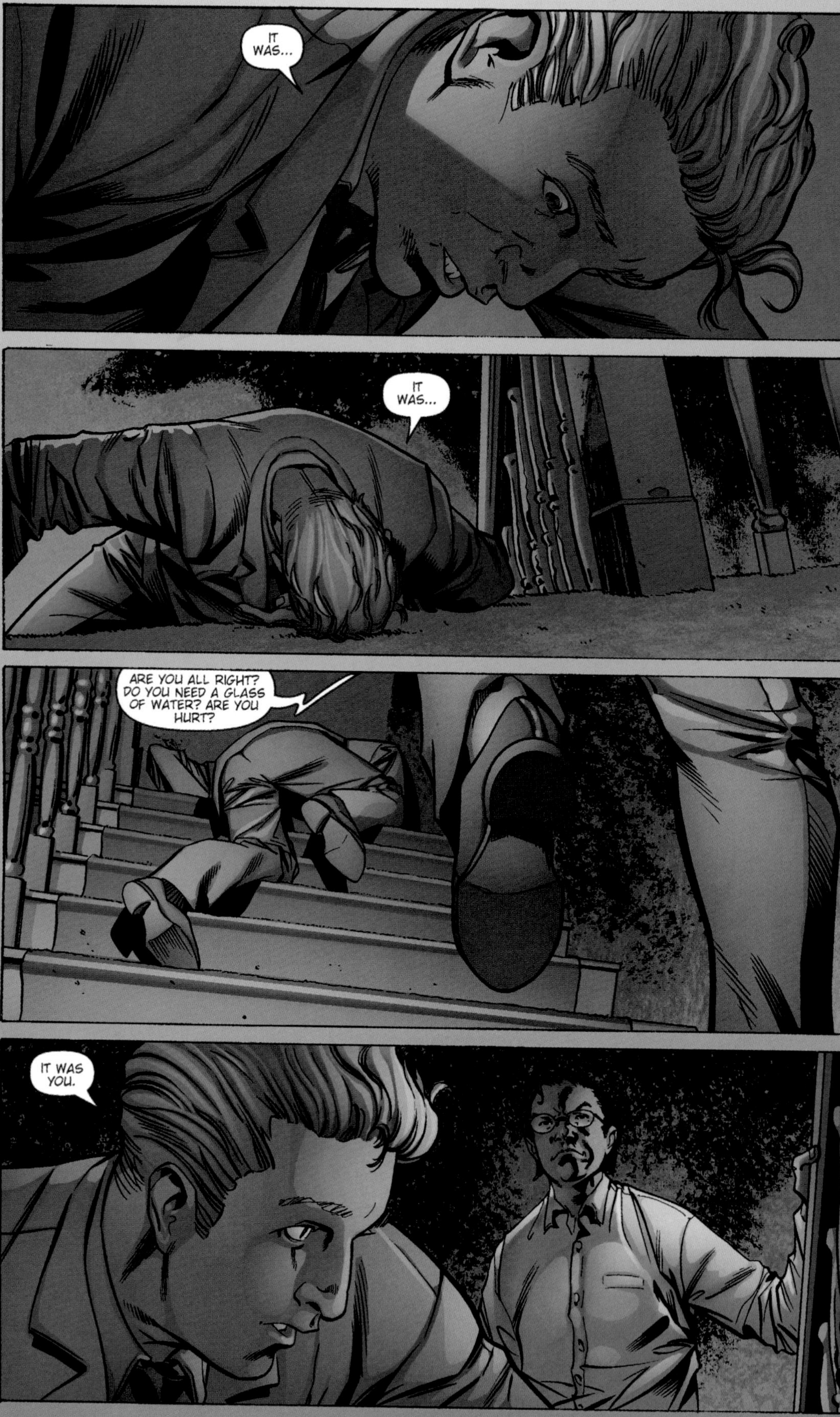
IT WAS...
IT WAS...
ARE YOU ALL RIGHT? DO YOU NEED A GLASS OF WATER? ARE YOU HURT?
IT WAS YOU.

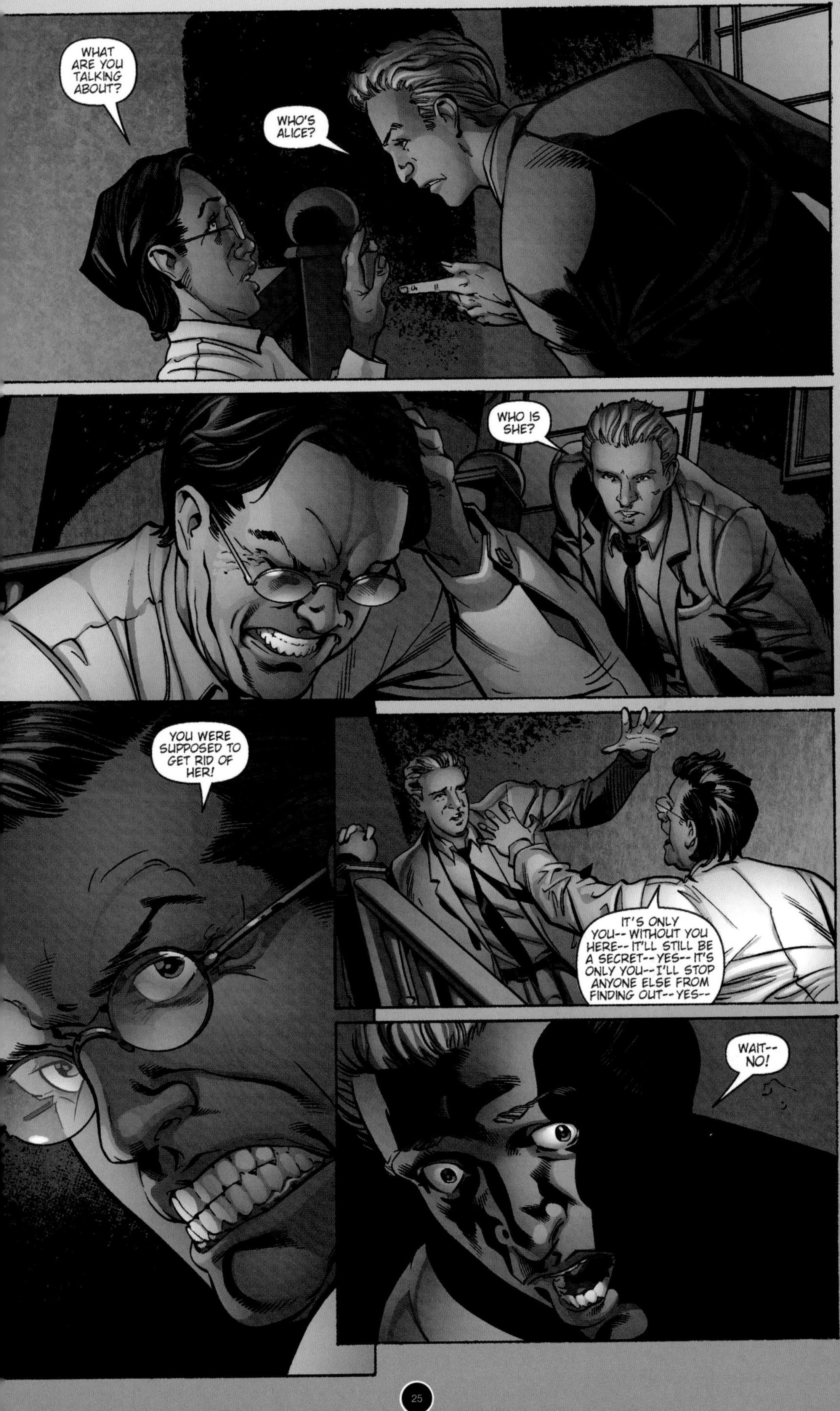
WHAT ARE YOU TALKING ABOUT?
WHO'S ALICE?
WHO IS SHE?
YOU WERE SUPPOSED TO GET RID OF HER!
IT'S ONLY YOU-- WITHOUT YOU HERE-- IT'LL STILL BE A SECRET-- YES-- IT'S ONLY YOU-- I'LL STOP ANYONE ELSE FROM FINDING OUT-- YES--
WAIT-- NO!

TO BE
CONTINUED...

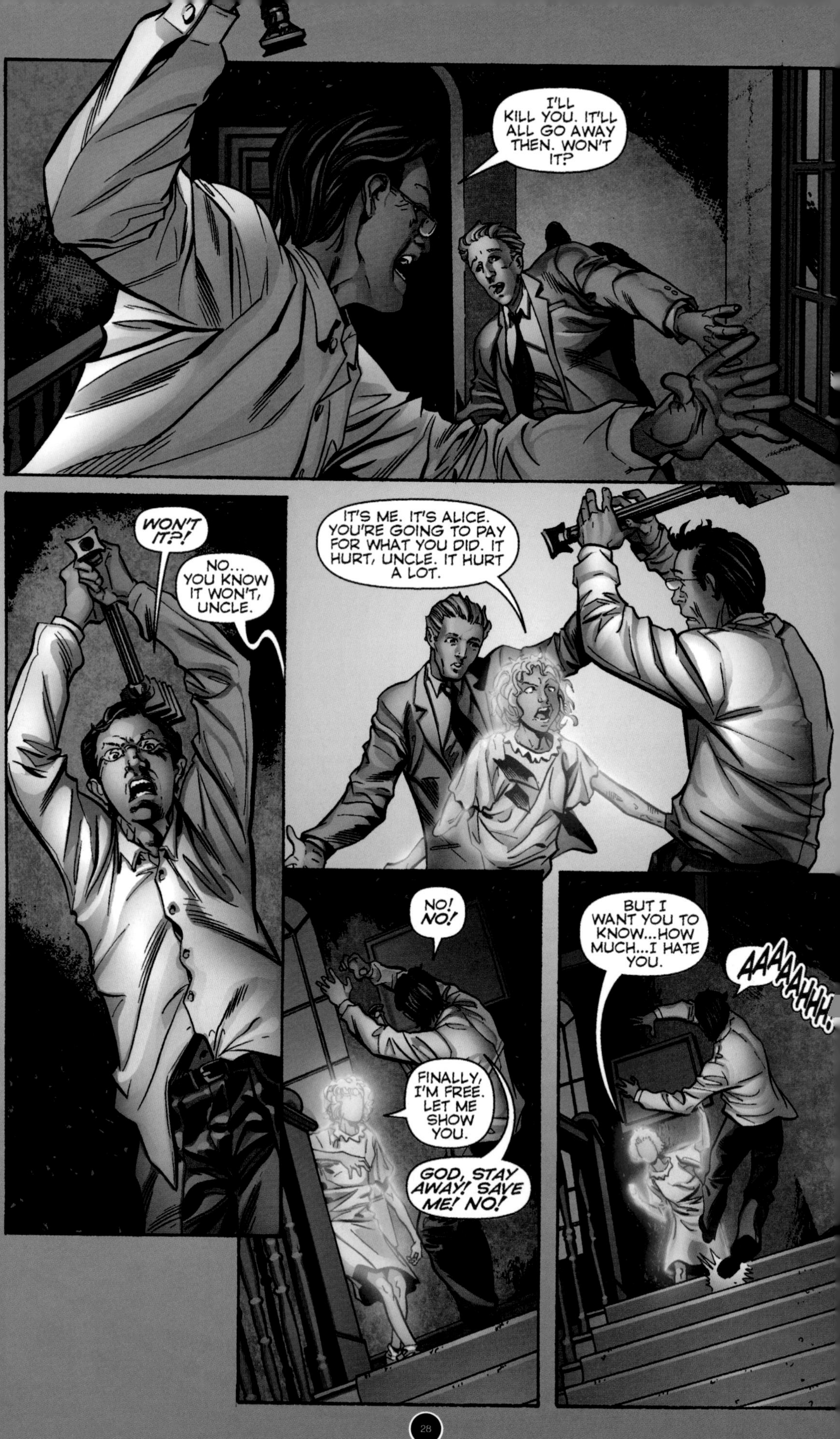
I'LL KILL YOU. IT'LL ALL GO AWAY THEN. WON'T IT?
WON'T IT?!
NO... YOU KNOW IT WON'T, UNCLE.
IT'S ME. IT'S ALICE. YOU'RE GOING TO PAY FOR WHAT YOU DID. IT HURT, UNCLE. IT HURT A LOT.
NO! NO!
FINALLY, I'M FREE. LET ME SHOW YOU.
GOD, STAY AWAY! SAVE ME! NO!
BUT I WANT YOU TO KNOW...HOW MUCH...I HATE YOU.
AAAAAHHH..

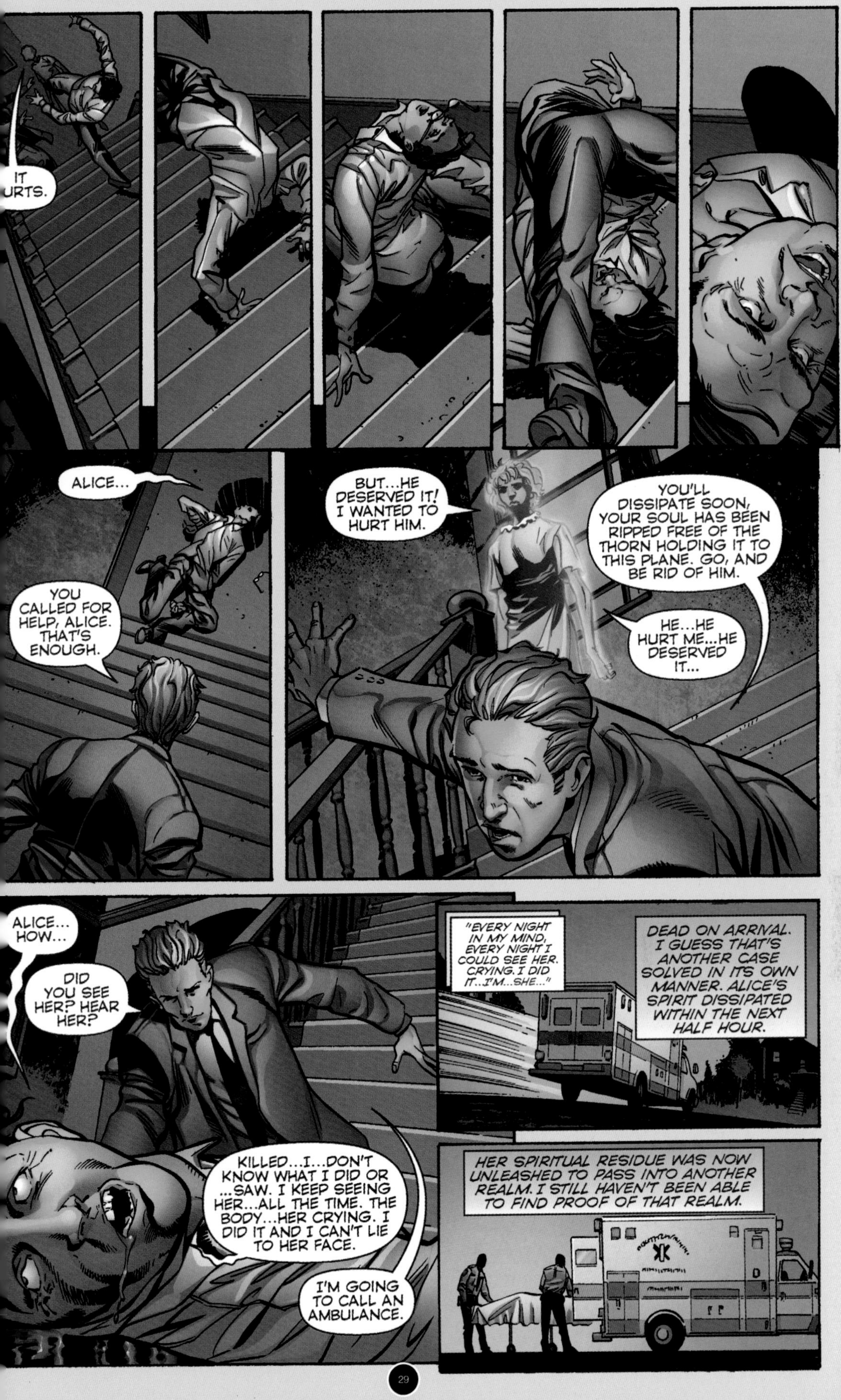

IT URTS.
ALICE...
YOU CALLED FOR HELP, ALICE. THAT'S ENOUGH.
BUT...HE DESERVED IT! I WANTED TO HURT HIM.
YOU'LL DISSIPATE SOON, YOUR SOUL HAS BEEN RIPPED FREE OF THE THORN HOLDING IT TO THIS PLANE. GO, AND BE RID OF HIM.
HE...HE HURT ME...HE DESERVED IT...
ALICE... HOW...
DID YOU SEE HER? HEAR HER?
KILLED...I...DON'T KNOW WHAT I DID OR ...SAW. I KEEP SEEING HER...ALL THE TIME. THE BODY...HER CRYING. I DID IT AND I CAN'T LIE TO HER FACE.
I'M GOING TO CALL AN AMBULANCE.
"EVERY NIGHT IN MY MIND, EVERY NIGHT I COULD SEE HER. CRYING. I DID IT...I'M...SHE..."
DEAD ON ARRIVAL. I GUESS THAT'S ANOTHER CASE SOLVED IN ITS OWN MANNER. ALICE'S SPIRIT DISSIPATED WITHIN THE NEXT HALF HOUR.
HER SPIRITUAL RESIDUE WAS NOW UNLEASHED TO PASS INTO ANOTHER REALM. I STILL HAVEN'T BEEN ABLE TO FIND PROOF OF THAT REALM.

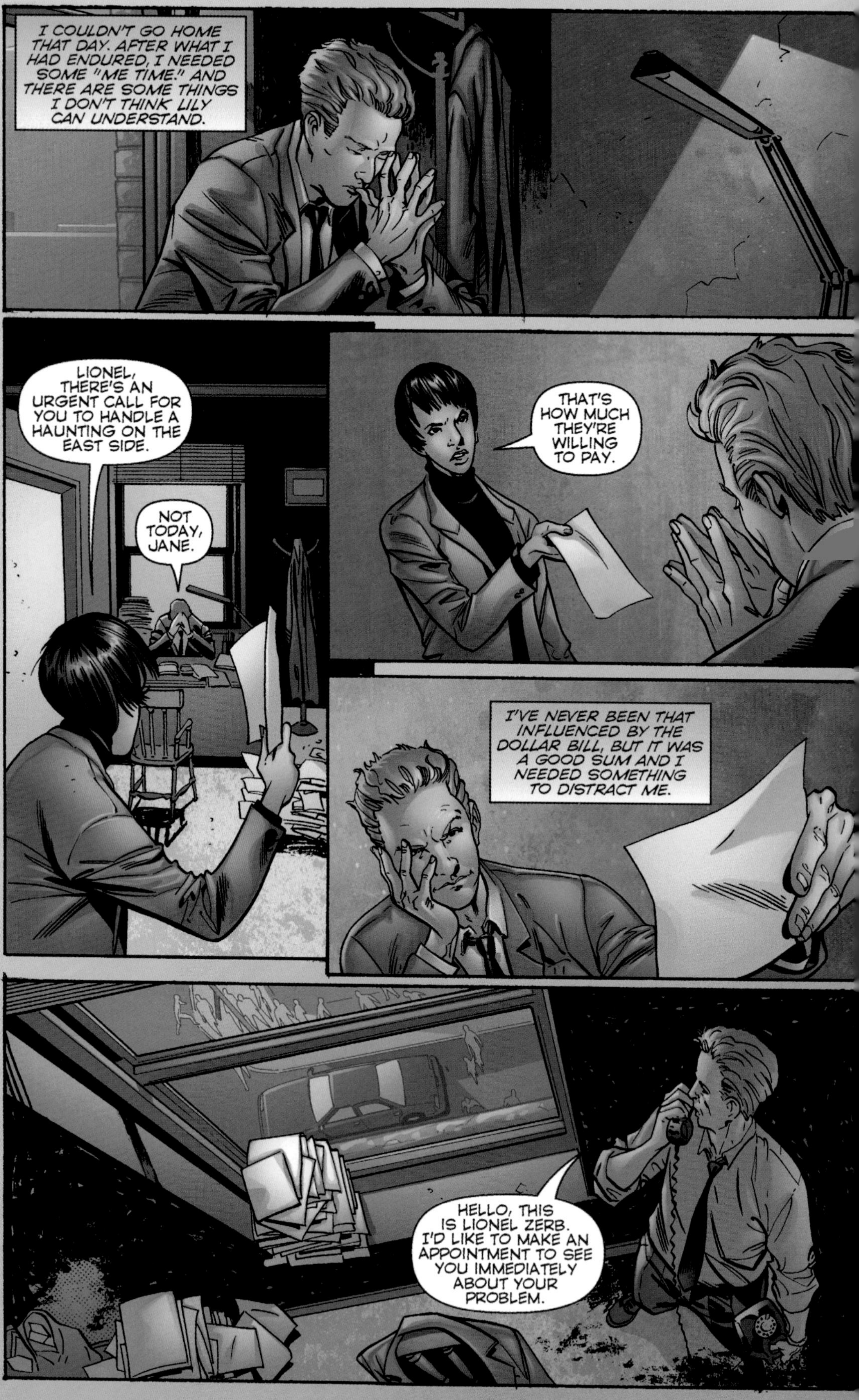

I COULDN'T GO HOME THAT DAY. AFTER WHAT I HAD ENDURED, I NEEDED SOME "ME TIME." AND THERE ARE SOME THINGS I DON'T THINK LILY CAN UNDERSTAND.
LIONEL, THERE'S AN URGENT CALL FOR YOU TO HANDLE A HAUNTING ON THE EAST SIDE.
NOT TODAY, JANE.
THAT'S HOW MUCH THEY'RE WILLING TO PAY.
I'VE NEVER BEEN THAT INFLUENCED BY THE DOLLAR BILL, BUT IT WAS A GOOD SUM AND I NEEDED SOMETHING TO DISTRACT ME.
HELLO, THIS IS LIONEL ZERB. I'D LIKE TO MAKE AN APPOINTMENT TO SEE YOU IMMEDIATELY ABOUT YOUR PROBLEM.

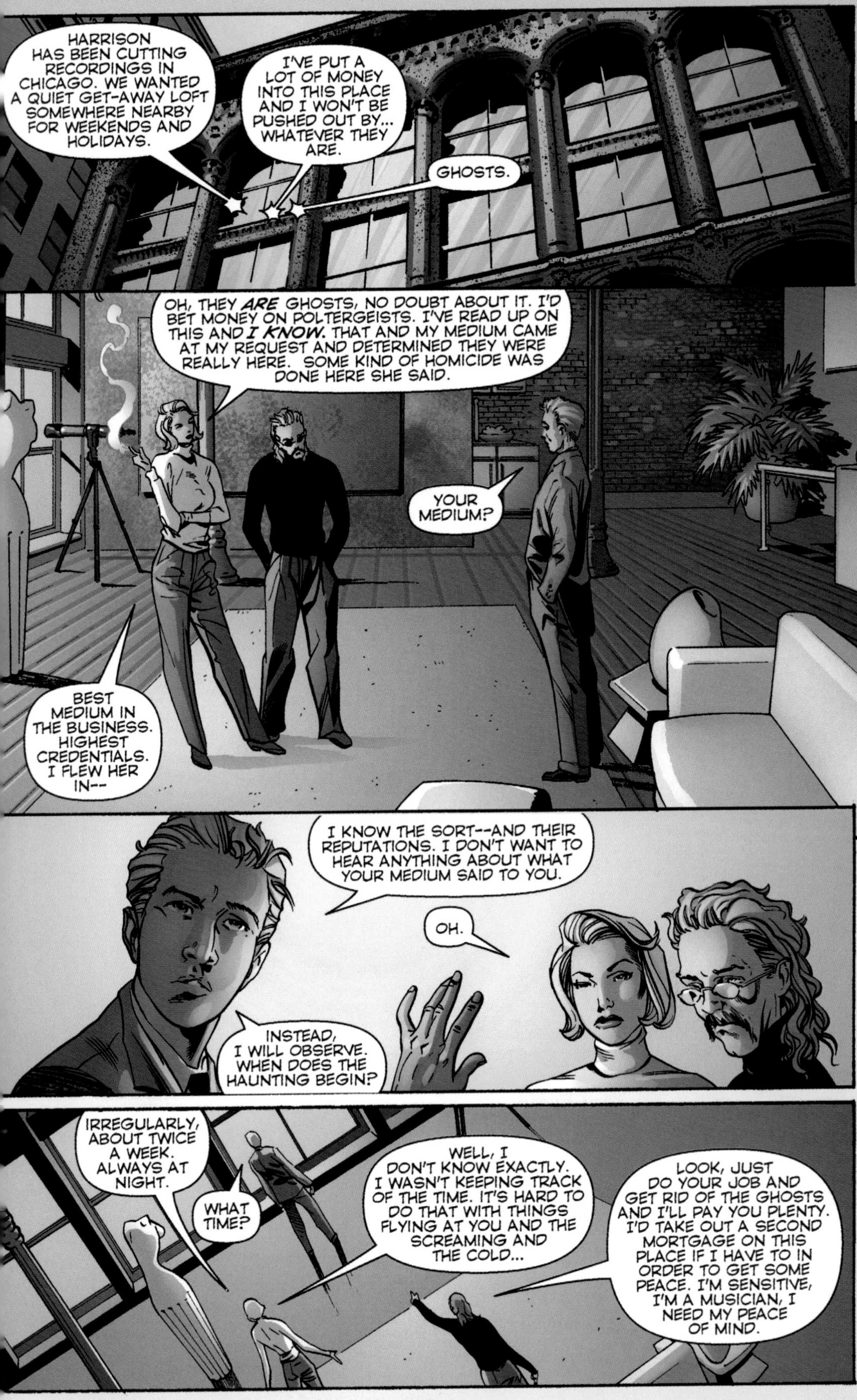
HARRISON HAS BEEN CUTTING RECORDINGS IN CHICAGO. WE WANTED A QUIET GET-AWAY LOFT SOMEWHERE NEARBY FOR WEEKENDS AND HOLIDAYS.
I'VE PUT A LOT OF MONEY INTO THIS PLACE AND I WON'T BE PUSHED OUT BY... WHATEVER THEY ARE.
GHOSTS.
OH, THEY *ARE* GHOSTS, NO DOUBT ABOUT IT. I'D BET MONEY ON POLTERGEISTS. I'VE READ UP ON THIS AND *I KNOW.* THAT AND MY MEDIUM CAME AT MY REQUEST AND DETERMINED THEY WERE REALLY HERE. SOME KIND OF HOMICIDE WAS DONE HERE SHE SAID.
YOUR MEDIUM?
BEST MEDIUM IN THE BUSINESS. HIGHEST CREDENTIALS. I FLEW HER IN--
I KNOW THE SORT--AND THEIR REPUTATIONS. I DON'T WANT TO HEAR ANYTHING ABOUT WHAT YOUR MEDIUM SAID TO YOU.
OH.
INSTEAD, I WILL OBSERVE. WHEN DOES THE HAUNTING BEGIN?
IRREGULARLY, ABOUT TWICE A WEEK. ALWAYS AT NIGHT.
WHAT TIME?
WELL, I DON'T KNOW EXACTLY. I WASN'T KEEPING TRACK OF THE TIME. IT'S HARD TO DO THAT WITH THINGS FLYING AT YOU AND THE SCREAMING AND THE COLD...
LOOK, JUST DO YOUR JOB AND GET RID OF THE GHOSTS AND I'LL PAY YOU PLENTY. I'D TAKE OUT A SECOND MORTGAGE ON THIS PLACE IF I HAVE TO IN ORDER TO GET SOME PEACE. I'M SENSITIVE, I'M A MUSICIAN, I NEED MY PEACE OF MIND.

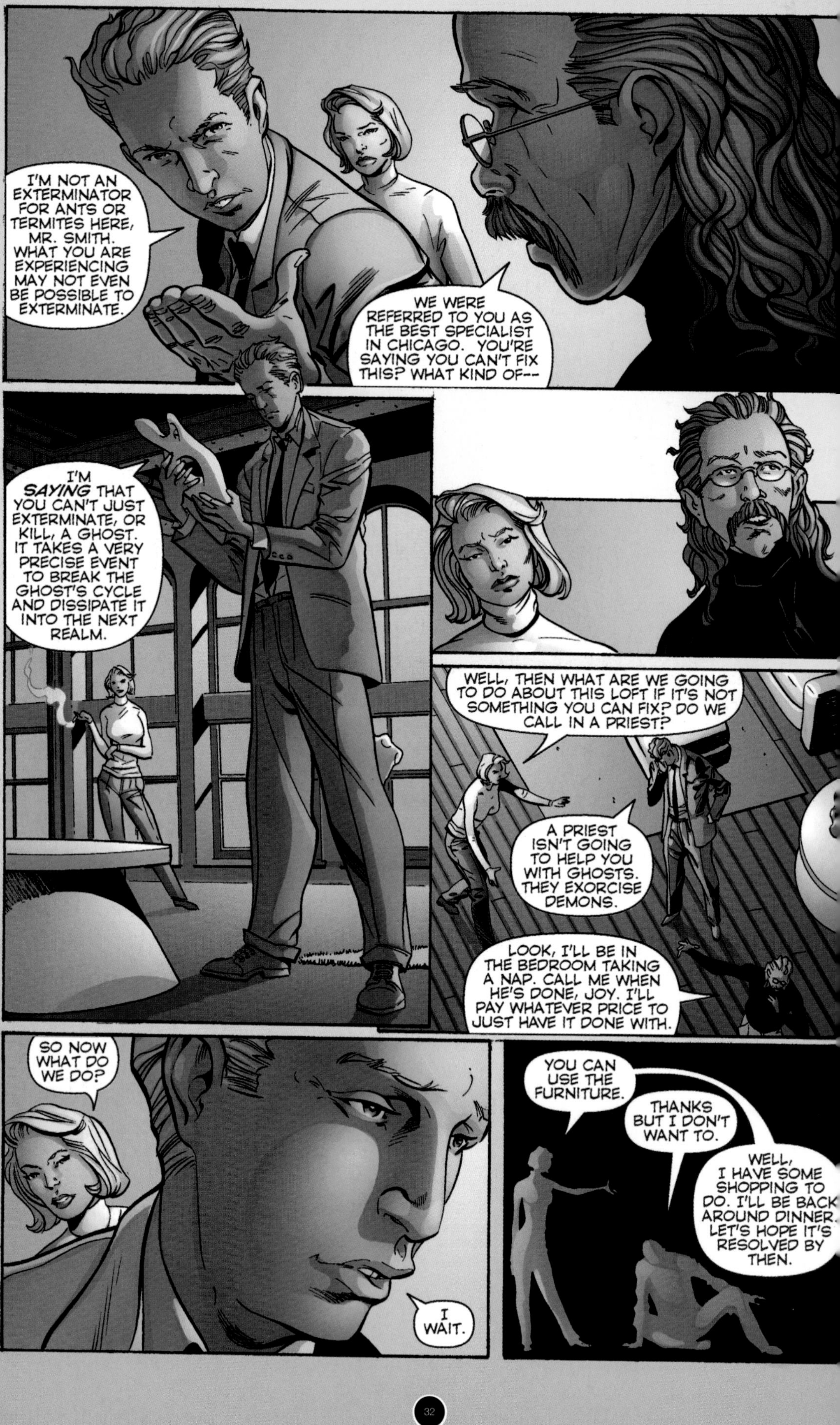
I'M NOT AN EXTERMINATOR FOR ANTS OR TERMITES HERE, MR. SMITH. WHAT YOU ARE EXPERIENCING MAY NOT EVEN BE POSSIBLE TO EXTERMINATE.
WE WERE REFERRED TO YOU AS THE BEST SPECIALIST IN CHICAGO. YOU'RE SAYING YOU CAN'T FIX THIS? WHAT KIND OF--
I'M *SAYING* THAT YOU CAN'T JUST EXTERMINATE, OR KILL, A GHOST. IT TAKES A VERY PRECISE EVENT TO BREAK THE GHOST'S CYCLE AND DISSIPATE IT INTO THE NEXT REALM.
WELL, THEN WHAT ARE WE GOING TO DO ABOUT THIS LOFT IF IT'S NOT SOMETHING YOU CAN FIX? DO WE CALL IN A PRIEST?
A PRIEST ISN'T GOING TO HELP YOU WITH GHOSTS. THEY EXORCISE DEMONS.
LOOK, I'LL BE IN THE BEDROOM TAKING A NAP. CALL ME WHEN HE'S DONE, JOY. I'LL PAY WHATEVER PRICE TO JUST HAVE IT DONE WITH.
SO NOW WHAT DO WE DO?
I WAIT.
YOU CAN USE THE FURNITURE.
THANKS BUT I DON'T WANT TO.
WELL, I HAVE SOME SHOPPING TO DO. I'LL BE BACK AROUND DINNER. LET'S HOPE IT'S RESOLVED BY THEN.

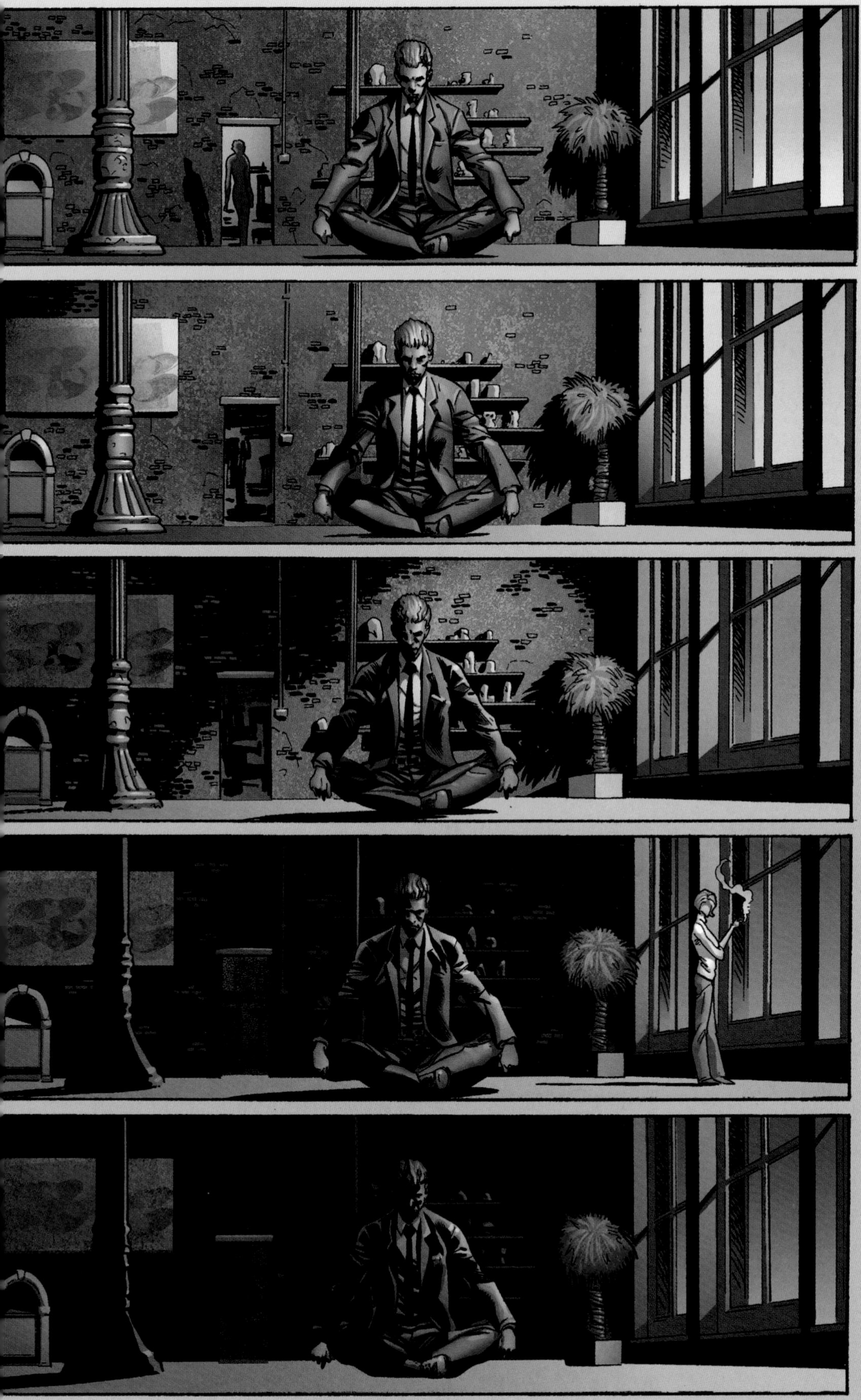

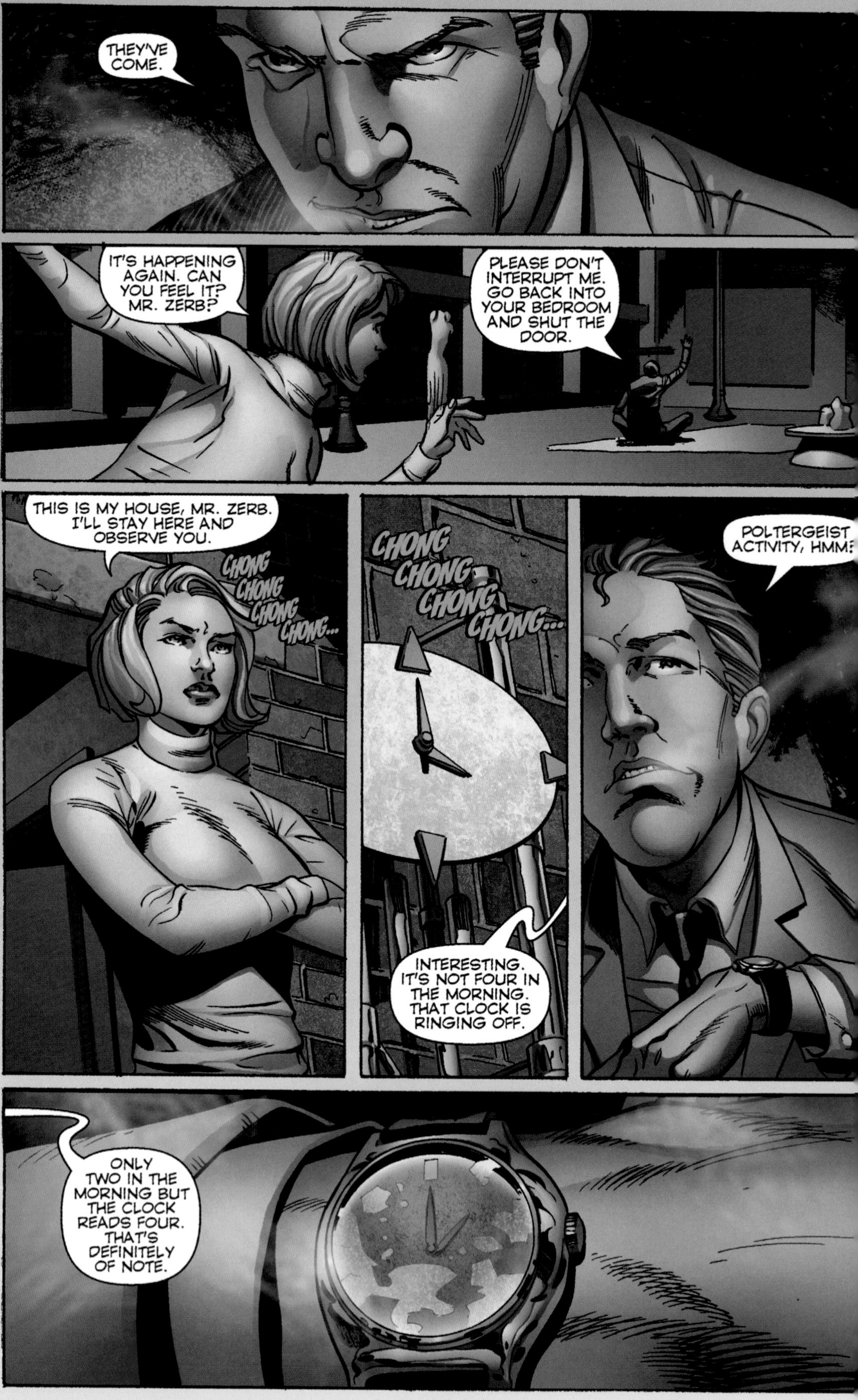
THEY'VE COME.
IT'S HAPPENING AGAIN. CAN YOU FEEL IT? MR. ZERB?
PLEASE DON'T INTERRUPT ME. GO BACK INTO YOUR BEDROOM AND SHUT THE DOOR.
THIS IS MY HOUSE, MR. ZERB. I'LL STAY HERE AND OBSERVE YOU.
CHONG CHONG CHONG CHONG...
CHONG CHONG CHONG CHONG...
POLTERGEIST ACTIVITY, HMM?
INTERESTING. IT'S NOT FOUR IN THE MORNING. THAT CLOCK IS RINGING OFF.
ONLY TWO IN THE MORNING BUT THE CLOCK READS FOUR. THAT'S DEFINITELY OF NOTE.

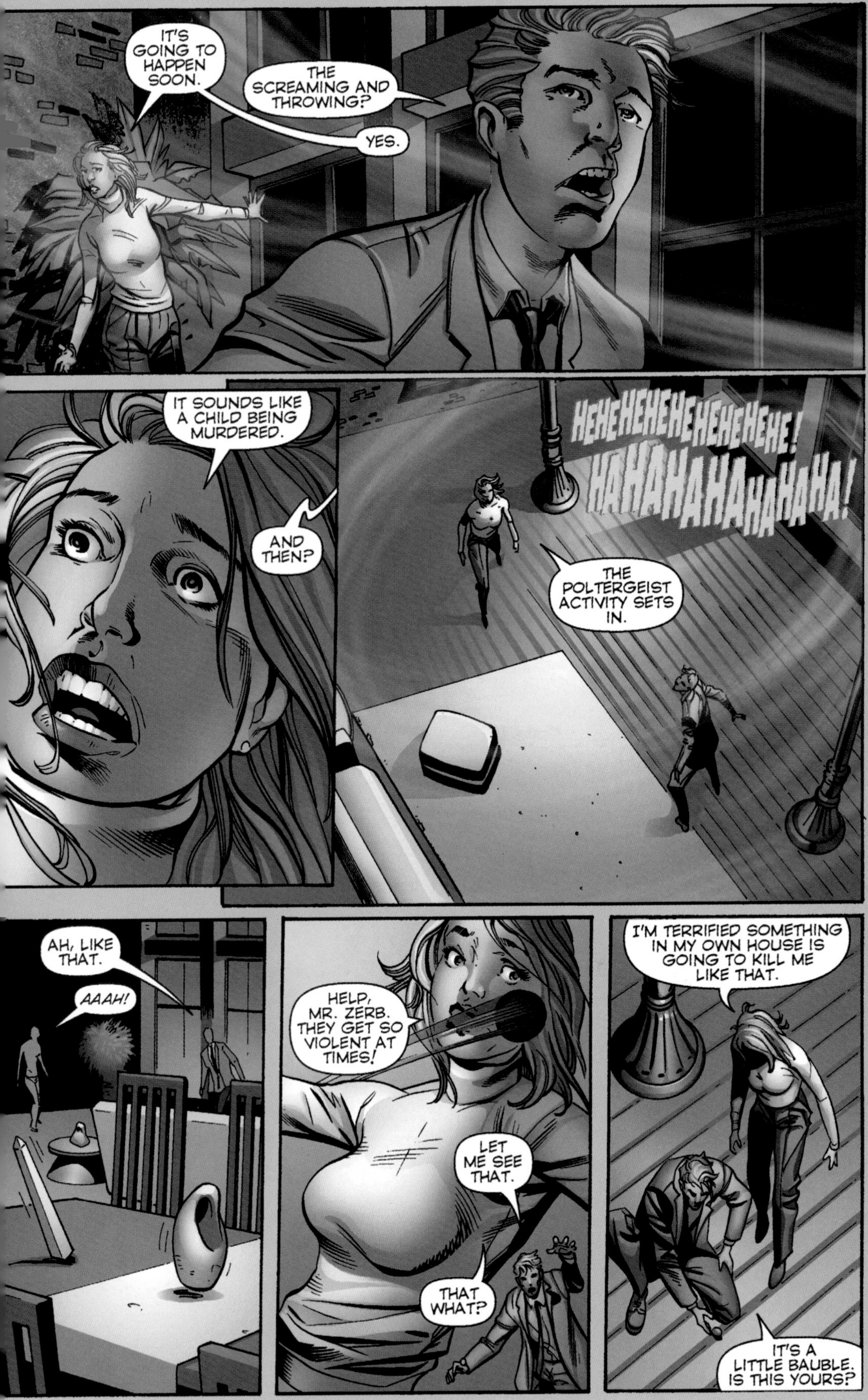
IT'S GOING TO HAPPEN SOON.
THE SCREAMING AND THROWING?
YES.
IT SOUNDS LIKE A CHILD BEING MURDERED.
AND THEN?
HEHEHEHEHEHEHEHEHE! HAHAHAHAHAHAHAHA!
THE POLTERGEIST ACTIVITY SETS IN.
AH, LIKE THAT.
AAAH!
HELP, MR. ZERB. THEY GET SO VIOLENT AT TIMES!
LET ME SEE THAT.
THAT WHAT?
I'M TERRIFIED SOMETHING IN MY OWN HOUSE IS GOING TO KILL ME LIKE THAT.
IT'S A LITTLE BAUBLE. IS THIS YOURS?

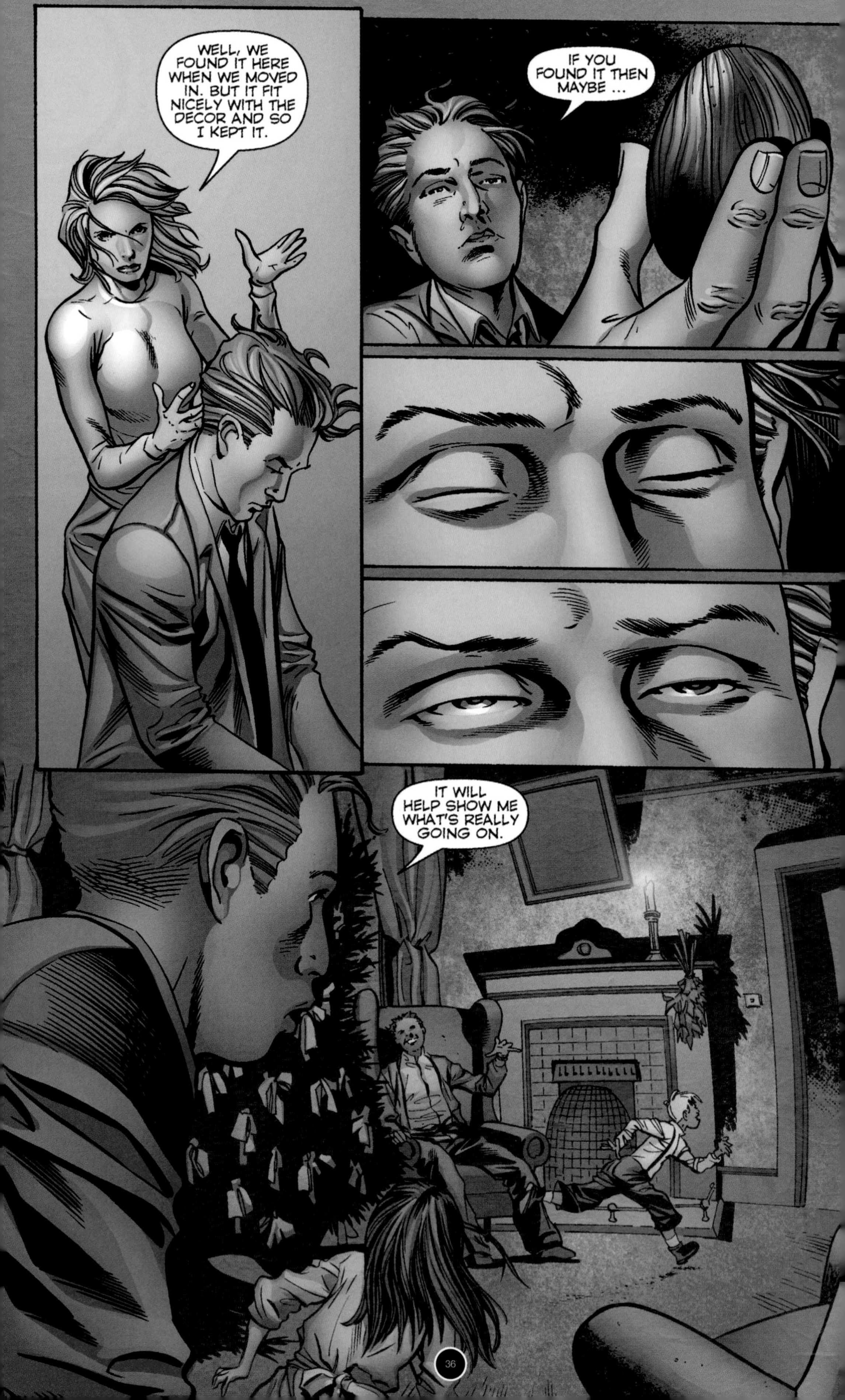
WELL, WE FOUND IT HERE WHEN WE MOVED IN. BUT IT FIT NICELY WITH THE DECOR AND SO I KEPT IT.
IF YOU FOUND IT THEN MAYBE ...
IT WILL HELP SHOW ME WHAT'S REALLY GOING ON.

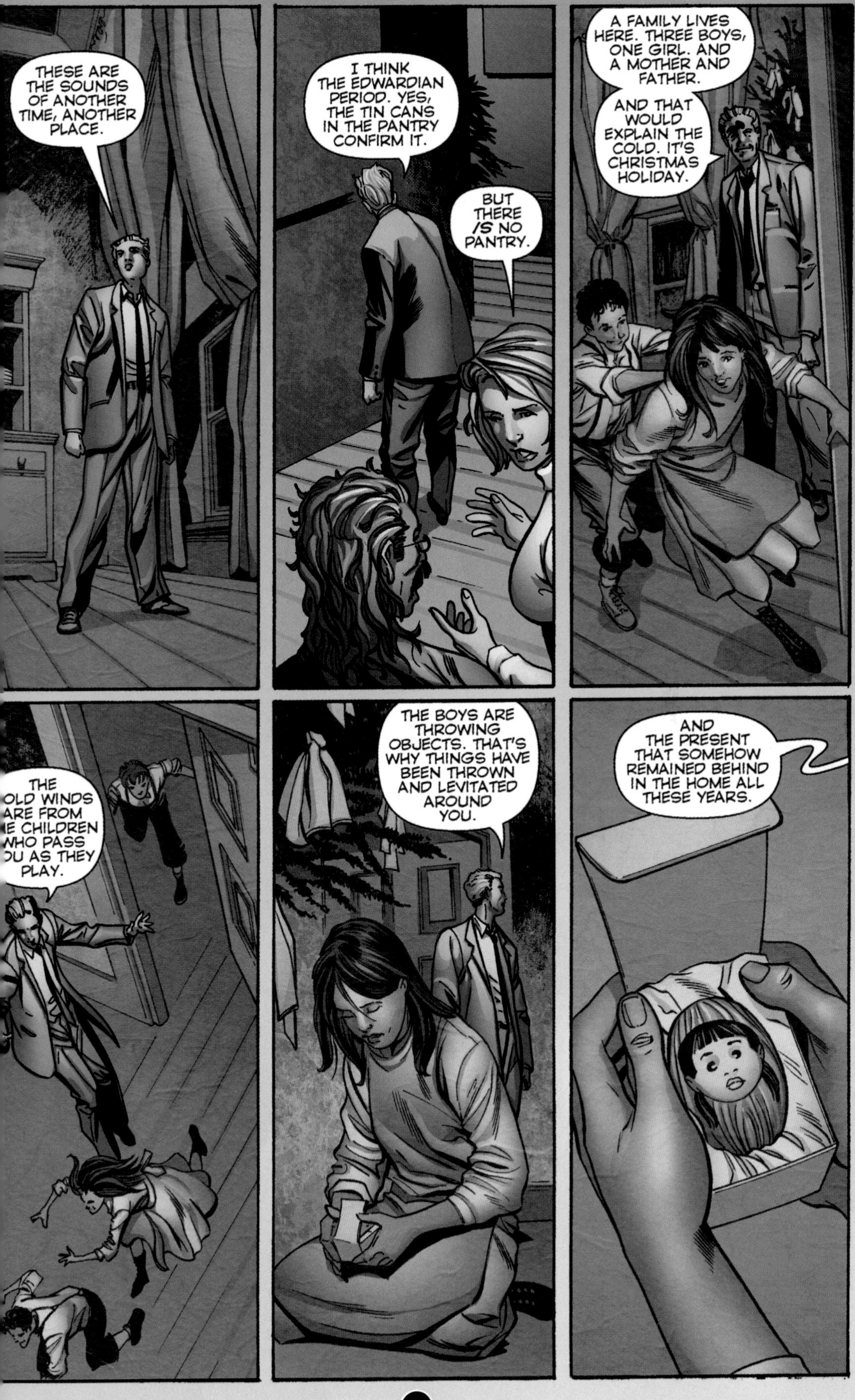
THESE ARE THE SOUNDS OF ANOTHER TIME, ANOTHER PLACE.
I THINK THE EDWARDIAN PERIOD. YES, THE TIN CANS IN THE PANTRY CONFIRM IT.
BUT THERE *IS* NO PANTRY.
A FAMILY LIVES HERE. THREE BOYS, ONE GIRL. AND A MOTHER AND FATHER.
AND THAT WOULD EXPLAIN THE COLD. IT'S CHRISTMAS HOLIDAY.
THE OLD WINDS ARE FROM THE CHILDREN WHO PASS YOU AS THEY PLAY.
THE BOYS ARE THROWING OBJECTS. THAT'S WHY THINGS HAVE BEEN THROWN AND LEVITATED AROUND YOU.
AND THE PRESENT THAT SOMEHOW REMAINED BEHIND IN THE HOME ALL THESE YEARS.

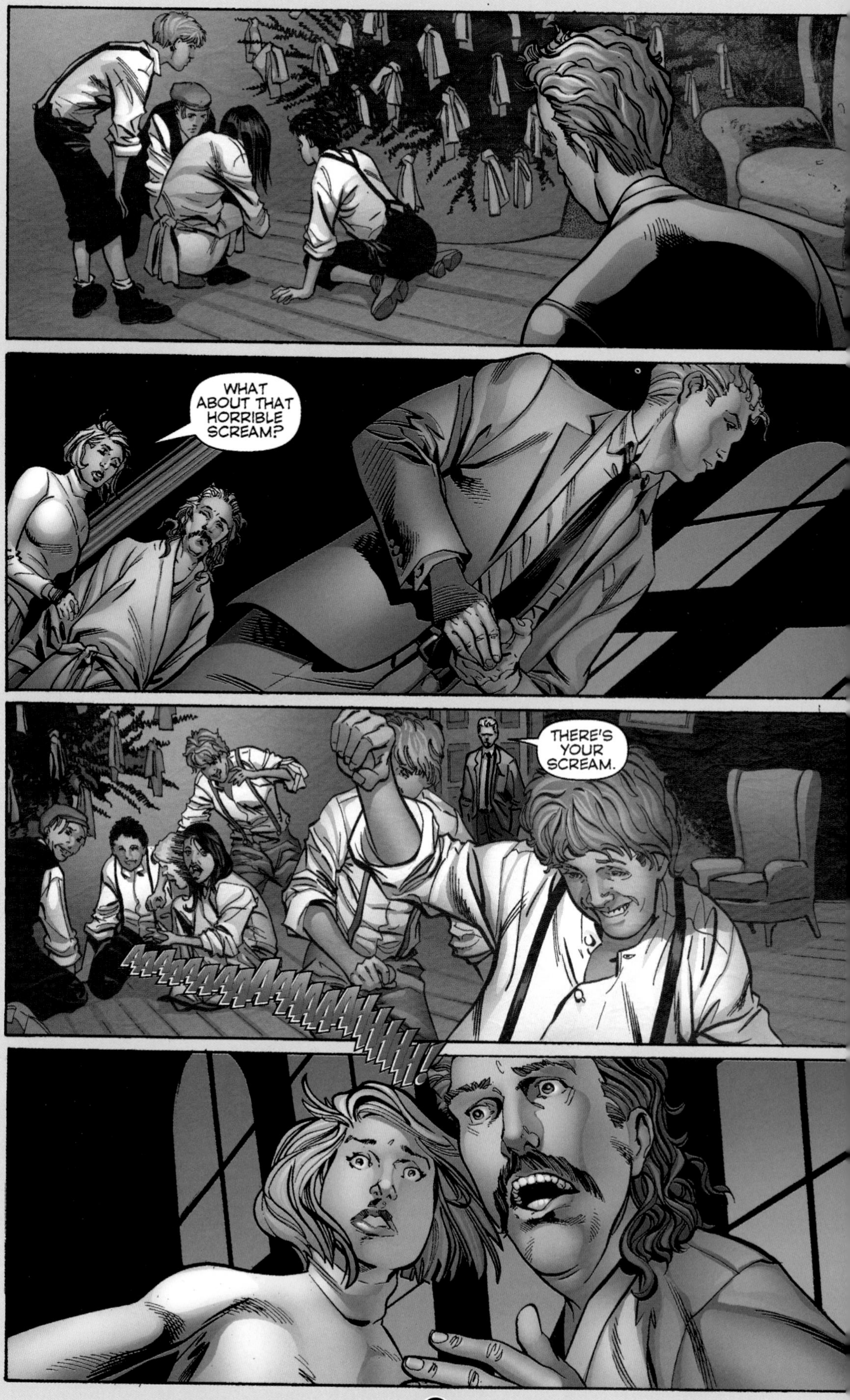
WHAT ABOUT THAT HORRIBLE SCREAM?
THERE'S YOUR SCREAM.
AAAAAAAAAAAAAAAAAHHHHHH!

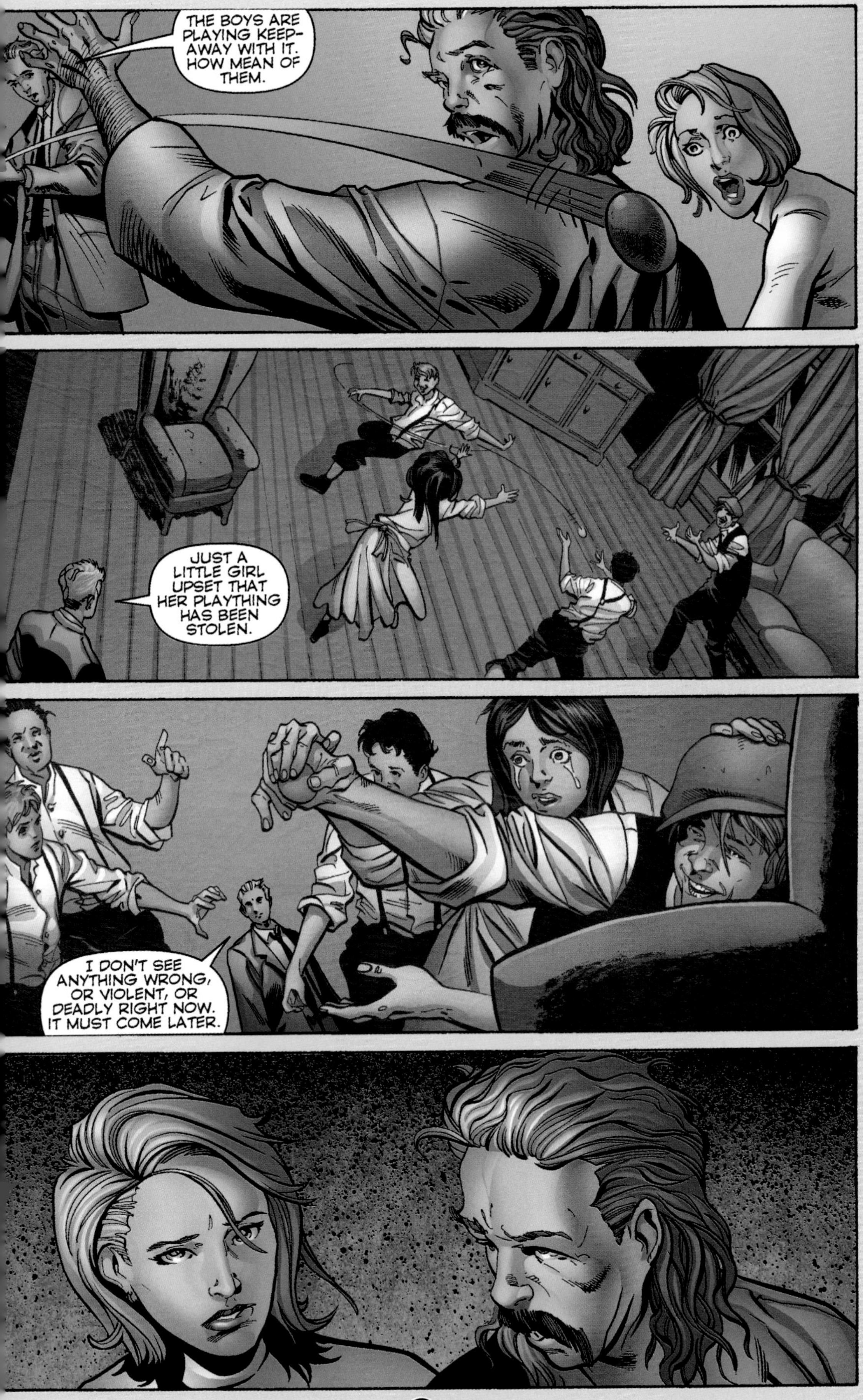
THE BOYS ARE PLAYING KEEP-AWAY WITH IT. HOW MEAN OF THEM.
JUST A LITTLE GIRL UPSET THAT HER PLAYTHING HAS BEEN STOLEN.
I DON'T SEE ANYTHING WRONG, OR VIOLENT, OR DEADLY RIGHT NOW. IT MUST COME LATER.

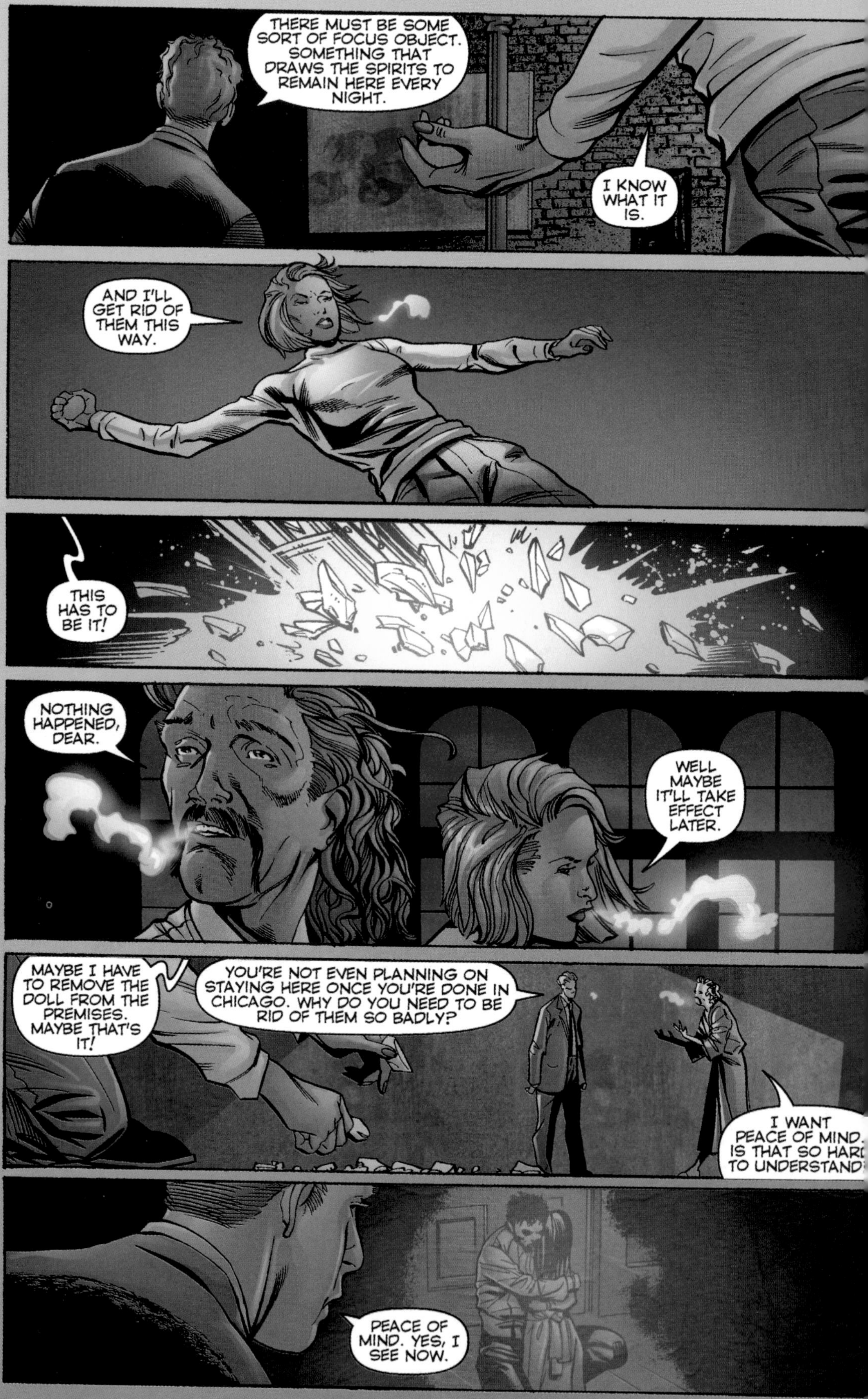
THERE MUST BE SOME SORT OF FOCUS OBJECT. SOMETHING THAT DRAWS THE SPIRITS TO REMAIN HERE EVERY NIGHT.
I KNOW WHAT IT IS.
AND I'LL GET RID OF THEM THIS WAY.
THIS HAS TO BE IT!
NOTHING HAPPENED, DEAR.
WELL MAYBE IT'LL TAKE EFFECT LATER.
MAYBE I HAVE TO REMOVE THE DOLL FROM THE PREMISES. MAYBE THAT'S IT!
YOU'RE NOT EVEN PLANNING ON STAYING HERE ONCE YOU'RE DONE IN CHICAGO. WHY DO YOU NEED TO BE RID OF THEM SO BADLY?
I WANT PEACE OF MIND. IS THAT SO HAR
TO UNDERSTAND
PEACE OF MIND. YES, I SEE NOW.

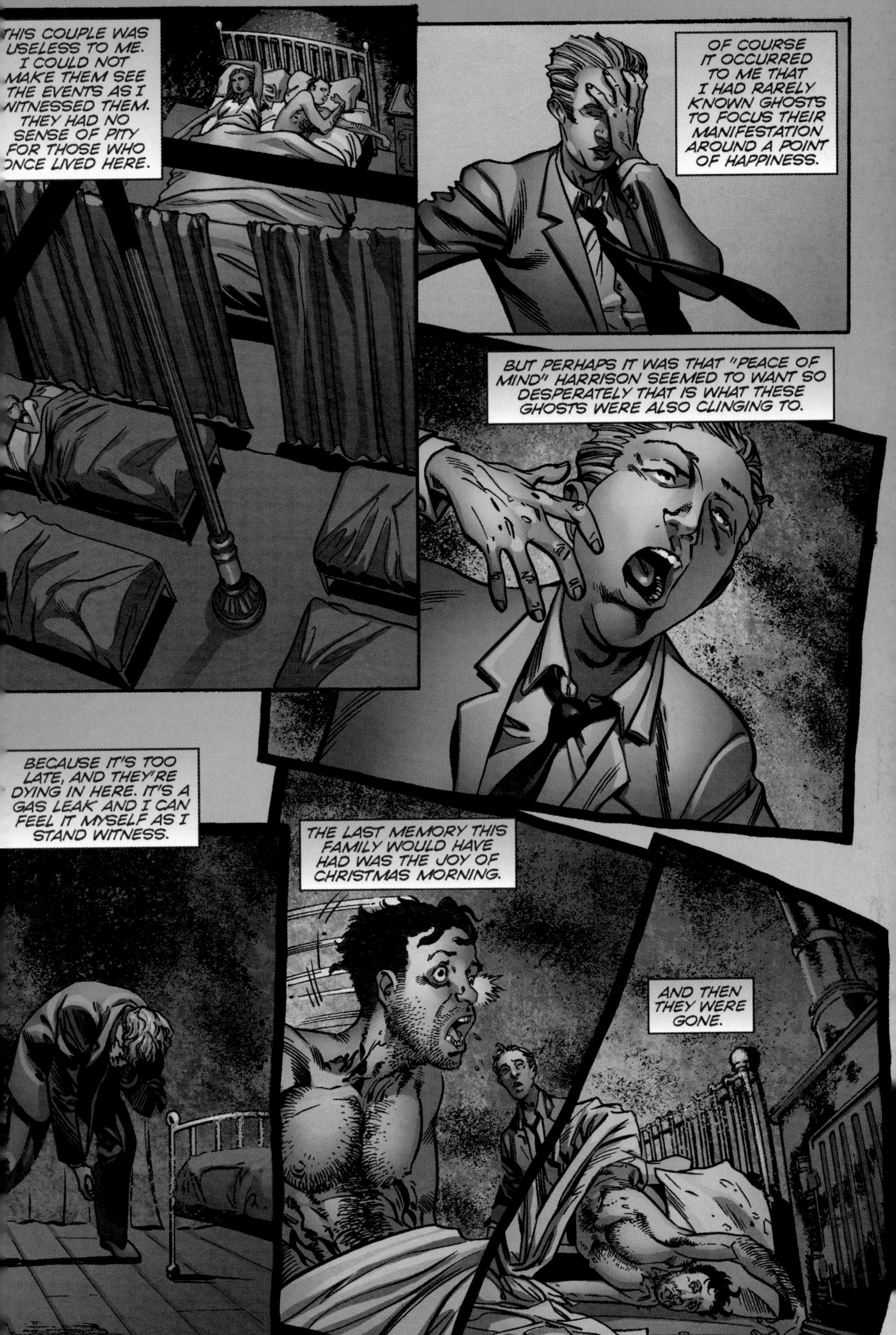
THIS COUPLE WAS USELESS TO ME. I COULD NOT MAKE THEM SEE THE EVENTS AS I WITNESSED THEM. THEY HAD NO SENSE OF PITY FOR THOSE WHO ONCE LIVED HERE.
OF COURSE IT OCCURRED TO ME THAT I HAD RARELY KNOWN GHOSTS TO FOCUS THEIR MANIFESTATION AROUND A POINT OF HAPPINESS.
BUT PERHAPS IT WAS THAT "PEACE OF MIND" HARRISON SEEMED TO WANT SO DESPERATELY THAT IS WHAT THESE GHOSTS WERE ALSO CLINGING TO.
BECAUSE IT'S TOO LATE, AND THEY'RE DYING IN HERE. IT'S A GAS LEAK AND I CAN FEEL IT MYSELF AS I STAND WITNESS.
THE LAST MEMORY THIS FAMILY WOULD HAVE HAD WAS THE JOY OF CHRISTMAS MORNING.
AND THEN THEY WERE GONE.

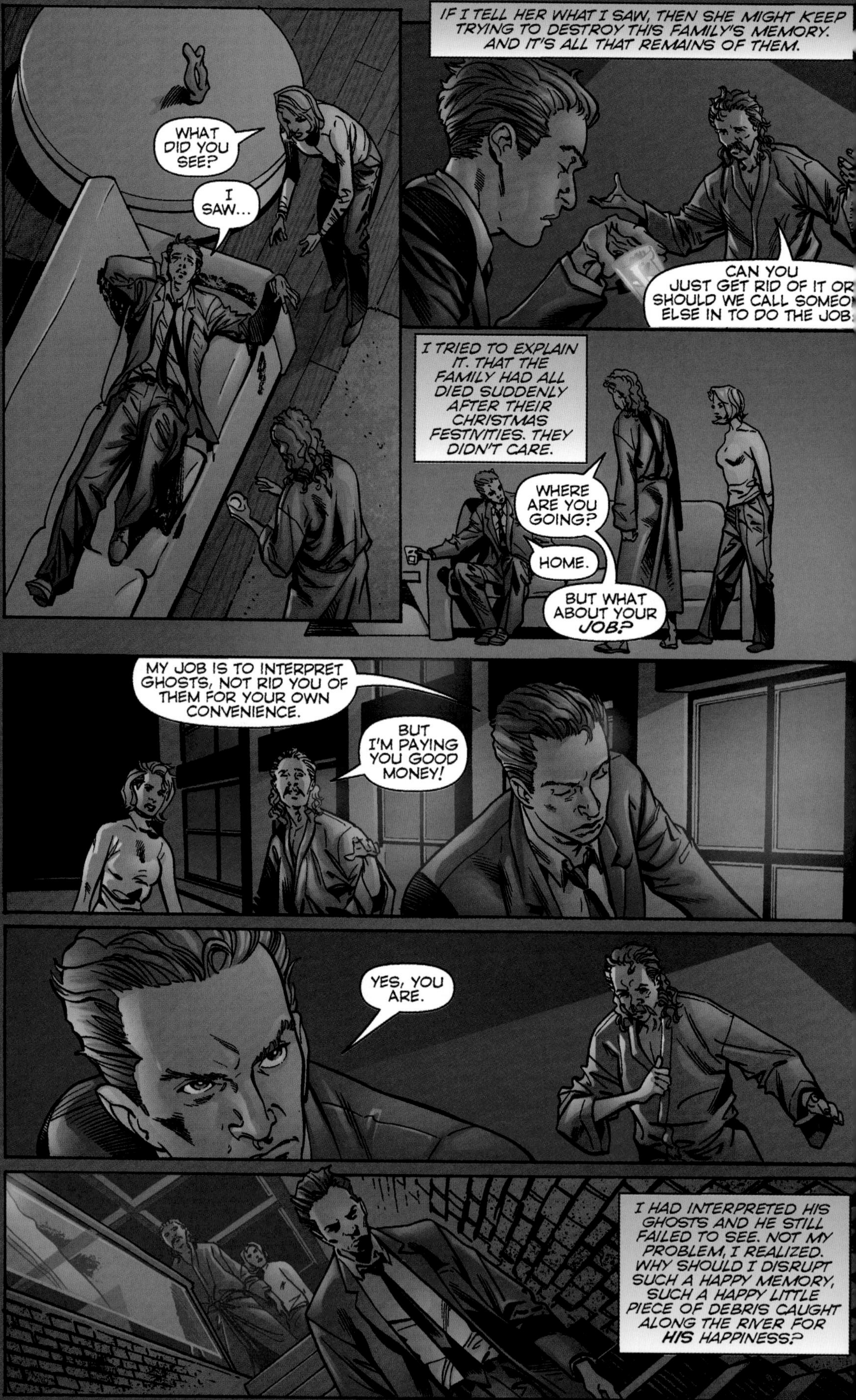
WHAT DID YOU SEE?
I SAW...
IF I TELL HER WHAT I SAW, THEN SHE MIGHT KEEP TRYING TO DESTROY THIS FAMILY'S MEMORY. AND IT'S ALL THAT REMAINS OF THEM.
CAN YOU JUST GET RID OF IT OR SHOULD WE CALL SOMEO ELSE IN TO DO THE JOB
I TRIED TO EXPLAIN IT. THAT THE FAMILY HAD ALL DIED SUDDENLY AFTER THEIR CHRISTMAS FESTIVITIES. THEY DIDN'T CARE.
WHERE ARE YOU GOING?
HOME.
BUT WHAT ABOUT YOUR JOB?
MY JOB IS TO INTERPRET GHOSTS, NOT RID YOU OF THEM FOR YOUR OWN CONVENIENCE.
BUT I'M PAYING YOU GOOD MONEY!
YES, YOU ARE.
I HAD INTERPRETED HIS GHOSTS AND HE STILL FAILED TO SEE. NOT MY PROBLEM, I REALIZED. WHY SHOULD I DISRUPT SUCH A HAPPY MEMORY, SUCH A HAPPY LITTLE PIECE OF DEBRIS CAUGHT ALONG THE RIVER FOR HIS HAPPINESS?

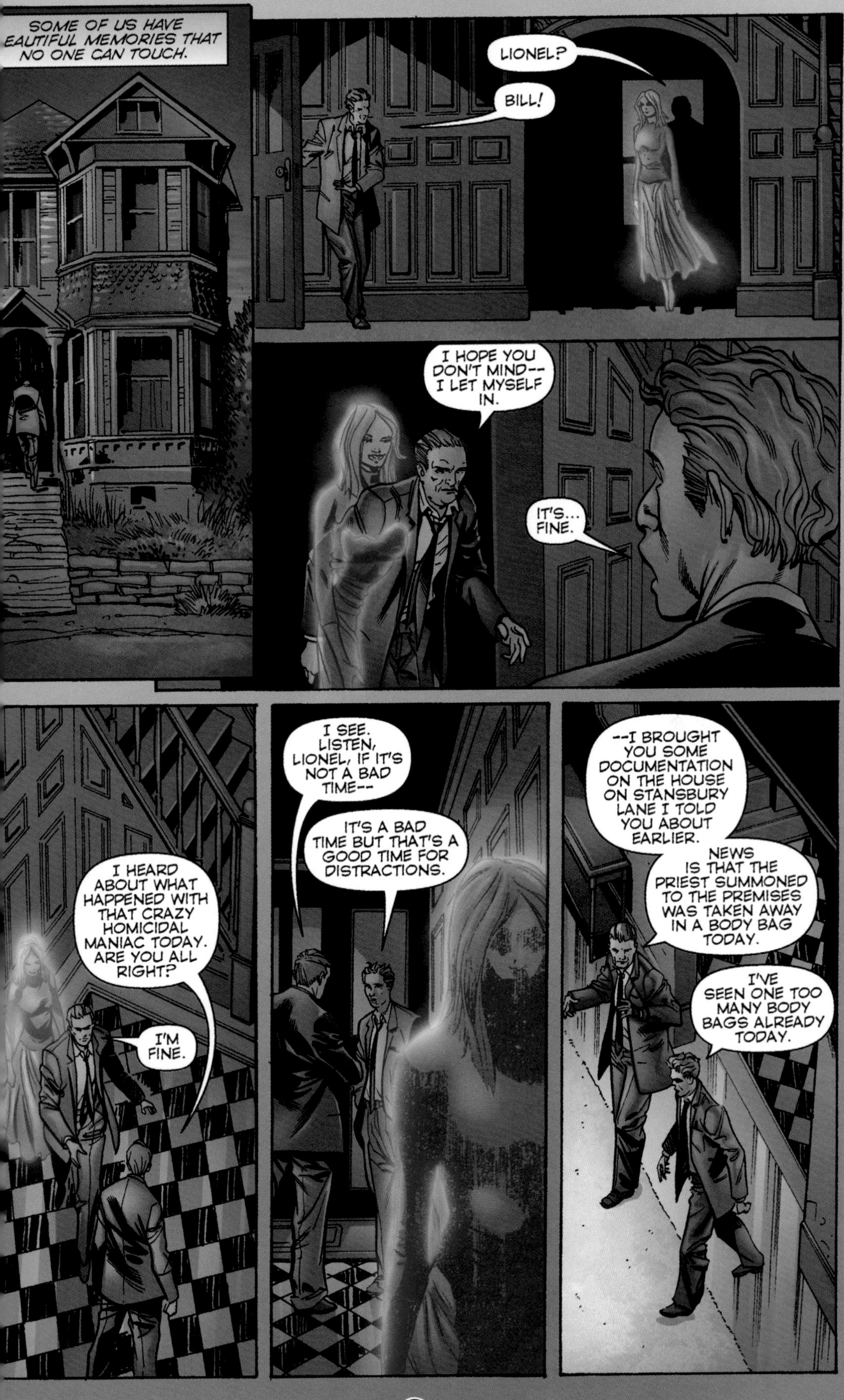
SOME OF US HAVE BEAUTIFUL MEMORIES THAT NO ONE CAN TOUCH.
LIONEL?
BILL!
I HOPE YOU DON'T MIND-- I LET MYSELF IN.
IT'S... FINE.
I HEARD ABOUT WHAT HAPPENED WITH THAT CRAZY HOMICIDAL MANIAC TODAY. ARE YOU ALL RIGHT?
I'M FINE.
I SEE. LISTEN, LIONEL, IF IT'S NOT A BAD TIME--
IT'S A BAD TIME BUT THAT'S A GOOD TIME FOR DISTRACTIONS.
--I BROUGHT YOU SOME DOCUMENTATION ON THE HOUSE ON STANSBURY LANE I TOLD YOU ABOUT EARLIER.
NEWS IS THAT THE PRIEST SUMMONED TO THE PREMISES WAS TAKEN AWAY IN A BODY BAG TODAY.
I'VE SEEN ONE TOO MANY BODY BAGS ALREADY TODAY.

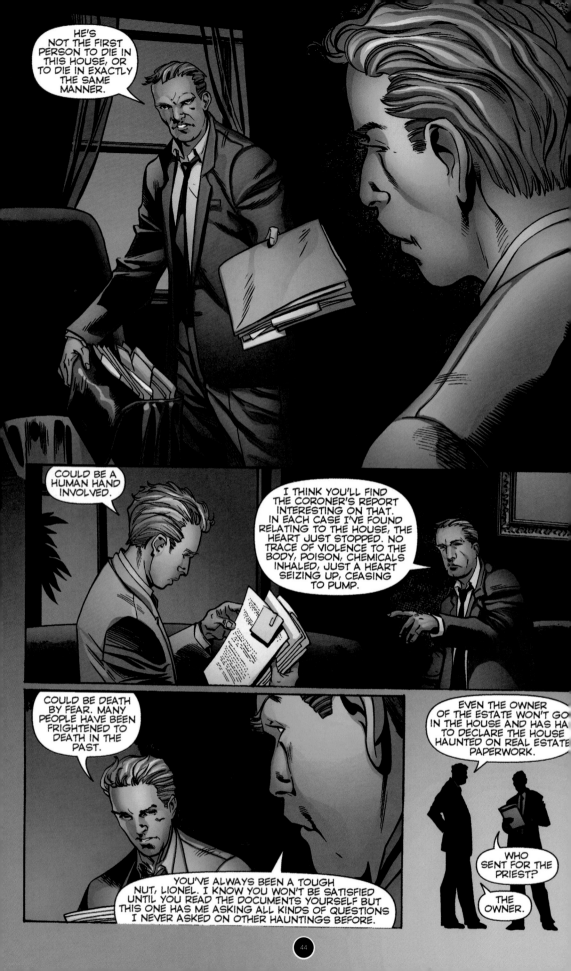

HE'S NOT THE FIRST PERSON TO DIE IN THIS HOUSE, OR TO DIE IN EXACTLY THE SAME MANNER.

COULD BE A HUMAN HAND INVOLVED.

I THINK YOU'LL FIND THE CORONER'S REPORT INTERESTING ON THAT. IN EACH CASE I'VE FOUND RELATING TO THE HOUSE, THE HEART JUST STOPPED. NO TRACE OF VIOLENCE TO THE BODY, POISON, CHEMICALS INHALED, JUST A HEART SEIZING UP, CEASING TO PUMP.

COULD BE DEATH BY FEAR. MANY PEOPLE HAVE BEEN FRIGHTENED TO DEATH IN THE PAST.

EVEN THE OWNER OF THE ESTATE WON'T GO IN THE HOUSE AND HAS HA TO DECLARE THE HOUSE HAUNTED ON REAL ESTATE PAPERWORK.

YOU'VE ALWAYS BEEN A TOUGH NUT, LIONEL. I KNOW YOU WON'T BE SATISFIED UNTIL YOU READ THE DOCUMENTS YOURSELF BUT THIS ONE HAS ME ASKING ALL KINDS OF QUESTIONS I NEVER ASKED ON OTHER HAUNTINGS BEFORE.

WHO SENT FOR THE PRIEST?

THE OWNER.

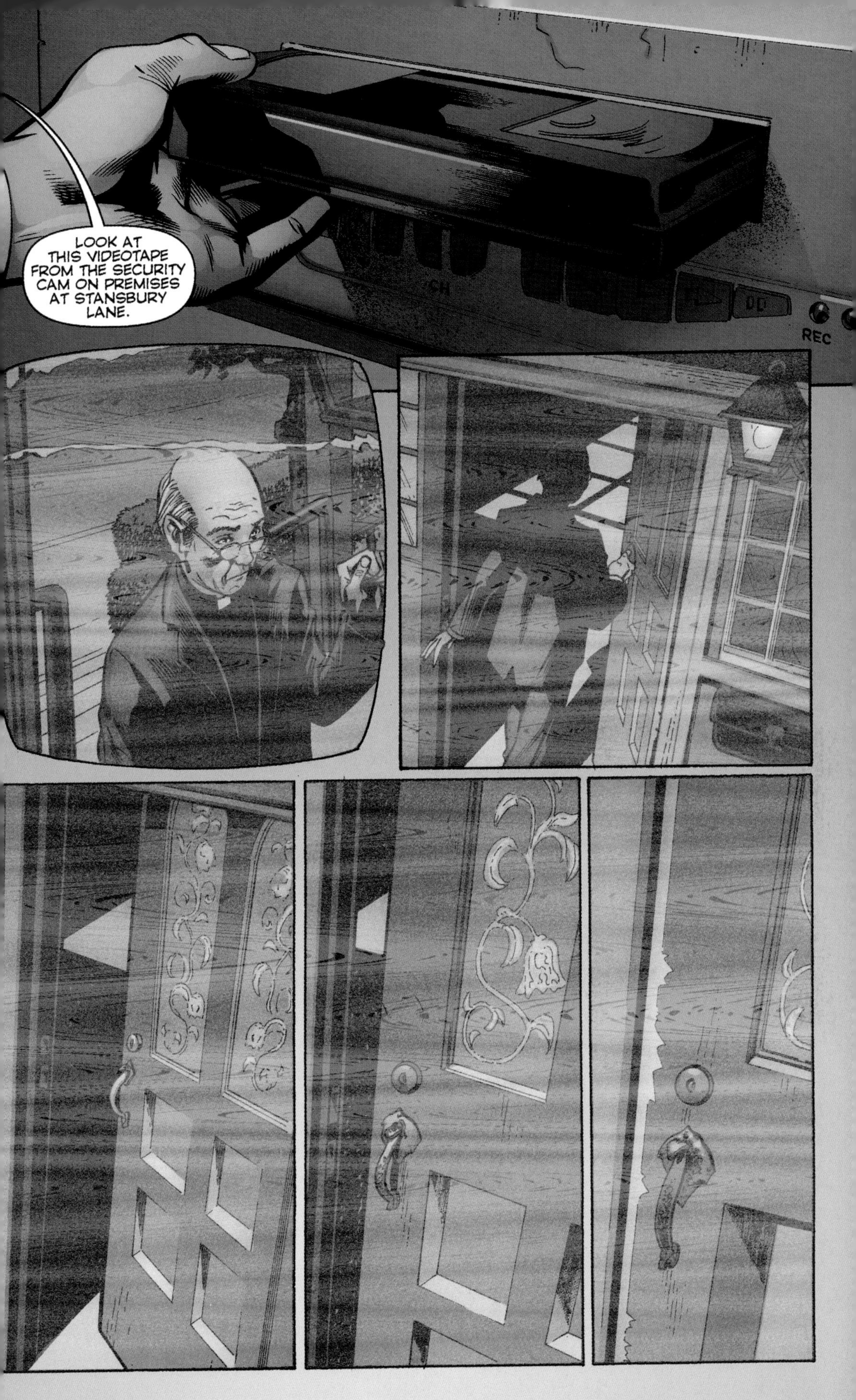
LOOK AT THIS VIDEOTAPE FROM THE SECURITY CAM ON PREMISES AT STANSBURY LANE.
CH
REC

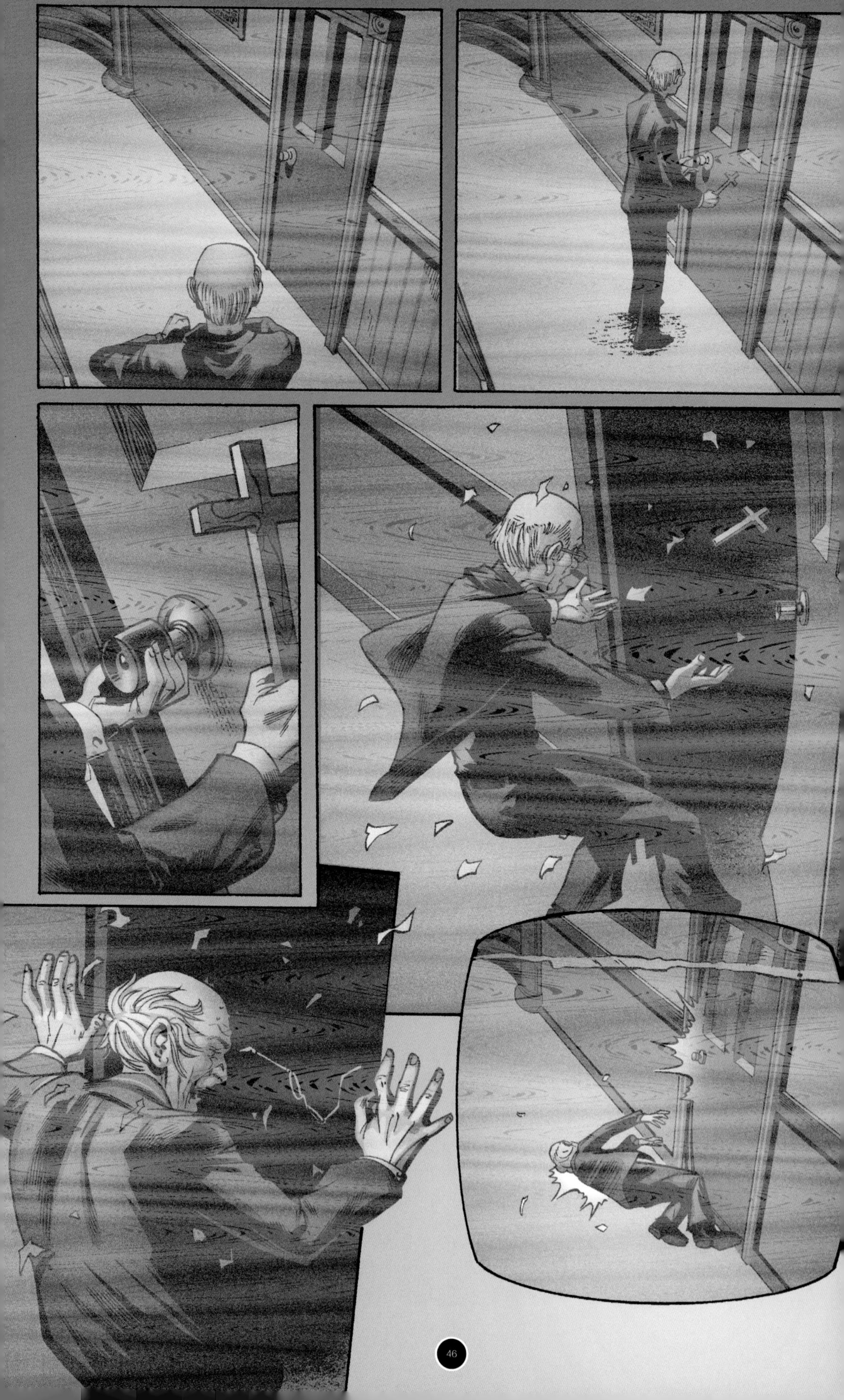

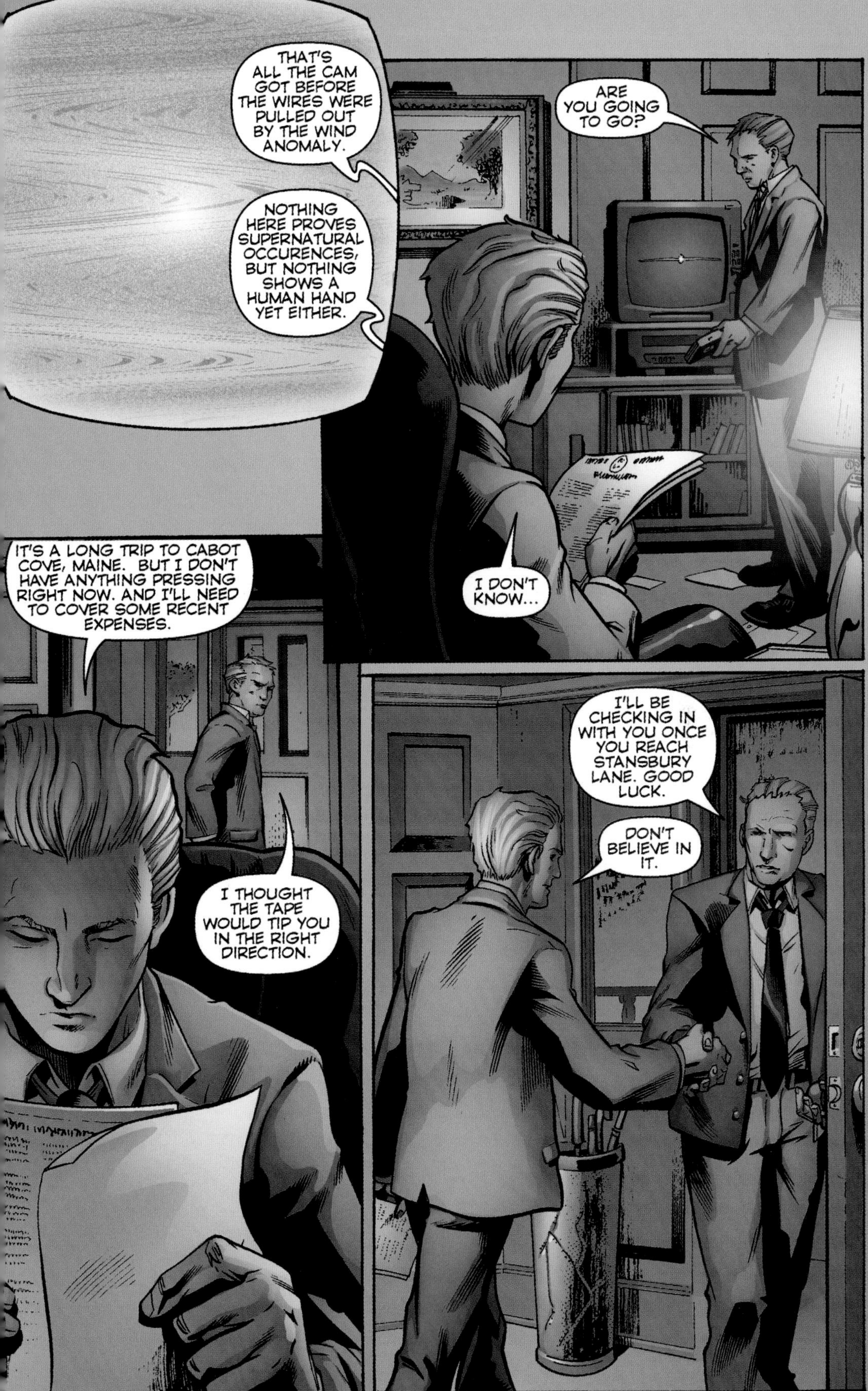
THAT'S ALL THE CAM GOT BEFORE THE WIRES WERE PULLED OUT BY THE WIND ANOMALY.
NOTHING HERE PROVES SUPERNATURAL OCCURENCES, BUT NOTHING SHOWS A HUMAN HAND YET EITHER.
ARE YOU GOING TO GO?
I DON'T KNOW...
IT'S A LONG TRIP TO CABOT COVE, MAINE. BUT I DON'T HAVE ANYTHING PRESSING RIGHT NOW. AND I'LL NEED TO COVER SOME RECENT EXPENSES.
I THOUGHT THE TAPE WOULD TIP YOU IN THE RIGHT DIRECTION.
I'LL BE CHECKING IN WITH YOU ONCE YOU REACH STANSBURY LANE. GOOD LUCK.
DON'T BELIEVE IN IT.

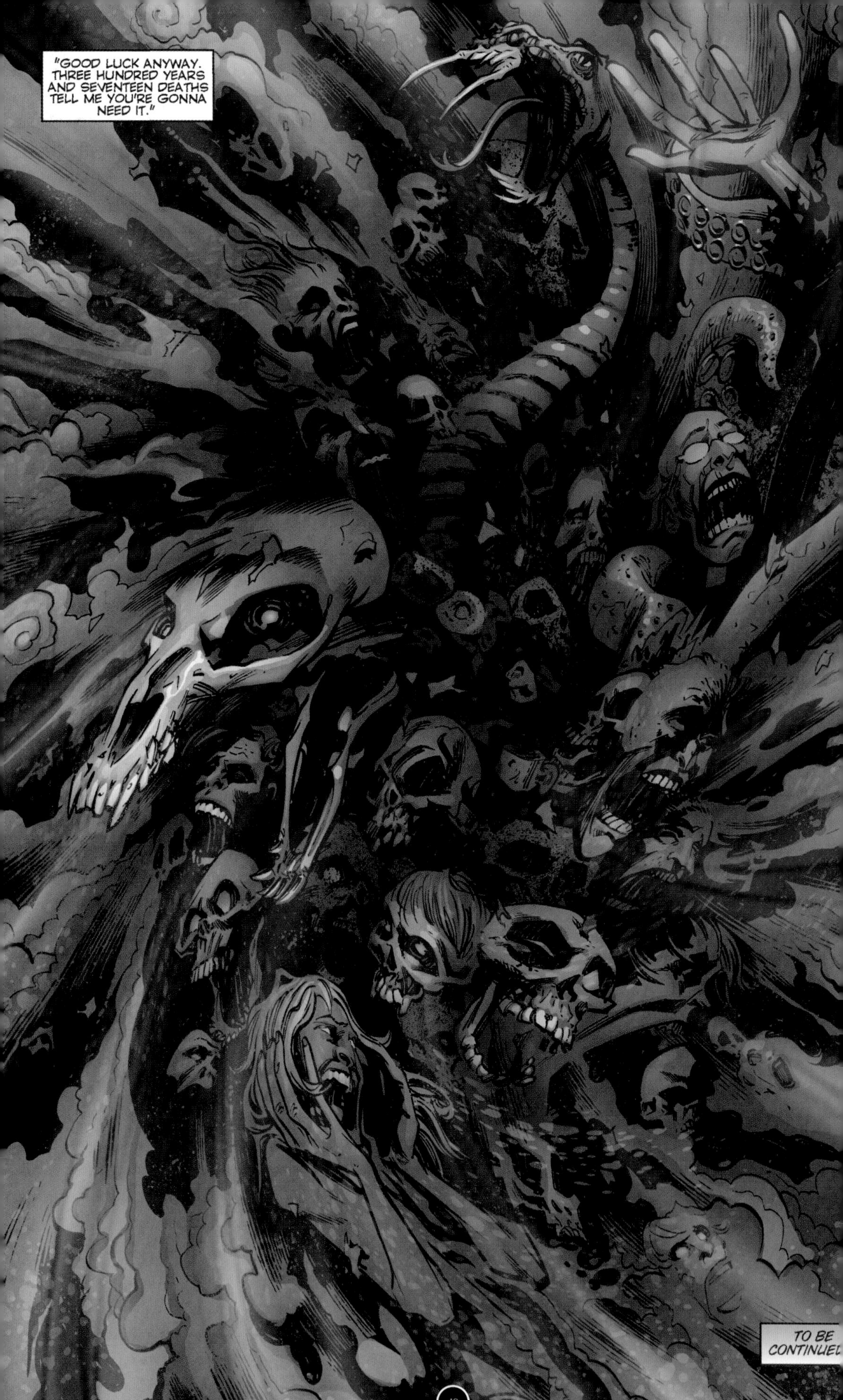
"GOOD LUCK ANYWAY. THREE HUNDRED YEARS AND SEVENTEEN DEATHS TELL ME YOU'RE GONNA NEED IT."
TO BE CONTINUED

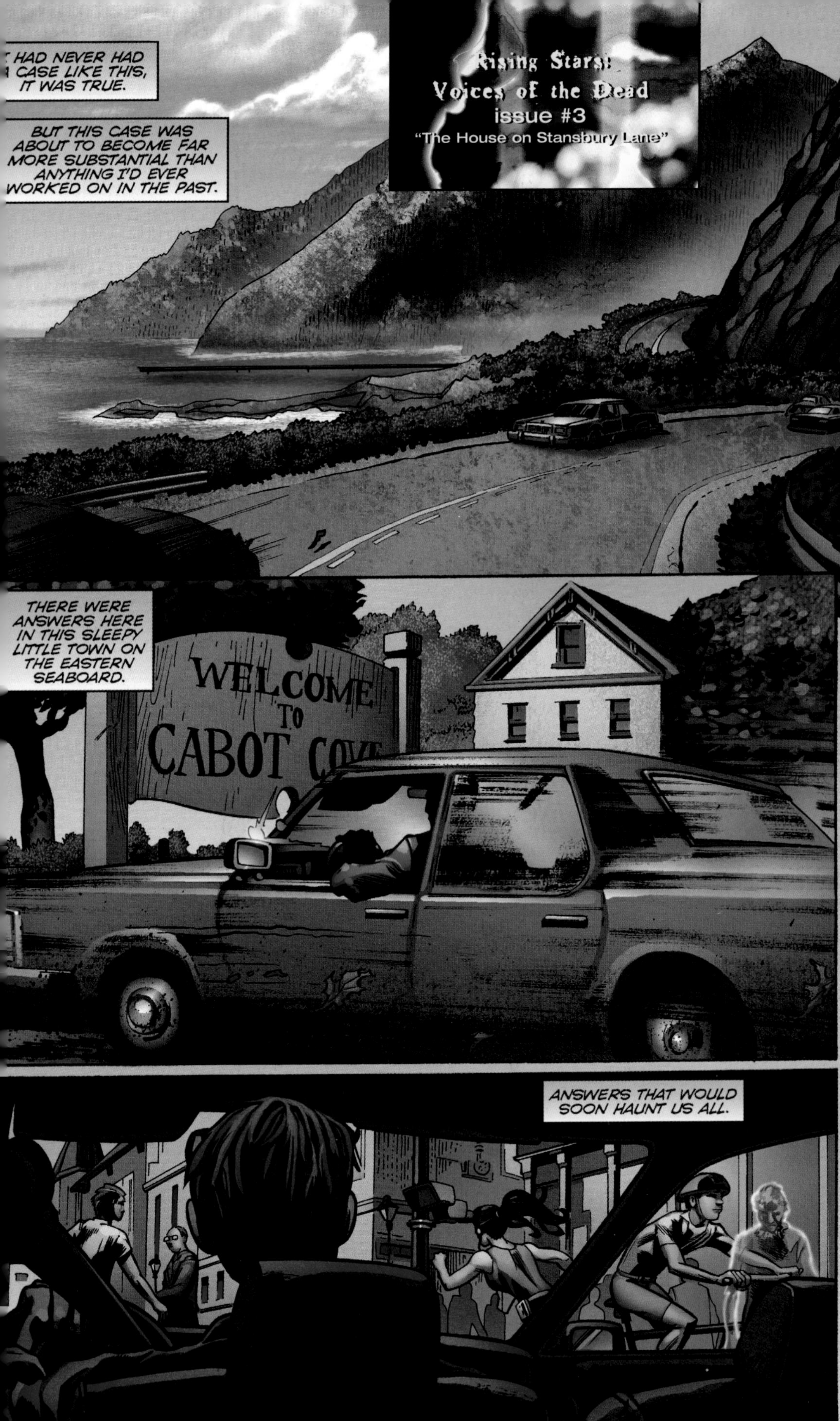
Rising Stars:
Voices of the Dead
issue #3
"The House on Stansbury Lane"
HAD NEVER HAD CASE LIKE THIS, IT WAS TRUE.
BUT THIS CASE WAS ABOUT TO BECOME FAR MORE SUBSTANTIAL THAN ANYTHING I'D EVER WORKED ON IN THE PAST.
THERE WERE ANSWERS HERE IN THIS SLEEPY LITTLE TOWN ON THE EASTERN SEABOARD.
WELCOME TO CABOT COVE
ANSWERS THAT WOULD SOON HAUNT US ALL.

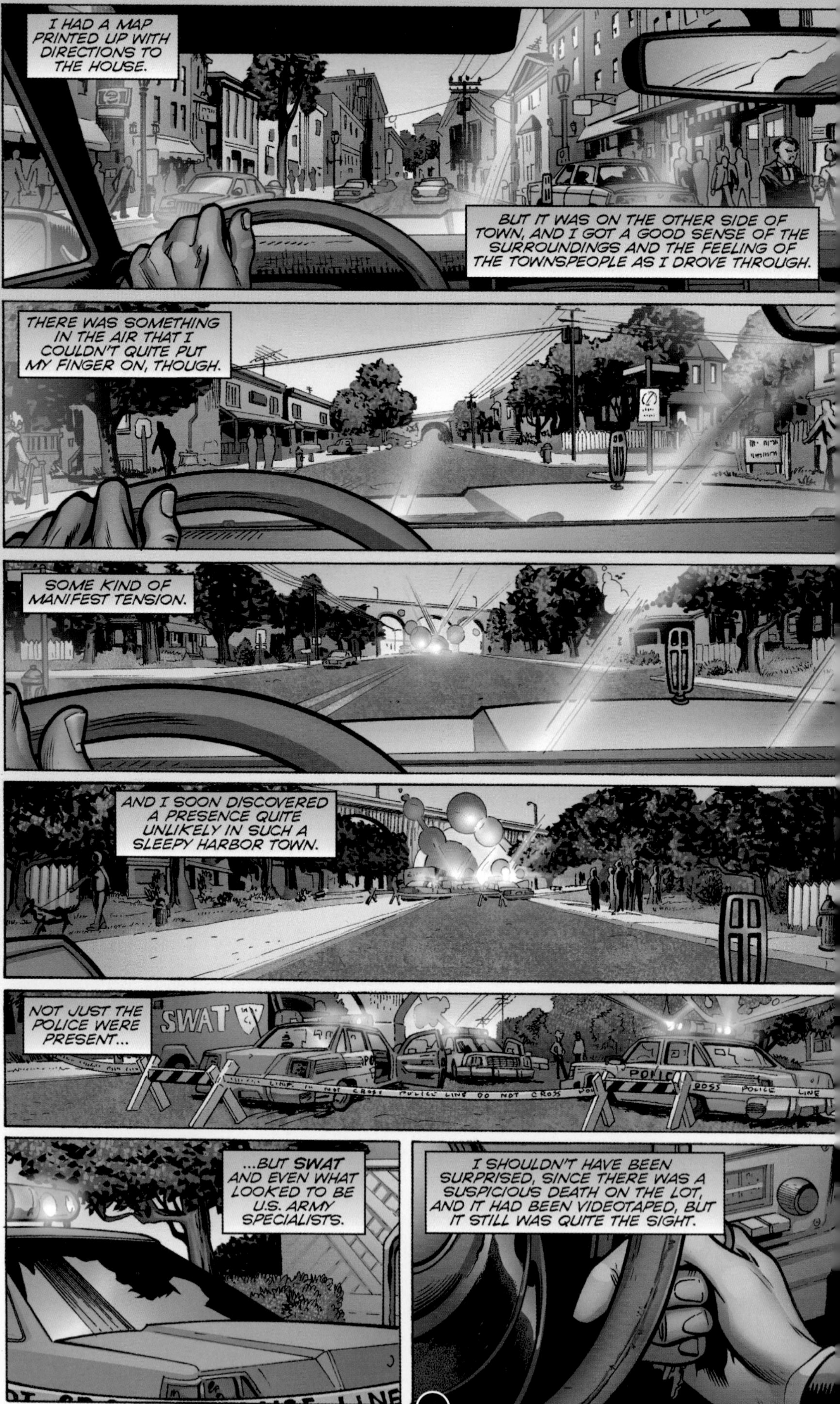
I HAD A MAP PRINTED UP WITH DIRECTIONS TO THE HOUSE.
BUT IT WAS ON THE OTHER SIDE OF TOWN, AND I GOT A GOOD SENSE OF THE SURROUNDINGS AND THE FEELING OF THE TOWNSPEOPLE AS I DROVE THROUGH.
THERE WAS SOMETHING IN THE AIR THAT I COULDN'T QUITE PUT MY FINGER ON, THOUGH.
SOME KIND OF MANIFEST TENSION.
AND I SOON DISCOVERED A PRESENCE QUITE UNLIKELY IN SUCH A SLEEPY HARBOR TOWN.
NOT JUST THE POLICE WERE PRESENT...
SWAT
...BUT SWAT AND EVEN WHAT LOOKED TO BE U.S. ARMY SPECIALISTS.
I SHOULDN'T HAVE BEEN SURPRISED, SINCE THERE WAS A SUSPICIOUS DEATH ON THE LOT, AND IT HAD BEEN VIDEOTAPED, BUT IT STILL WAS QUITE THE SIGHT.

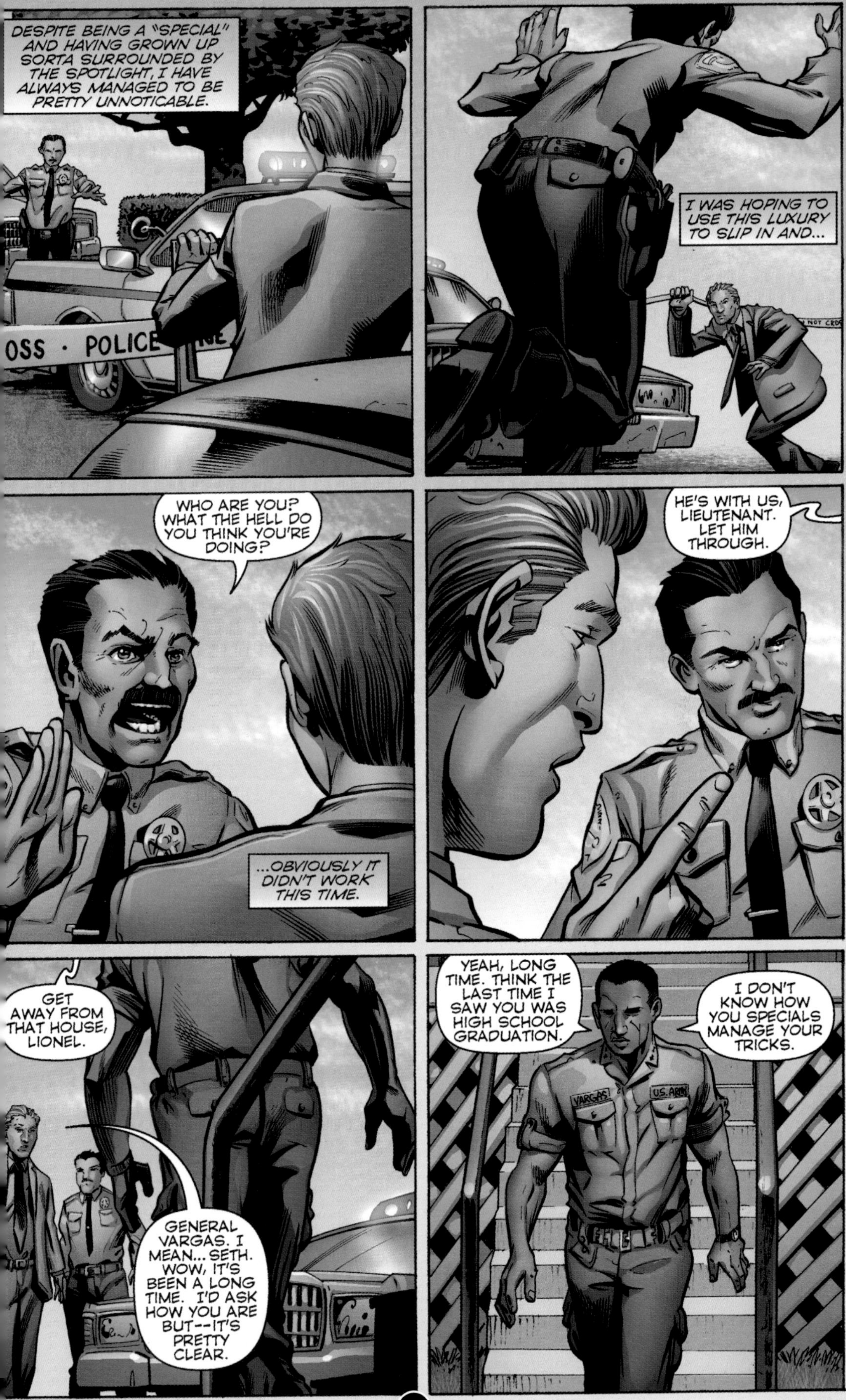

DESPITE BEING A "SPECIAL" AND HAVING GROWN UP SORTA SURROUNDED BY THE SPOTLIGHT, I HAVE ALWAYS MANAGED TO BE PRETTY UNNOTICABLE.
OSS · POLICE
I WAS HOPING TO USE THIS LUXURY TO SLIP IN AND...
WHO ARE YOU? WHAT THE HELL DO YOU THINK YOU'RE DOING?
...OBVIOUSLY IT DIDN'T WORK THIS TIME.
HE'S WITH US, LIEUTENANT. LET HIM THROUGH.
GET AWAY FROM THAT HOUSE, LIONEL.
GENERAL VARGAS. I MEAN... SETH. WOW, IT'S BEEN A LONG TIME. I'D ASK HOW YOU ARE BUT--IT'S PRETTY CLEAR.
YEAH, LONG TIME. THINK THE LAST TIME I SAW YOU WAS HIGH SCHOOL GRADUATION.
I DON'T KNOW HOW YOU SPECIALS MANAGE YOUR TRICKS.
VARGAS
U.S. ARMY

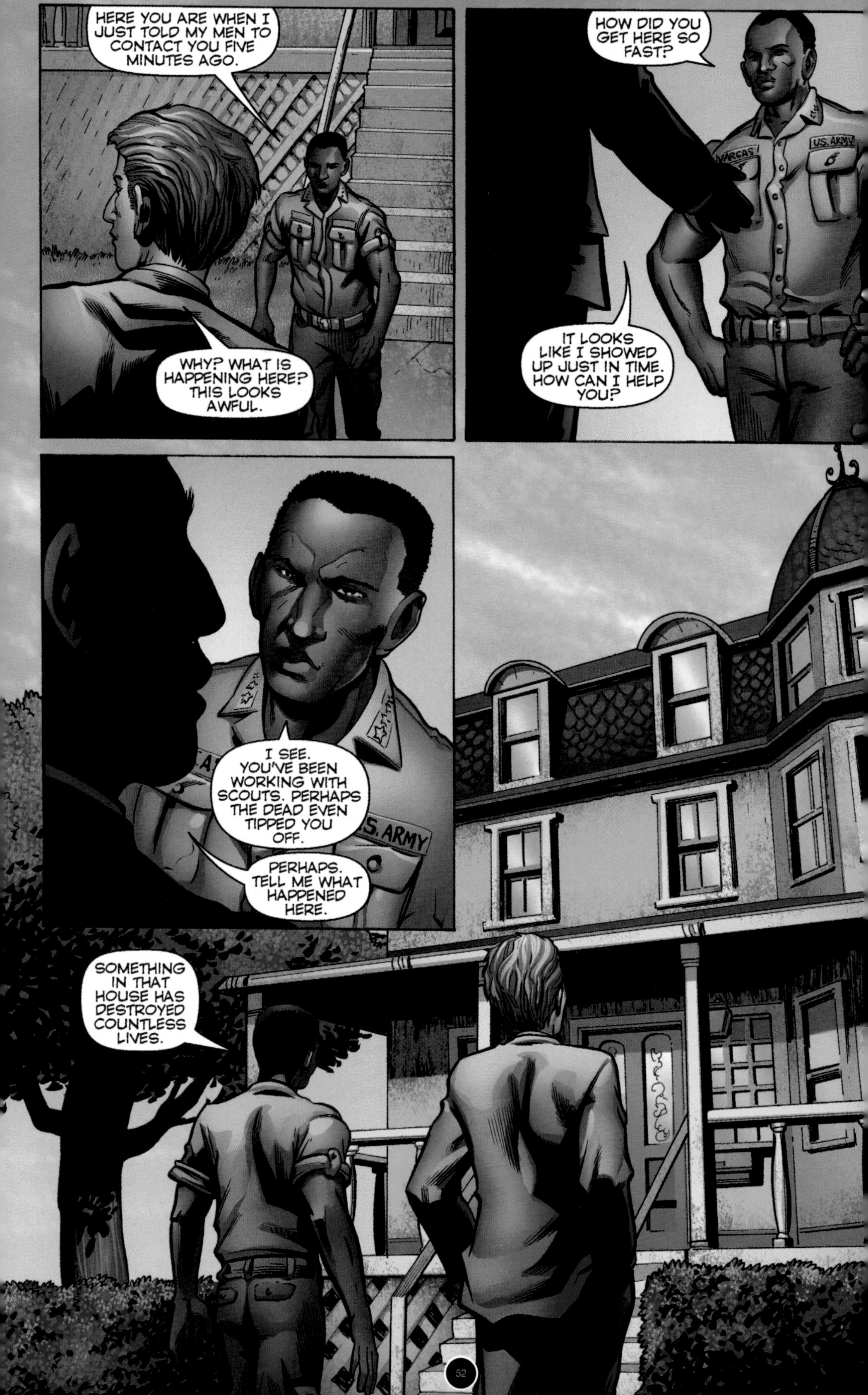

HERE YOU ARE WHEN I JUST TOLD MY MEN TO CONTACT YOU FIVE MINUTES AGO.
WHY? WHAT IS HAPPENING HERE? THIS LOOKS AWFUL.
HOW DID YOU GET HERE SO FAST?
IT LOOKS LIKE I SHOWED UP JUST IN TIME. HOW CAN I HELP YOU?
I SEE. YOU'VE BEEN WORKING WITH SCOUTS. PERHAPS THE DEAD EVEN TIPPED YOU OFF.
PERHAPS. TELL ME WHAT HAPPENED HERE.
SOMETHING IN THAT HOUSE HAS DESTROYED COUNTLESS LIVES.

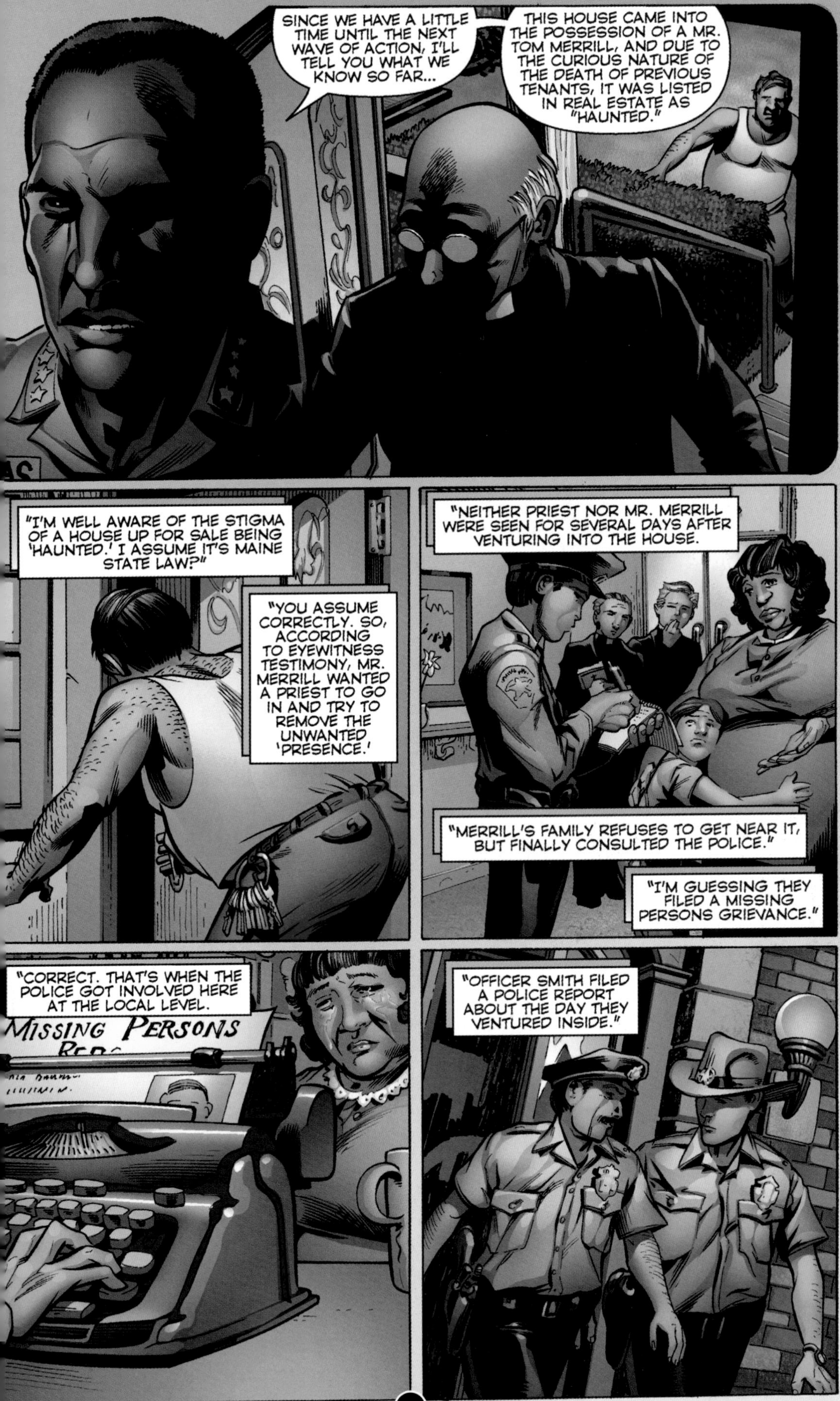
SINCE WE HAVE A LITTLE TIME UNTIL THE NEXT WAVE OF ACTION, I'LL TELL YOU WHAT WE KNOW SO FAR...
THIS HOUSE CAME INTO THE POSSESSION OF A MR. TOM MERRILL, AND DUE TO THE CURIOUS NATURE OF THE DEATH OF PREVIOUS TENANTS, IT WAS LISTED IN REAL ESTATE AS "HAUNTED."
"I'M WELL AWARE OF THE STIGMA OF A HOUSE UP FOR SALE BEING 'HAUNTED.' I ASSUME IT'S MAINE STATE LAW?"
"YOU ASSUME CORRECTLY. SO, ACCORDING TO EYEWITNESS TESTIMONY, MR. MERRILL WANTED A PRIEST TO GO IN AND TRY TO REMOVE THE UNWANTED 'PRESENCE.'
"NEITHER PRIEST NOR MR. MERRILL WERE SEEN FOR SEVERAL DAYS AFTER VENTURING INTO THE HOUSE.
"MERRILL'S FAMILY REFUSES TO GET NEAR IT, BUT FINALLY CONSULTED THE POLICE."
"I'M GUESSING THEY FILED A MISSING PERSONS GRIEVANCE."
"CORRECT. THAT'S WHEN THE POLICE GOT INVOLVED HERE AT THE LOCAL LEVEL.
MISSING PERSONS
"OFFICER SMITH FILED A POLICE REPORT ABOUT THE DAY THEY VENTURED INSIDE."

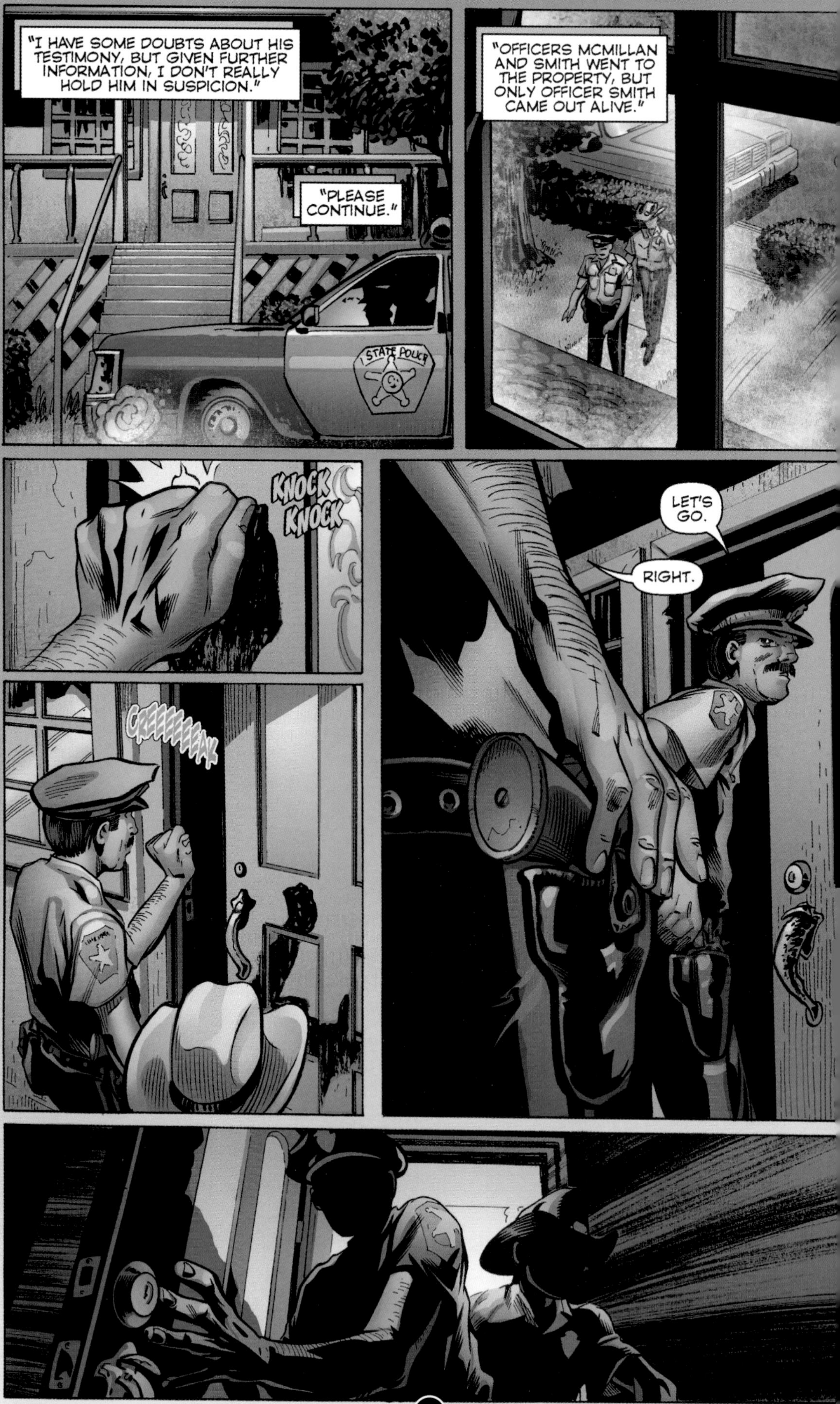
"I HAVE SOME DOUBTS ABOUT HIS TESTIMONY, BUT GIVEN FURTHER INFORMATION, I DON'T REALLY HOLD HIM IN SUSPICION."
"PLEASE CONTINUE."
STATE POLICE
"OFFICERS MCMILLAN AND SMITH WENT TO THE PROPERTY, BUT ONLY OFFICER SMITH CAME OUT ALIVE."
KNOCK KNOCK
LET'S GO.
RIGHT.
CREEEEEEEAK

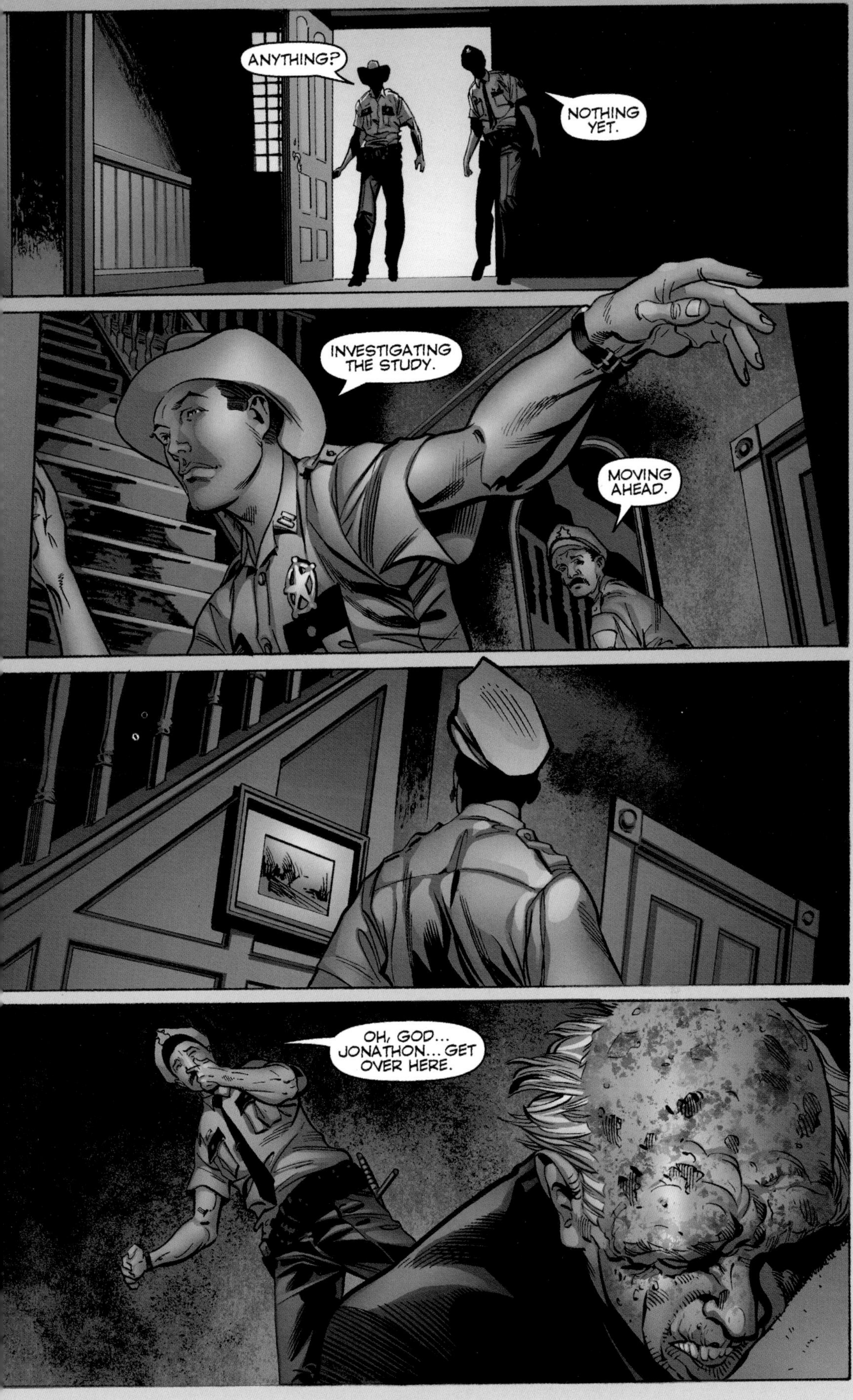
ANYTHING?
NOTHING YET.
INVESTIGATING THE STUDY.
MOVING AHEAD.
OH, GOD... JONATHON... GET OVER HERE.

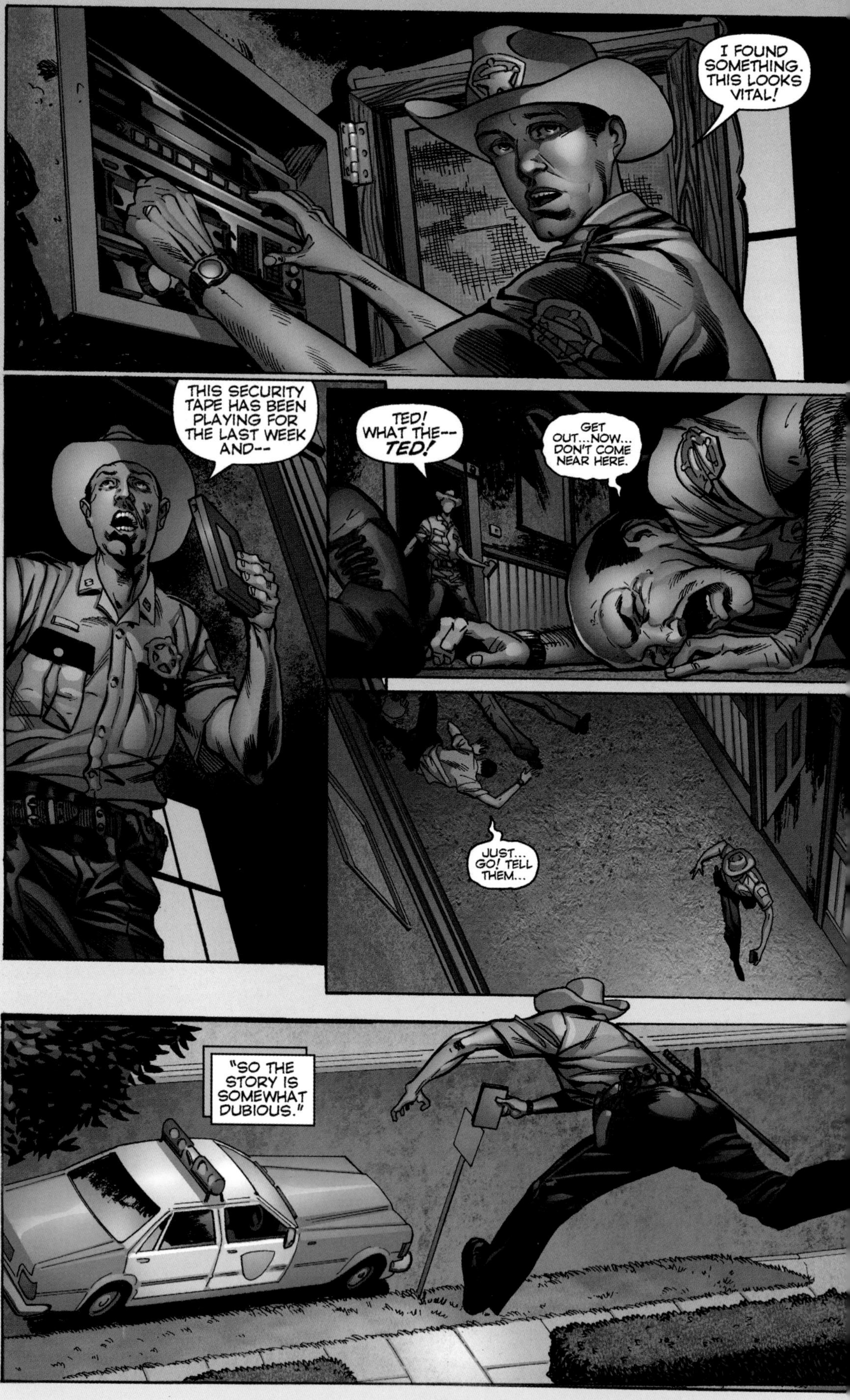

I FOUND SOMETHING. THIS LOOKS VITAL!
THIS SECURITY TAPE HAS BEEN PLAYING FOR THE LAST WEEK AND--
TED! WHAT THE-- TED!
GET OUT...NOW... DON'T COME NEAR HERE.
JUST... GO! TELL THEM...
"SO THE STORY IS SOMEWHAT DUBIOUS."

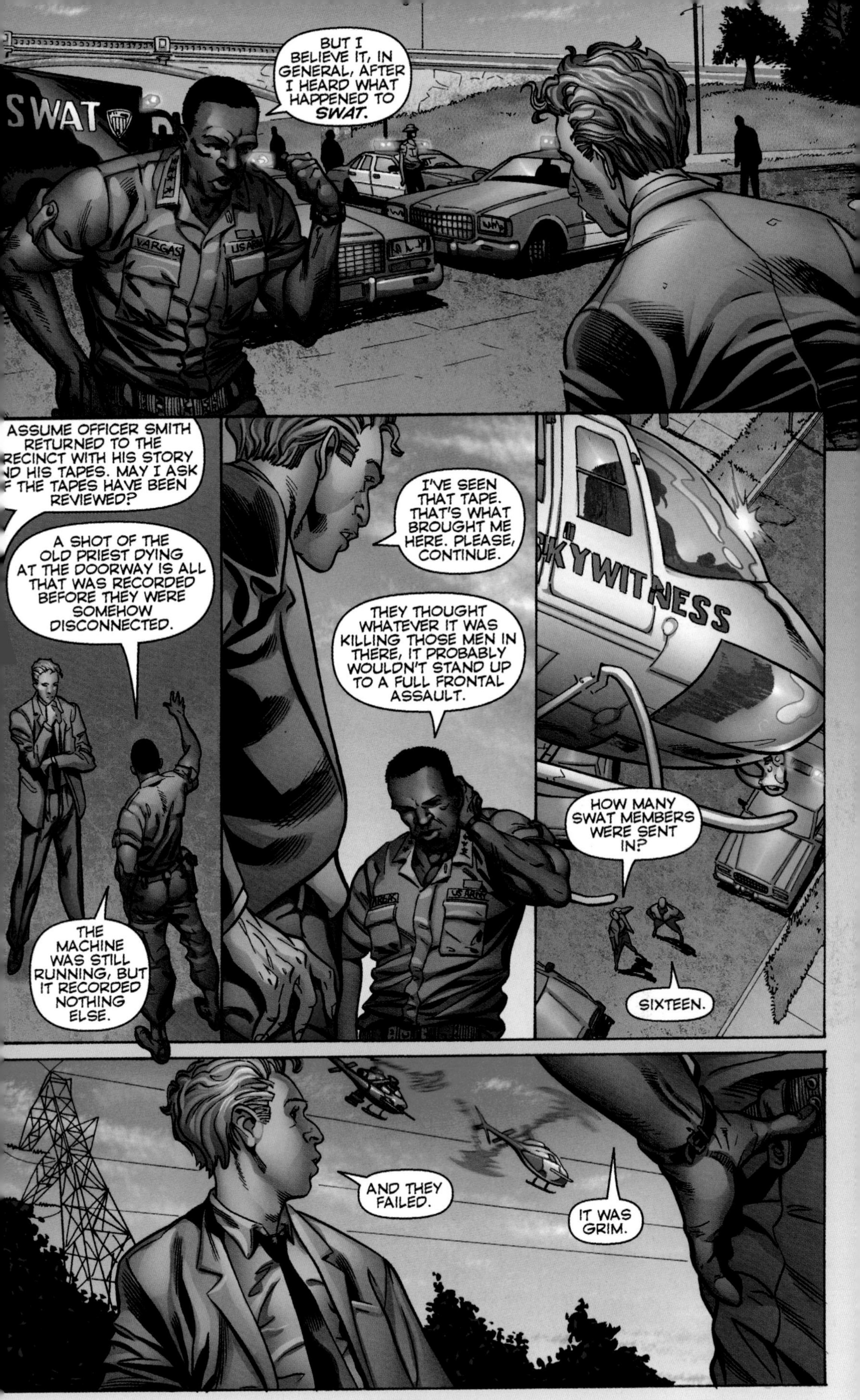
BUT I BELIEVE IT, IN GENERAL, AFTER I HEARD WHAT HAPPENED TO SWAT.
SWAT
VARGAS
US ARMY
ASSUME OFFICER SMITH RETURNED TO THE RECINCT WITH HIS STORY ND HIS TAPES. MAY I ASK F THE TAPES HAVE BEEN REVIEWED?
A SHOT OF THE OLD PRIEST DYING AT THE DOORWAY IS ALL THAT WAS RECORDED BEFORE THEY WERE SOMEHOW DISCONNECTED.
THE MACHINE WAS STILL RUNNING, BUT IT RECORDED NOTHING ELSE.
I'VE SEEN THAT TAPE. THAT'S WHAT BROUGHT ME HERE. PLEASE, CONTINUE.
THEY THOUGHT WHATEVER IT WAS KILLING THOSE MEN IN THERE, IT PROBABLY WOULDN'T STAND UP TO A FULL FRONTAL ASSAULT.
KYWITNESS
HOW MANY SWAT MEMBERS WERE SENT IN?
SIXTEEN.
AND THEY FAILED.
IT WAS GRIM.

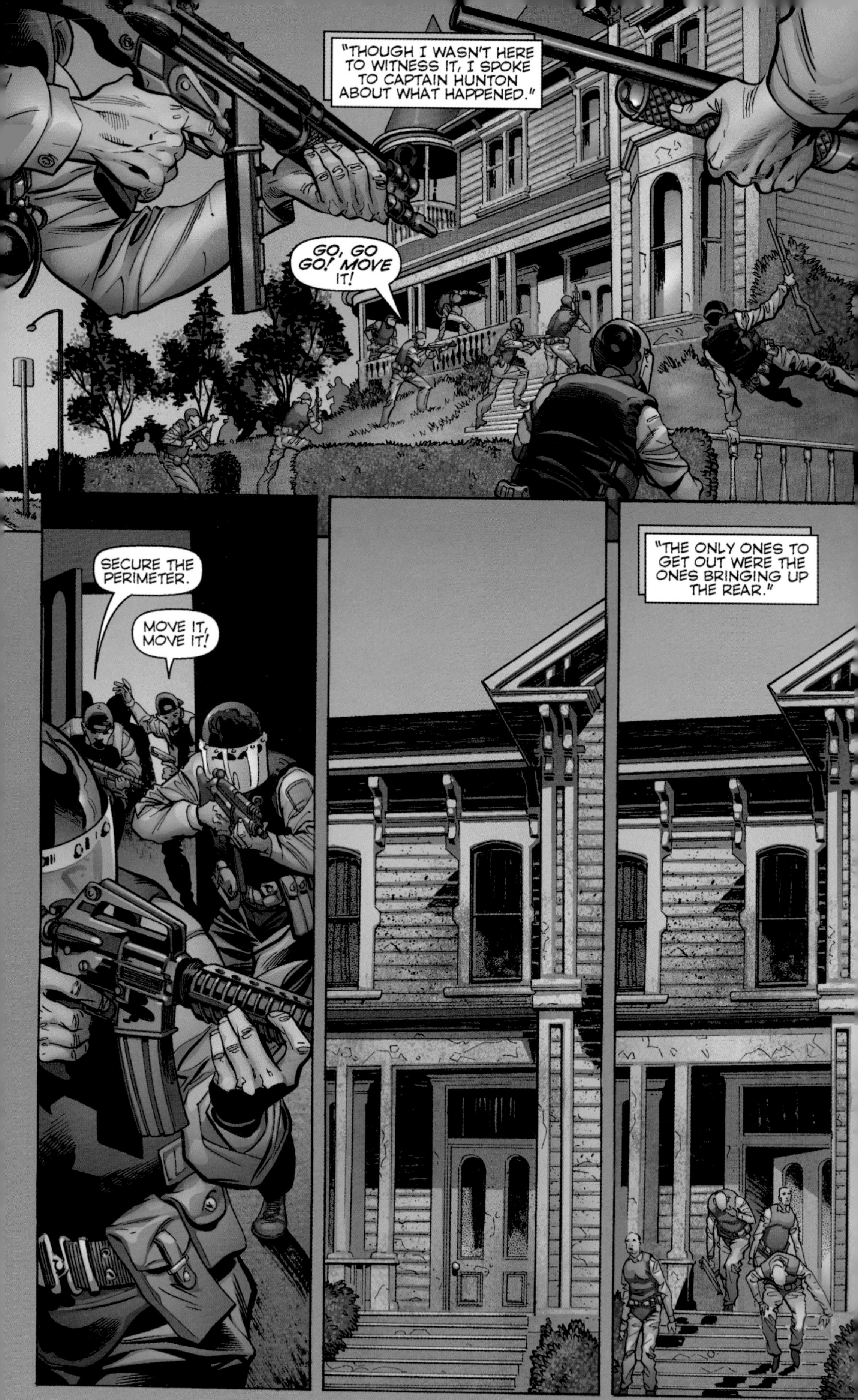
"THOUGH I WASN'T HERE TO WITNESS IT, I SPOKE TO CAPTAIN HUNTON ABOUT WHAT HAPPENED."
GO, GO GO! MOVE IT!
SECURE THE PERIMETER.
MOVE IT, MOVE IT!
"THE ONLY ONES TO GET OUT WERE THE ONES BRINGING UP THE REAR."

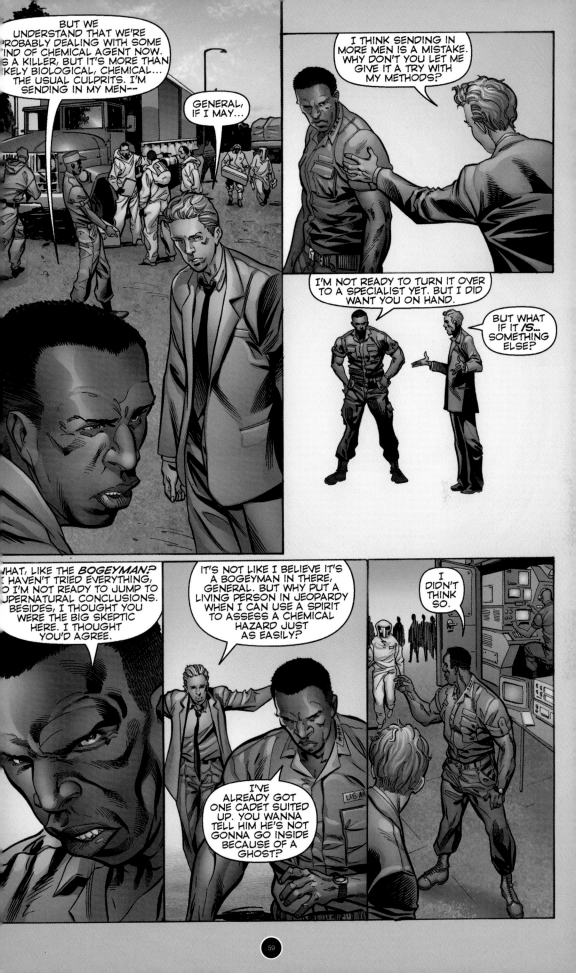

BUT WE UNDERSTAND THAT WE'RE PROBABLY DEALING WITH SOME KIND OF CHEMICAL AGENT NOW. IS A KILLER, BUT IT'S MORE THAN LIKELY BIOLOGICAL, CHEMICAL... THE USUAL CULPRITS. I'M SENDING IN MY MEN--

GENERAL, IF I MAY...

I THINK SENDING IN MORE MEN IS A MISTAKE. WHY DON'T YOU LET ME GIVE IT A TRY WITH MY METHODS?

I'M NOT READY TO TURN IT OVER TO A SPECIALIST YET. BUT I DID WANT YOU ON HAND.

BUT WHAT IF IT *IS*... SOMETHING ELSE?

WHAT, LIKE THE *BOGEYMAN?* I HAVEN'T TRIED EVERYTHING, SO I'M NOT READY TO JUMP TO SUPERNATURAL CONCLUSIONS. BESIDES, I THOUGHT YOU WERE THE BIG SKEPTIC HERE. I THOUGHT YOU'D AGREE.

IT'S NOT LIKE I BELIEVE IT'S A BOGEYMAN IN THERE, GENERAL. BUT WHY PUT A LIVING PERSON IN JEOPARDY WHEN I CAN USE A SPIRIT TO ASSESS A CHEMICAL HAZARD JUST AS EASILY?

I DIDN'T THINK SO.

I'VE ALREADY GOT ONE CADET SUITED UP. YOU WANNA TELL HIM HE'S NOT GONNA GO INSIDE BECAUSE OF A GHOST?

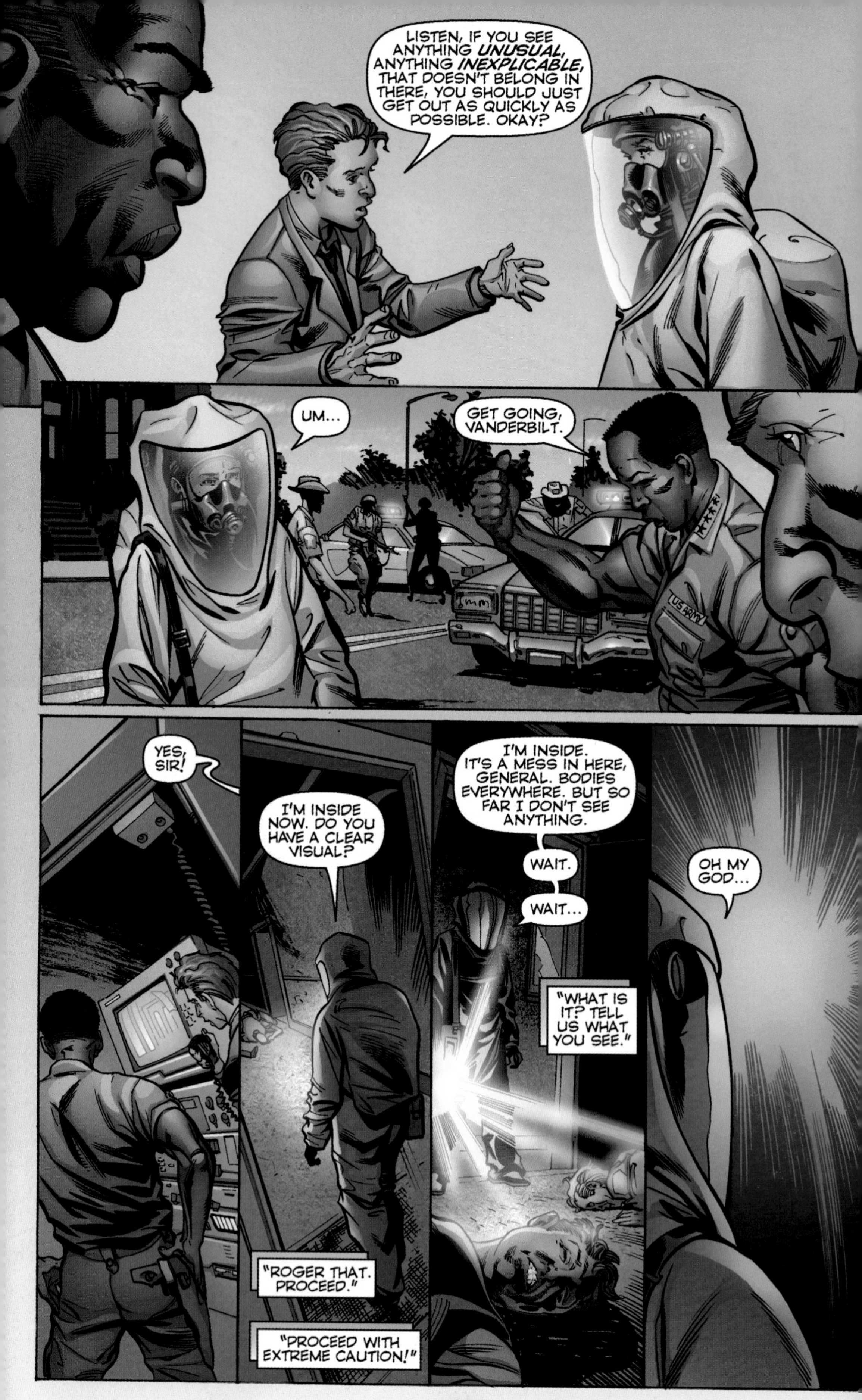
LISTEN, IF YOU SEE ANYTHING *UNUSUAL*, ANYTHING *INEXPLICABLE*, THAT DOESN'T BELONG IN THERE, YOU SHOULD JUST GET OUT AS QUICKLY AS POSSIBLE. OKAY?
UM...
GET GOING, VANDERBILT.
US ARMY
YES, SIR!
I'M INSIDE NOW. DO YOU HAVE A CLEAR VISUAL?
"ROGER THAT. PROCEED."
"PROCEED WITH EXTREME CAUTION!"
I'M INSIDE. IT'S A MESS IN HERE, GENERAL. BODIES EVERYWHERE. BUT SO FAR I DON'T SEE ANYTHING.
WAIT.
WAIT...
"WHAT IS IT? TELL US WHAT YOU SEE."
OH MY GOD...

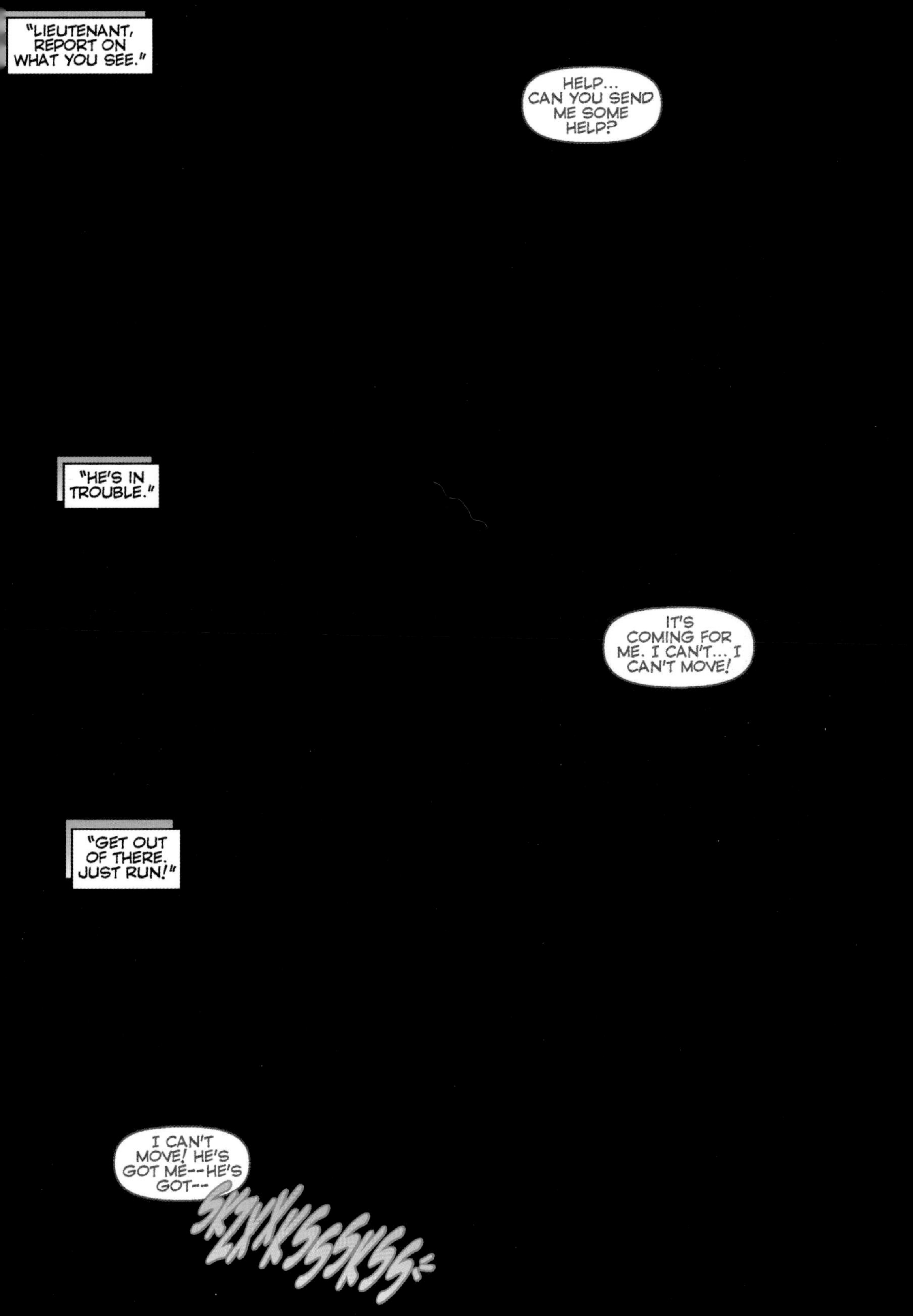
"LIEUTENANT, REPORT ON WHAT YOU SEE."
HELP... CAN YOU SEND ME SOME HELP?
"HE'S IN TROUBLE."
IT'S COMING FOR ME. I CAN'T... I CAN'T MOVE!
"GET OUT OF THERE. JUST RUN!"
I CAN'T MOVE! HE'S GOT ME--HE'S GOT--

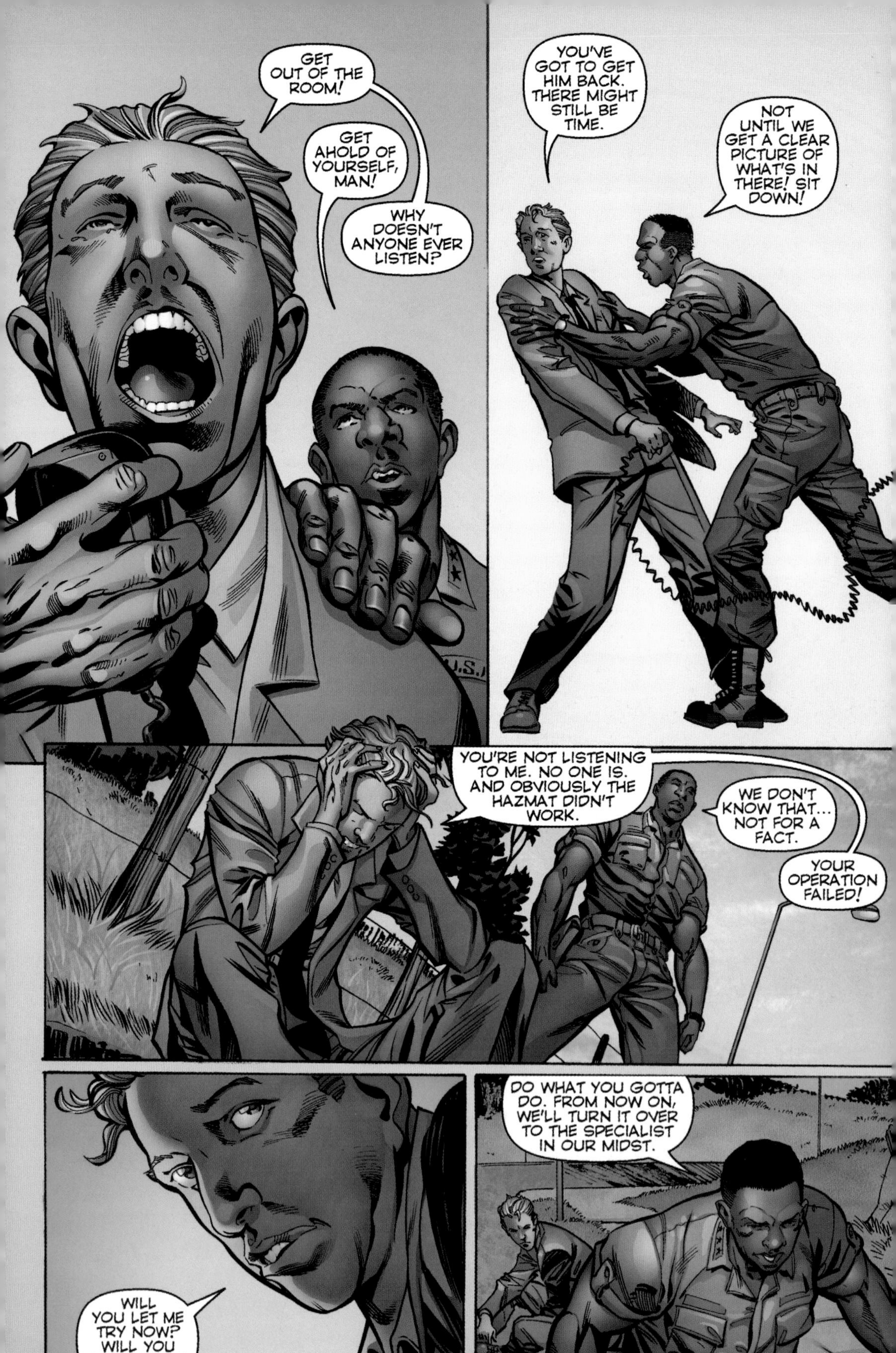
GET OUT OF THE ROOM!
GET AHOLD OF YOURSELF, MAN!
WHY DOESN'T ANYONE EVER LISTEN?
YOU'VE GOT TO GET HIM BACK. THERE MIGHT STILL BE TIME.
NOT UNTIL WE GET A CLEAR PICTURE OF WHAT'S IN THERE! SIT DOWN!
YOU'RE NOT LISTENING TO ME. NO ONE IS. AND OBVIOUSLY THE HAZMAT DIDN'T WORK.
WE DON'T KNOW THAT... NOT FOR A FACT.
YOUR OPERATION FAILED!
WILL YOU LET ME TRY NOW? WILL YOU STOP DOING THIS?
DO WHAT YOU GOTTA DO. FROM NOW ON, WE'LL TURN IT OVER TO THE SPECIALIST IN OUR MIDST.

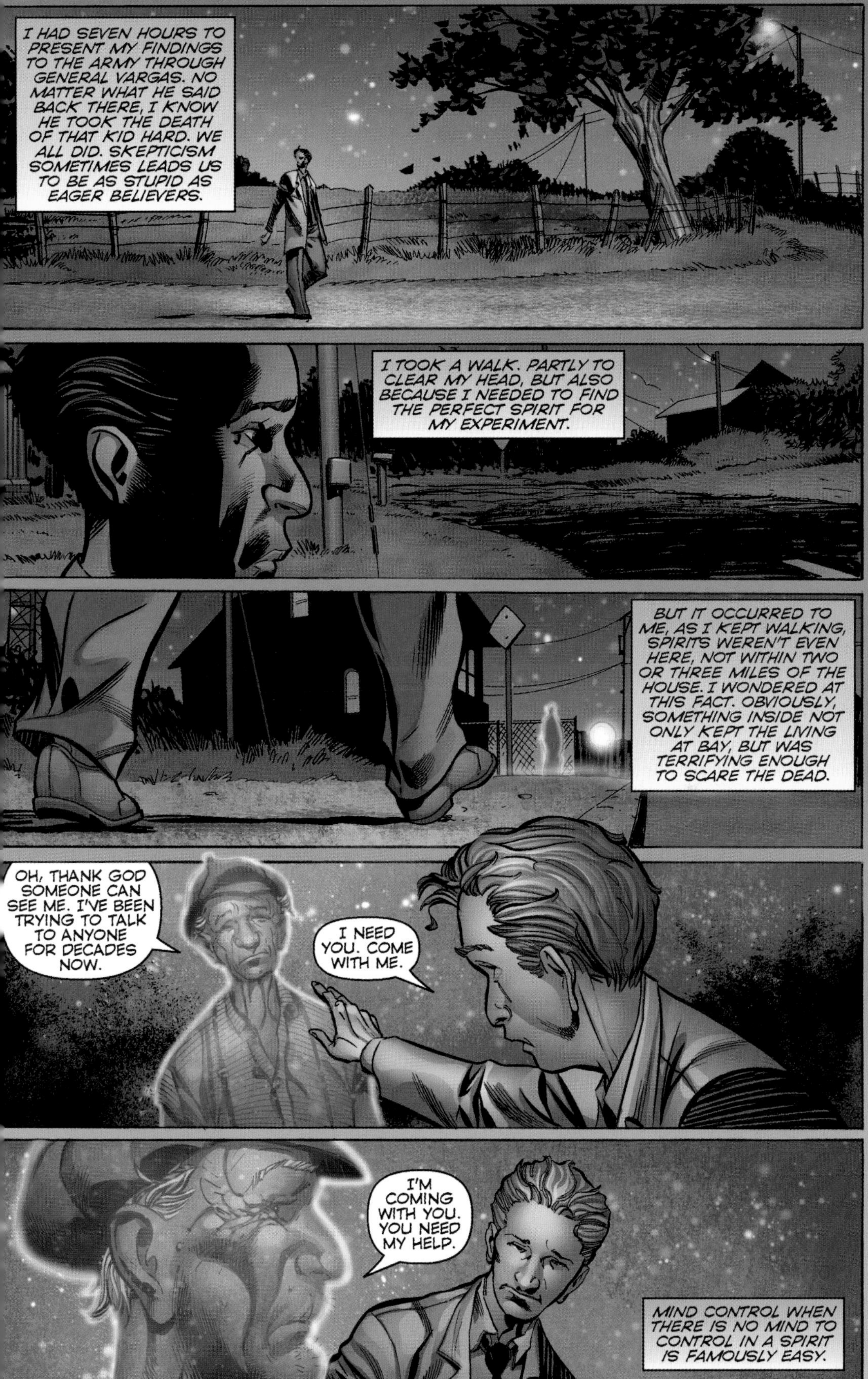
I HAD SEVEN HOURS TO PRESENT MY FINDINGS TO THE ARMY THROUGH GENERAL VARGAS. NO MATTER WHAT HE SAID BACK THERE, I KNOW HE TOOK THE DEATH OF THAT KID HARD. WE ALL DID. SKEPTICISM SOMETIMES LEADS US TO BE AS STUPID AS EAGER BELIEVERS.
I TOOK A WALK. PARTLY TO CLEAR MY HEAD, BUT ALSO BECAUSE I NEEDED TO FIND THE PERFECT SPIRIT FOR MY EXPERIMENT.
BUT IT OCCURRED TO ME, AS I KEPT WALKING, SPIRITS WEREN'T EVEN HERE, NOT WITHIN TWO OR THREE MILES OF THE HOUSE. I WONDERED AT THIS FACT. OBVIOUSLY, SOMETHING INSIDE NOT ONLY KEPT THE LIVING AT BAY, BUT WAS TERRIFYING ENOUGH TO SCARE THE DEAD.
OH, THANK GOD SOMEONE CAN SEE ME. I'VE BEEN TRYING TO TALK TO ANYONE FOR DECADES NOW.
I NEED YOU. COME WITH ME.
I'M COMING WITH YOU. YOU NEED MY HELP.
MIND CONTROL WHEN THERE IS NO MIND TO CONTROL IN A SPIRIT IS FAMOUSLY EASY.

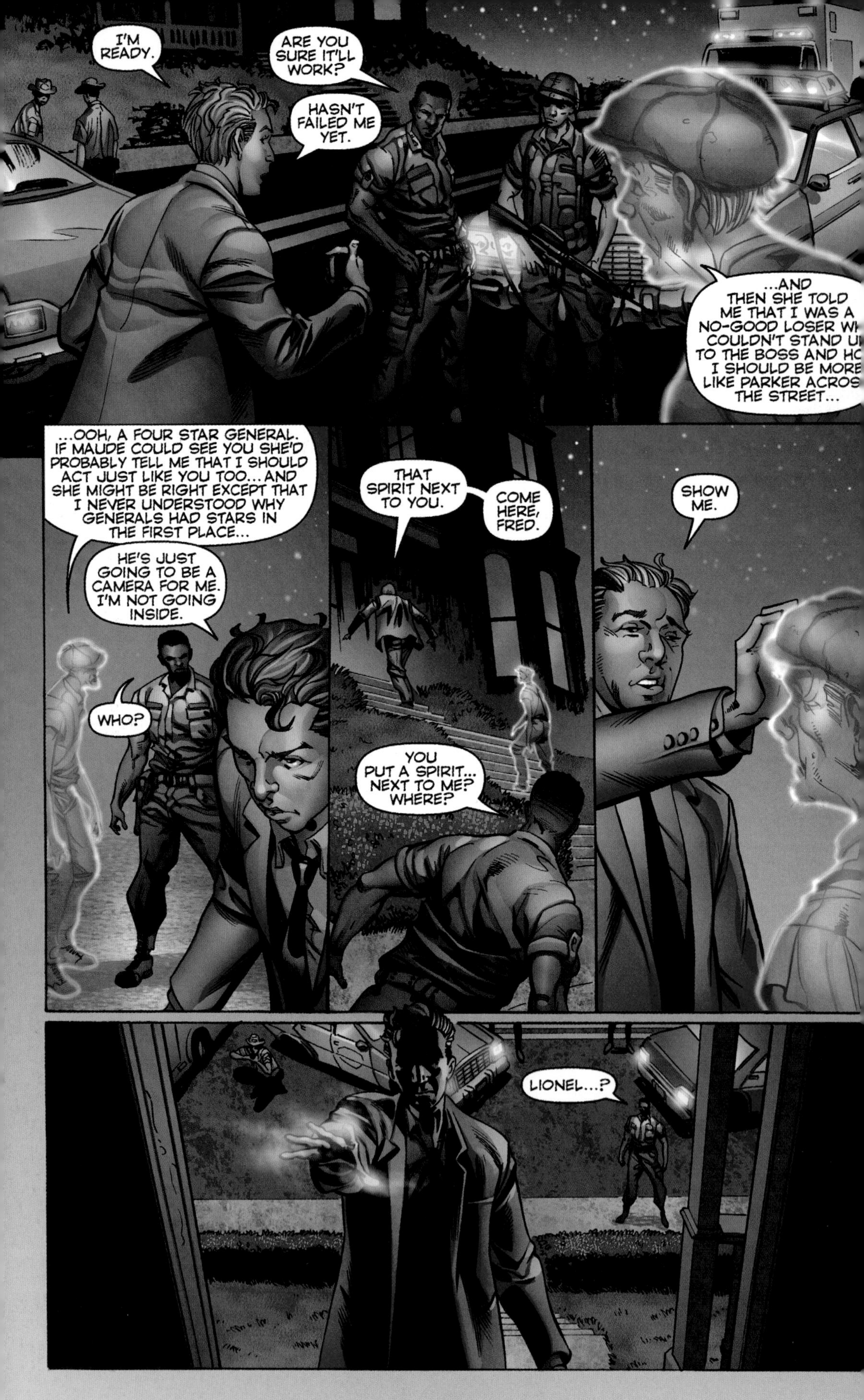

I'M READY.
ARE YOU SURE IT'LL WORK?
HASN'T FAILED ME YET.
...AND THEN SHE TOLD ME THAT I WAS A NO-GOOD LOSER WH COULDN'T STAND U TO THE BOSS AND HO I SHOULD BE MORE LIKE PARKER ACROS THE STREET...
...OOH, A FOUR STAR GENERAL. IF MAUDE COULD SEE YOU SHE'D PROBABLY TELL ME THAT I SHOULD ACT JUST LIKE YOU TOO... AND SHE MIGHT BE RIGHT EXCEPT THAT I NEVER UNDERSTOOD WHY GENERALS HAD STARS IN THE FIRST PLACE...
HE'S JUST GOING TO BE A CAMERA FOR ME. I'M NOT GOING INSIDE.
WHO?
THAT SPIRIT NEXT TO YOU.
COME HERE, FRED.
YOU PUT A SPIRIT... NEXT TO ME? WHERE?
SHOW ME.
LIONEL...?

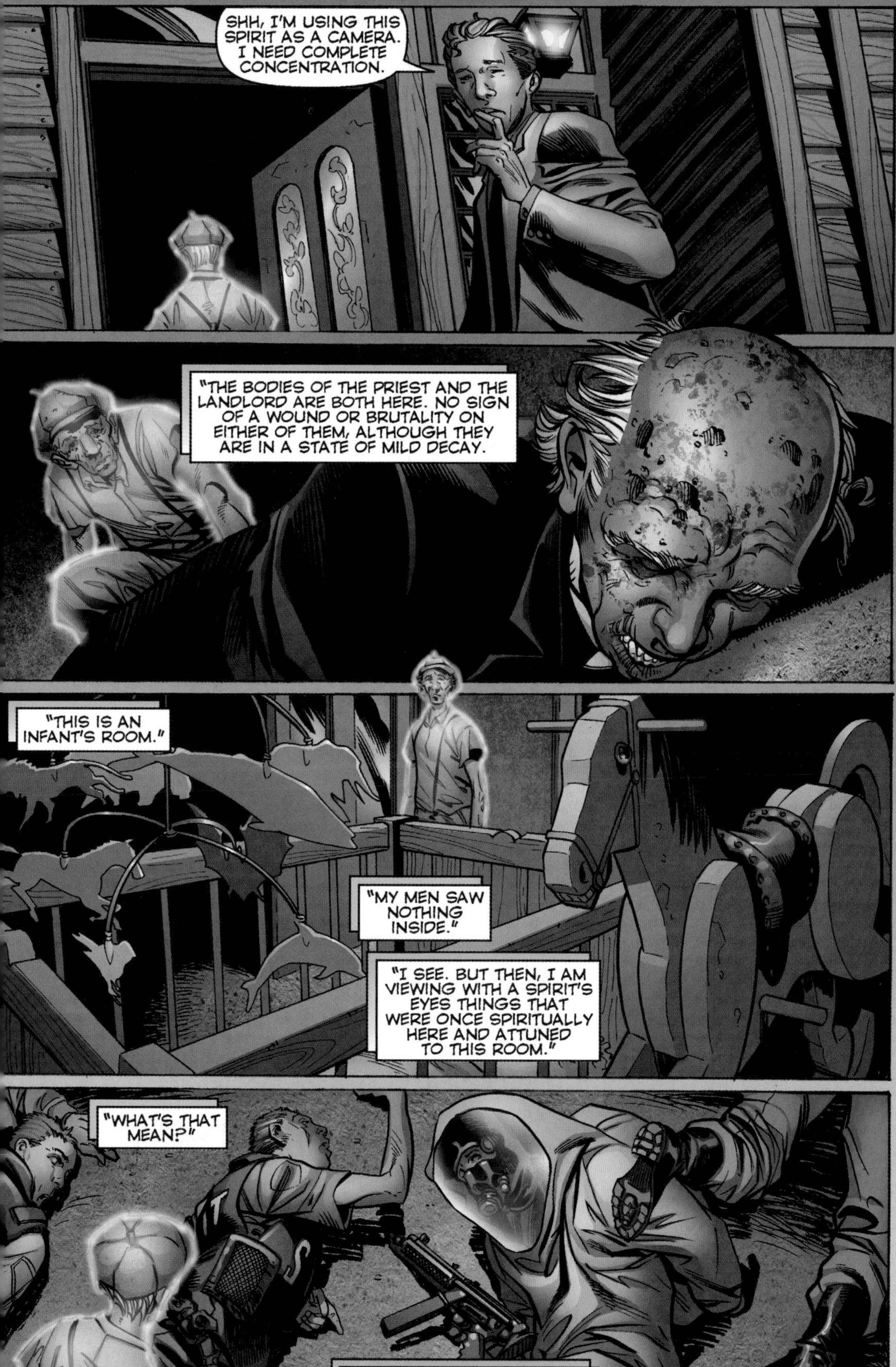
SHH, I'M USING THIS SPIRIT AS A CAMERA. I NEED COMPLETE CONCENTRATION.
"THE BODIES OF THE PRIEST AND THE LANDLORD ARE BOTH HERE. NO SIGN OF A WOUND OR BRUTALITY ON EITHER OF THEM, ALTHOUGH THEY ARE IN A STATE OF MILD DECAY.
"THIS IS AN INFANT'S ROOM."
"MY MEN SAW NOTHING INSIDE."
"I SEE. BUT THEN, I AM VIEWING WITH A SPIRIT'S EYES THINGS THAT WERE ONCE SPIRITUALLY HERE AND ATTUNED TO THIS ROOM."
"WHAT'S THAT MEAN?"
"I DON'T KNOW YET. BUT I'M SURPRISED TO SEE SO MUCH DEATH IN SUCH A PLACE."

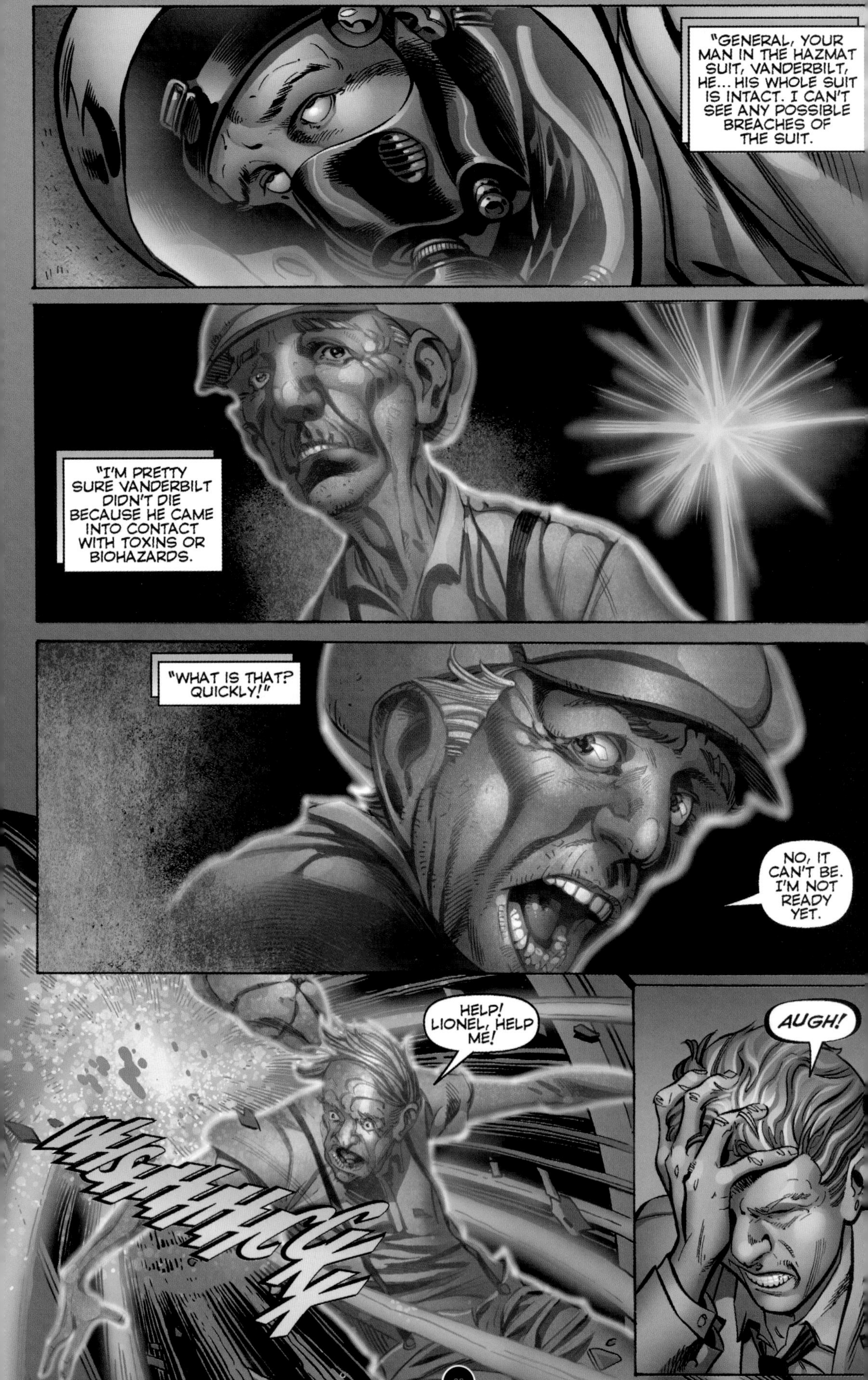
"GENERAL, YOUR MAN IN THE HAZMAT SUIT, VANDERBILT, HE... HIS WHOLE SUIT IS INTACT. I CAN'T SEE ANY POSSIBLE BREACHES OF THE SUIT.
"I'M PRETTY SURE VANDERBILT DIDN'T DIE BECAUSE HE CAME INTO CONTACT WITH TOXINS OR BIOHAZARDS.
"WHAT IS THAT? QUICKLY!"
NO, IT CAN'T BE. I'M NOT READY YET.
HELP! LIONEL, HELP ME!
AUGH!

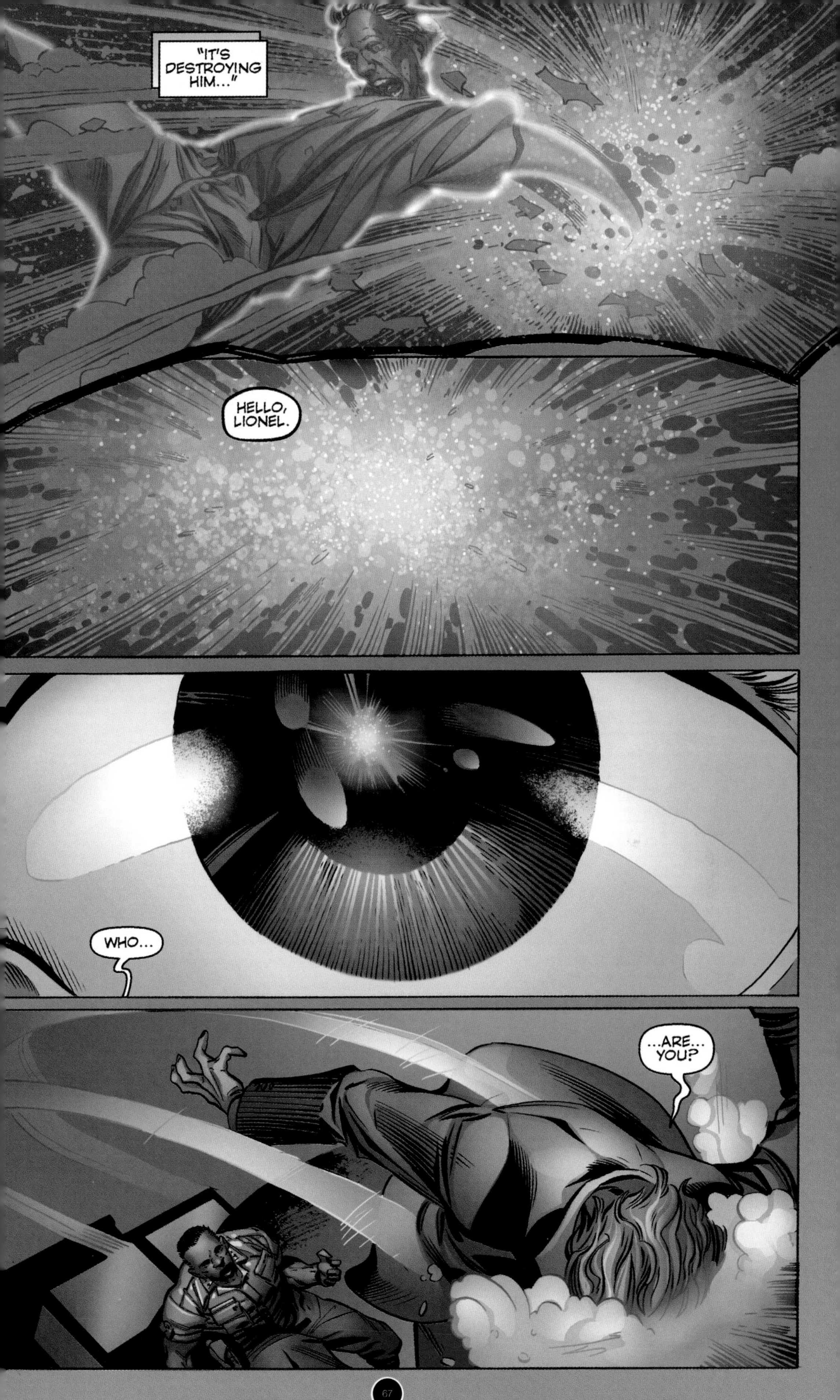
"IT'S DESTROYING HIM..."
HELLO, LIONEL.
WHO...
...ARE... YOU?

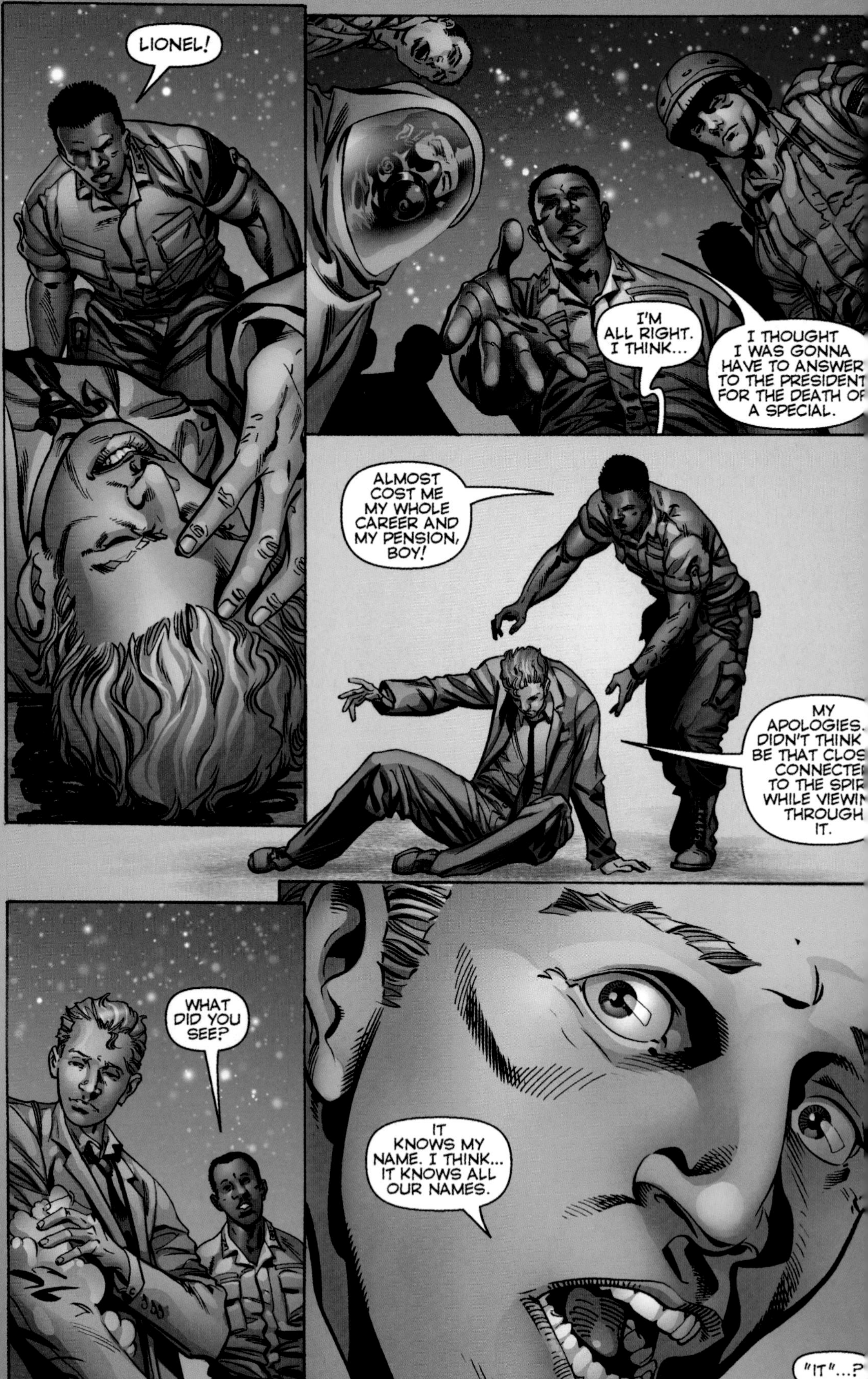
LIONEL!
I'M ALL RIGHT. I THINK...
I THOUGHT I WAS GONNA HAVE TO ANSWER TO THE PRESIDENT FOR THE DEATH OF A SPECIAL.
ALMOST COST ME MY WHOLE CAREER AND MY PENSION, BOY!
MY APOLOGIES. DIDN'T THINK BE THAT CLOS CONNECTE TO THE SPIR WHILE VIEWIN THROUGH IT.
WHAT DID YOU SEE?
IT KNOWS MY NAME. I THINK... IT KNOWS ALL OUR NAMES.
"IT"...?

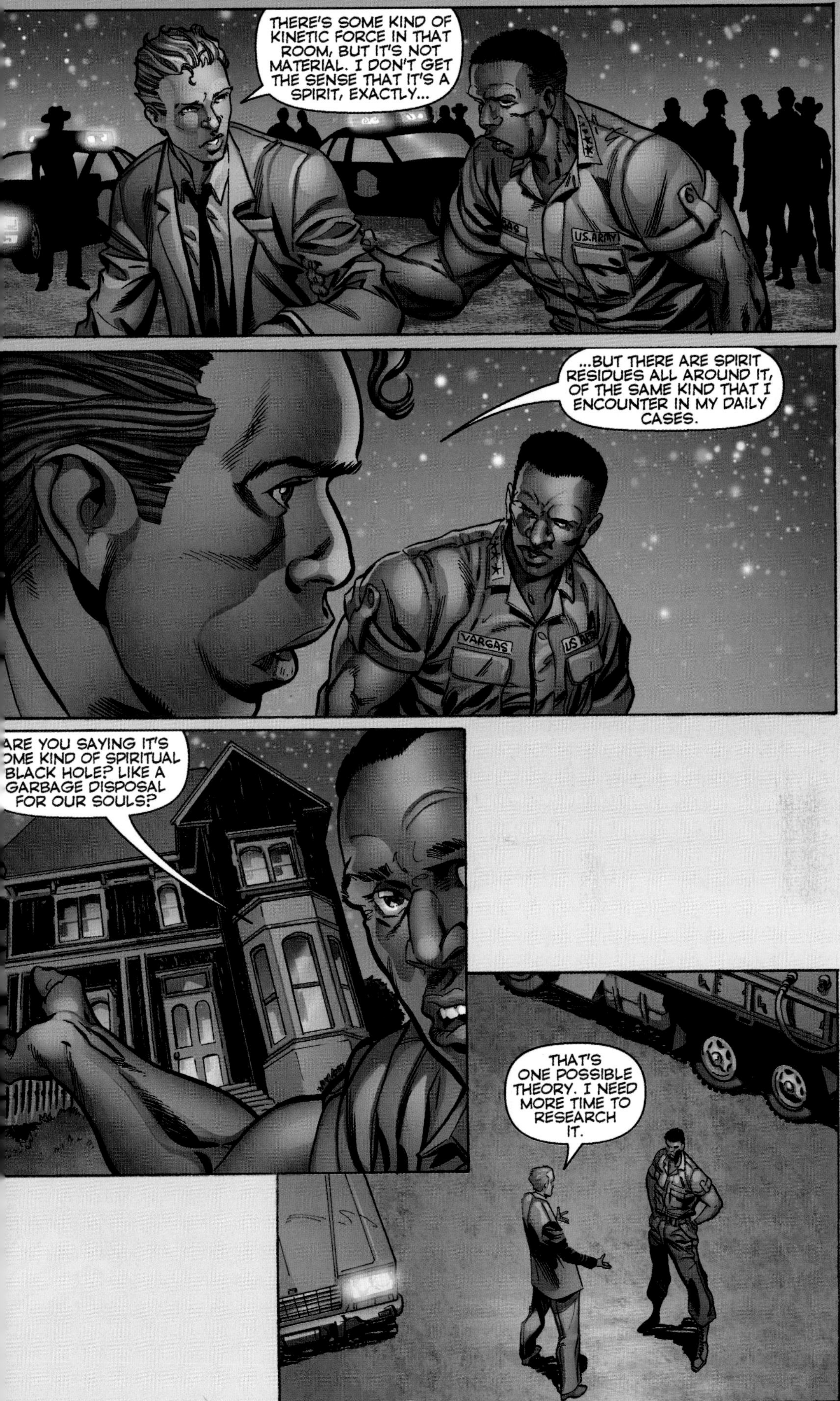
THERE'S SOME KIND OF KINETIC FORCE IN THAT ROOM, BUT IT'S NOT MATERIAL. I DON'T GET THE SENSE THAT IT'S A SPIRIT, EXACTLY...
U.S. ARMY
...BUT THERE ARE SPIRIT RESIDUES ALL AROUND IT, OF THE SAME KIND THAT I ENCOUNTER IN MY DAILY CASES.
VARGAS
ARE YOU SAYING IT'S SOME KIND OF SPIRITUAL BLACK HOLE? LIKE A GARBAGE DISPOSAL FOR OUR SOULS?
THAT'S ONE POSSIBLE THEORY. I NEED MORE TIME TO RESEARCH IT.

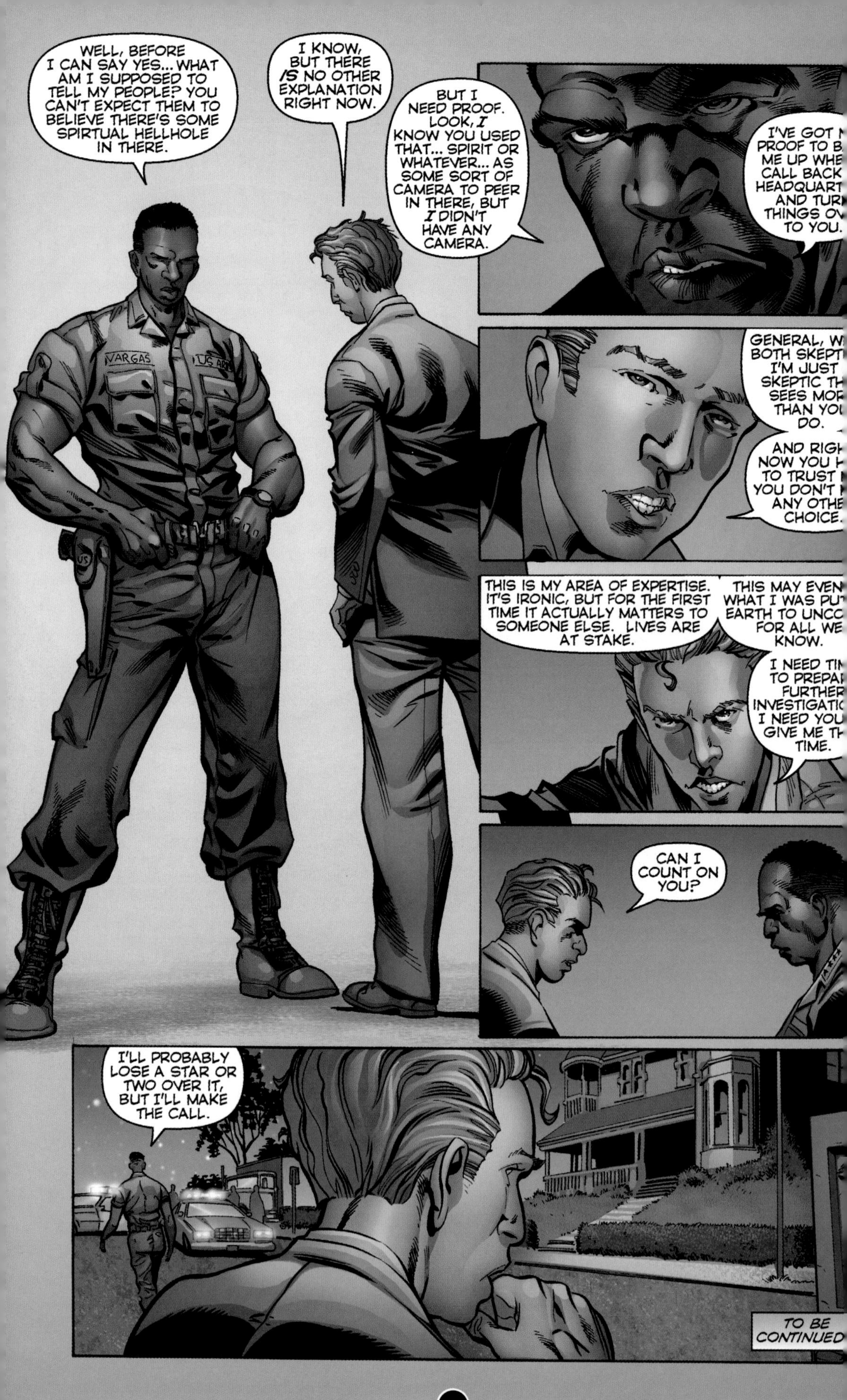
WELL, BEFORE I CAN SAY YES... WHAT AM I SUPPOSED TO TELL MY PEOPLE? YOU CAN'T EXPECT THEM TO BELIEVE THERE'S SOME SPIRTUAL HELLHOLE IN THERE.
I KNOW, BUT THERE *IS* NO OTHER EXPLANATION RIGHT NOW.
BUT I NEED PROOF. LOOK, *I* KNOW YOU USED THAT... SPIRIT OR WHATEVER... AS SOME SORT OF CAMERA TO PEER IN THERE, BUT *I* DIDN'T HAVE ANY CAMERA.
VARGAS
US AR
I'VE GOT PROOF TO B ME UP WHE CALL BACK HEADQUART AND TUR THINGS OV TO YOU.
GENERAL, W BOTH SKEPT I'M JUST SKEPTIC TH SEES MOR THAN YOU DO.
AND RIGH NOW YOU H TO TRUST YOU DON'T ANY OTHE CHOICE.
THIS IS MY AREA OF EXPERTISE. IT'S IRONIC, BUT FOR THE FIRST TIME IT ACTUALLY MATTERS TO SOMEONE ELSE. LIVES ARE AT STAKE.
THIS MAY EVEN WHAT I WAS PUT EARTH TO UNCO FOR ALL WE KNOW.
I NEED TIM TO PREPA FURTHER INVESTIGATIC I NEED YOU GIVE ME TH TIME.
CAN I COUNT ON YOU?
I'LL PROBABLY LOSE A STAR OR TWO OVER IT, BUT I'LL MAKE THE CALL.
TO BE CONTINUED

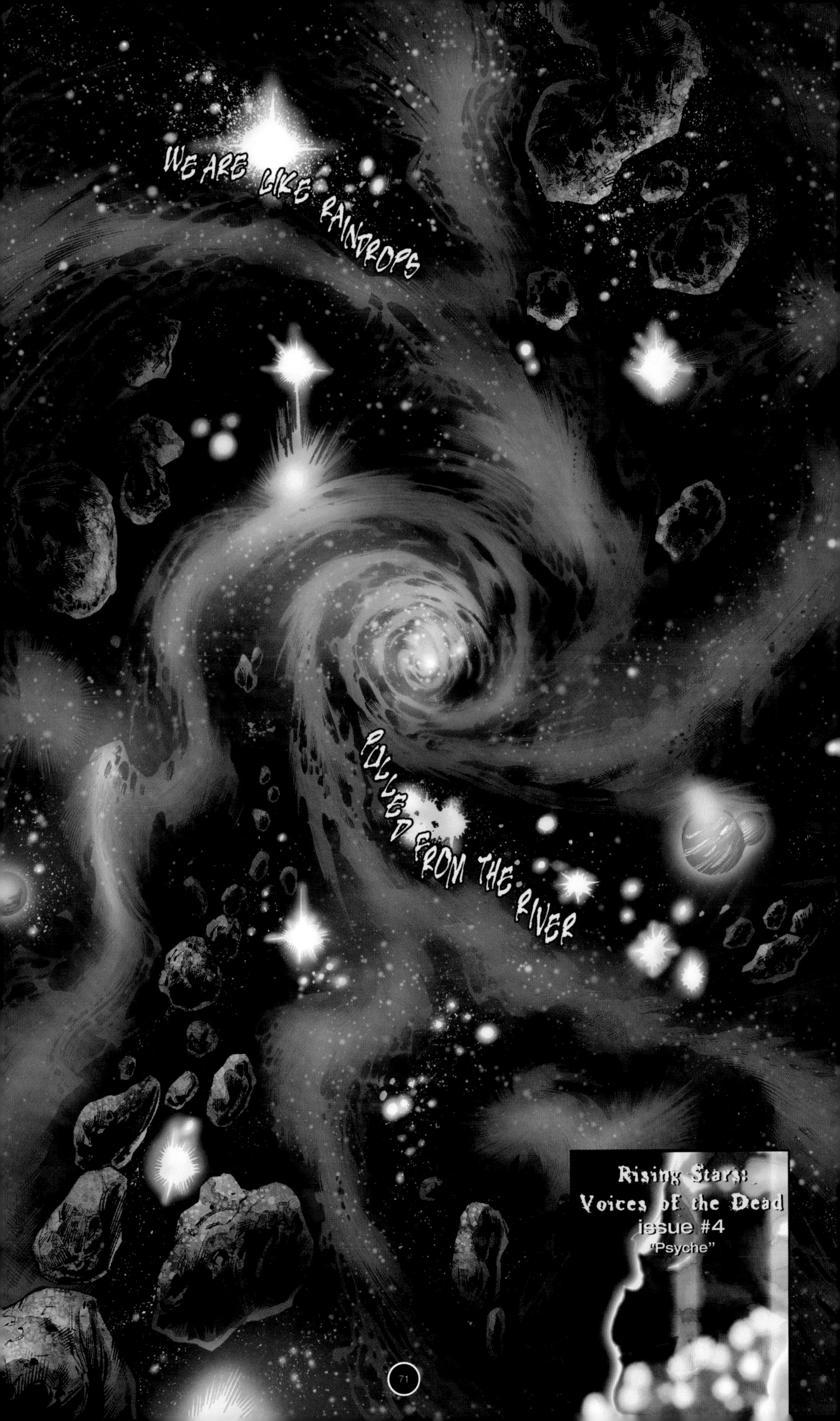

WE ARE LIKE RAINDROPS
PULLED FROM THE RIVER
Rising Stars:
Voices of the Dead
issue #4
"Psyche"

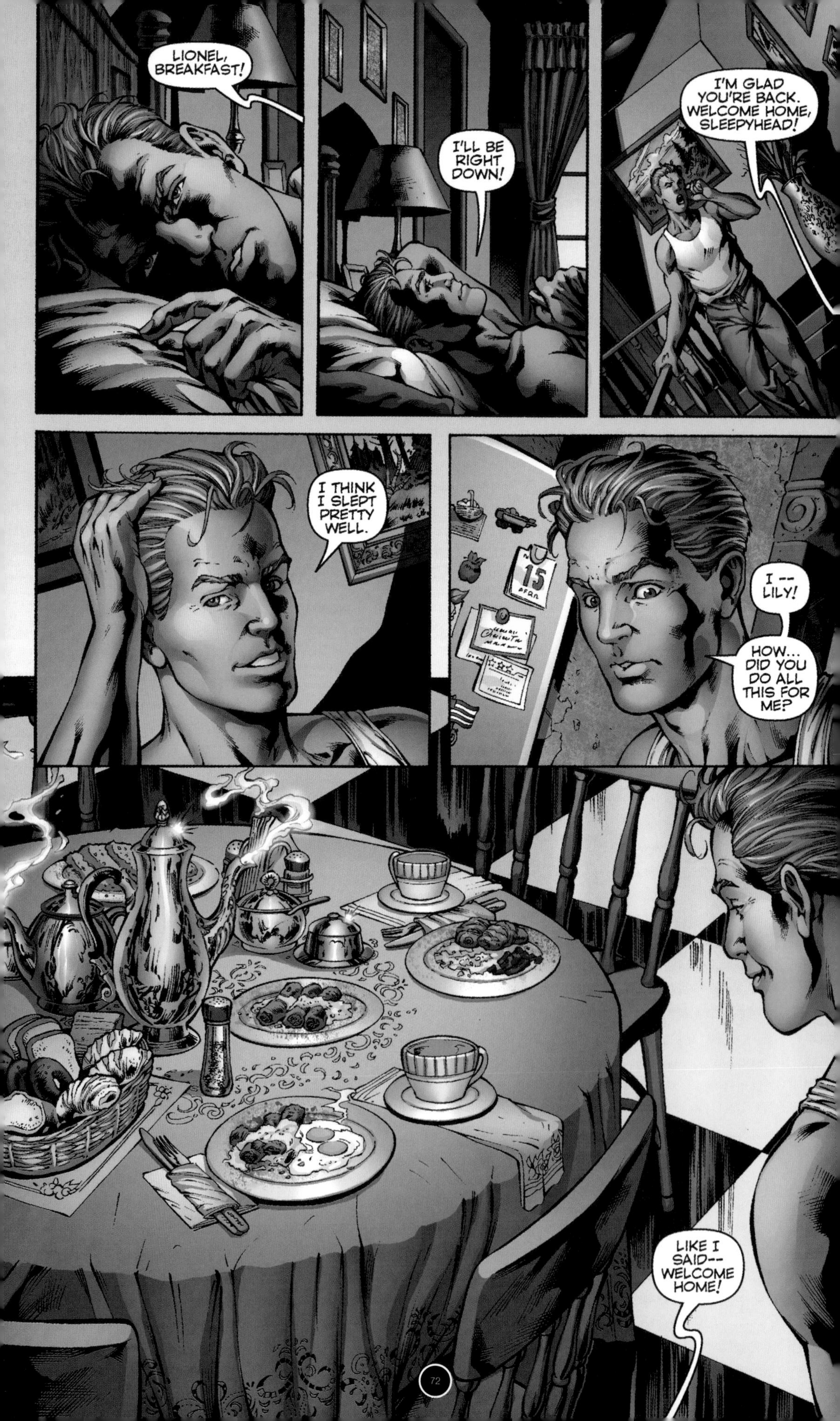

LIONEL, BREAKFAST!
I'LL BE RIGHT DOWN!
I'M GLAD YOU'RE BACK. WELCOME HOME, SLEEPYHEAD!
I THINK I SLEPT PRETTY WELL.
I -- LILY!
HOW... DID YOU DO ALL THIS FOR ME?
LIKE I SAID-- WELCOME HOME!

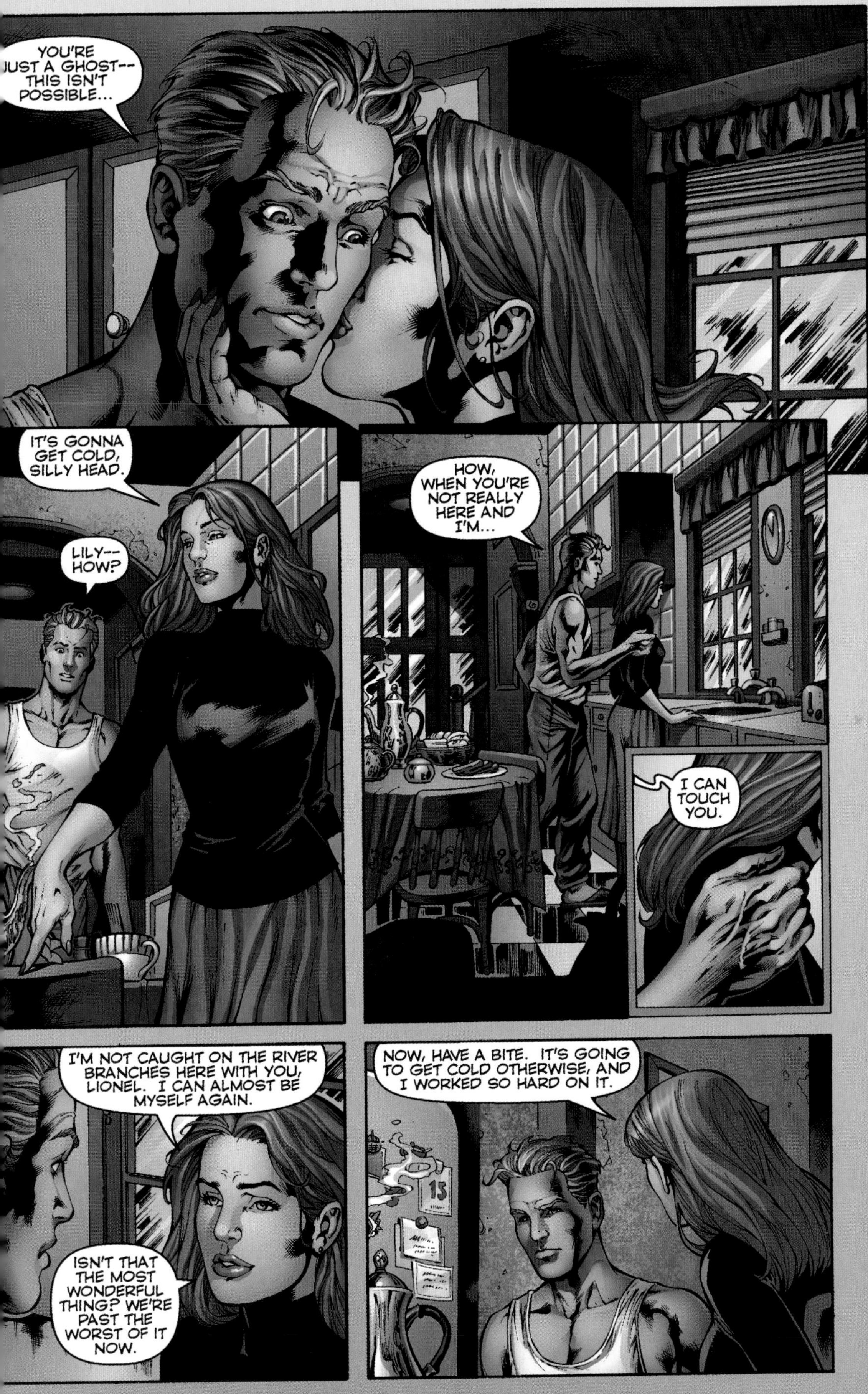
YOU'RE JUST A GHOST-- THIS ISN'T POSSIBLE...
IT'S GONNA GET COLD, SILLY HEAD.
LILY-- HOW?
HOW, WHEN YOU'RE NOT REALLY HERE AND I'M...
I CAN TOUCH YOU.
I'M NOT CAUGHT ON THE RIVER BRANCHES HERE WITH YOU, LIONEL. I CAN ALMOST BE MYSELF AGAIN.
ISN'T THAT THE MOST WONDERFUL THING? WE'RE PAST THE WORST OF IT NOW.
NOW, HAVE A BITE. IT'S GOING TO GET COLD OTHERWISE, AND I WORKED SO HARD ON IT.
15

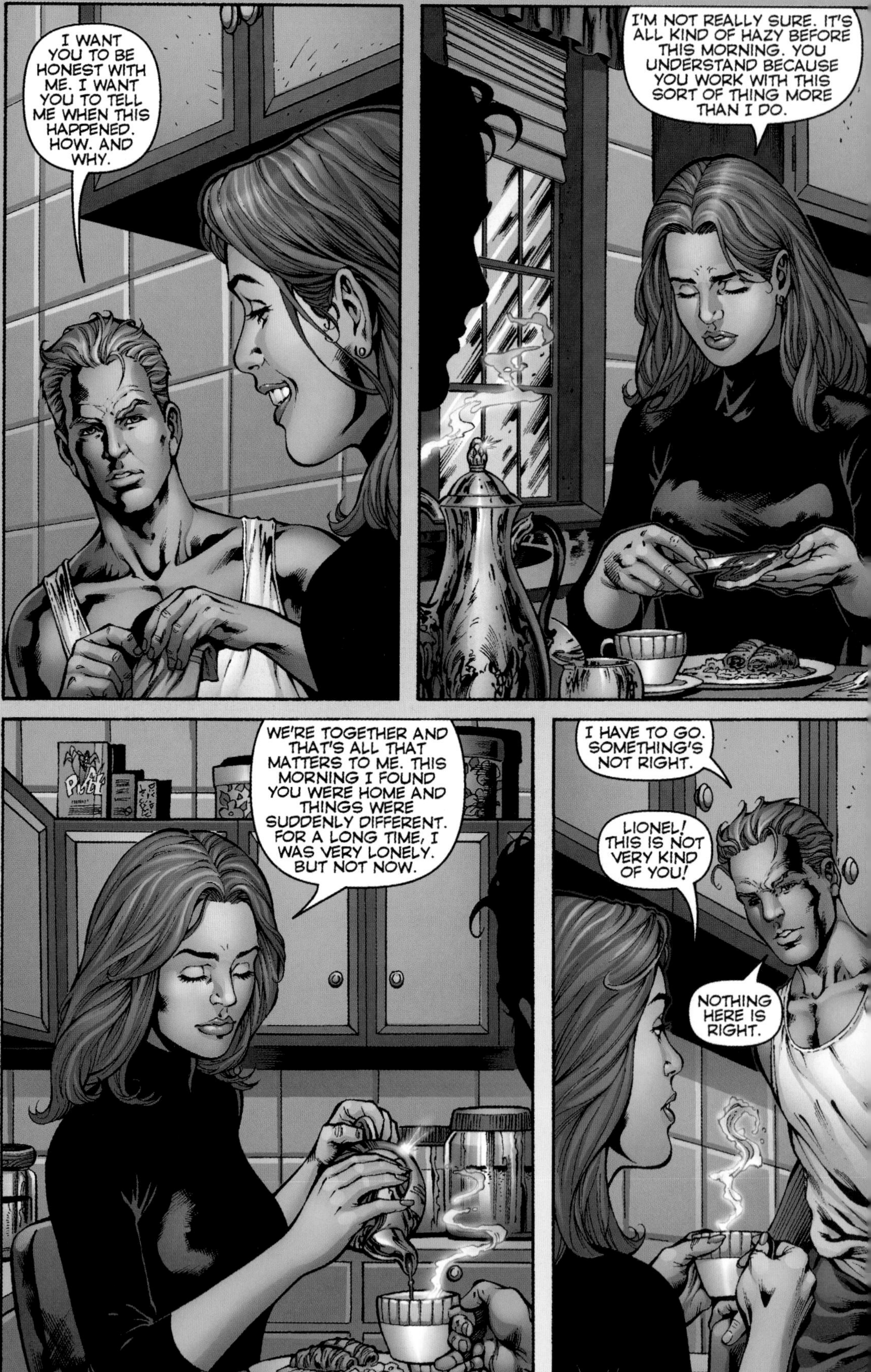
I WANT YOU TO BE HONEST WITH ME. I WANT YOU TO TELL ME WHEN THIS HAPPENED. HOW. AND WHY.
I'M NOT REALLY SURE. IT'S ALL KIND OF HAZY BEFORE THIS MORNING. YOU UNDERSTAND BECAUSE YOU WORK WITH THIS SORT OF THING MORE THAN I DO.
WE'RE TOGETHER AND THAT'S ALL THAT MATTERS TO ME. THIS MORNING I FOUND YOU WERE HOME AND THINGS WERE SUDDENLY DIFFERENT. FOR A LONG TIME, I WAS VERY LONELY. BUT NOT NOW.
I HAVE TO GO. SOMETHING'S NOT RIGHT.
LIONEL! THIS IS NOT VERY KIND OF YOU!
NOTHING HERE IS RIGHT.

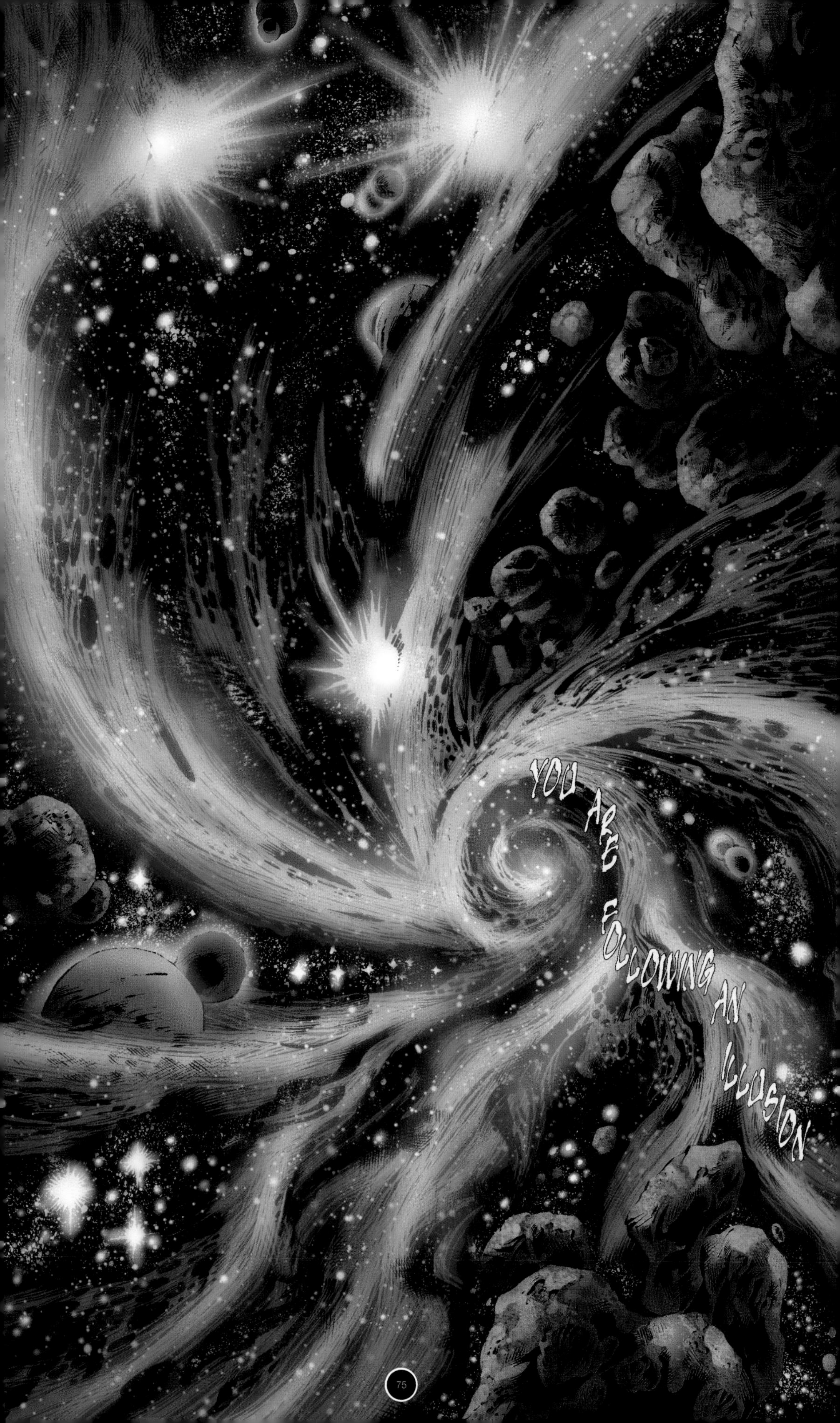
YOU ARE FOLLOWING AN ILLUSION

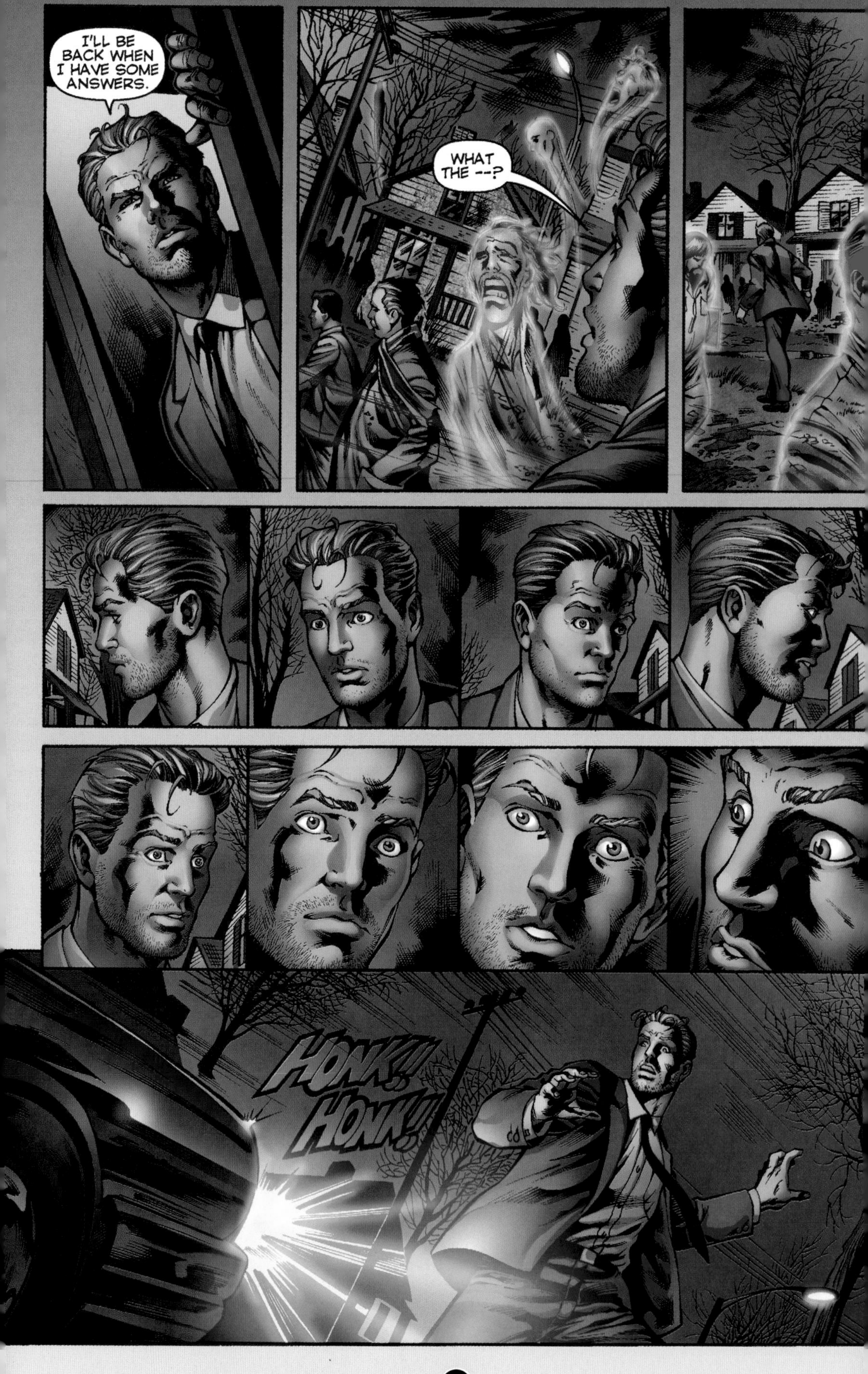
I'LL BE BACK WHEN I HAVE SOME ANSWERS.
WHAT THE --?
HONK!!
HONK!!

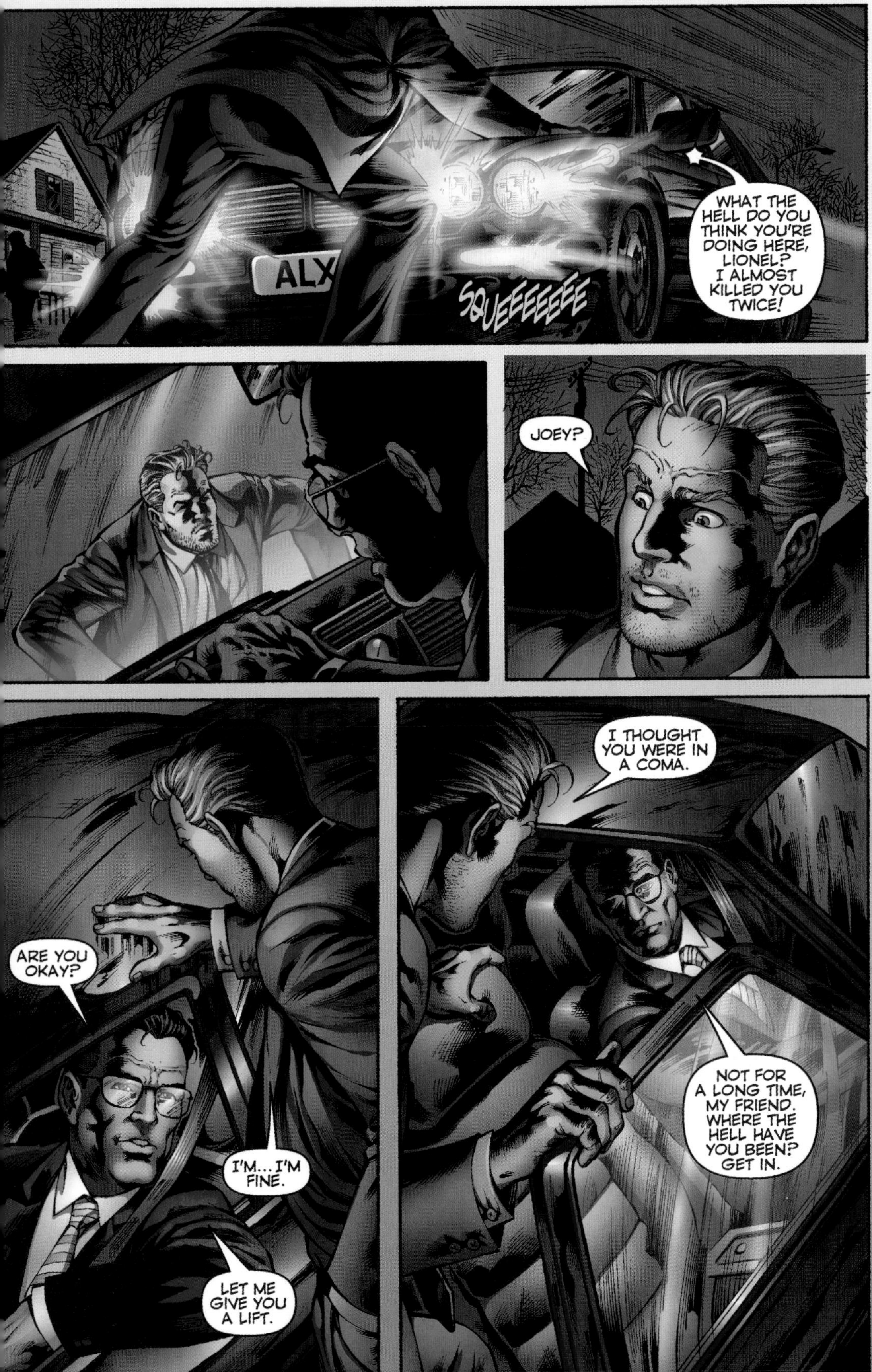
SQUEEEEEEE
WHAT THE HELL DO YOU THINK YOU'RE DOING HERE, LIONEL? I ALMOST KILLED YOU TWICE!
JOEY?
ARE YOU OKAY?
I'M... I'M FINE.
LET ME GIVE YOU A LIFT.
I THOUGHT YOU WERE IN A COMA.
NOT FOR A LONG TIME, MY FRIEND. WHERE THE HELL HAVE YOU BEEN? GET IN.

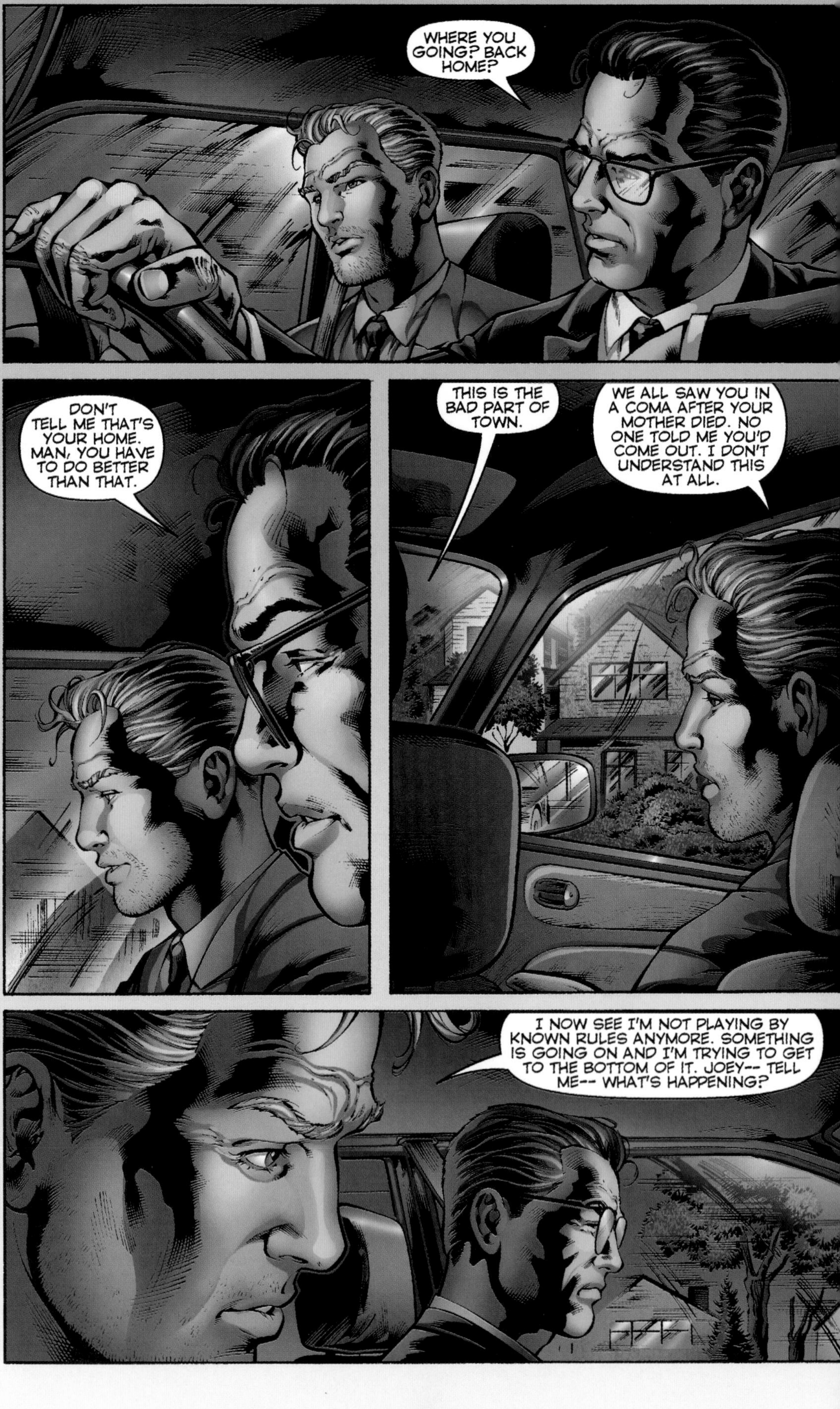
WHERE YOU GOING? BACK HOME?
DON'T TELL ME THAT'S YOUR HOME. MAN, YOU HAVE TO DO BETTER THAN THAT.
THIS IS THE BAD PART OF TOWN.
WE ALL SAW YOU IN A COMA AFTER YOUR MOTHER DIED. NO ONE TOLD ME YOU'D COME OUT. I DON'T UNDERSTAND THIS AT ALL.
I NOW SEE I'M NOT PLAYING BY KNOWN RULES ANYMORE. SOMETHING IS GOING ON AND I'M TRYING TO GET TO THE BOTTOM OF IT. JOEY-- TELL ME-- WHAT'S HAPPENING?

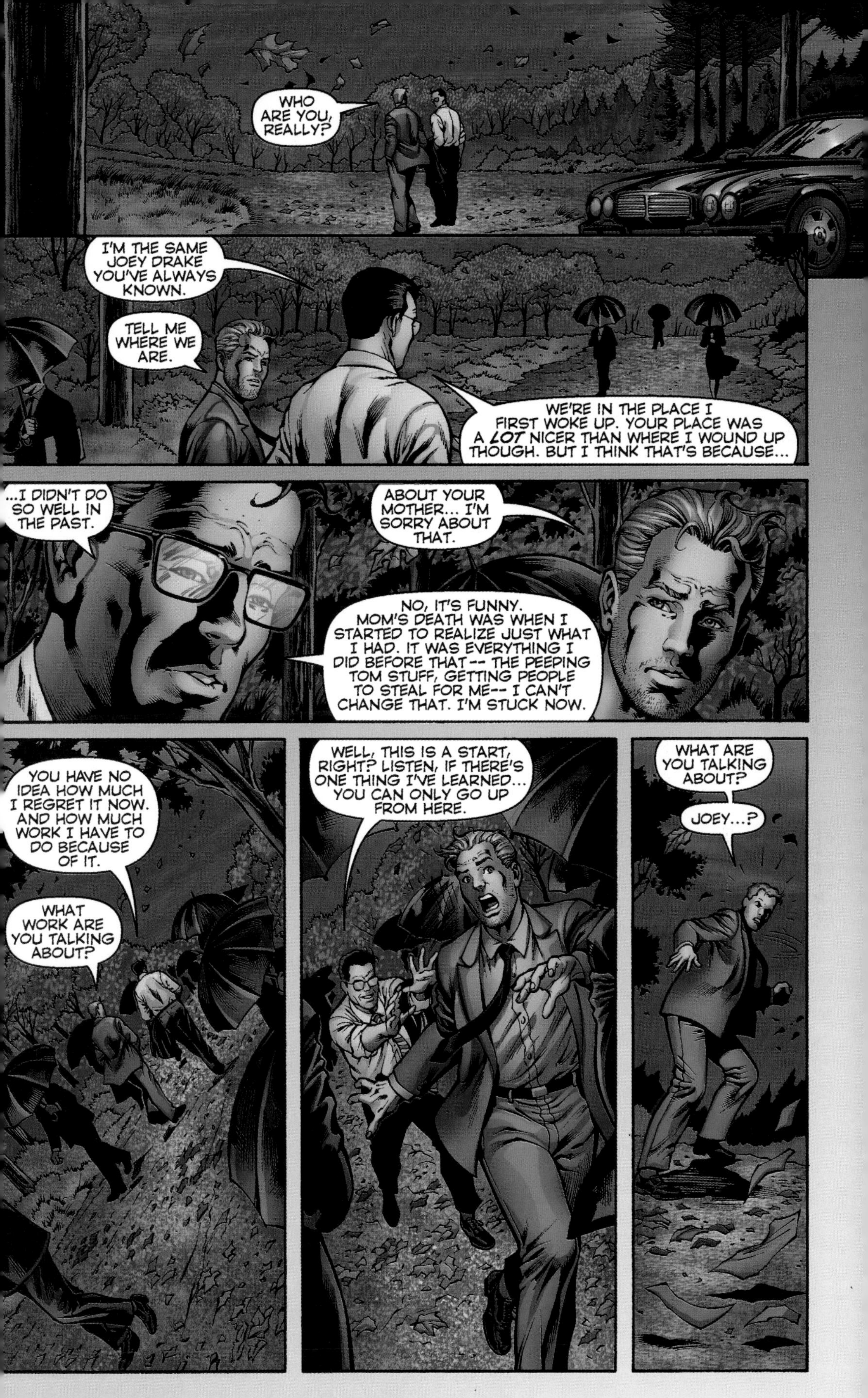
WHO ARE YOU, REALLY?
I'M THE SAME JOEY DRAKE YOU'VE ALWAYS KNOWN.
TELL ME WHERE WE ARE.
WE'RE IN THE PLACE I FIRST WOKE UP. YOUR PLACE WAS A LOT NICER THAN WHERE I WOUND UP THOUGH. BUT I THINK THAT'S BECAUSE...
...I DIDN'T DO SO WELL IN THE PAST.
ABOUT YOUR MOTHER... I'M SORRY ABOUT THAT.
NO, IT'S FUNNY. MOM'S DEATH WAS WHEN I STARTED TO REALIZE JUST WHAT I HAD. IT WAS EVERYTHING I DID BEFORE THAT-- THE PEEPING TOM STUFF, GETTING PEOPLE TO STEAL FOR ME-- I CAN'T CHANGE THAT. I'M STUCK NOW.
YOU HAVE NO IDEA HOW MUCH I REGRET IT NOW. AND HOW MUCH WORK I HAVE TO DO BECAUSE OF IT.
WHAT WORK ARE YOU TALKING ABOUT?
WELL, THIS IS A START, RIGHT? LISTEN, IF THERE'S ONE THING I'VE LEARNED... YOU CAN ONLY GO UP FROM HERE.
WHAT ARE YOU TALKING ABOUT?
JOEY...?

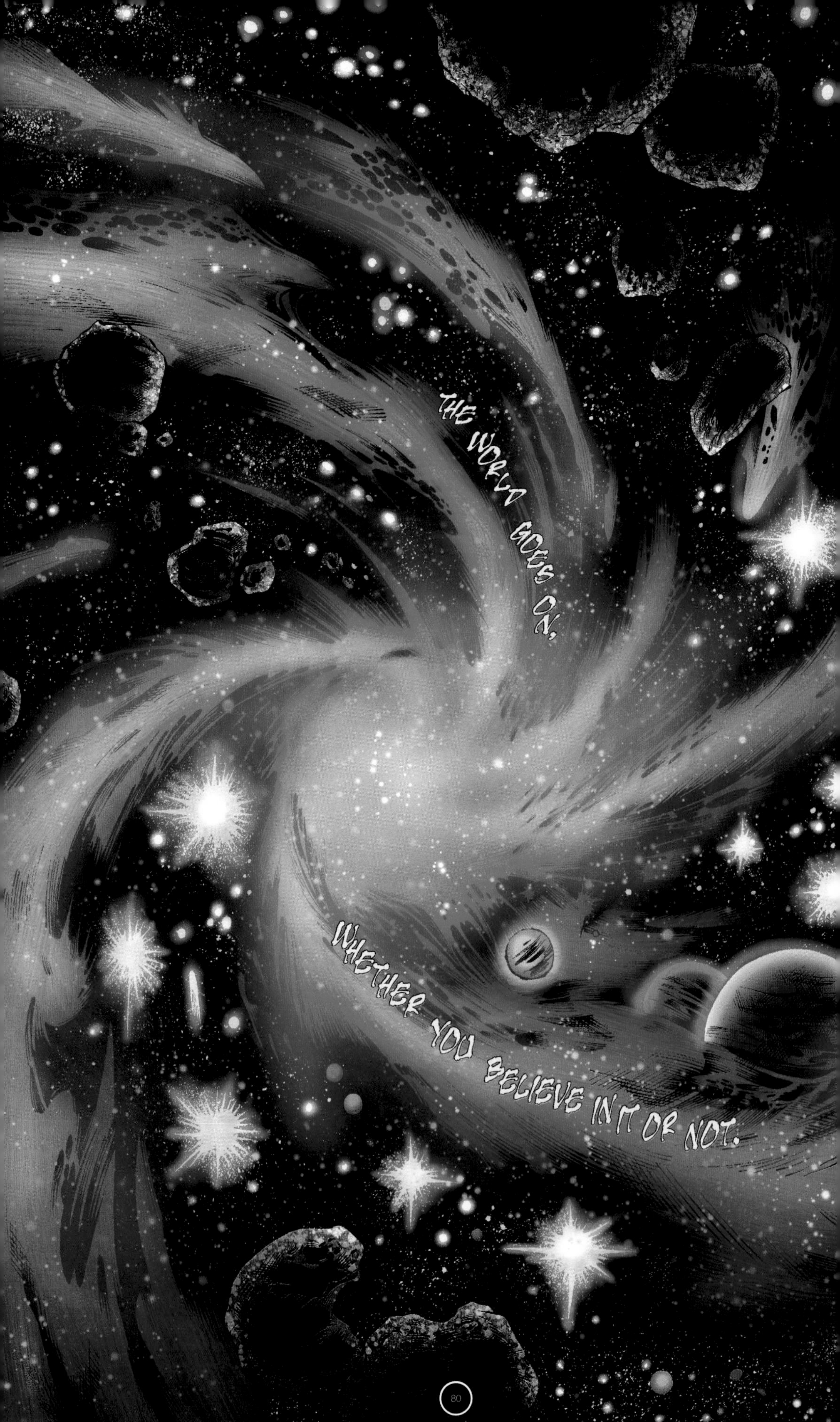
THE WORLD GOES ON,
WHETHER YOU BELIEVE IN IT OR NOT.

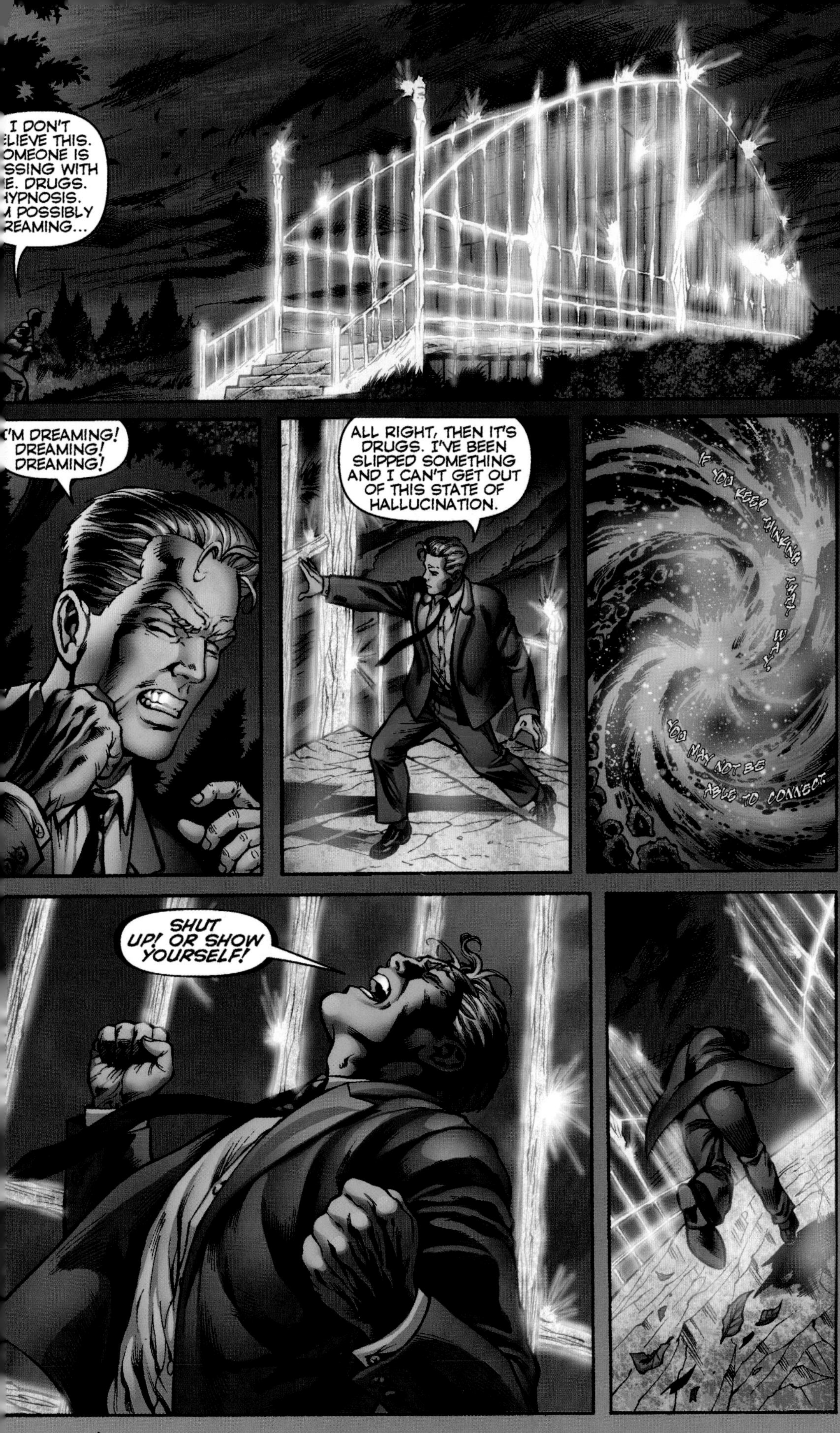
I DON'T ELIEVE THIS. OMEONE IS SSING WITH E. DRUGS. HYPNOSIS. M POSSIBLY REAMING...
'M DREAMING! DREAMING! DREAMING!
ALL RIGHT, THEN IT'S DRUGS. I'VE BEEN SLIPPED SOMETHING AND I CAN'T GET OUT OF THIS STATE OF HALLUCINATION.
IF YOU KEEP THINKING THAT WAY,
YOU MAY NOT BE ABLE TO CONNECT.
SHUT UP! OR SHOW YOURSELF!

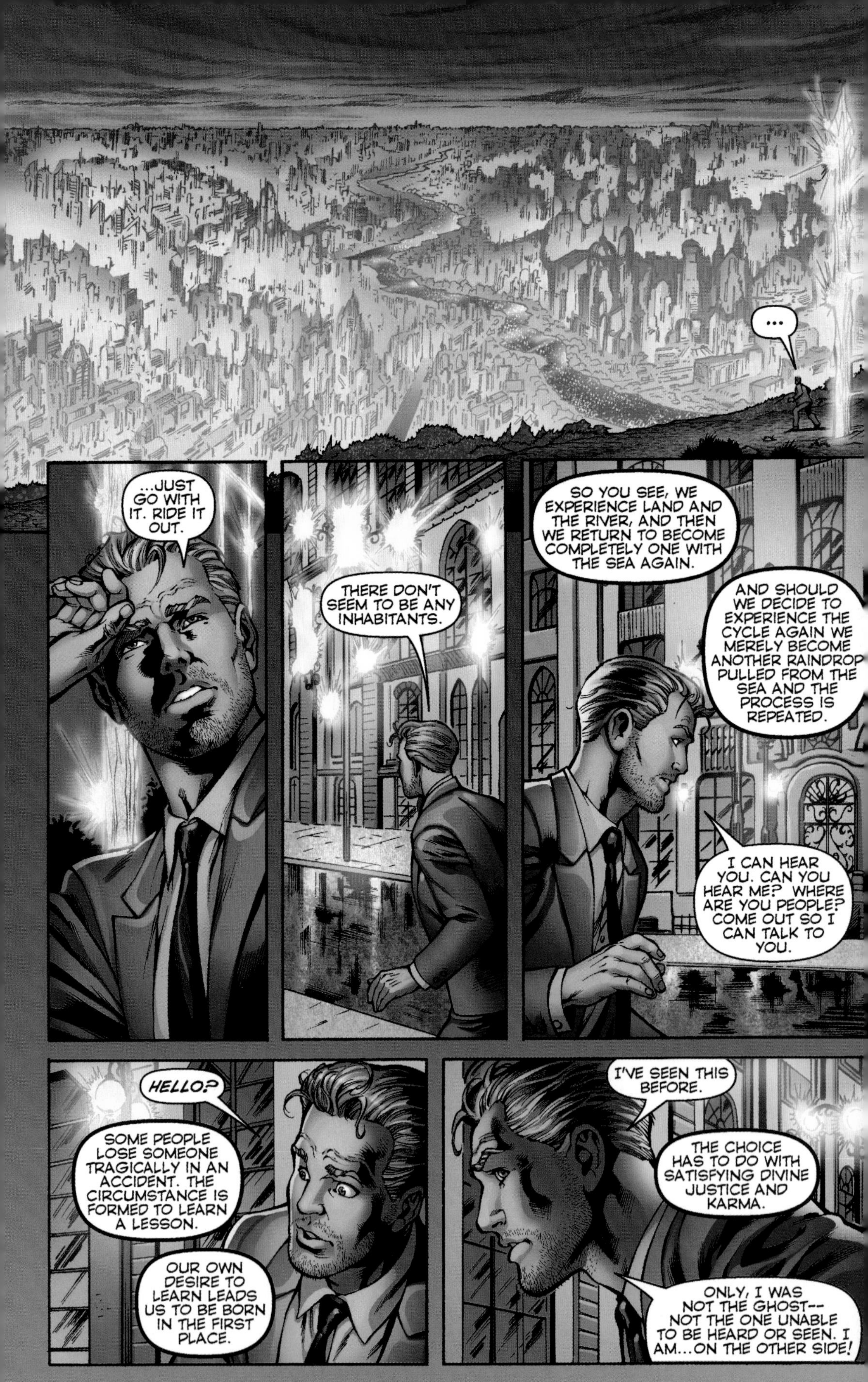
...
...JUST GO WITH IT. RIDE IT OUT.
THERE DON'T SEEM TO BE ANY INHABITANTS.
SO YOU SEE, WE EXPERIENCE LAND AND THE RIVER, AND THEN WE RETURN TO BECOME COMPLETELY ONE WITH THE SEA AGAIN.
AND SHOULD WE DECIDE TO EXPERIENCE THE CYCLE AGAIN WE MERELY BECOME ANOTHER RAINDROP PULLED FROM THE SEA AND THE PROCESS IS REPEATED.
I CAN HEAR YOU. CAN YOU HEAR ME? WHERE ARE YOU PEOPLE? COME OUT SO I CAN TALK TO YOU.
HELLO?
SOME PEOPLE LOSE SOMEONE TRAGICALLY IN AN ACCIDENT. THE CIRCUMSTANCE IS FORMED TO LEARN A LESSON.
OUR OWN DESIRE TO LEARN LEADS US TO BE BORN IN THE FIRST PLACE.
I'VE SEEN THIS BEFORE.
THE CHOICE HAS TO DO WITH SATISFYING DIVINE JUSTICE AND KARMA.
ONLY, I WAS NOT THE GHOST-- NOT THE ONE UNABLE TO BE HEARD OR SEEN. I AM...ON THE OTHER SIDE!

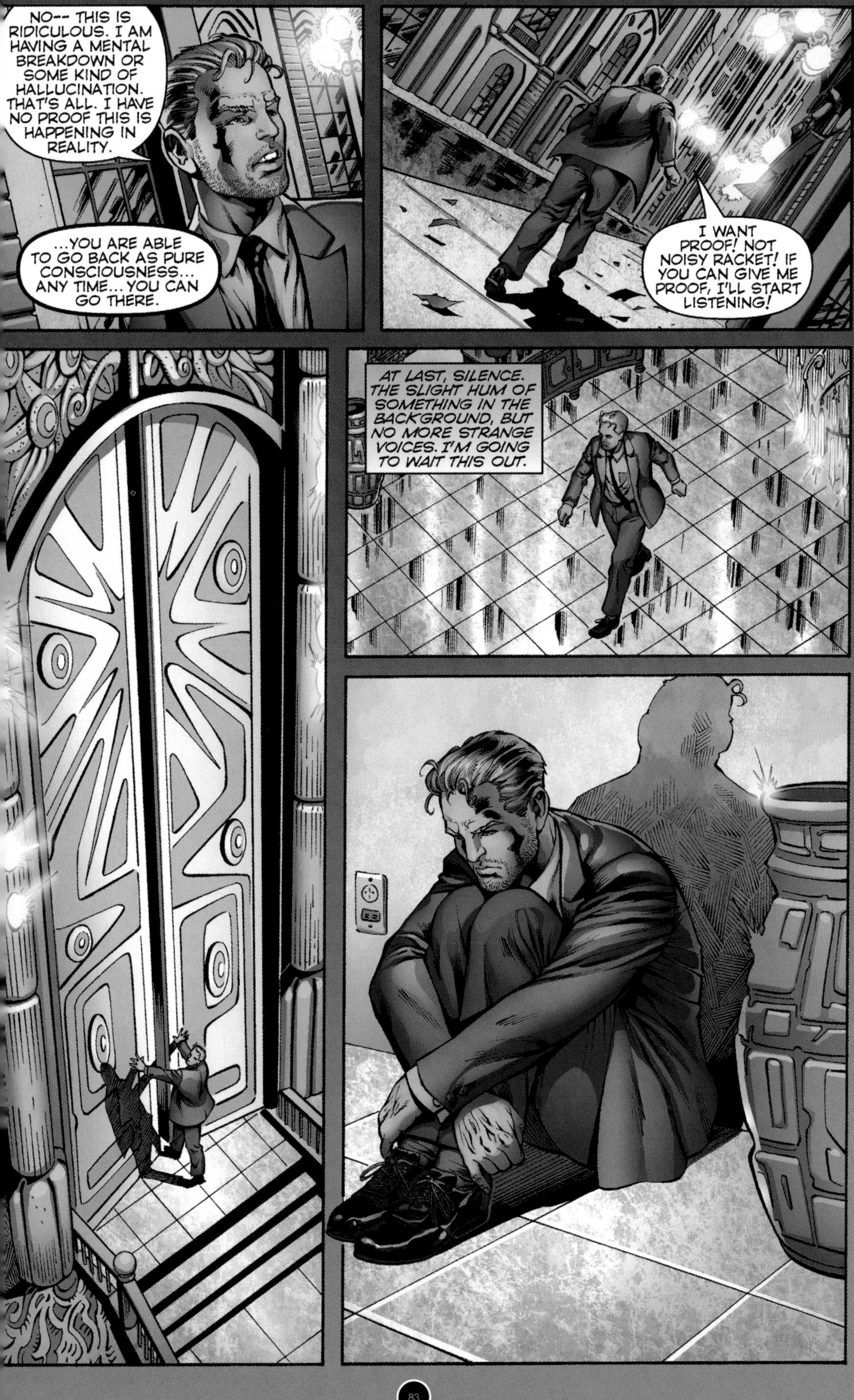
NO-- THIS IS RIDICULOUS. I AM HAVING A MENTAL BREAKDOWN OR SOME KIND OF HALLUCINATION. THAT'S ALL. I HAVE NO PROOF THIS IS HAPPENING IN REALITY.
...YOU ARE ABLE TO GO BACK AS PURE CONSCIOUSNESS... ANY TIME... YOU CAN GO THERE.
I WANT PROOF! NOT NOISY RACKET! IF YOU CAN GIVE ME PROOF, I'LL START LISTENING!
AT LAST, SILENCE. THE SLIGHT HUM OF SOMETHING IN THE BACKGROUND, BUT NO MORE STRANGE VOICES. I'M GOING TO WAIT THIS OUT.

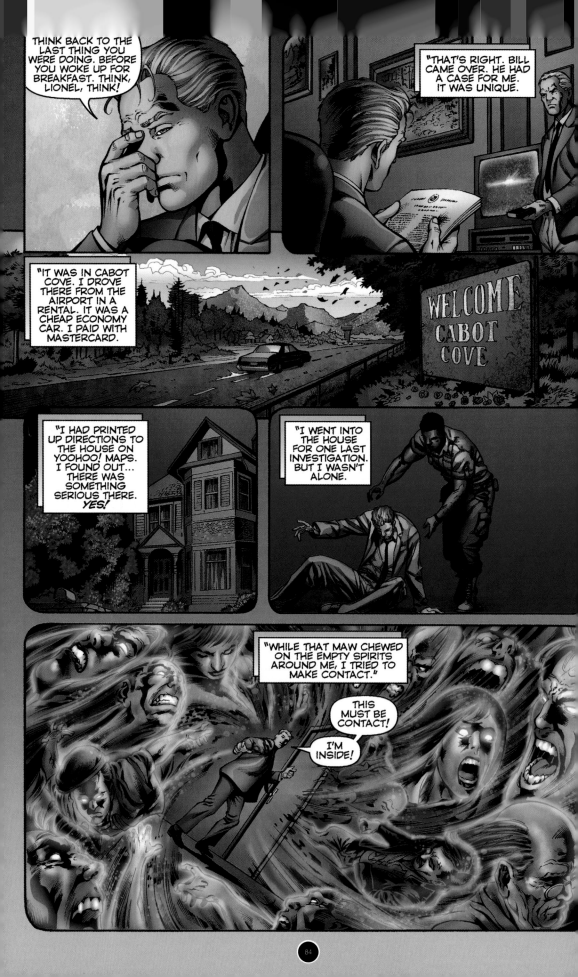

THINK BACK TO THE LAST THING YOU WERE DOING. BEFORE YOU WOKE UP FOR BREAKFAST. THINK, LIONEL, THINK!

"THAT'S RIGHT. BILL CAME OVER. HE HAD A CASE FOR ME. IT WAS UNIQUE.

"IT WAS IN CABOT COVE. I DROVE THERE FROM THE AIRPORT IN A RENTAL. IT WAS A CHEAP ECONOMY CAR. I PAID WITH MASTERCARD.

WELCOME CABOT COVE

"I HAD PRINTED UP DIRECTIONS TO THE HOUSE ON YOOHOO! MAPS. I FOUND OUT... THERE WAS SOMETHING SERIOUS THERE. YES!

"I WENT INTO THE HOUSE FOR ONE LAST INVESTIGATION. BUT I WASN'T ALONE.

"WHILE THAT MAW CHEWED ON THE EMPTY SPIRITS AROUND ME, I TRIED TO MAKE CONTACT."

THIS MUST BE CONTACT!

I'M INSIDE!

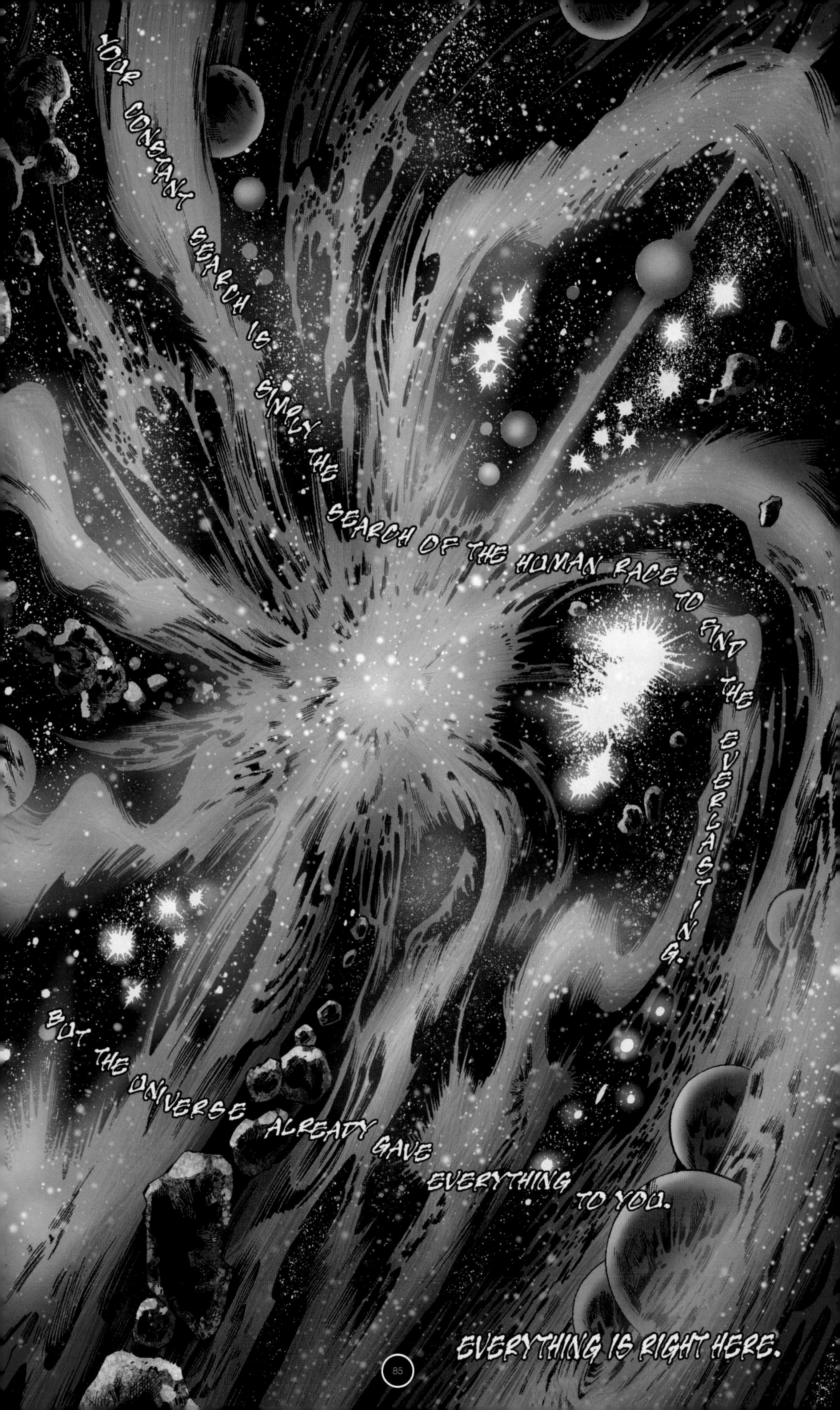
YOUR CONSTANT SEARCH IS SIMPLY THE SEARCH OF THE HUMAN RACE TO FIND THE EVERLASTING.
BUT THE UNIVERSE ALREADY GAVE EVERYTHING TO YOU.
EVERYTHING IS RIGHT HERE.

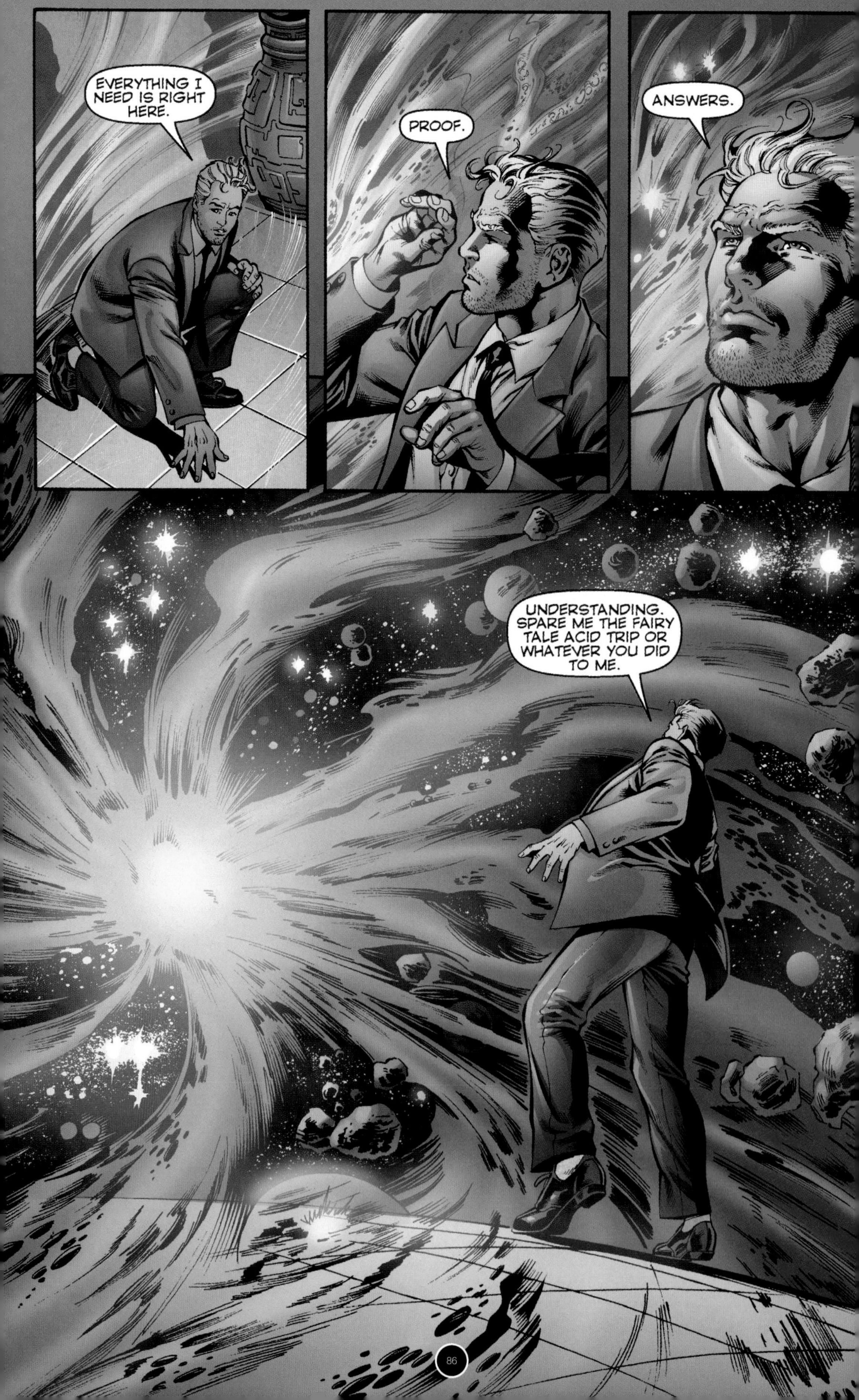
EVERYTHING I NEED IS RIGHT HERE.
PROOF.
ANSWERS.
UNDERSTANDING. SPARE ME THE FAIRY TALE ACID TRIP OR WHATEVER YOU DID TO ME.

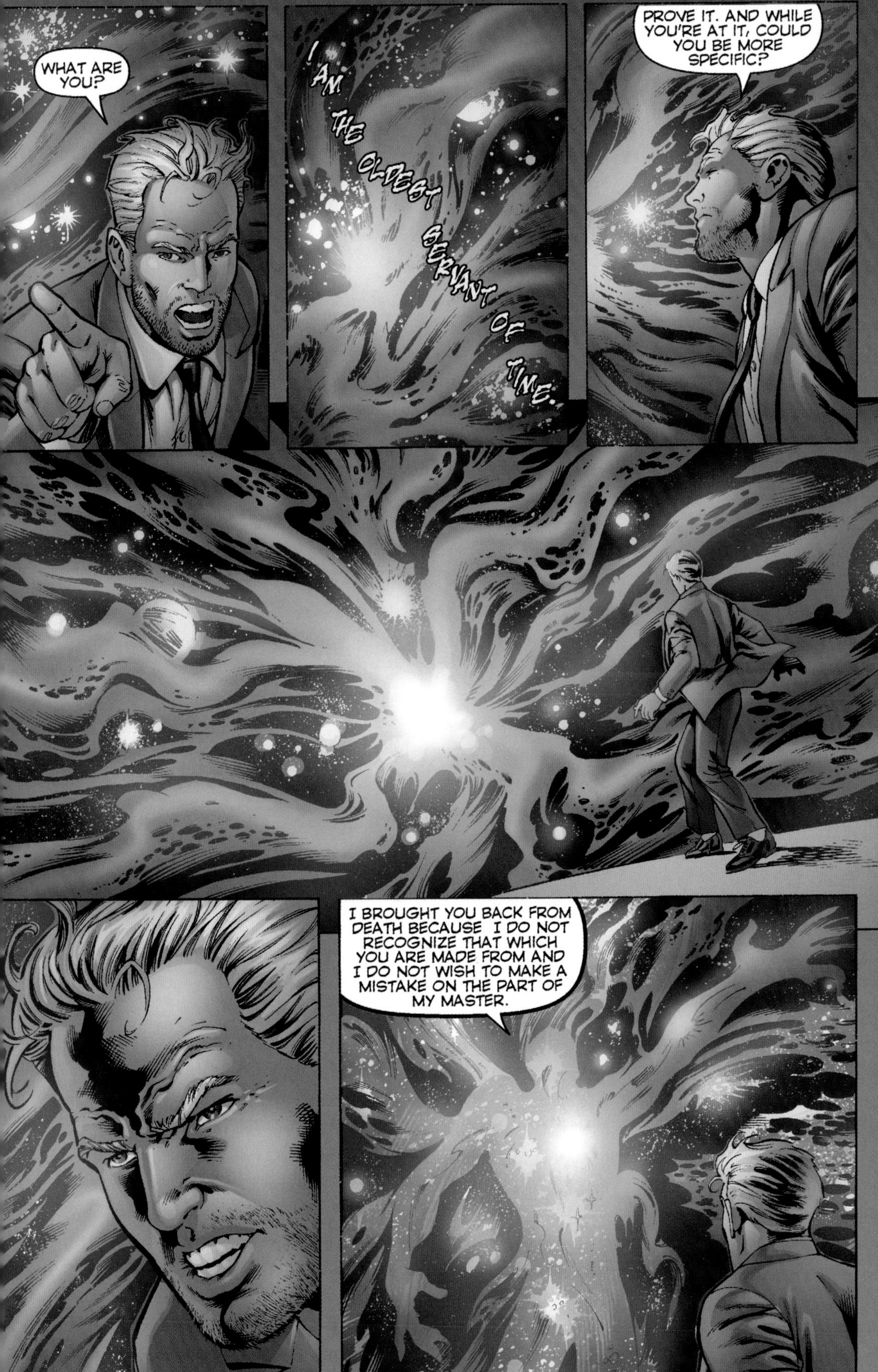

WHAT ARE YOU?
I AM THE OLDEST SERVANT OF TIME.
PROVE IT. AND WHILE YOU'RE AT IT, COULD YOU BE MORE SPECIFIC?
I BROUGHT YOU BACK FROM DEATH BECAUSE I DO NOT RECOGNIZE THAT WHICH YOU ARE MADE FROM AND I DO NOT WISH TO MAKE A MISTAKE ON THE PART OF MY MASTER.

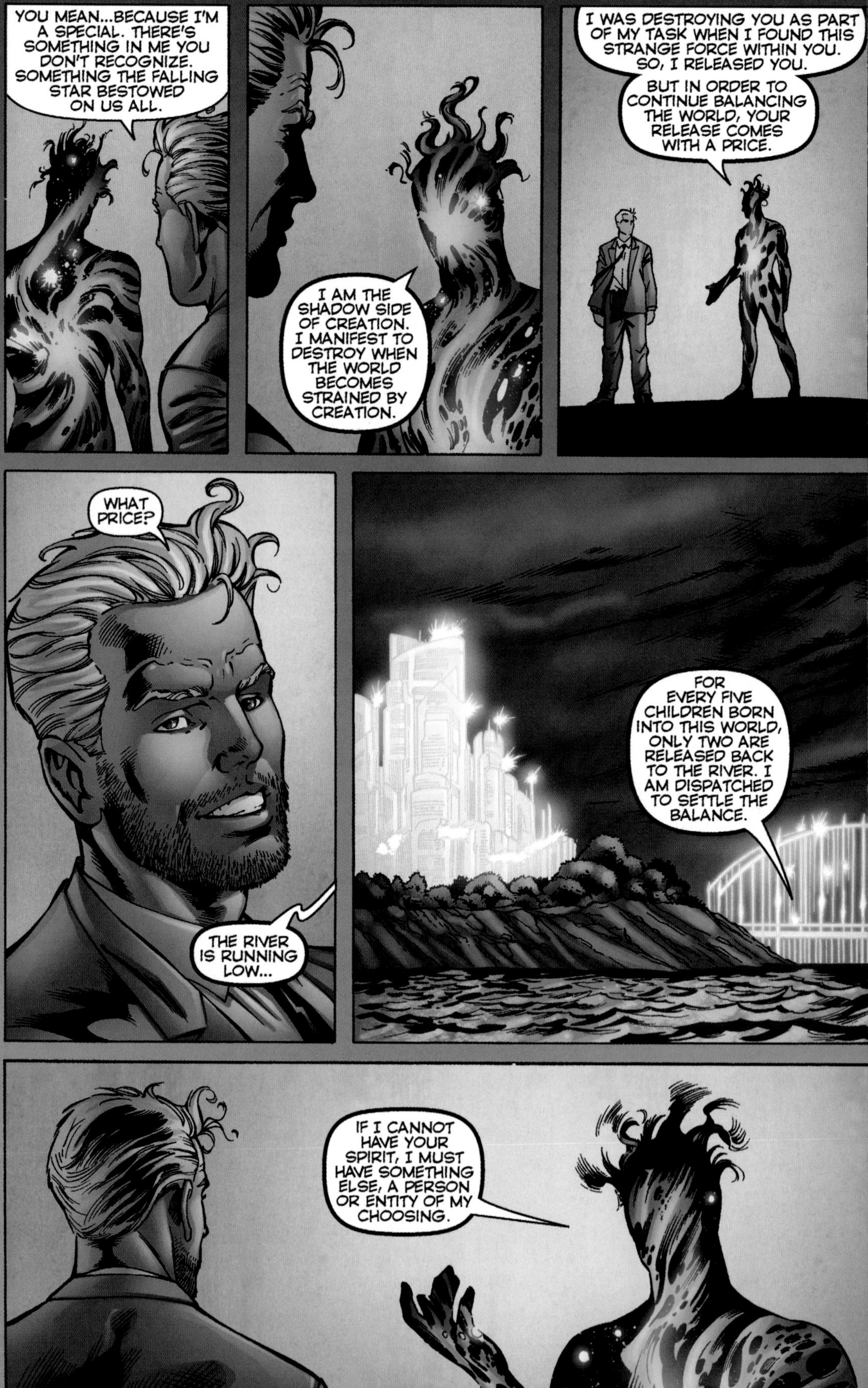
YOU MEAN...BECAUSE I'M A SPECIAL. THERE'S SOMETHING IN ME YOU DON'T RECOGNIZE. SOMETHING THE FALLING STAR BESTOWED ON US ALL.
I AM THE SHADOW SIDE OF CREATION. I MANIFEST TO DESTROY WHEN THE WORLD BECOMES STRAINED BY CREATION.
I WAS DESTROYING YOU AS PART OF MY TASK WHEN I FOUND THIS STRANGE FORCE WITHIN YOU. SO, I RELEASED YOU.
BUT IN ORDER TO CONTINUE BALANCING THE WORLD, YOUR RELEASE COMES WITH A PRICE.
WHAT PRICE?
THE RIVER IS RUNNING LOW...
FOR EVERY FIVE CHILDREN BORN INTO THIS WORLD, ONLY TWO ARE RELEASED BACK TO THE RIVER. I AM DISPATCHED TO SETTLE THE BALANCE.
IF I CANNOT HAVE YOUR SPIRIT, I MUST HAVE SOMETHING ELSE, A PERSON OR ENTITY OF MY CHOOSING.

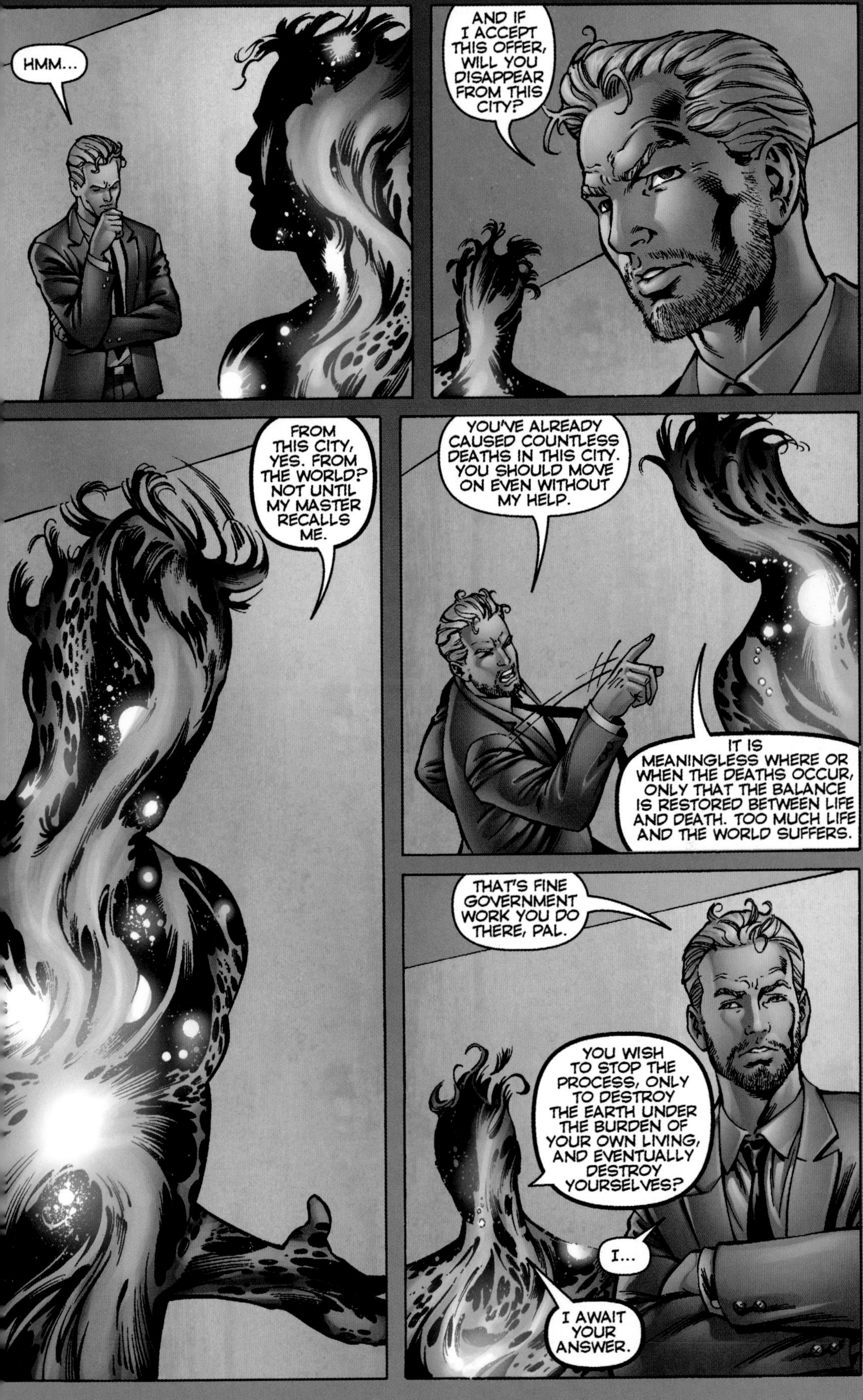
HMM...
AND IF I ACCEPT THIS OFFER, WILL YOU DISAPPEAR FROM THIS CITY?
FROM THIS CITY, YES. FROM THE WORLD? NOT UNTIL MY MASTER RECALLS ME.
YOU'VE ALREADY CAUSED COUNTLESS DEATHS IN THIS CITY. YOU SHOULD MOVE ON EVEN WITHOUT MY HELP.
IT IS MEANINGLESS WHERE OR WHEN THE DEATHS OCCUR, ONLY THAT THE BALANCE IS RESTORED BETWEEN LIFE AND DEATH. TOO MUCH LIFE AND THE WORLD SUFFERS.
THAT'S FINE GOVERNMENT WORK YOU DO THERE, PAL.
YOU WISH TO STOP THE PROCESS, ONLY TO DESTROY THE EARTH UNDER THE BURDEN OF YOUR OWN LIVING, AND EVENTUALLY DESTROY YOURSELVES?
I...
I AWAIT YOUR ANSWER.

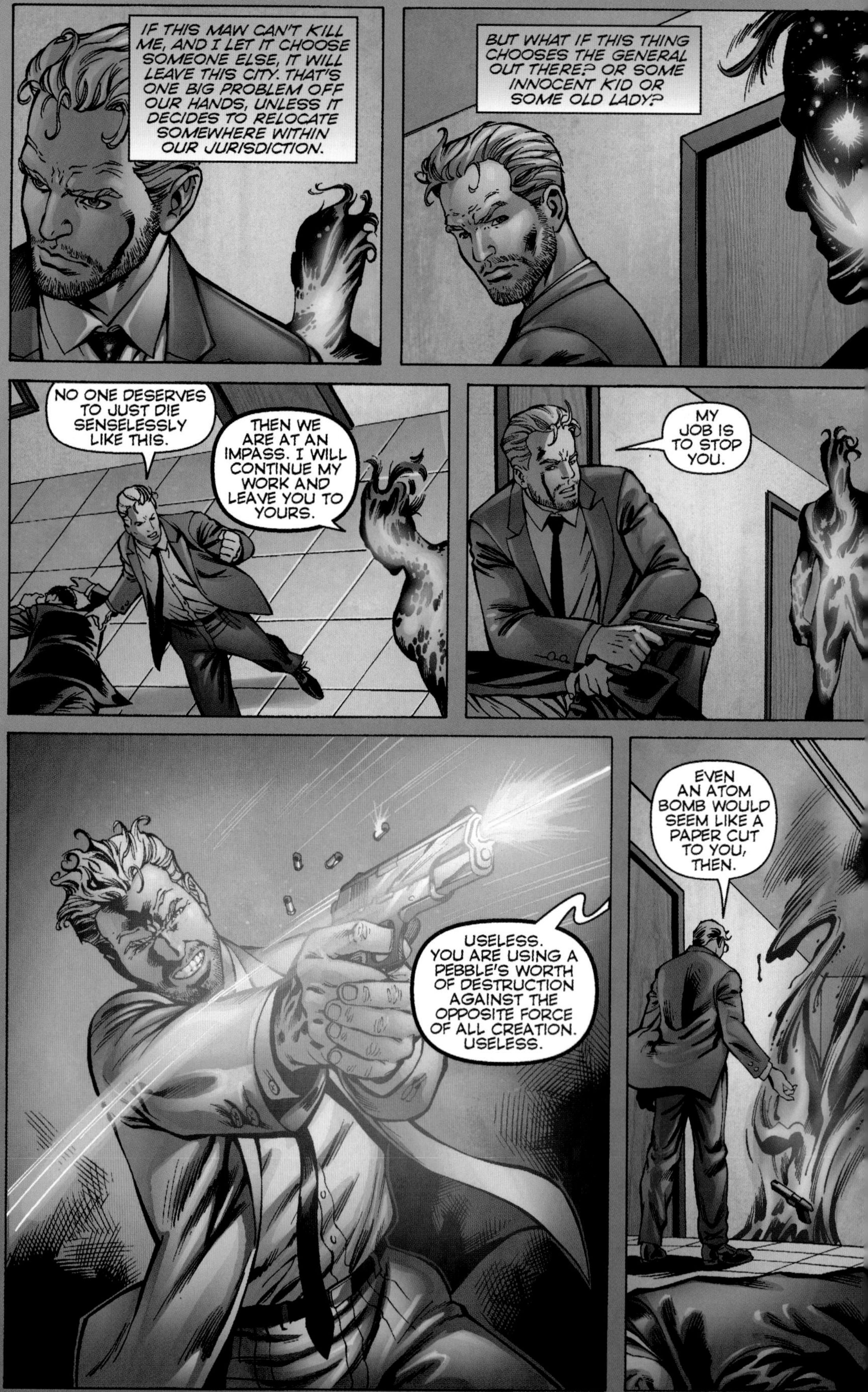
IF THIS MAW CAN'T KILL ME, AND I LET IT CHOOSE SOMEONE ELSE, IT WILL LEAVE THIS CITY. THAT'S ONE BIG PROBLEM OFF OUR HANDS, UNLESS IT DECIDES TO RELOCATE SOMEWHERE WITHIN OUR JURISDICTION.
BUT WHAT IF THIS THING CHOOSES THE GENERAL OUT THERE? OR SOME INNOCENT KID OR SOME OLD LADY?
NO ONE DESERVES TO JUST DIE SENSELESSLY LIKE THIS.
THEN WE ARE AT AN IMPASS. I WILL CONTINUE MY WORK AND LEAVE YOU TO YOURS.
MY JOB IS TO STOP YOU.
USELESS. YOU ARE USING A PEBBLE'S WORTH OF DESTRUCTION AGAINST THE OPPOSITE FORCE OF ALL CREATION. USELESS.
EVEN AN ATOM BOMB WOULD SEEM LIKE A PAPER CUT TO YOU, THEN.

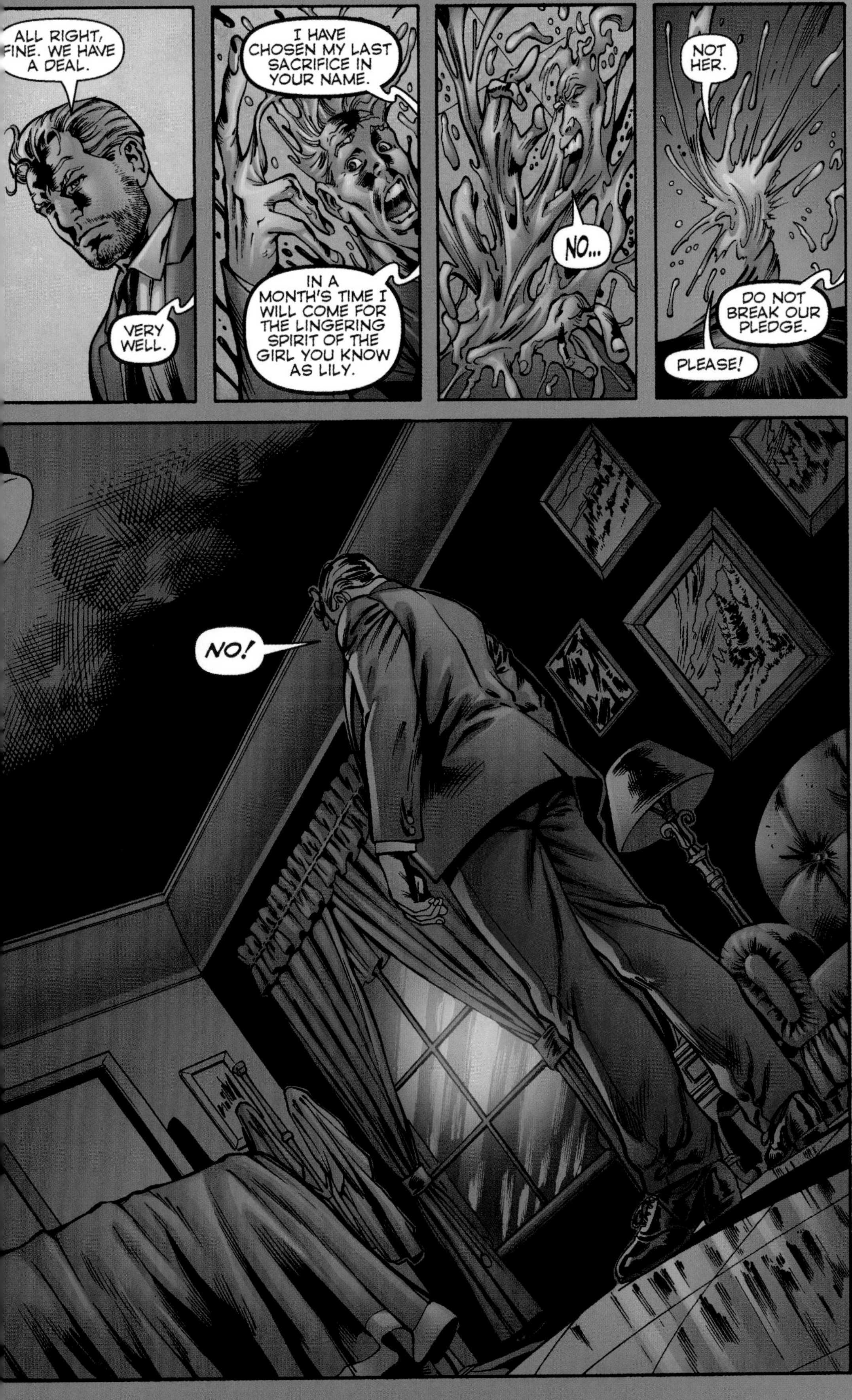
ALL RIGHT, FINE. WE HAVE A DEAL.
VERY WELL.
I HAVE CHOSEN MY LAST SACRIFICE IN YOUR NAME.
IN A MONTH'S TIME I WILL COME FOR THE LINGERING SPIRIT OF THE GIRL YOU KNOW AS LILY.
NO...
NOT HER.
DO NOT BREAK OUR PLEDGE.
PLEASE!
NO!

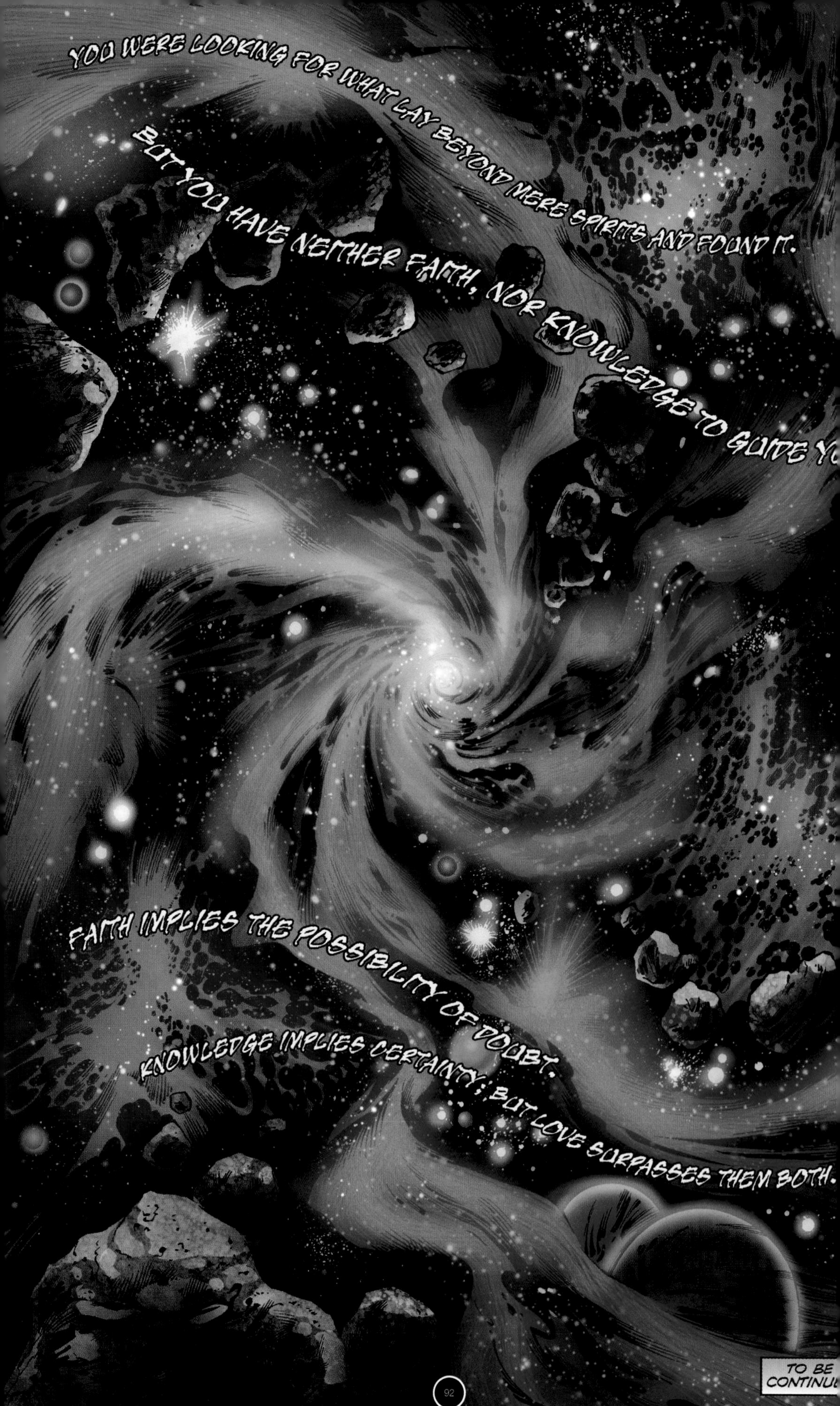
YOU WERE LOOKING FOR WHAT LAY BEYOND MERE SPIRITS AND FOUND IT.
BUT YOU HAVE NEITHER FAITH, NOR KNOWLEDGE TO GUIDE YOU
FAITH IMPLIES THE POSSIBILITY OF DOUBT.
KNOWLEDGE IMPLIES CERTAINTY; BUT LOVE SURPASSES THEM BOTH.
TO BE CONTINUED

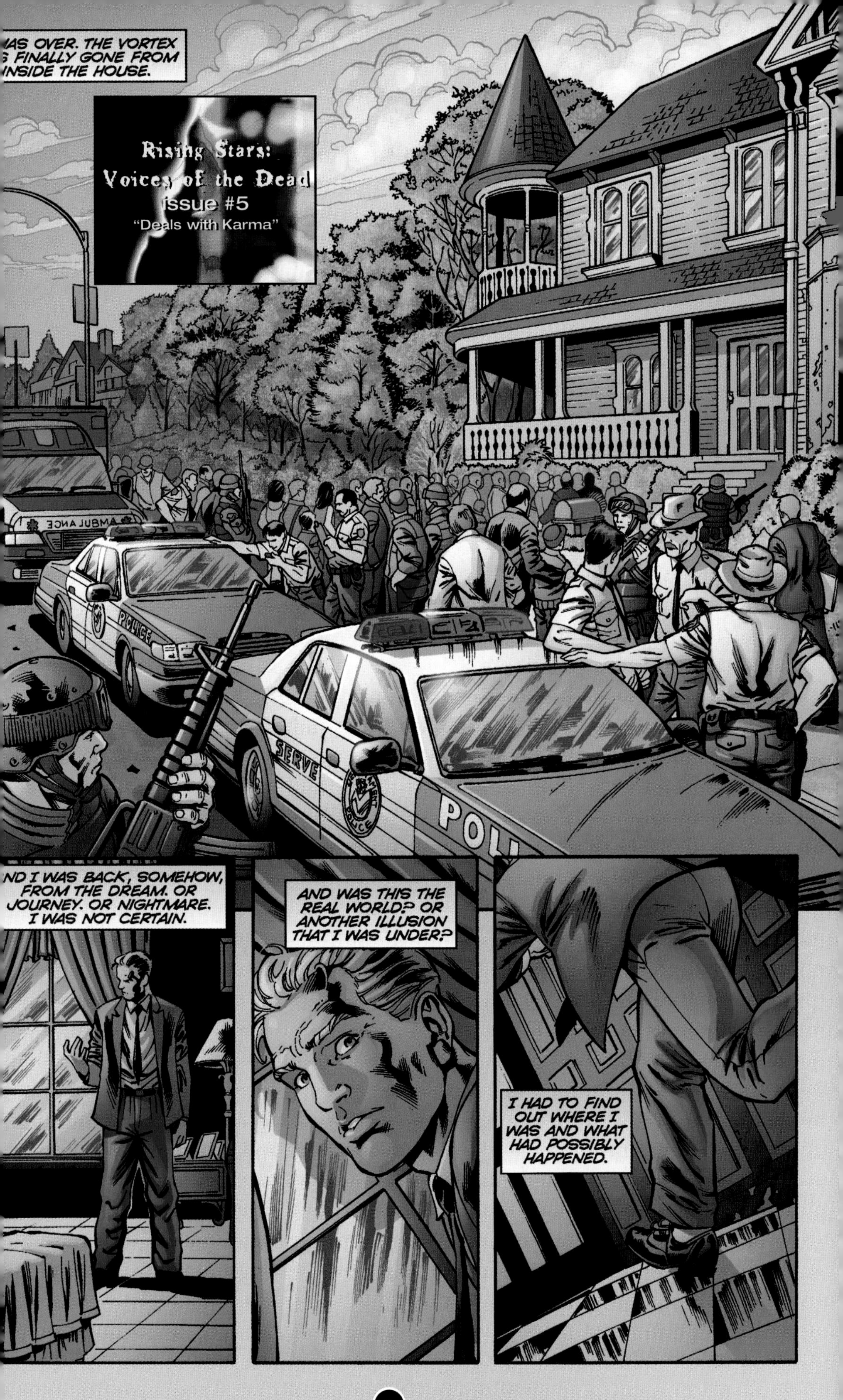

AS OVER. THE VORTEX S FINALLY GONE FROM INSIDE THE HOUSE.
Rising Stars: Voices of the Dead
issue #5
"Deals with Karma"
AMBULANCE
POLICE
SERVE
POLI
ND I WAS BACK, SOMEHOW, FROM THE DREAM. OR JOURNEY. OR NIGHTMARE. I WAS NOT CERTAIN.
AND WAS THIS THE REAL WORLD? OR ANOTHER ILLUSION THAT I WAS UNDER?
I HAD TO FIND OUT WHERE I WAS AND WHAT HAD POSSIBLY HAPPENED.

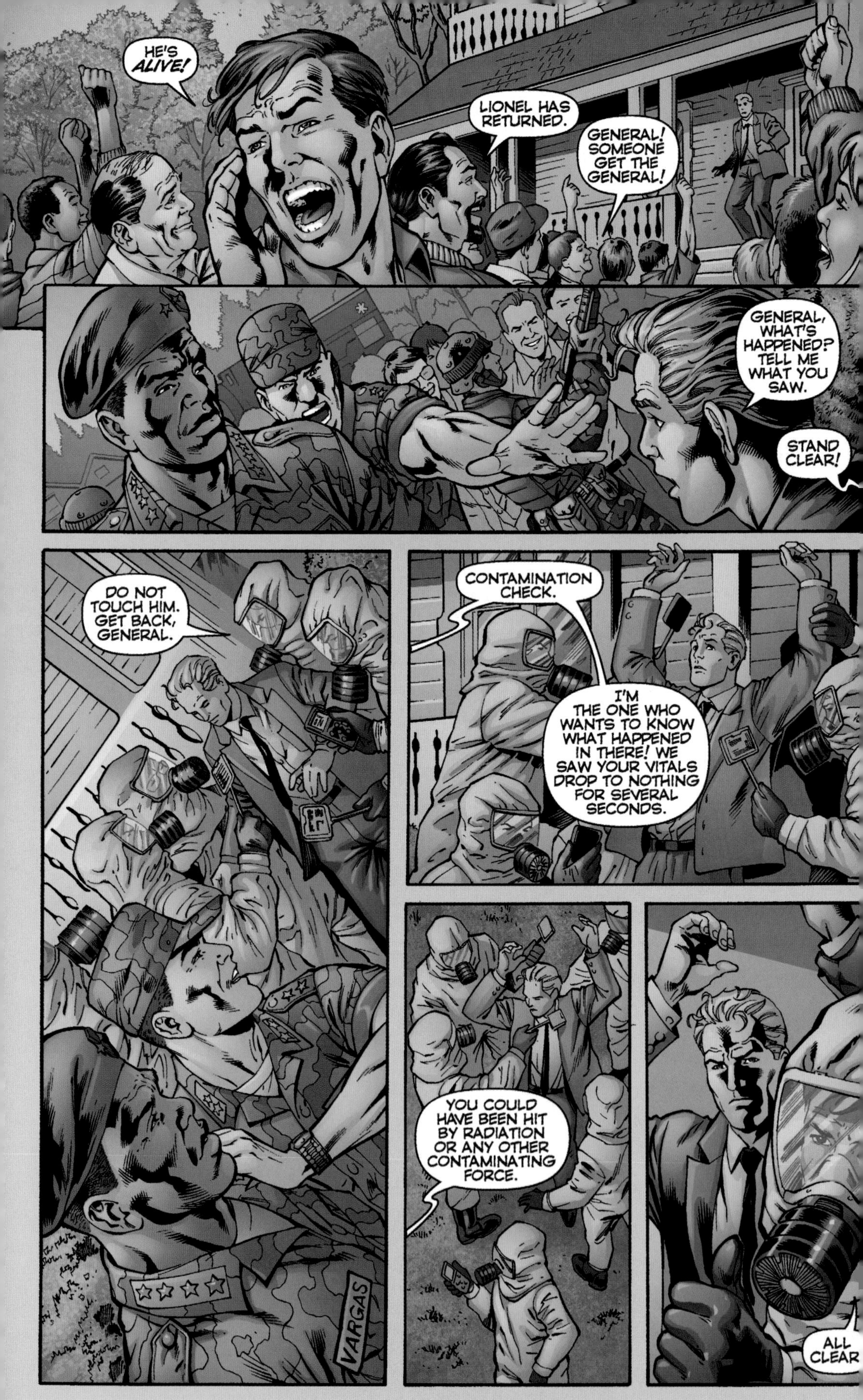
HE'S ALIVE!
LIONEL HAS RETURNED.
GENERAL! SOMEONE GET THE GENERAL!
GENERAL, WHAT'S HAPPENED? TELL ME WHAT YOU SAW.
STAND CLEAR!
DO NOT TOUCH HIM. GET BACK, GENERAL.
VARGAS
CONTAMINATION CHECK.
I'M THE ONE WHO WANTS TO KNOW WHAT HAPPENED IN THERE! WE SAW YOUR VITALS DROP TO NOTHING FOR SEVERAL SECONDS.
YOU COULD HAVE BEEN HIT BY RADIATION OR ANY OTHER CONTAMINATING FORCE.
ALL CLEAR

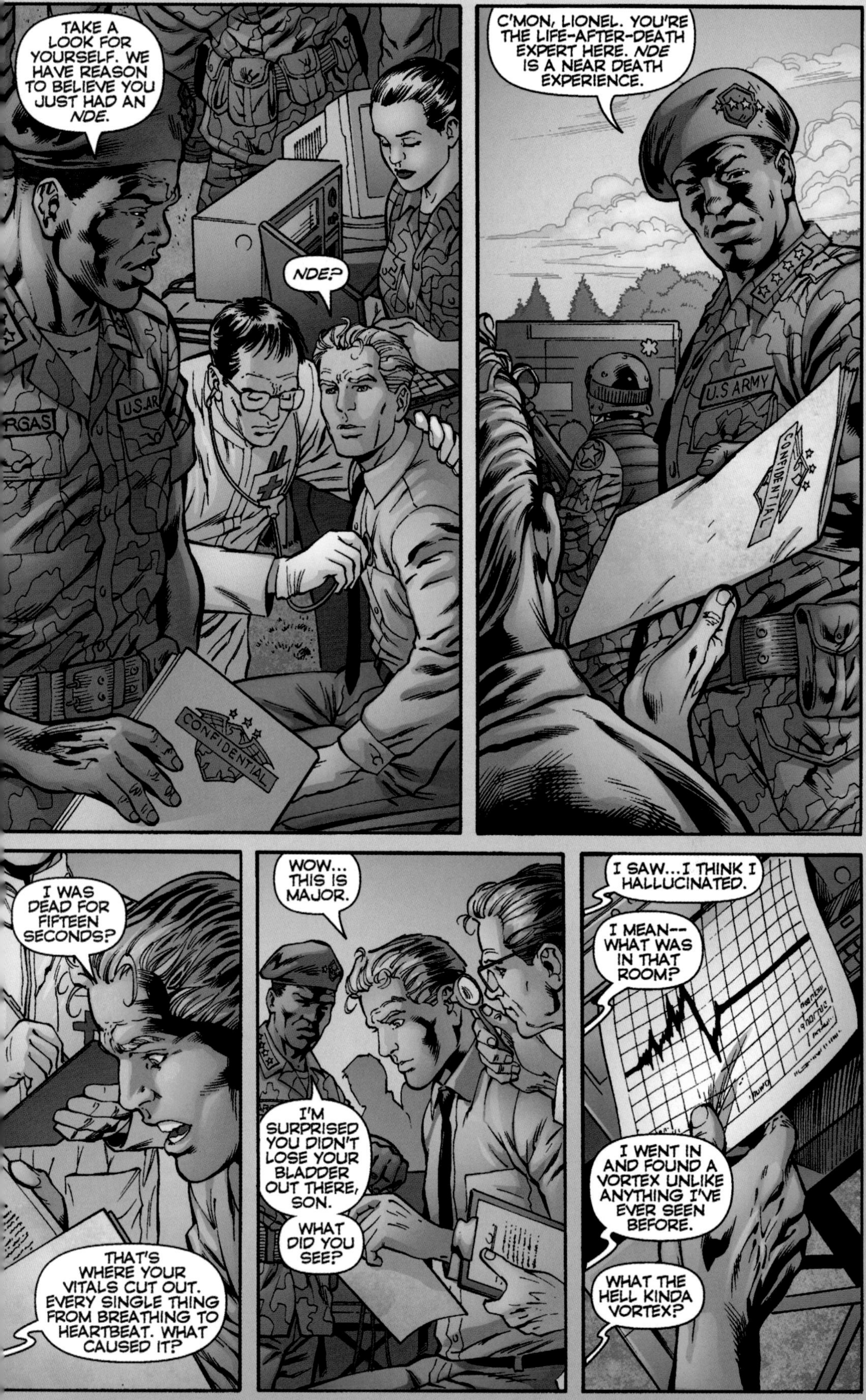
TAKE A LOOK FOR YOURSELF. WE HAVE REASON TO BELIEVE YOU JUST HAD AN NDE.
NDE?
C'MON, LIONEL. YOU'RE THE LIFE-AFTER-DEATH EXPERT HERE. NDE IS A NEAR DEATH EXPERIENCE.
U.S ARMY
CONFIDENTIAL
I WAS DEAD FOR FIFTEEN SECONDS?
THAT'S WHERE YOUR VITALS CUT OUT. EVERY SINGLE THING FROM BREATHING TO HEARTBEAT. WHAT CAUSED IT?
WOW... THIS IS MAJOR.
I'M SURPRISED YOU DIDN'T LOSE YOUR BLADDER OUT THERE, SON.
WHAT DID YOU SEE?
I SAW...I THINK I HALLUCINATED.
I MEAN-- WHAT WAS IN THAT ROOM?
I WENT IN AND FOUND A VORTEX UNLIKE ANYTHING I'VE EVER SEEN BEFORE.
WHAT THE HELL KINDA VORTEX?

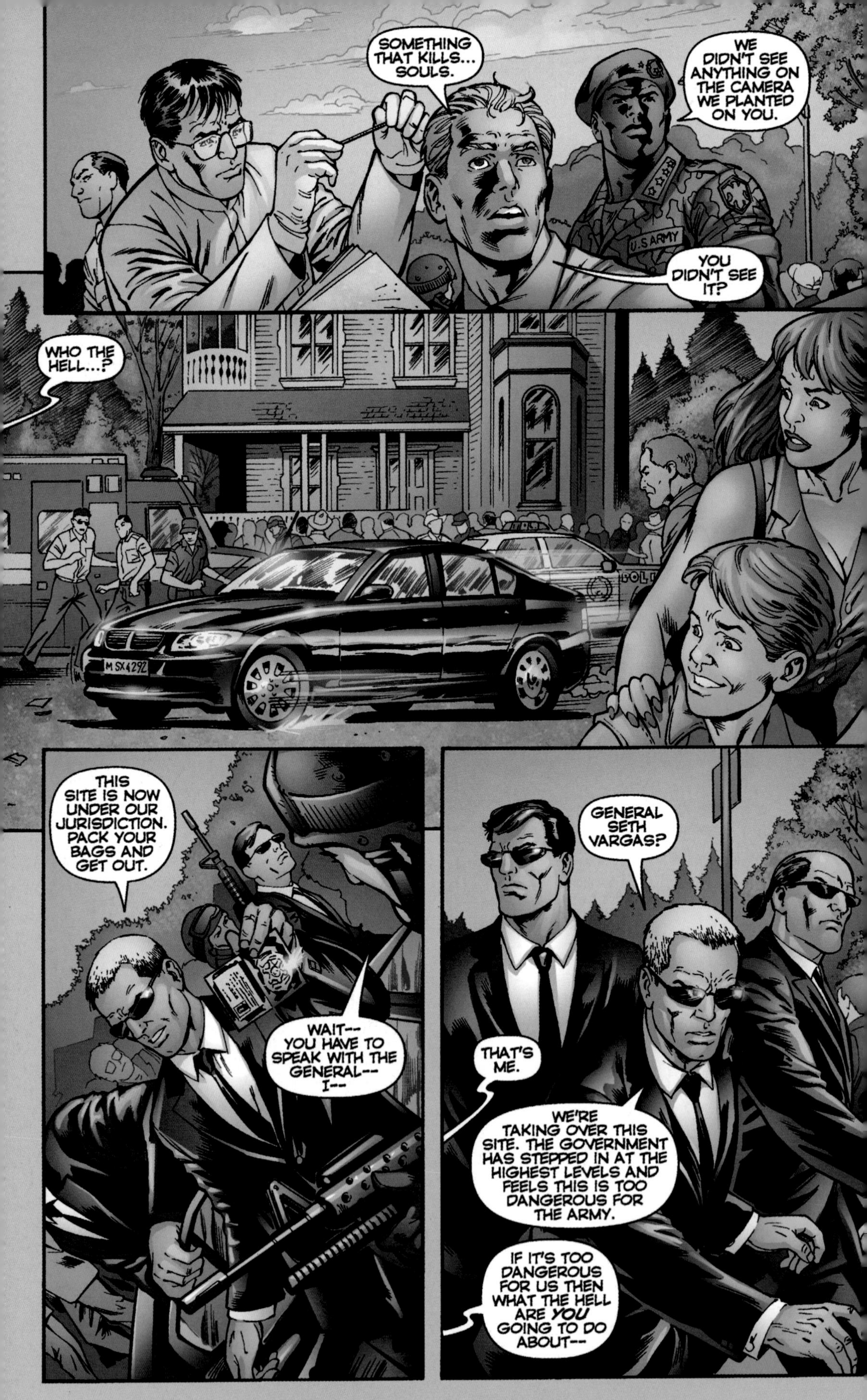
SOMETHING THAT KILLS... SOULS.
WE DIDN'T SEE ANYTHING ON THE CAMERA WE PLANTED ON YOU.
YOU DIDN'T SEE IT?
U.S. ARMY
WHO THE HELL...?
M SX 4292
THIS SITE IS NOW UNDER OUR JURISDICTION. PACK YOUR BAGS AND GET OUT.
WAIT-- YOU HAVE TO SPEAK WITH THE GENERAL-- I--
GENERAL SETH VARGAS?
THAT'S ME.
WE'RE TAKING OVER THIS SITE. THE GOVERNMENT HAS STEPPED IN AT THE HIGHEST LEVELS AND FEELS THIS IS TOO DANGEROUS FOR THE ARMY.
IF IT'S TOO DANGEROUS FOR US THEN WHAT THE HELL ARE *YOU* GOING TO DO ABOUT--

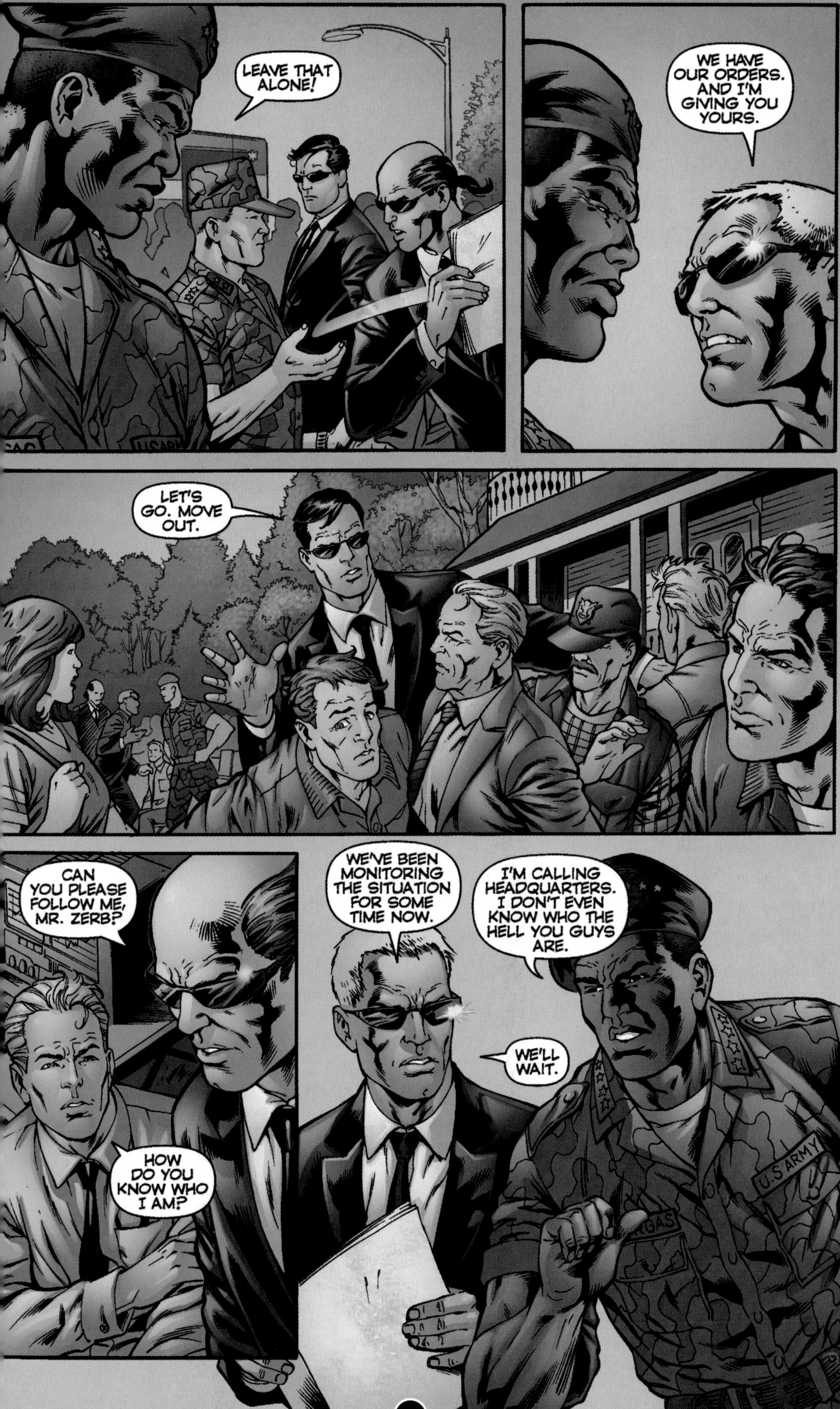

LEAVE THAT ALONE!
WE HAVE OUR ORDERS. AND I'M GIVING YOU YOURS.
LET'S GO. MOVE OUT.
CAN YOU PLEASE FOLLOW ME, MR. ZERB?
HOW DO YOU KNOW WHO I AM?
WE'VE BEEN MONITORING THE SITUATION FOR SOME TIME NOW.
I'M CALLING HEADQUARTERS. I DON'T EVEN KNOW WHO THE HELL YOU GUYS ARE.
WE'LL WAIT.
U.S ARMY

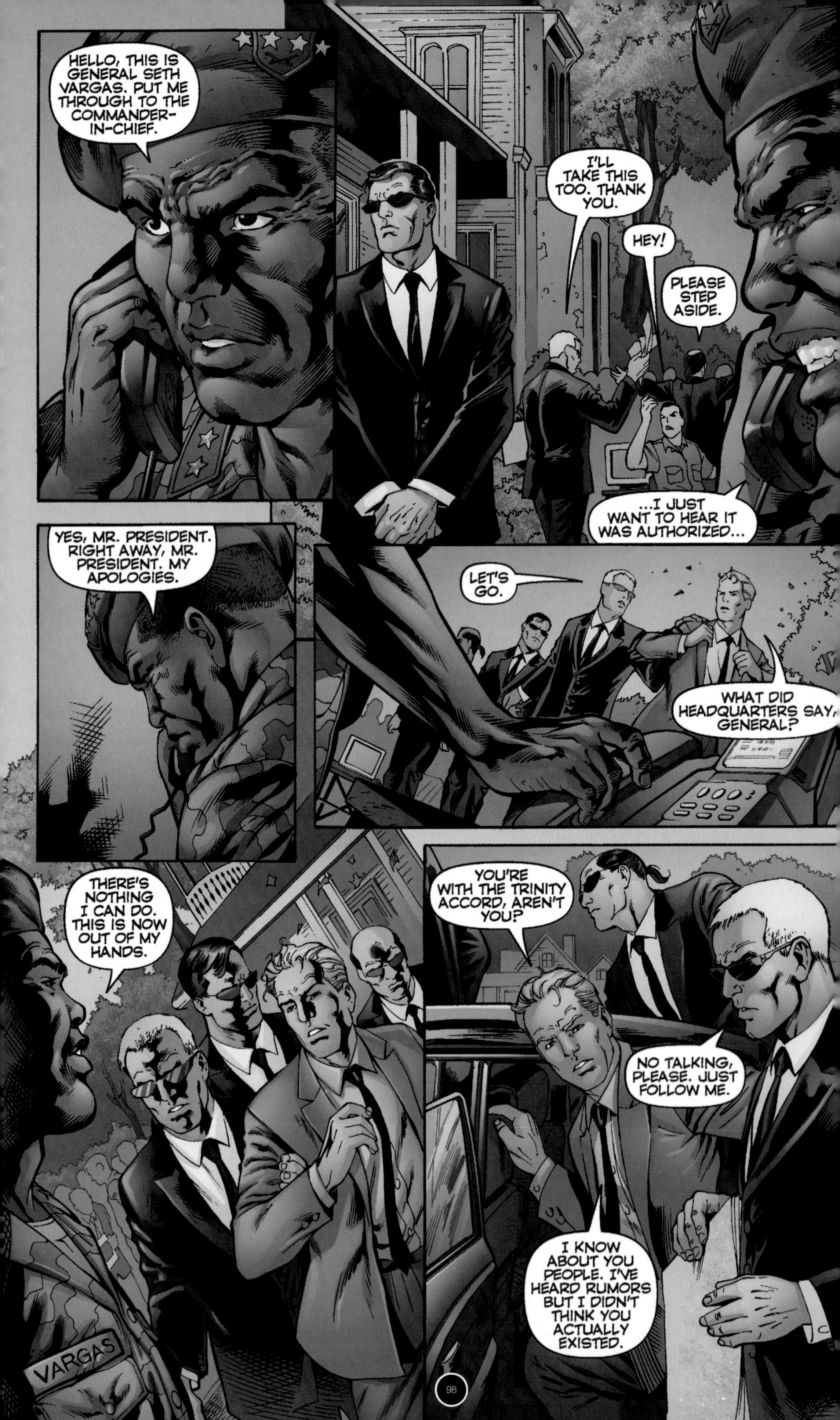

HELLO, THIS IS GENERAL SETH VARGAS. PUT ME THROUGH TO THE COMMANDER-IN-CHIEF.
I'LL TAKE THIS TOO. THANK YOU.
HEY!
PLEASE STEP ASIDE.
...I JUST WANT TO HEAR IT WAS AUTHORIZED...
YES, MR. PRESIDENT. RIGHT AWAY, MR. PRESIDENT. MY APOLOGIES.
LET'S GO.
WHAT DID HEADQUARTERS SAY, GENERAL?
THERE'S NOTHING I CAN DO. THIS IS NOW OUT OF MY HANDS.
VARGAS
YOU'RE WITH THE TRINITY ACCORD, AREN'T YOU?
NO TALKING, PLEASE. JUST FOLLOW ME.
I KNOW ABOUT YOU PEOPLE. I'VE HEARD RUMORS BUT I DIDN'T THINK YOU ACTUALLY EXISTED.

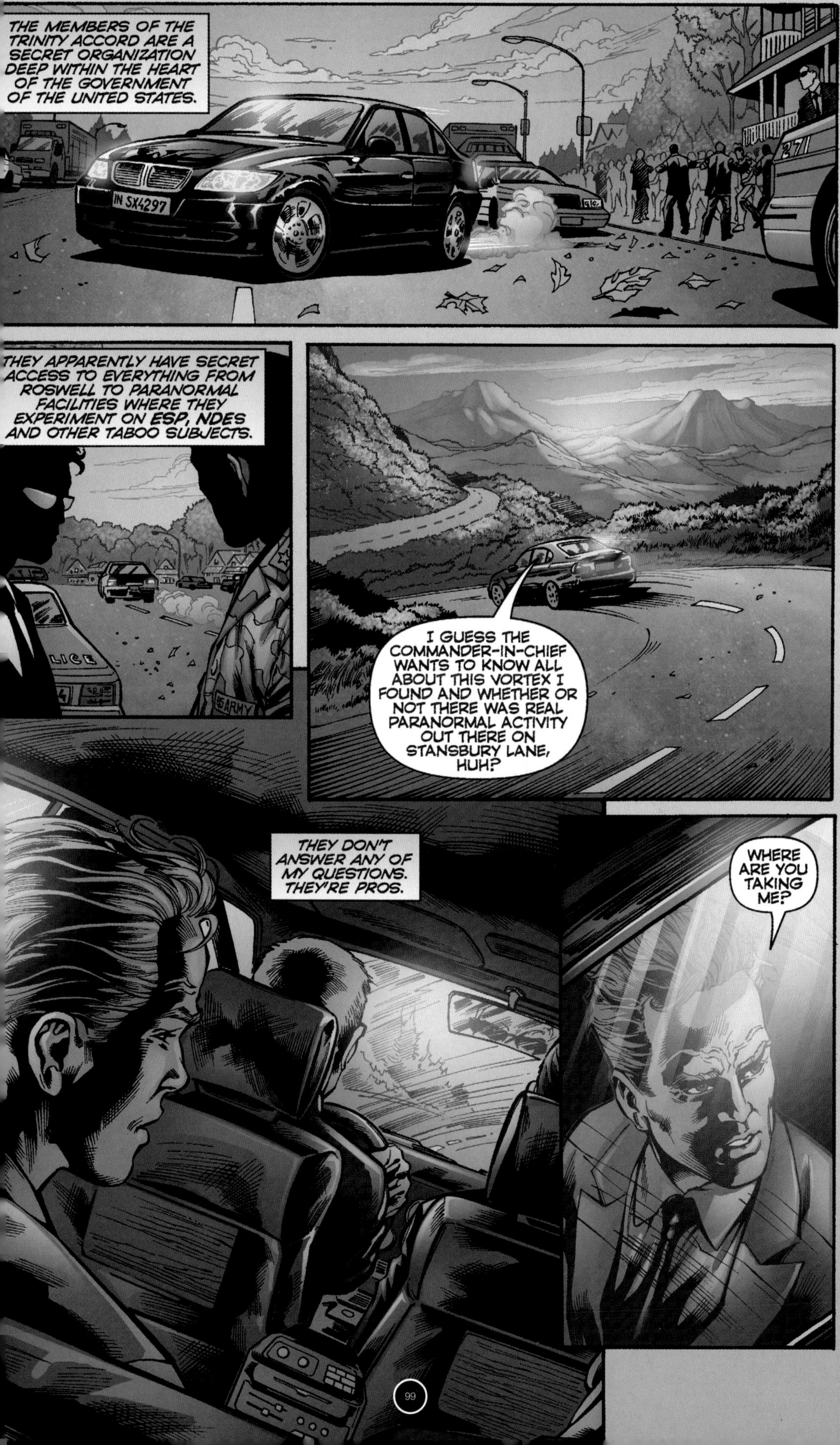
THE MEMBERS OF THE TRINITY ACCORD ARE A SECRET ORGANIZATION DEEP WITHIN THE HEART OF THE GOVERNMENT OF THE UNITED STATES.
IN SX4297
271
THEY APPARENTLY HAVE SECRET ACCESS TO EVERYTHING FROM ROSWELL TO PARANORMAL FACILITIES WHERE THEY EXPERIMENT ON ESP, NDES AND OTHER TABOO SUBJECTS.
LICE
US ARMY
I GUESS THE COMMANDER-IN-CHIEF WANTS TO KNOW ALL ABOUT THIS VORTEX I FOUND AND WHETHER OR NOT THERE WAS REAL PARANORMAL ACTIVITY OUT THERE ON STANSBURY LANE, HUH?
THEY DON'T ANSWER ANY OF MY QUESTIONS. THEY'RE PROS.
WHERE ARE YOU TAKING ME?

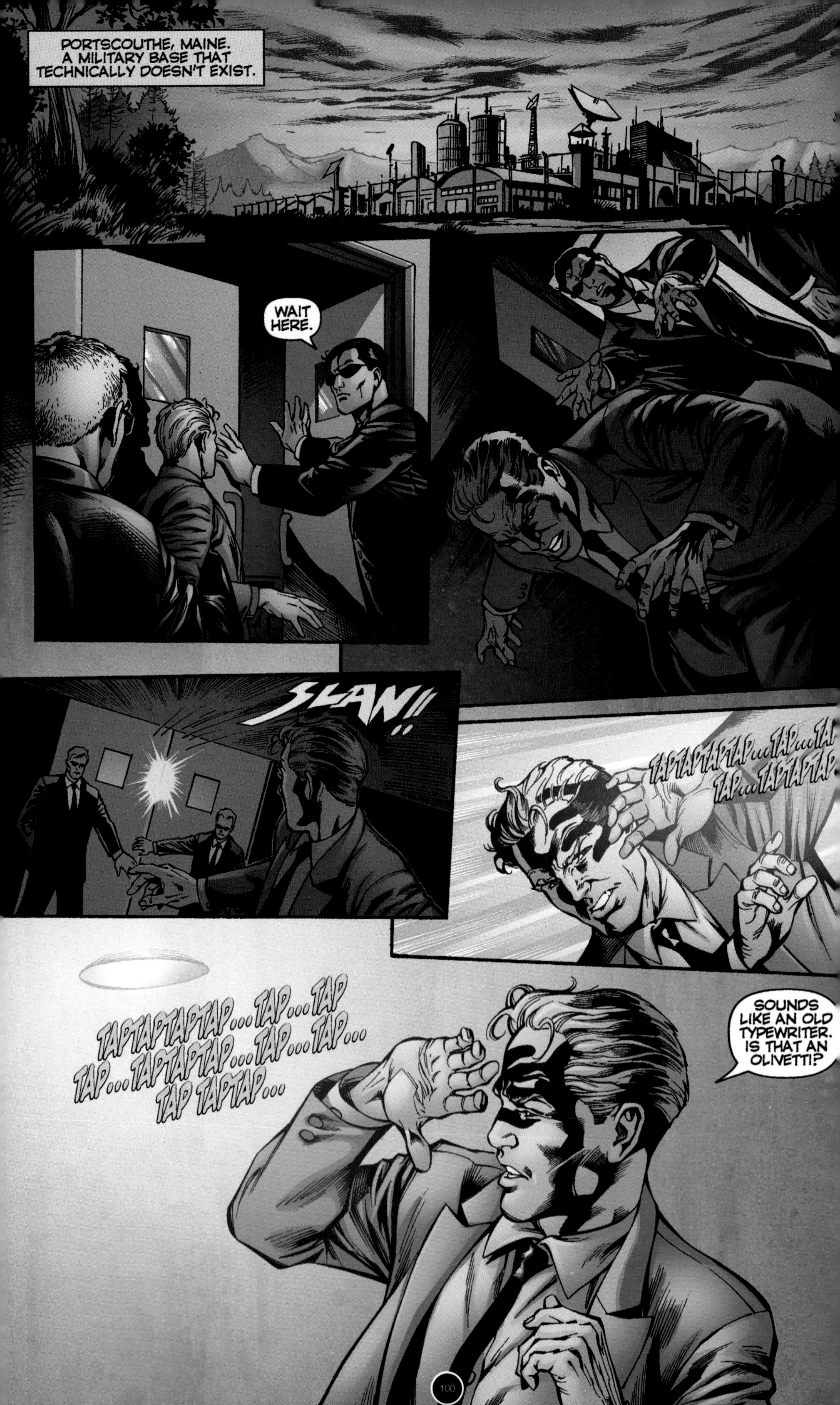
PORTSCOUTHE, MAINE. A MILITARY BASE THAT TECHNICALLY DOESN'T EXIST.
WAIT HERE.
SLAM!!
TAPTAPTAPTAP...TAP...TA
TAP...TAPTAPTAP
TAPTAPTAPTAP...TAP...TAP
TAP...TAPTAPTAP...TAP...TAP...
TAP TAPTAP...
SOUNDS LIKE AN OLD TYPEWRITER. IS THAT AN OLIVETTI?

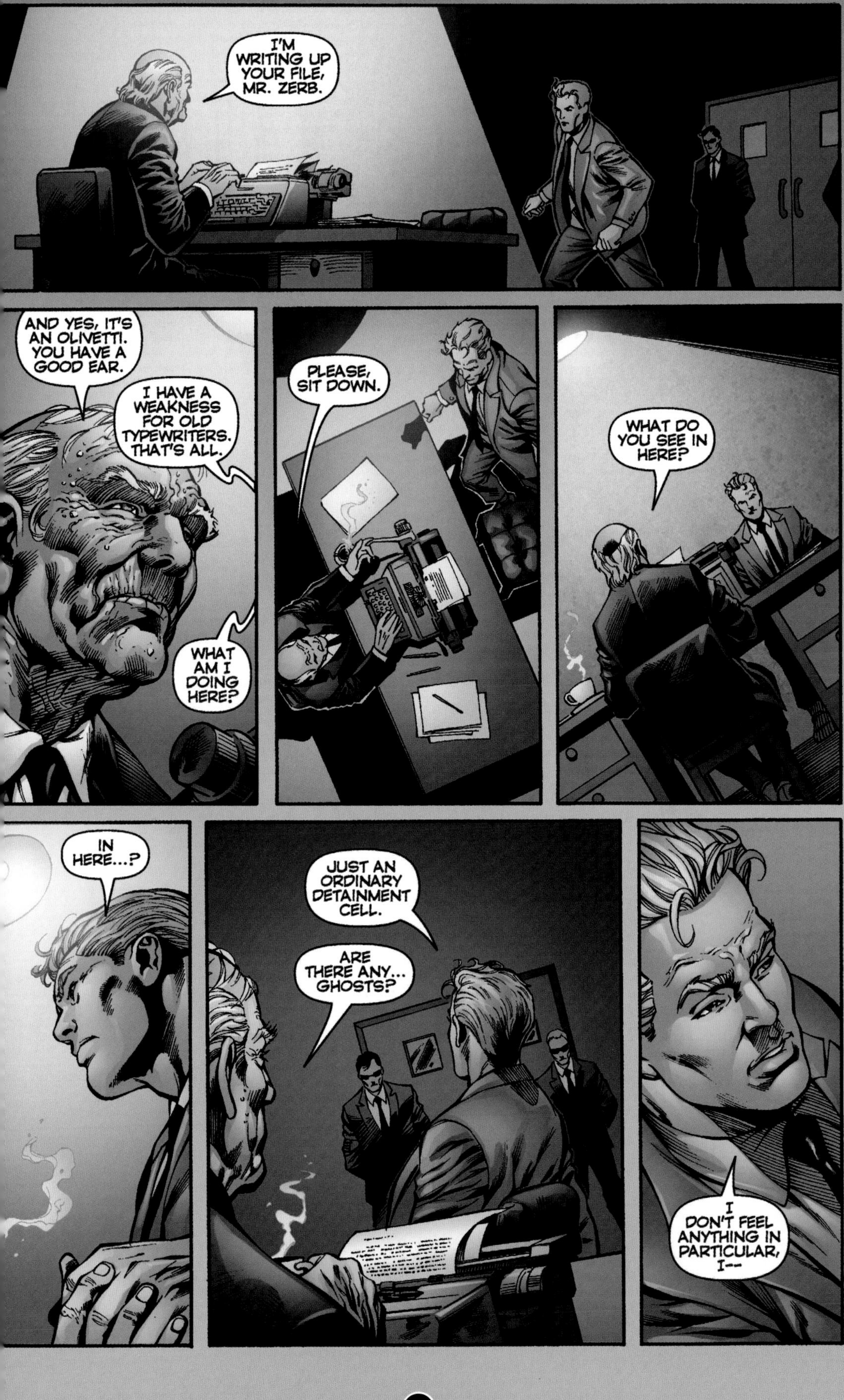
I'M WRITING UP YOUR FILE, MR. ZERB.
AND YES, IT'S AN OLIVETTI. YOU HAVE A GOOD EAR.
I HAVE A WEAKNESS FOR OLD TYPEWRITERS. THAT'S ALL.
WHAT AM I DOING HERE?
PLEASE, SIT DOWN.
WHAT DO YOU SEE IN HERE?
IN HERE...?
JUST AN ORDINARY DETAINMENT CELL.
ARE THERE ANY... GHOSTS?
I DON'T FEEL ANYTHING IN PARTICULAR, I--

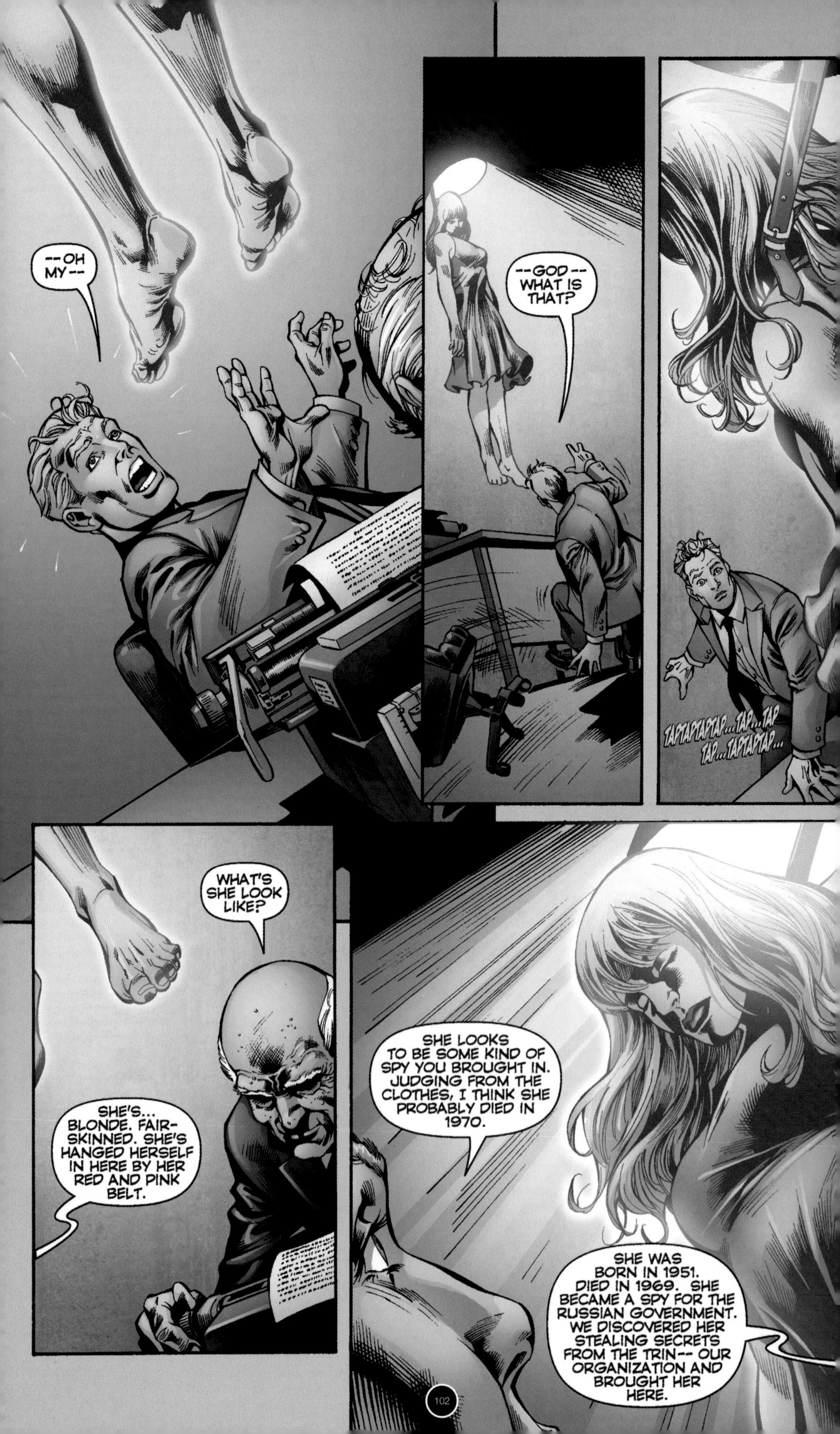
--OH MY--
--GOD--WHAT IS THAT?
TAPTAPTAPTAP...TAP...TAP TAP...TAPTAPTAP...
WHAT'S SHE LOOK LIKE?
SHE'S... BLONDE. FAIR-SKINNED. SHE'S HANGED HERSELF IN HERE BY HER RED AND PINK BELT.
SHE LOOKS TO BE SOME KIND OF SPY YOU BROUGHT IN. JUDGING FROM THE CLOTHES, I THINK SHE PROBABLY DIED IN 1970.
SHE WAS BORN IN 1951. DIED IN 1969. SHE BECAME A SPY FOR THE RUSSIAN GOVERNMENT. WE DISCOVERED HER STEALING SECRETS FROM THE TRIN-- OUR ORGANIZATION AND BROUGHT HER HERE.

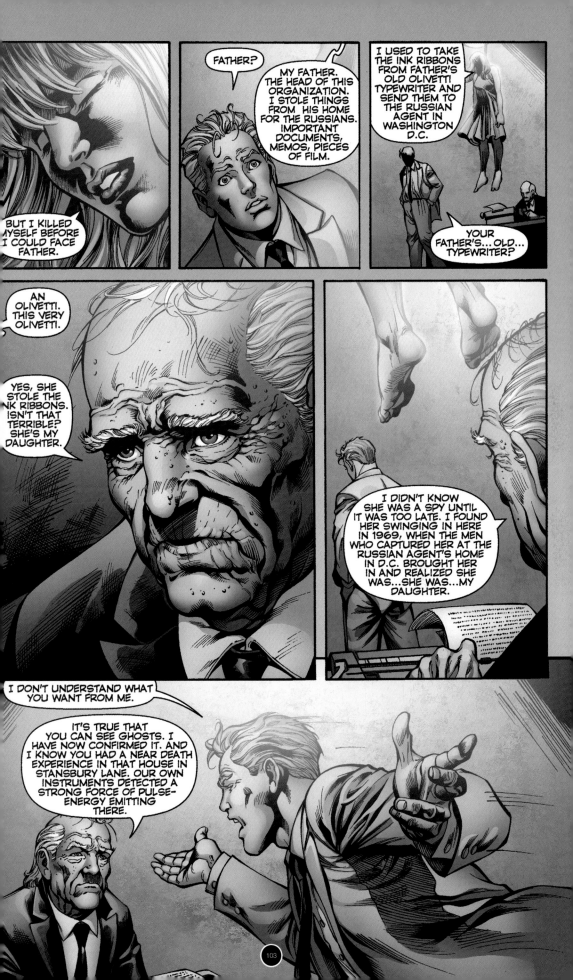

BUT I KILLED MYSELF BEFORE I COULD FACE FATHER.

FATHER?

MY FATHER. THE HEAD OF THIS ORGANIZATION. I STOLE THINGS FROM HIS HOME FOR THE RUSSIANS. IMPORTANT DOCUMENTS, MEMOS, PIECES OF FILM.

I USED TO TAKE THE INK RIBBONS FROM FATHER'S OLD OLIVETTI TYPEWRITER AND SEND THEM TO THE RUSSIAN AGENT IN WASHINGTON D.C.

YOUR FATHER'S... OLD... TYPEWRITER?

AN OLIVETTI. THIS VERY OLIVETTI.

YES, SHE STOLE THE INK RIBBONS. ISN'T THAT TERRIBLE? SHE'S MY DAUGHTER.

I DIDN'T KNOW SHE WAS A SPY UNTIL IT WAS TOO LATE. I FOUND HER SWINGING IN HERE IN 1969, WHEN THE MEN WHO CAPTURED HER AT THE RUSSIAN AGENT'S HOME IN D.C. BROUGHT HER IN AND REALIZED SHE WAS...SHE WAS...MY DAUGHTER.

I DON'T UNDERSTAND WHAT YOU WANT FROM ME.

IT'S TRUE THAT YOU CAN SEE GHOSTS. I HAVE NOW CONFIRMED IT. AND I KNOW YOU HAD A NEAR DEATH EXPERIENCE IN THAT HOUSE IN STANSBURY LANE. OUR OWN INSTRUMENTS DETECTED A STRONG FORCE OF PULSE-ENERGY EMITTING THERE.

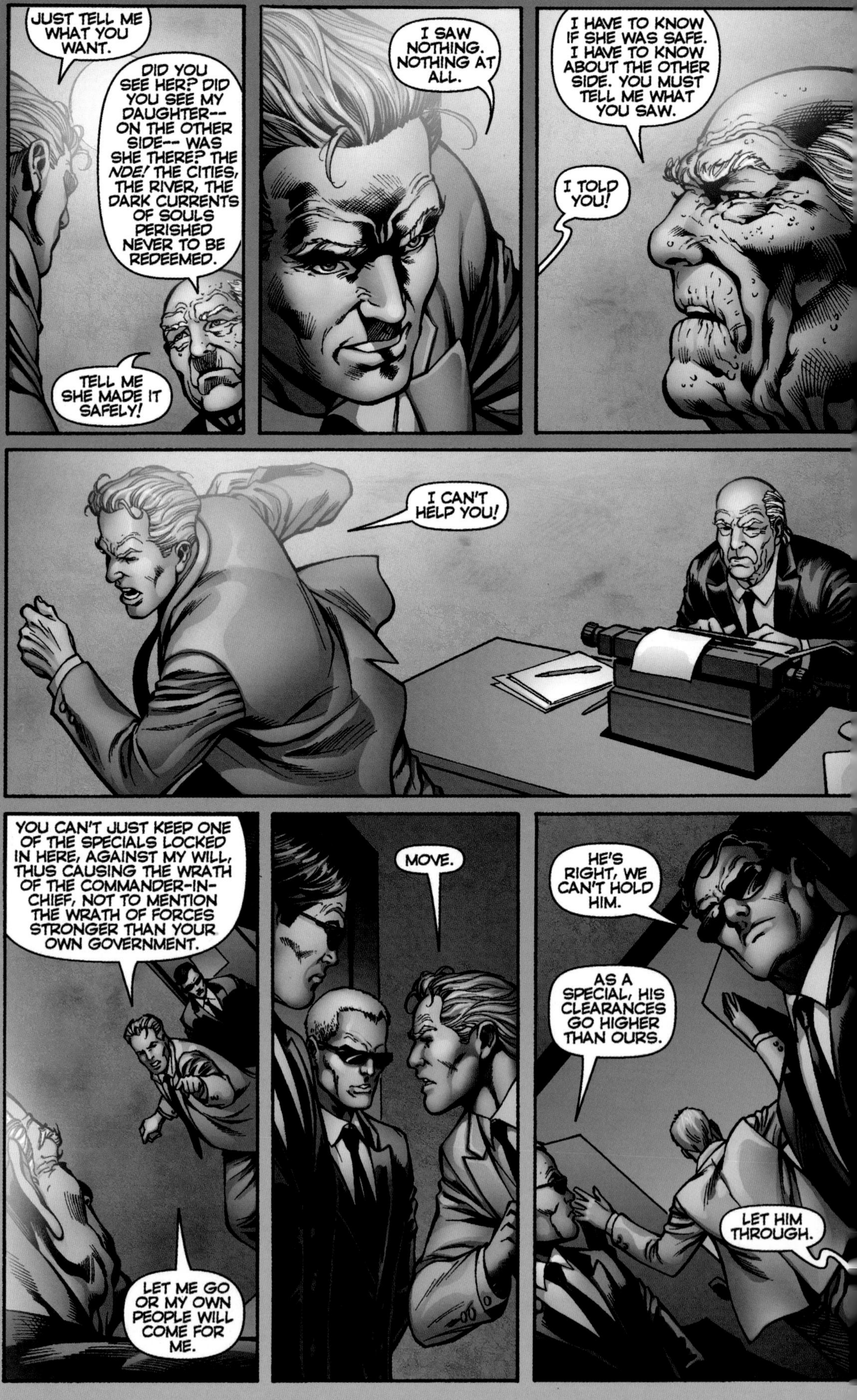
JUST TELL ME WHAT YOU WANT.
DID YOU SEE HER? DID YOU SEE MY DAUGHTER-- ON THE OTHER SIDE-- WAS SHE THERE? THE NDE! THE CITIES, THE RIVER, THE DARK CURRENTS OF SOULS PERISHED NEVER TO BE REDEEMED.
TELL ME SHE MADE IT SAFELY!
I SAW NOTHING. NOTHING AT ALL.
I HAVE TO KNOW IF SHE WAS SAFE. I HAVE TO KNOW ABOUT THE OTHER SIDE. YOU MUST TELL ME WHAT YOU SAW.
I TOLD YOU!
I CAN'T HELP YOU!
YOU CAN'T JUST KEEP ONE OF THE SPECIALS LOCKED IN HERE, AGAINST MY WILL, THUS CAUSING THE WRATH OF THE COMMANDER-IN-CHIEF, NOT TO MENTION THE WRATH OF FORCES STRONGER THAN YOUR OWN GOVERNMENT.
LET ME GO OR MY OWN PEOPLE WILL COME FOR ME.
MOVE.
HE'S RIGHT, WE CAN'T HOLD HIM.
AS A SPECIAL, HIS CLEARANCES GO HIGHER THAN OURS.
LET HIM THROUGH.

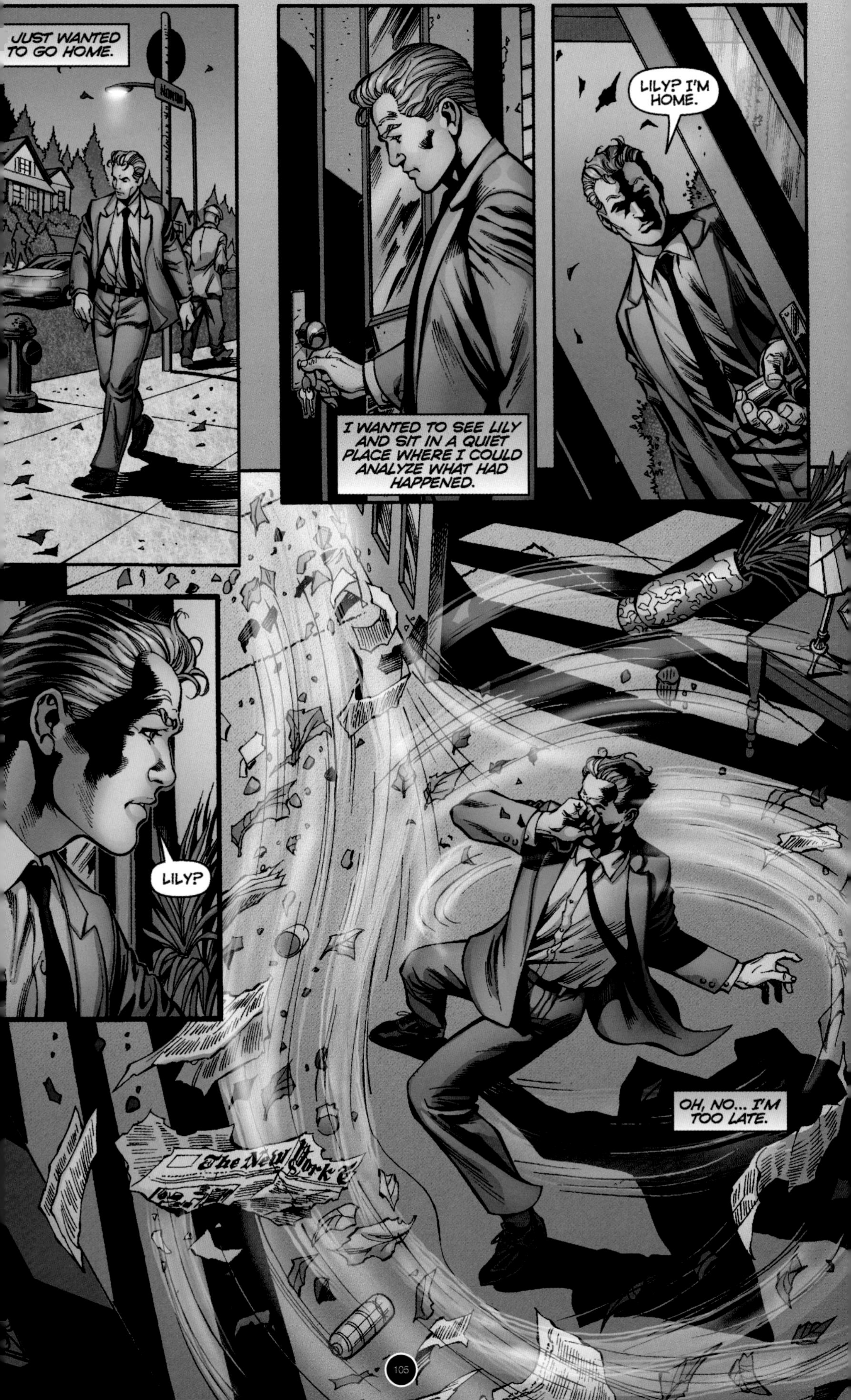
JUST WANTED TO GO HOME.
I WANTED TO SEE LILY AND SIT IN A QUIET PLACE WHERE I COULD ANALYZE WHAT HAD HAPPENED.
LILY? I'M HOME.
LILY?
OH, NO... I'M TOO LATE.

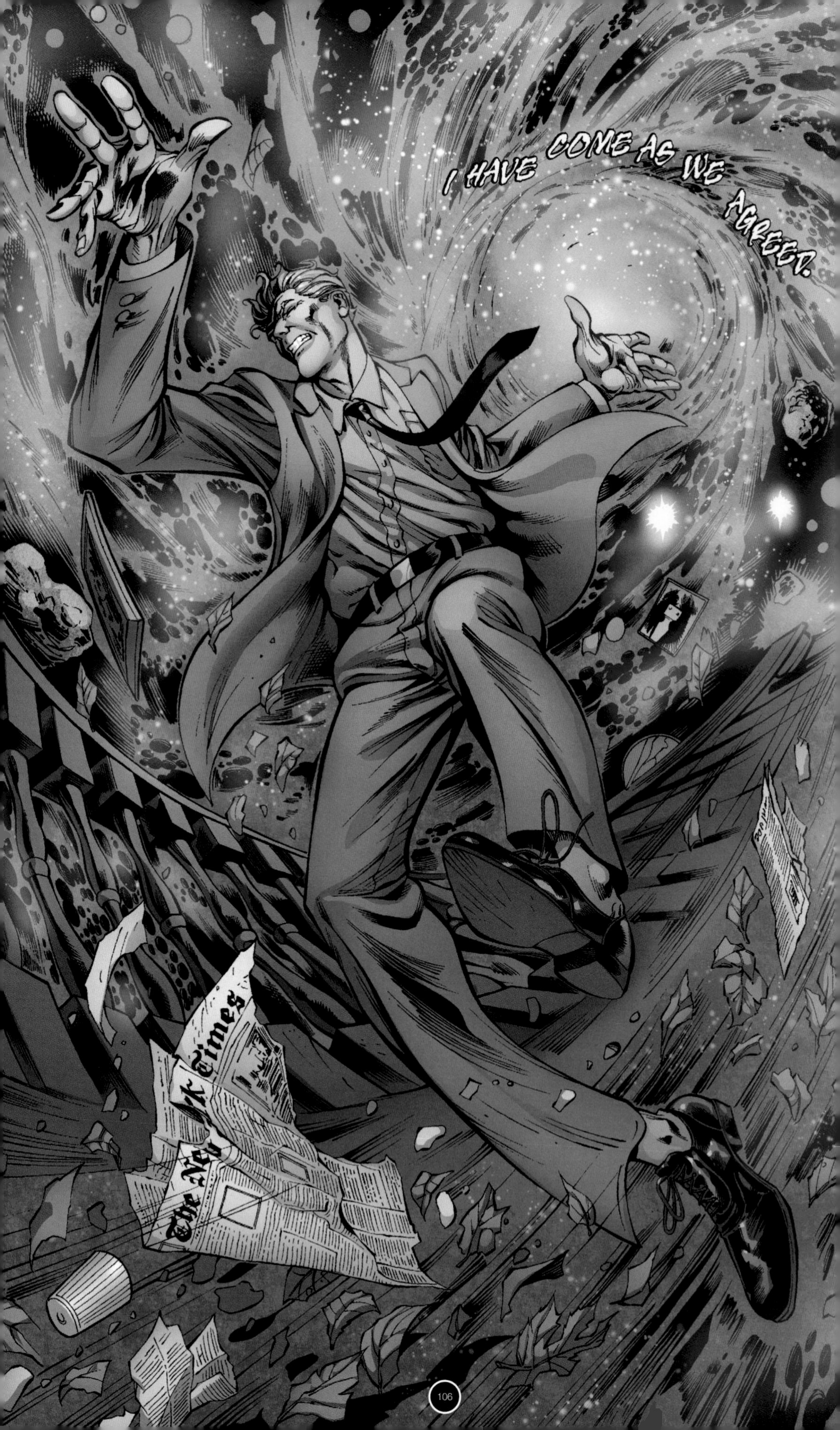
I HAVE COME AS WE AGREED.

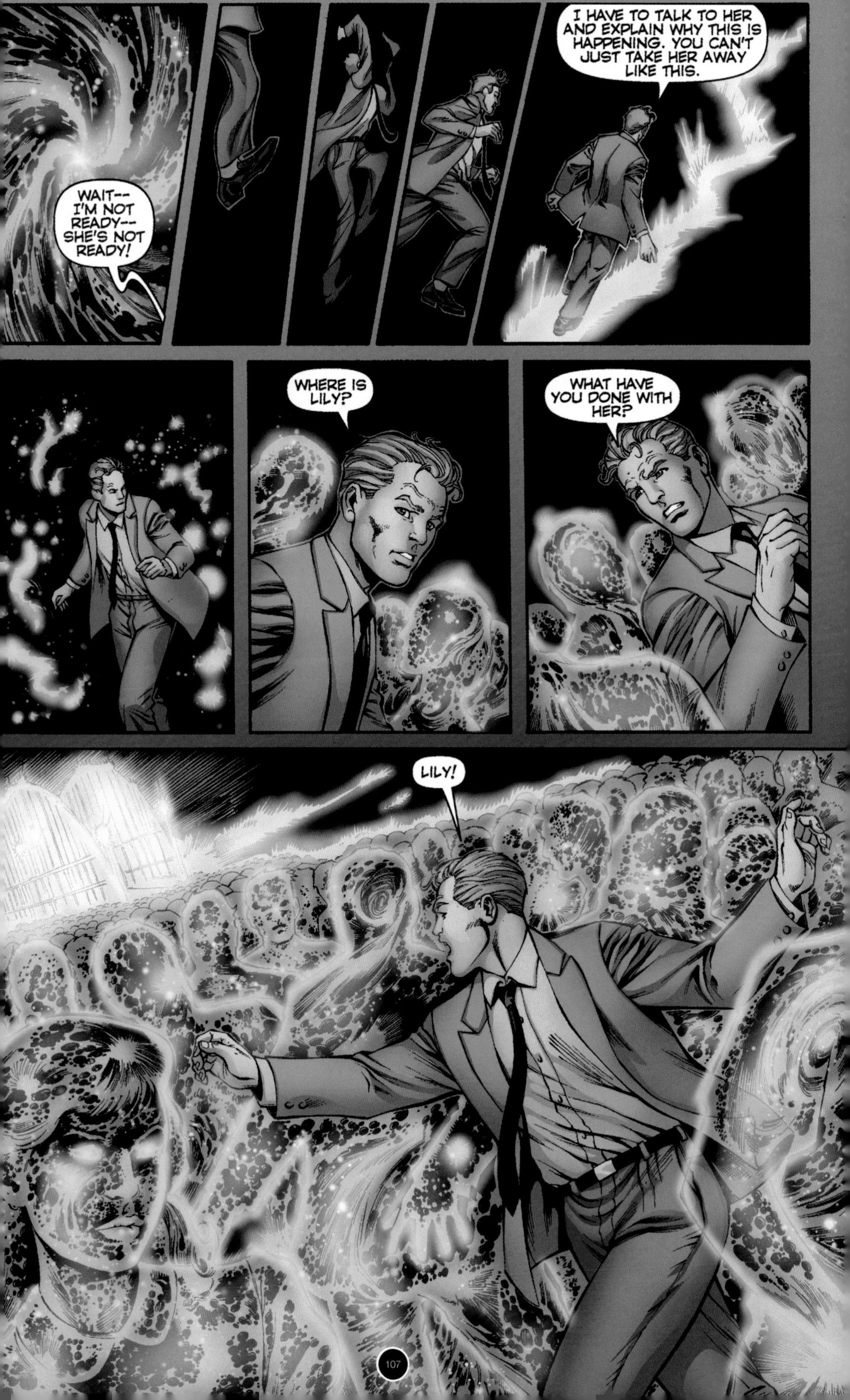
WAIT-- I'M NOT READY-- SHE'S NOT READY!
I HAVE TO TALK TO HER AND EXPLAIN WHY THIS IS HAPPENING. YOU CAN'T JUST TAKE HER AWAY LIKE THIS.
WHERE IS LILY?
WHAT HAVE YOU DONE WITH HER?
LILY!

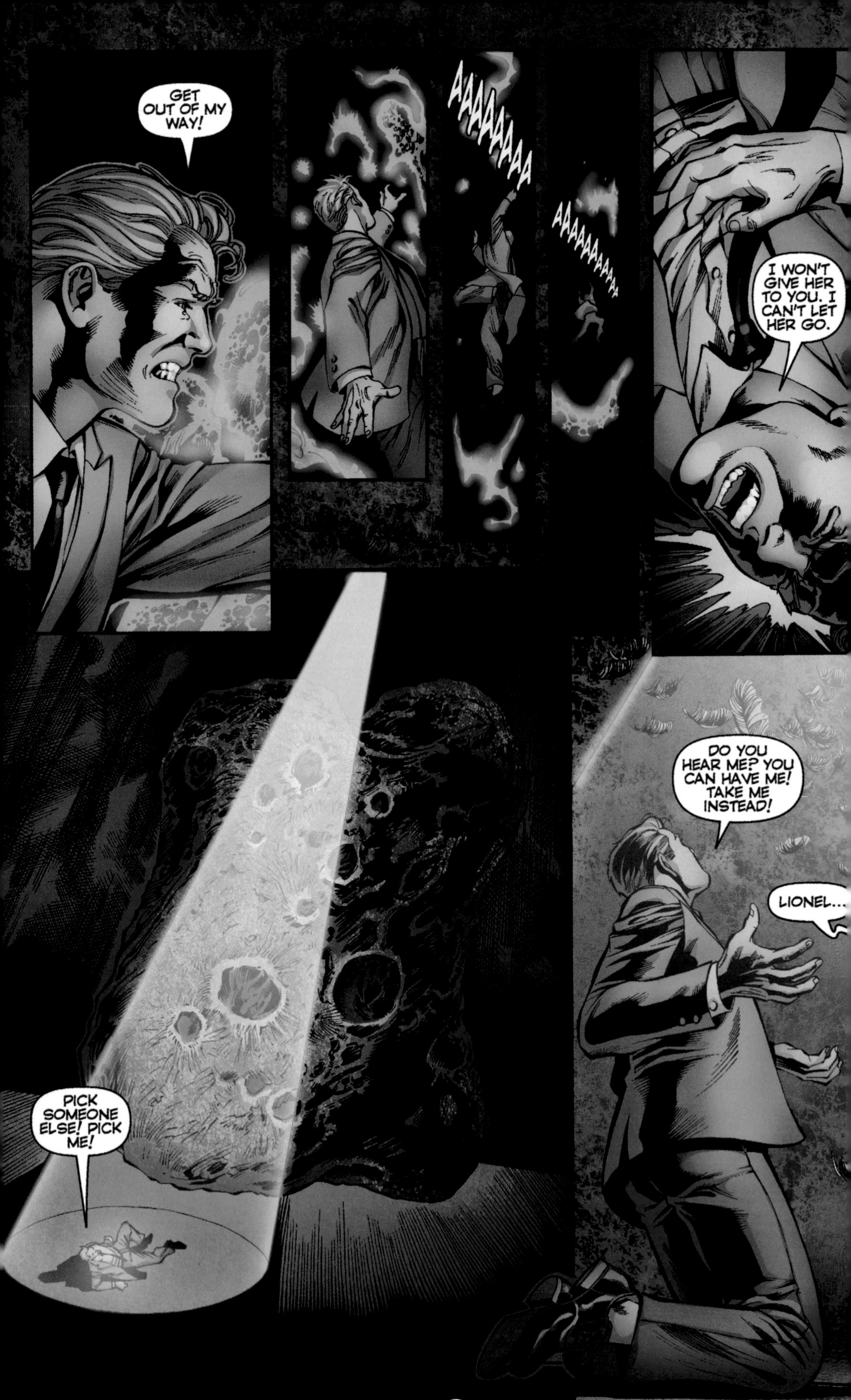

GET OUT OF MY WAY!
AAAAAAAAAA
AAAAAAAAAAA
I WON'T GIVE HER TO YOU. I CAN'T LET HER GO.
PICK SOMEONE ELSE! PICK ME!
DO YOU HEAR ME? YOU CAN HAVE ME! TAKE ME INSTEAD!
LIONEL...

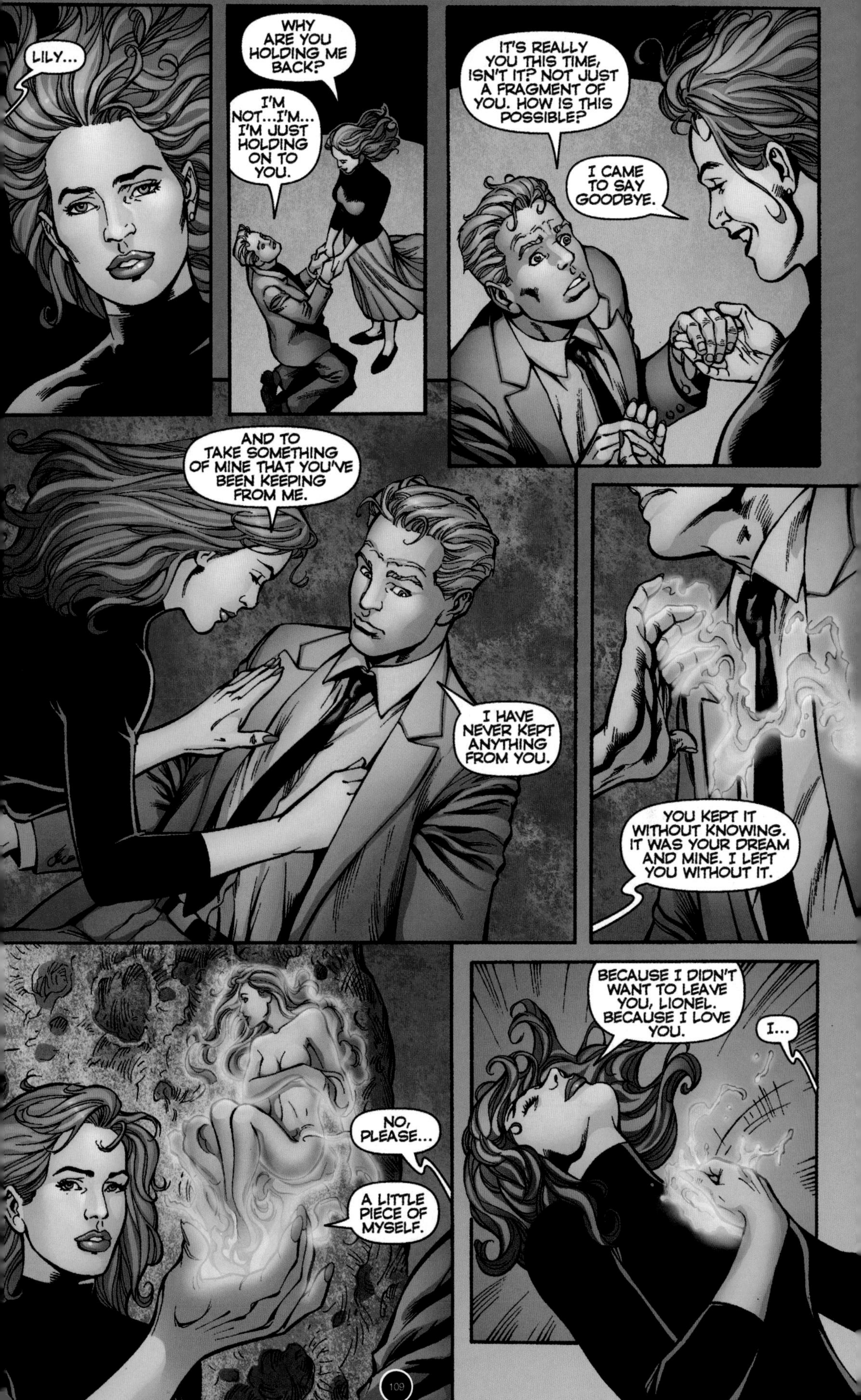
LILY...
WHY ARE YOU HOLDING ME BACK?
I'M NOT...I'M... I'M JUST HOLDING ON TO YOU.
IT'S REALLY YOU THIS TIME, ISN'T IT? NOT JUST A FRAGMENT OF YOU. HOW IS THIS POSSIBLE?
I CAME TO SAY GOODBYE.
AND TO TAKE SOMETHING OF MINE THAT YOU'VE BEEN KEEPING FROM ME.
I HAVE NEVER KEPT ANYTHING FROM YOU.
YOU KEPT IT WITHOUT KNOWING. IT WAS YOUR DREAM AND MINE. I LEFT YOU WITHOUT IT.
NO, PLEASE...
A LITTLE PIECE OF MYSELF.
BECAUSE I DIDN'T WANT TO LEAVE YOU, LIONEL. BECAUSE I LOVE YOU.
I...

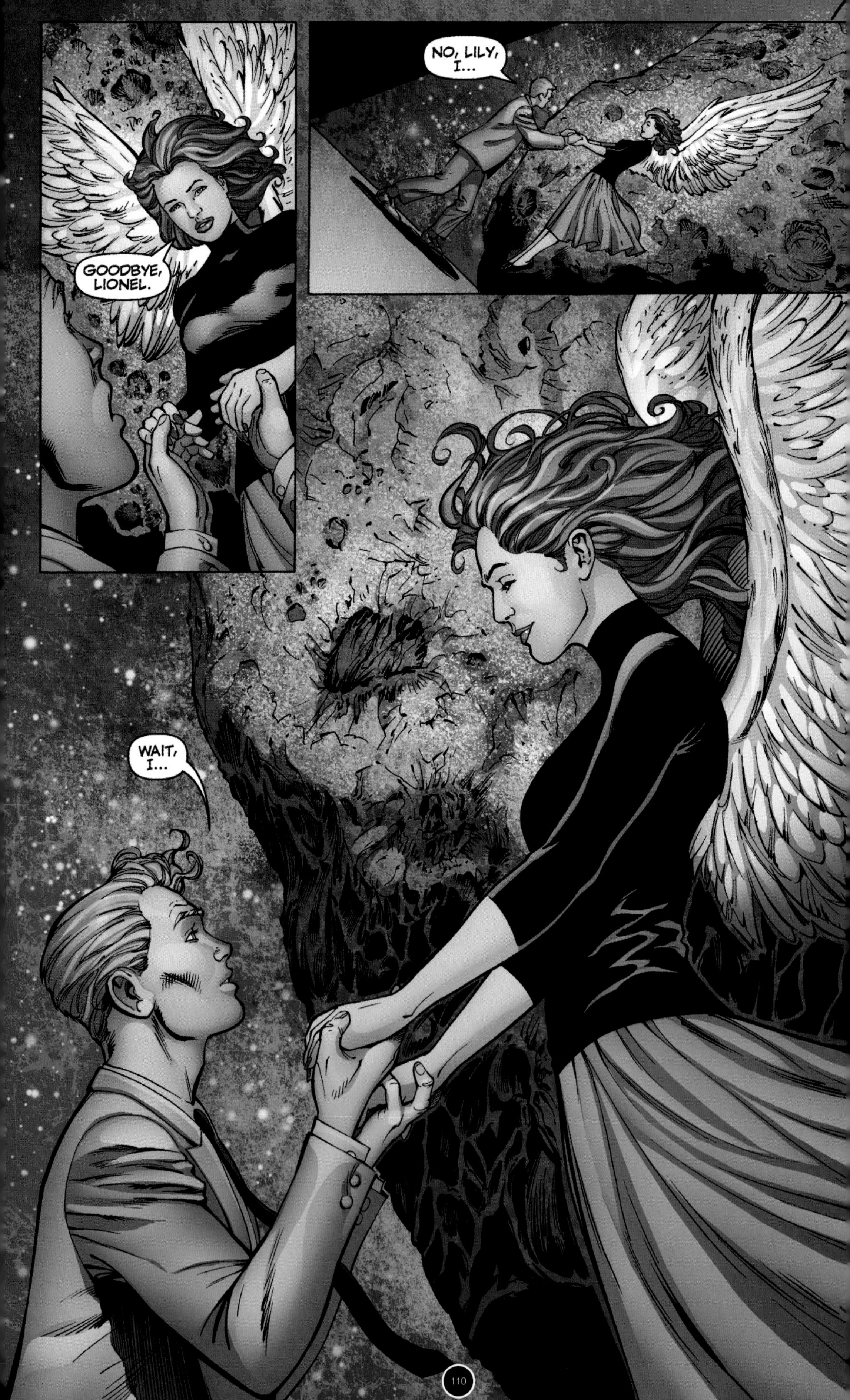
GOODBYE, LIONEL.
NO, LILY, I...
WAIT, I...

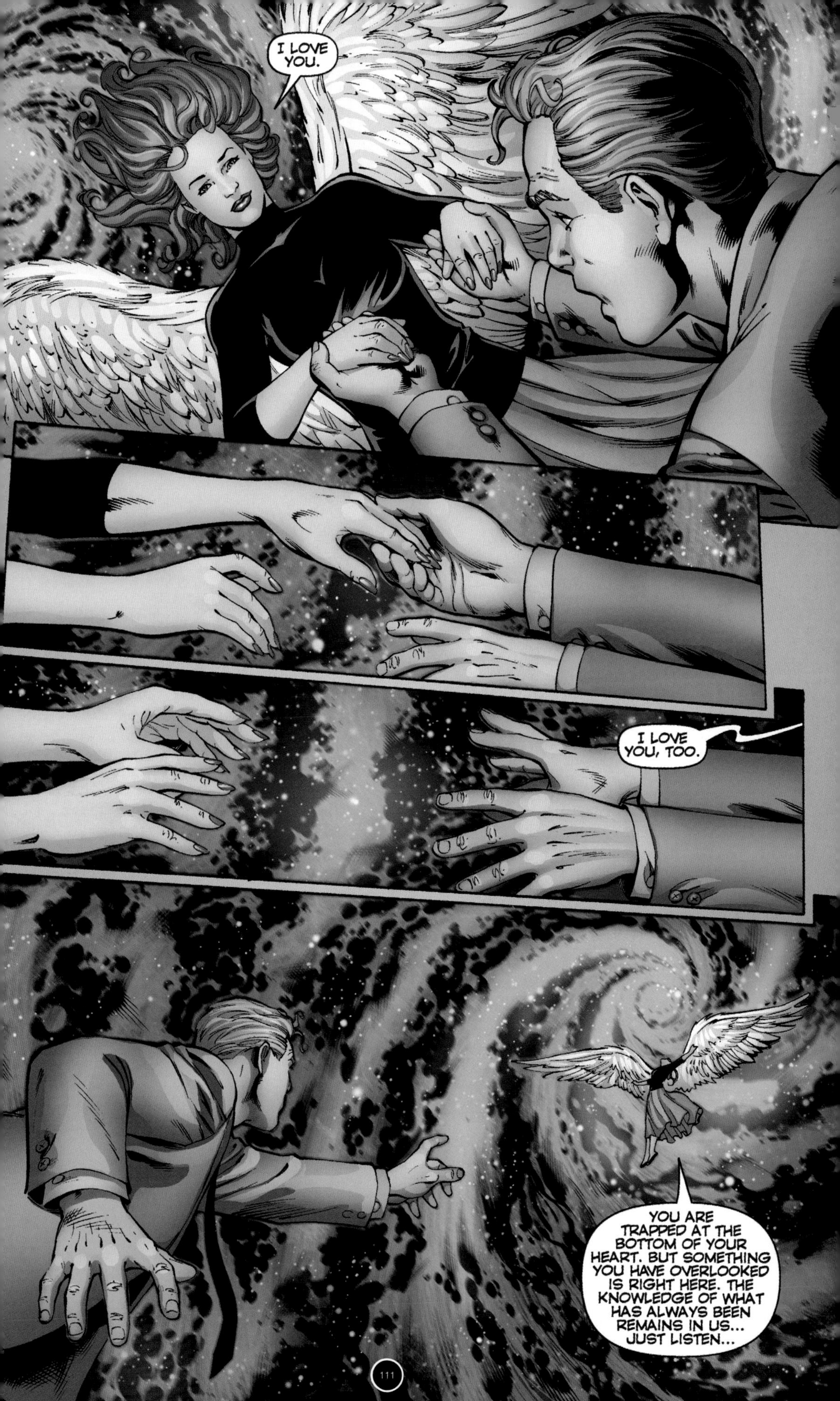
I LOVE YOU.
I LOVE YOU, TOO.
YOU ARE TRAPPED AT THE BOTTOM OF YOUR HEART. BUT SOMETHING YOU HAVE OVERLOOKED IS RIGHT HERE. THE KNOWLEDGE OF WHAT HAS ALWAYS BEEN REMAINS IN US... JUST LISTEN...

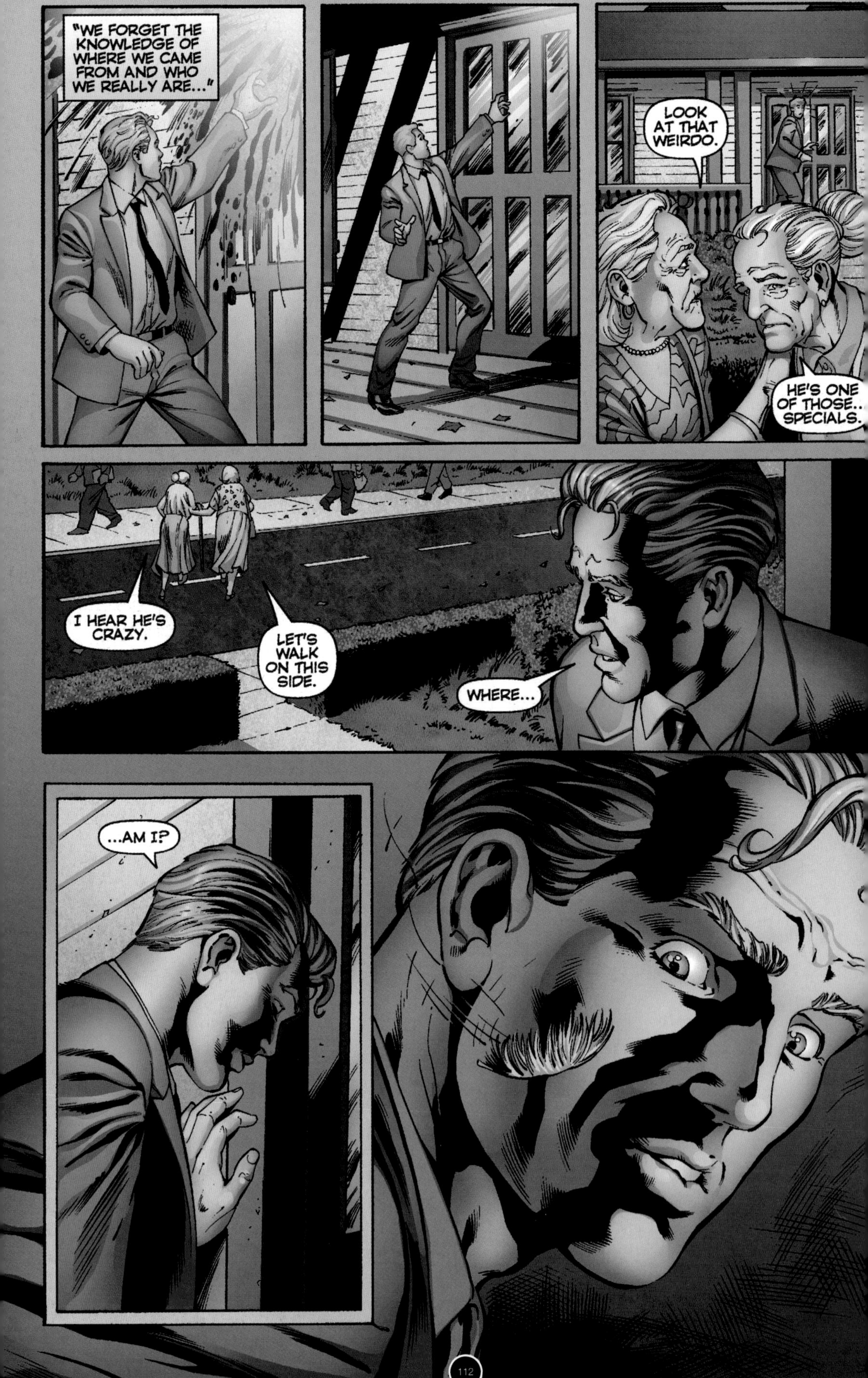
"WE FORGET THE KNOWLEDGE OF WHERE WE CAME FROM AND WHO WE REALLY ARE..."
LOOK AT THAT WEIRDO.
HE'S ONE OF THOSE.. SPECIALS.
I HEAR HE'S CRAZY.
LET'S WALK ON THIS SIDE.
WHERE...
...AM I?

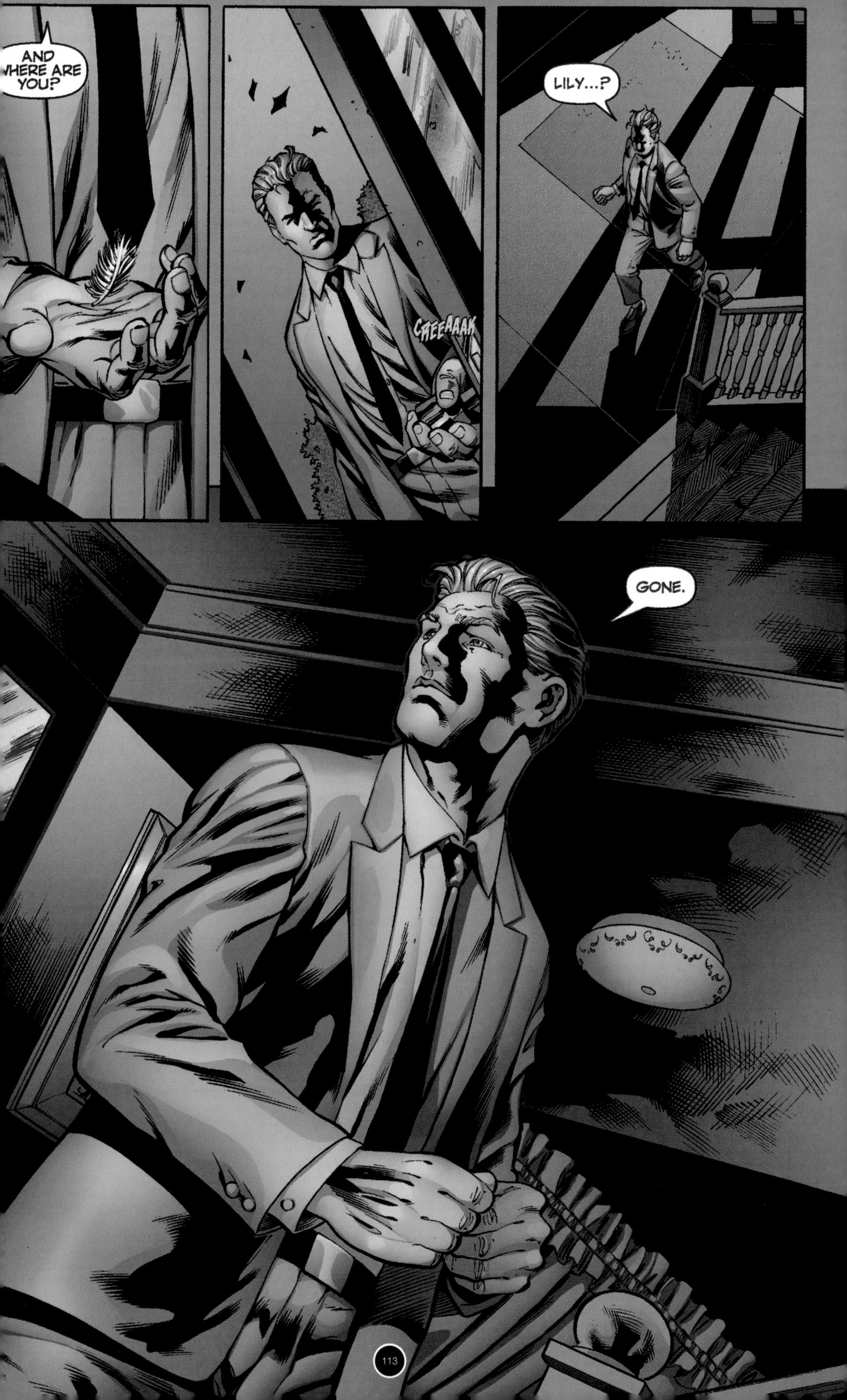
AND WHERE ARE YOU?
CREEAAAK
LILY...?
GONE.

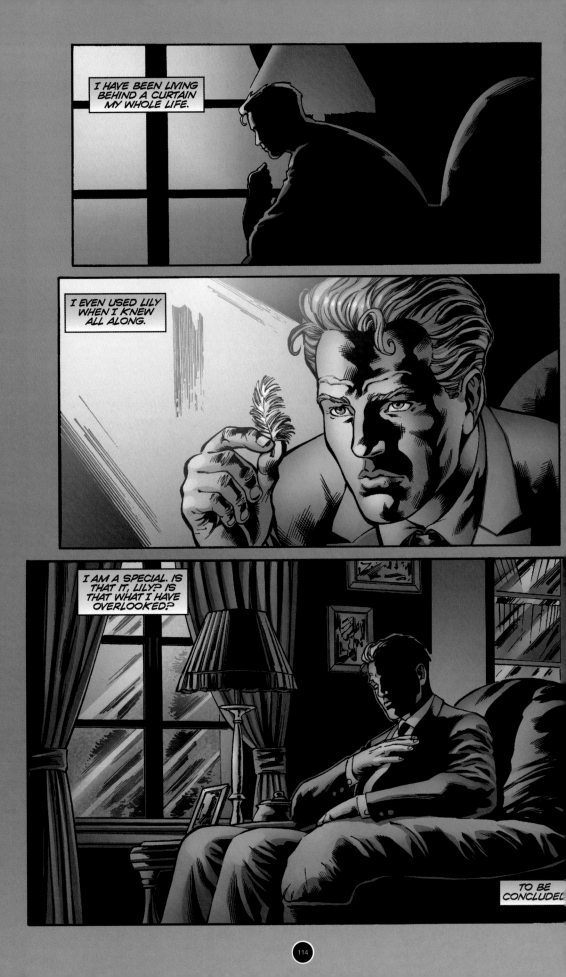

I HAVE BEEN LIVING BEHIND A CURTAIN MY WHOLE LIFE.

I EVEN USED LILY WHEN I KNEW ALL ALONG.

I AM A SPECIAL. IS THAT IT, LILY? IS THAT WHAT I HAVE OVERLOOKED?

TO BE CONCLUDED

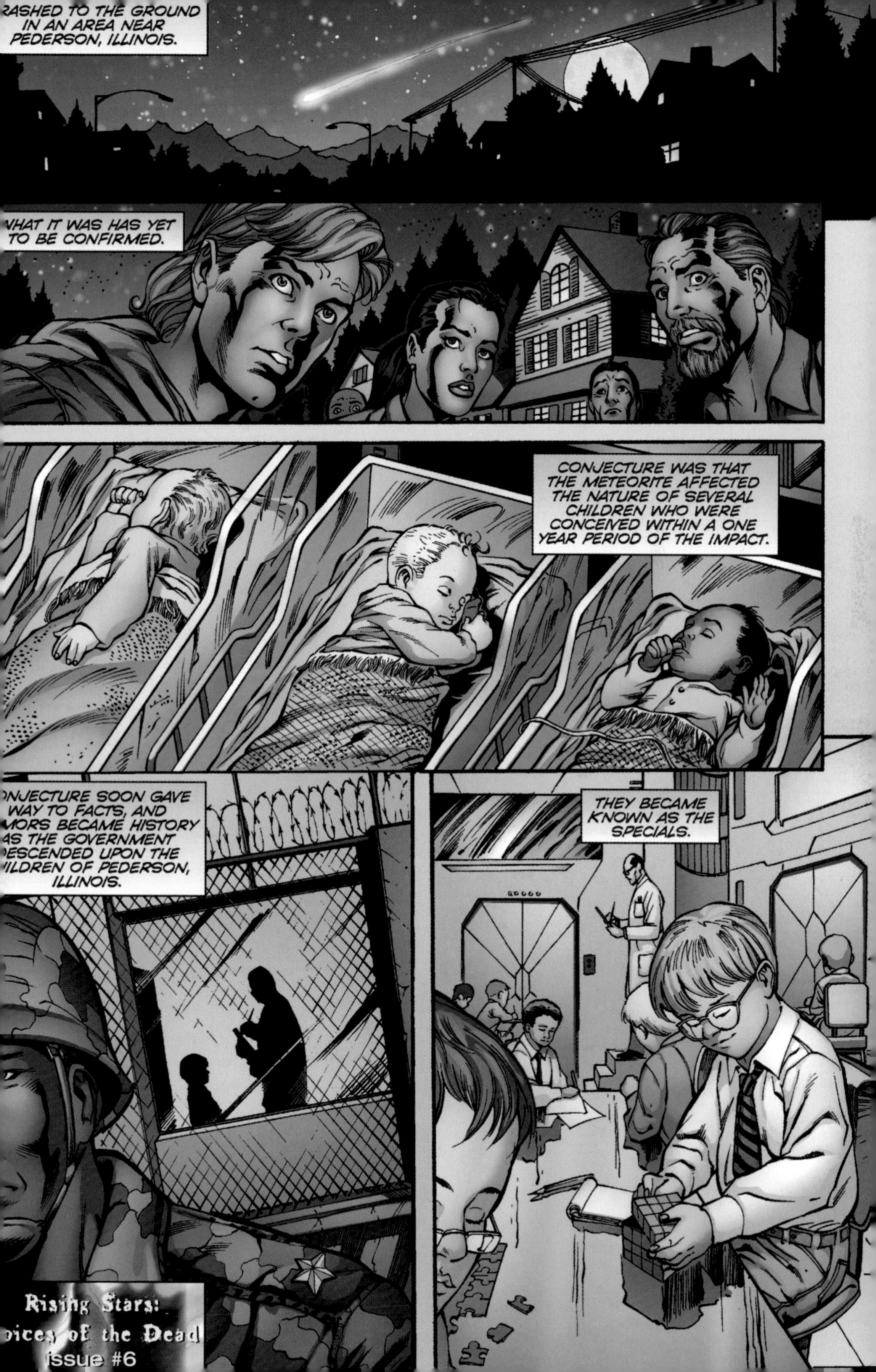
RASHED TO THE GROUND IN AN AREA NEAR PEDERSON, ILLINOIS.
WHAT IT WAS HAS YET TO BE CONFIRMED.
CONJECTURE WAS THAT THE METEORITE AFFECTED THE NATURE OF SEVERAL CHILDREN WHO WERE CONCEIVED WITHIN A ONE YEAR PERIOD OF THE IMPACT.
ONJECTURE SOON GAVE WAY TO FACTS, AND MORS BECAME HISTORY AS THE GOVERNMENT ESCENDED UPON THE ILDREN OF PEDERSON, ILLINOIS.
THEY BECAME KNOWN AS THE SPECIALS.
Rising Stars: oices of the Dead issue #6

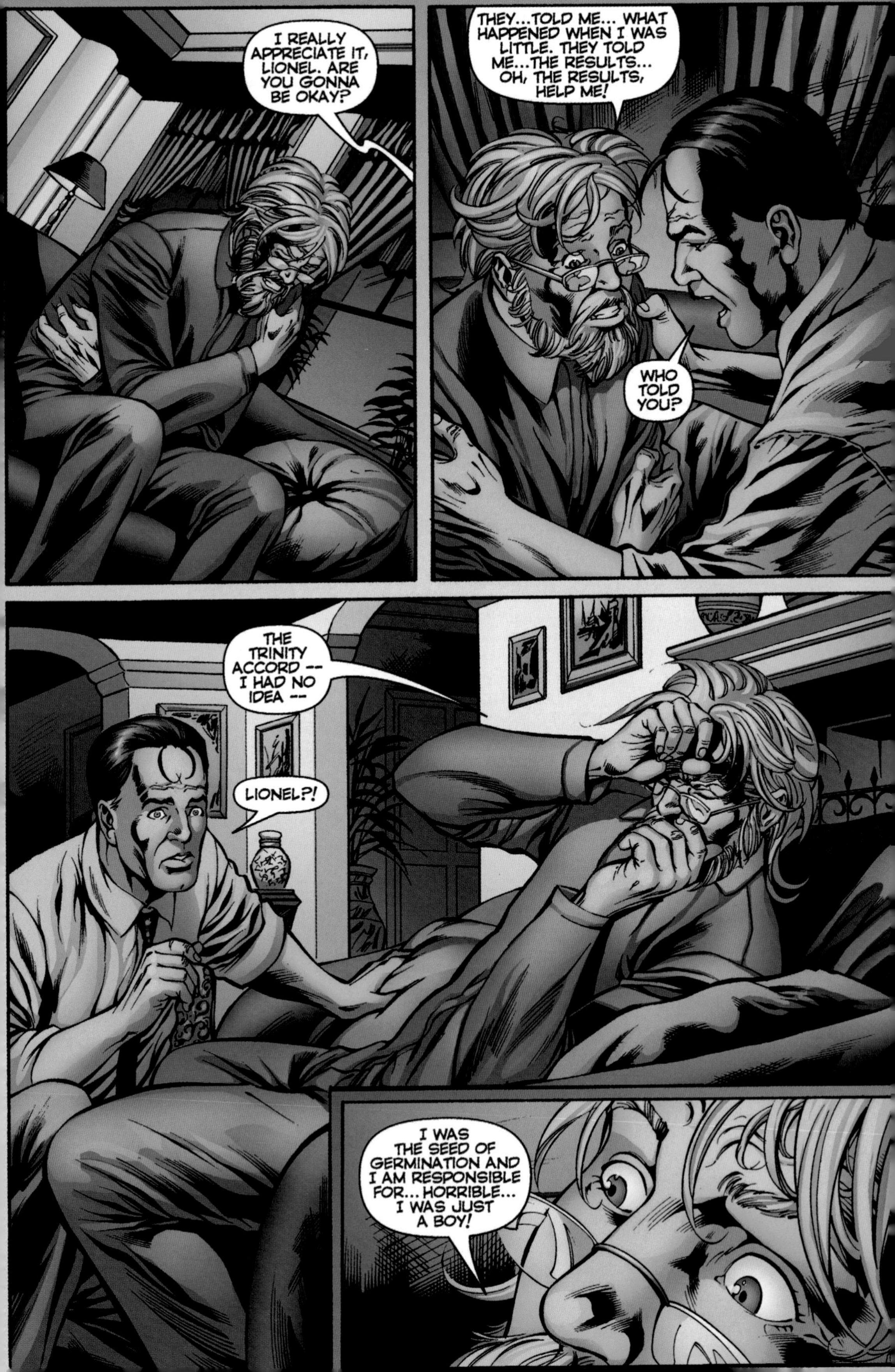
I REALLY APPRECIATE IT, LIONEL. ARE YOU GONNA BE OKAY?
THEY...TOLD ME... WHAT HAPPENED WHEN I WAS LITTLE. THEY TOLD ME...THE RESULTS... OH, THE RESULTS, HELP ME!
WHO TOLD YOU?
THE TRINITY ACCORD -- I HAD NO IDEA --
LIONEL?!
I WAS THE SEED OF GERMINATION AND I AM RESPONSIBLE FOR... HORRIBLE... I WAS JUST A BOY!

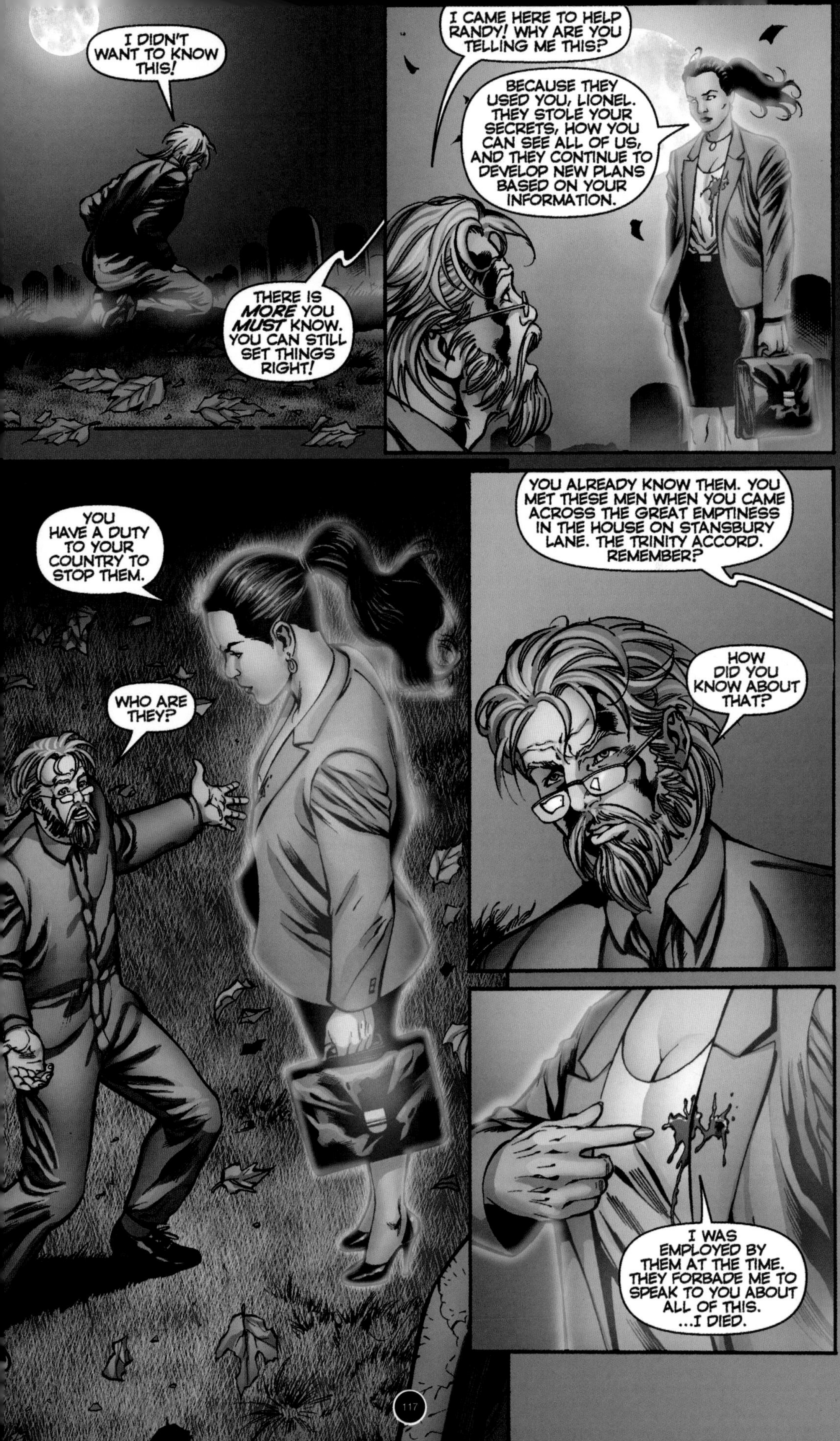
I DIDN'T WANT TO KNOW THIS!
I CAME HERE TO HELP RANDY! WHY ARE YOU TELLING ME THIS?
BECAUSE THEY USED YOU, LIONEL. THEY STOLE YOUR SECRETS, HOW YOU CAN SEE ALL OF US, AND THEY CONTINUE TO DEVELOP NEW PLANS BASED ON YOUR INFORMATION.
THERE IS MORE YOU MUST KNOW. YOU CAN STILL SET THINGS RIGHT!
YOU HAVE A DUTY TO YOUR COUNTRY TO STOP THEM.
WHO ARE THEY?
YOU ALREADY KNOW THEM. YOU MET THESE MEN WHEN YOU CAME ACROSS THE GREAT EMPTINESS IN THE HOUSE ON STANSBURY LANE. THE TRINITY ACCORD. REMEMBER?
HOW DID YOU KNOW ABOUT THAT?
I WAS EMPLOYED BY THEM AT THE TIME. THEY FORBADE ME TO SPEAK TO YOU ABOUT ALL OF THIS. ...I DIED.

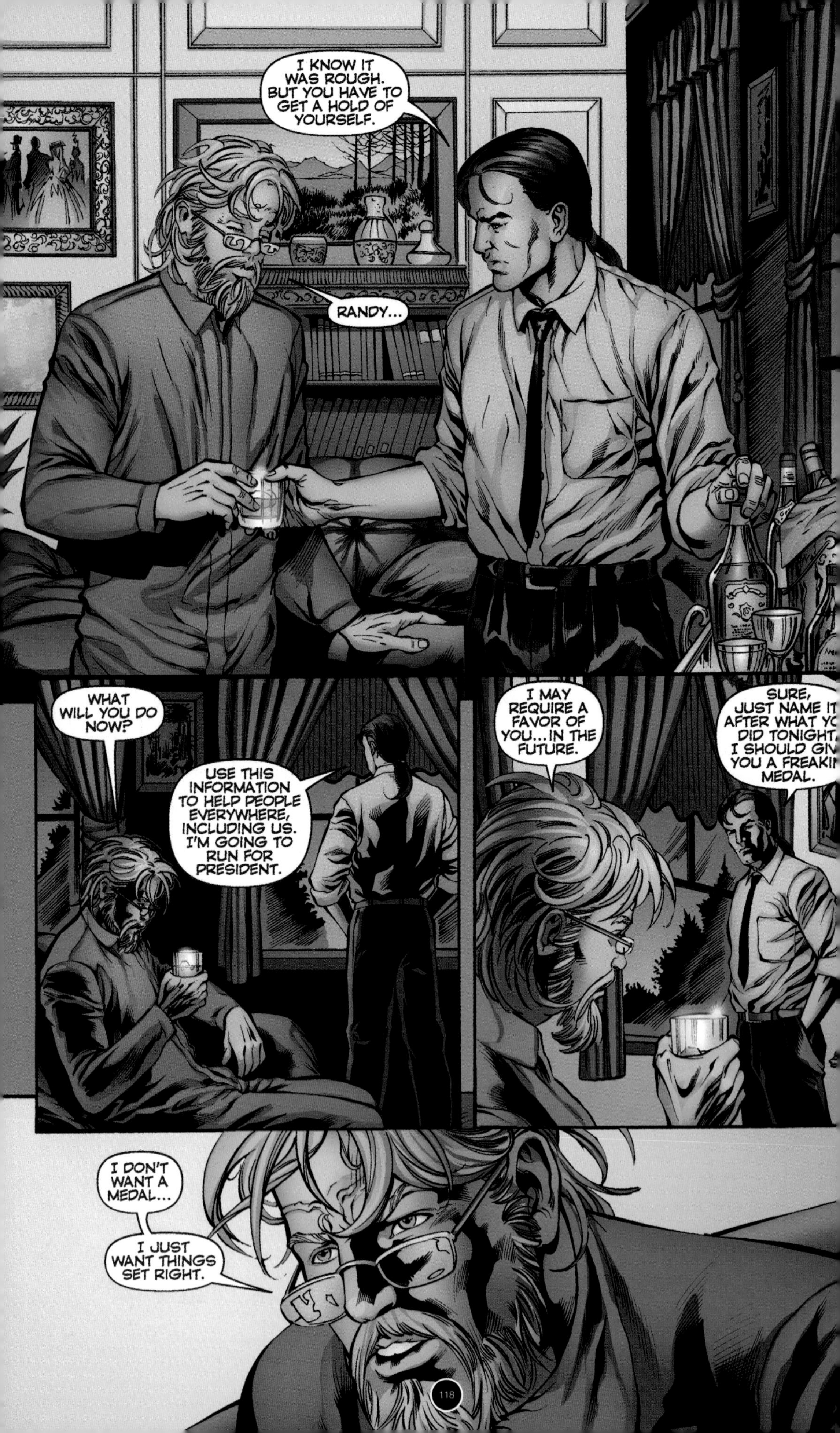
I KNOW IT WAS ROUGH. BUT YOU HAVE TO GET A HOLD OF YOURSELF.
RANDY...
WHAT WILL YOU DO NOW?
USE THIS INFORMATION TO HELP PEOPLE EVERYWHERE, INCLUDING US. I'M GOING TO RUN FOR PRESIDENT.
I MAY REQUIRE A FAVOR OF YOU...IN THE FUTURE.
I DON'T WANT A MEDAL...
I JUST WANT THINGS SET RIGHT.

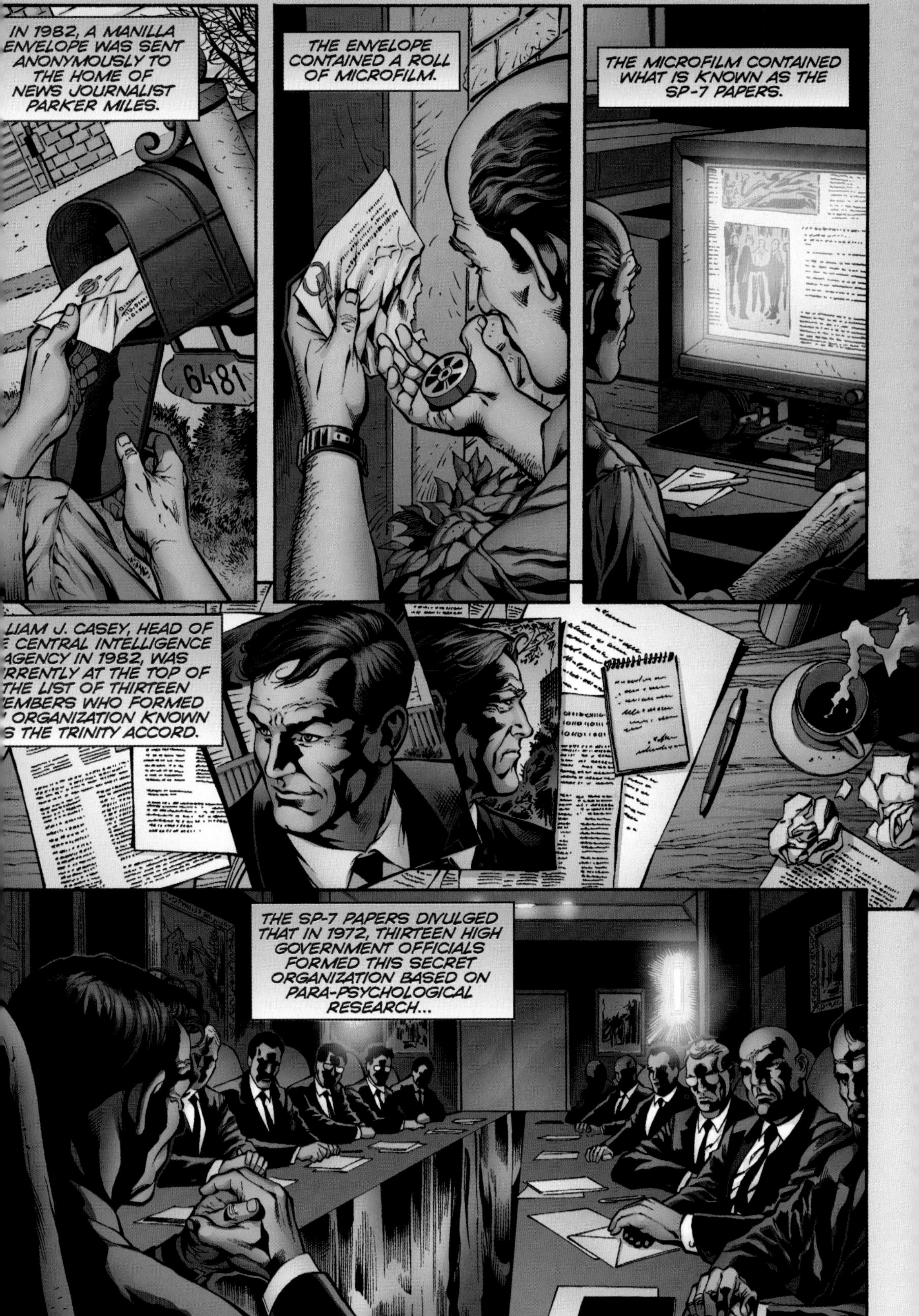
IN 1982, A MANILLA ENVELOPE WAS SENT ANONYMOUSLY TO THE HOME OF NEWS JOURNALIST PARKER MILES.
6481
THE ENVELOPE CONTAINED A ROLL OF MICROFILM.
THE MICROFILM CONTAINED WHAT IS KNOWN AS THE SP-7 PAPERS.
LIAM J. CASEY, HEAD OF E CENTRAL INTELLIGENCE AGENCY IN 1982, WAS RRENTLY AT THE TOP OF THE LIST OF THIRTEEN EMBERS WHO FORMED ORGANIZATION KNOWN S THE TRINITY ACCORD.
THE SP-7 PAPERS DIVULGED THAT IN 1972, THIRTEEN HIGH GOVERNMENT OFFICIALS FORMED THIS SECRET ORGANIZATION BASED ON PARA-PSYCHOLOGICAL RESEARCH...

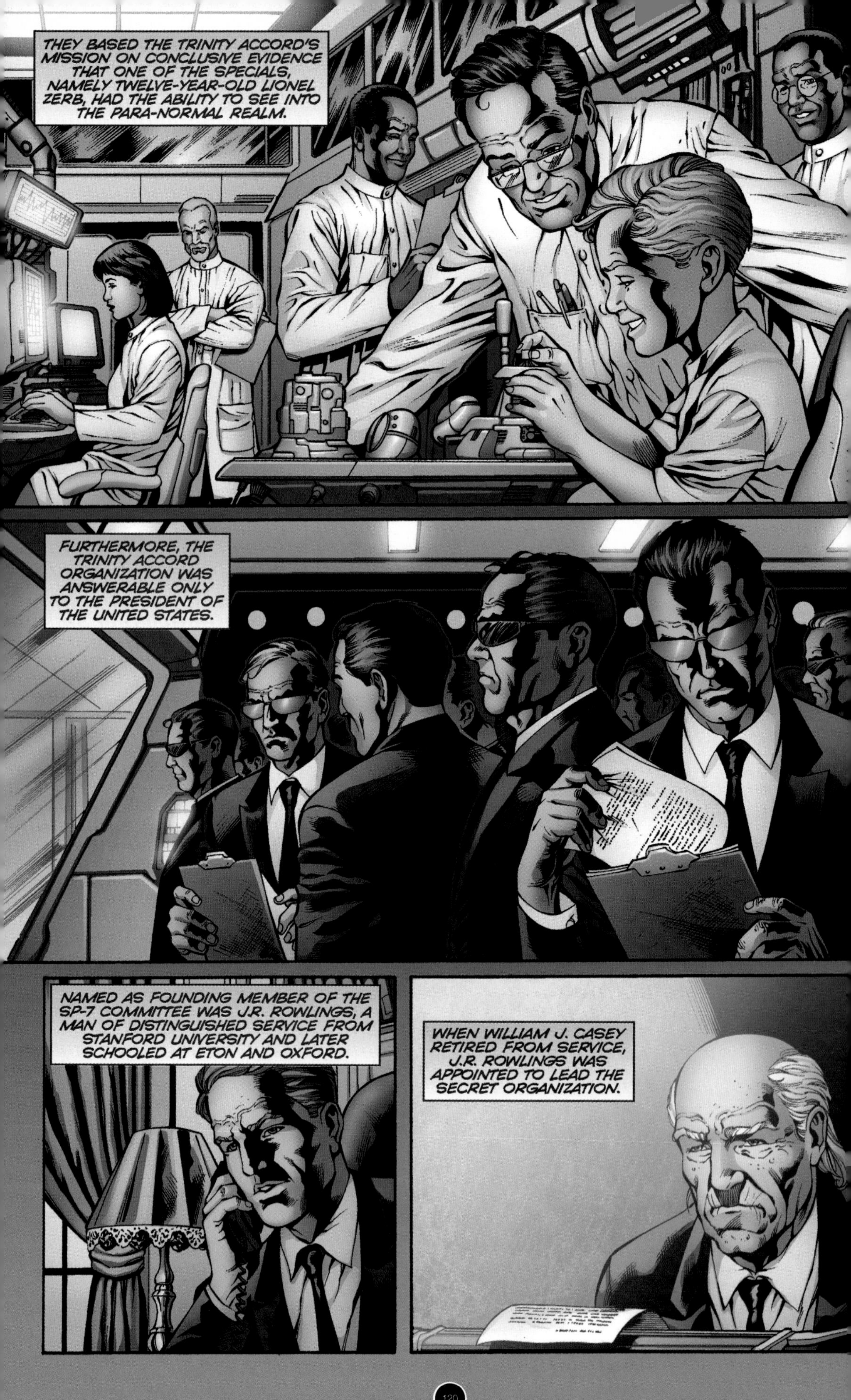
THEY BASED THE TRINITY ACCORD'S MISSION ON CONCLUSIVE EVIDENCE THAT ONE OF THE SPECIALS, NAMELY TWELVE-YEAR-OLD LIONEL ZERB, HAD THE ABILITY TO SEE INTO THE PARA-NORMAL REALM.
FURTHERMORE, THE TRINITY ACCORD ORGANIZATION WAS ANSWERABLE ONLY TO THE PRESIDENT OF THE UNITED STATES.
NAMED AS FOUNDING MEMBER OF THE SP-7 COMMITTEE WAS J.R. ROWLINGS, A MAN OF DISTINGUISHED SERVICE FROM STANFORD UNIVERSITY AND LATER SCHOOLED AT ETON AND OXFORD.
WHEN WILLIAM J. CASEY RETIRED FROM SERVICE, J.R. ROWLINGS WAS APPOINTED TO LEAD THE SECRET ORGANIZATION.

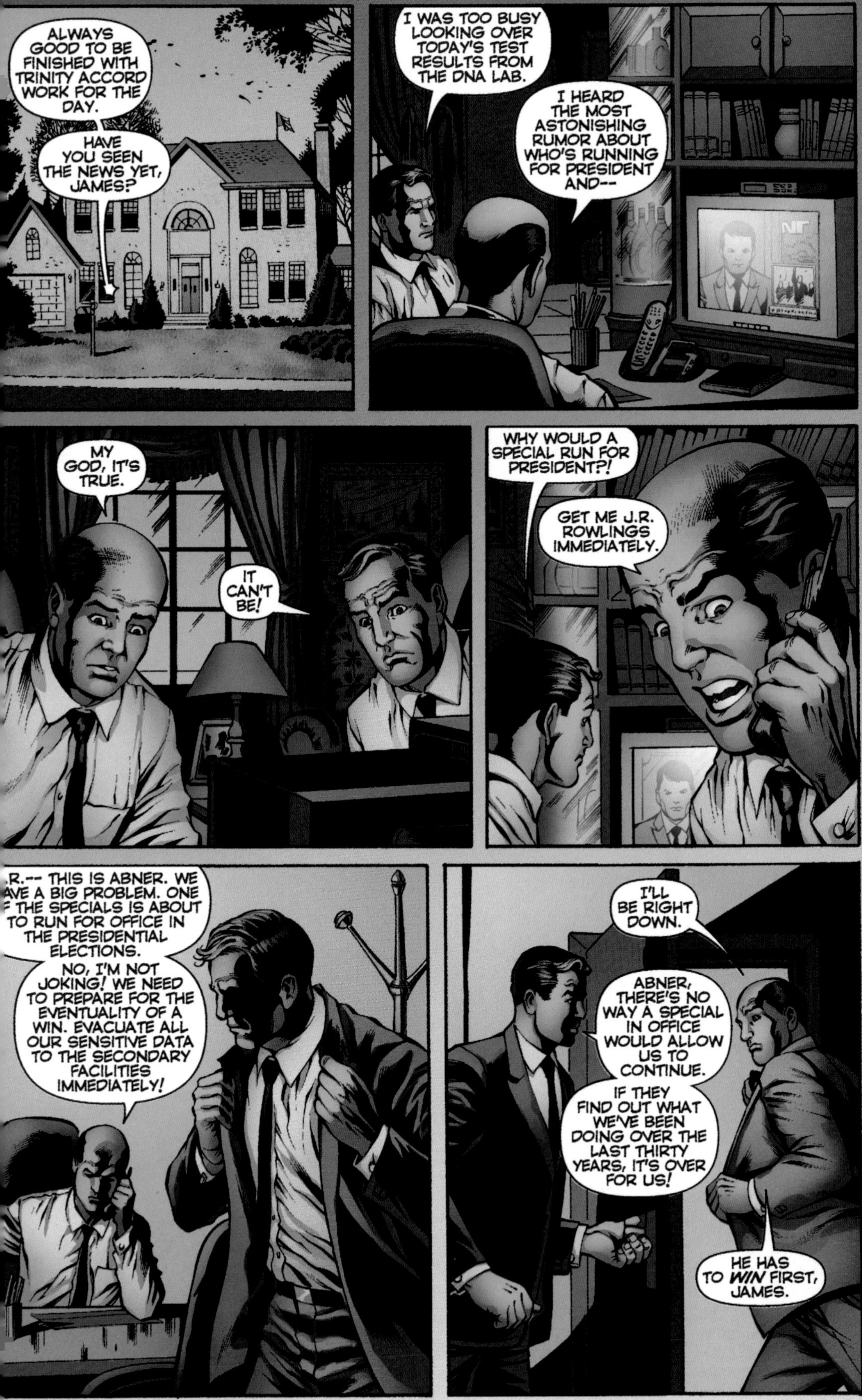
ALWAYS GOOD TO BE FINISHED WITH TRINITY ACCORD WORK FOR THE DAY.
HAVE YOU SEEN THE NEWS YET, JAMES?
I WAS TOO BUSY LOOKING OVER TODAY'S TEST RESULTS FROM THE DNA LAB.
I HEARD THE MOST ASTONISHING RUMOR ABOUT WHO'S RUNNING FOR PRESIDENT AND--
MY GOD, IT'S TRUE.
IT CAN'T BE!
WHY WOULD A SPECIAL RUN FOR PRESIDENT?!
GET ME J.R. ROWLINGS IMMEDIATELY.
R.-- THIS IS ABNER. WE AVE A BIG PROBLEM. ONE F THE SPECIALS IS ABOUT TO RUN FOR OFFICE IN THE PRESIDENTIAL ELECTIONS.
NO, I'M NOT JOKING! WE NEED TO PREPARE FOR THE EVENTUALITY OF A WIN. EVACUATE ALL OUR SENSITIVE DATA TO THE SECONDARY FACILITIES IMMEDIATELY!
I'LL BE RIGHT DOWN.
ABNER, THERE'S NO WAY A SPECIAL IN OFFICE WOULD ALLOW US TO CONTINUE.
IF THEY FIND OUT WHAT WE'VE BEEN DOING OVER THE LAST THIRTY YEARS, IT'S OVER FOR US!
HE HAS TO *WIN* FIRST, JAMES.

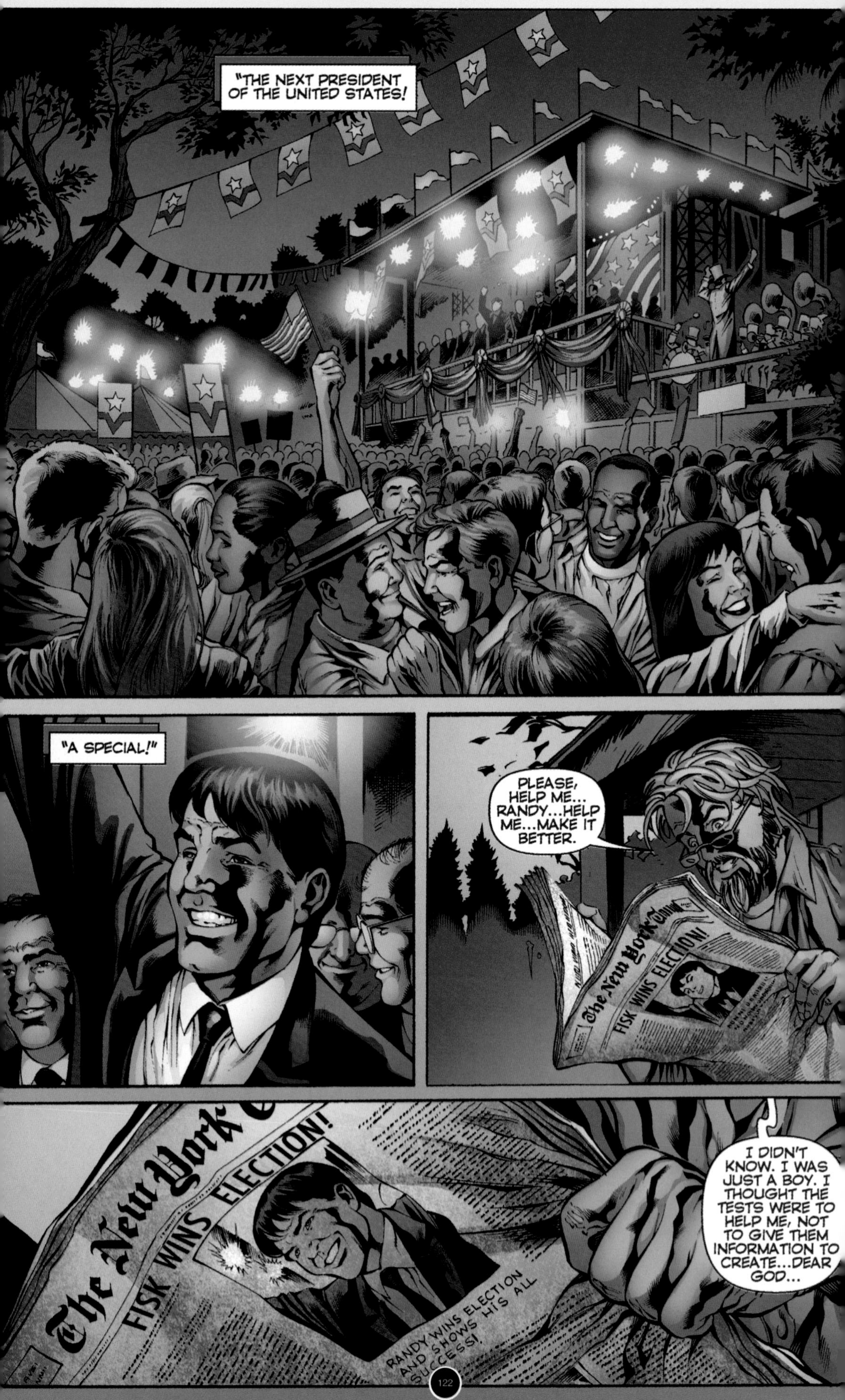
"THE NEXT PRESIDENT OF THE UNITED STATES!
"A SPECIAL!"
PLEASE, HELP ME... RANDY...HELP ME...MAKE IT BETTER.
The New York
FISK WINS ELECTION!
The New York
FISK WINS ELECTION!
RANDY WINS ELECTION AND SHOWS HIS ALL SUCCESS!
I DIDN'T KNOW. I WAS JUST A BOY. I THOUGHT THE TESTS WERE TO HELP ME, NOT TO GIVE THEM INFORMATION TO CREATE...DEAR GOD...

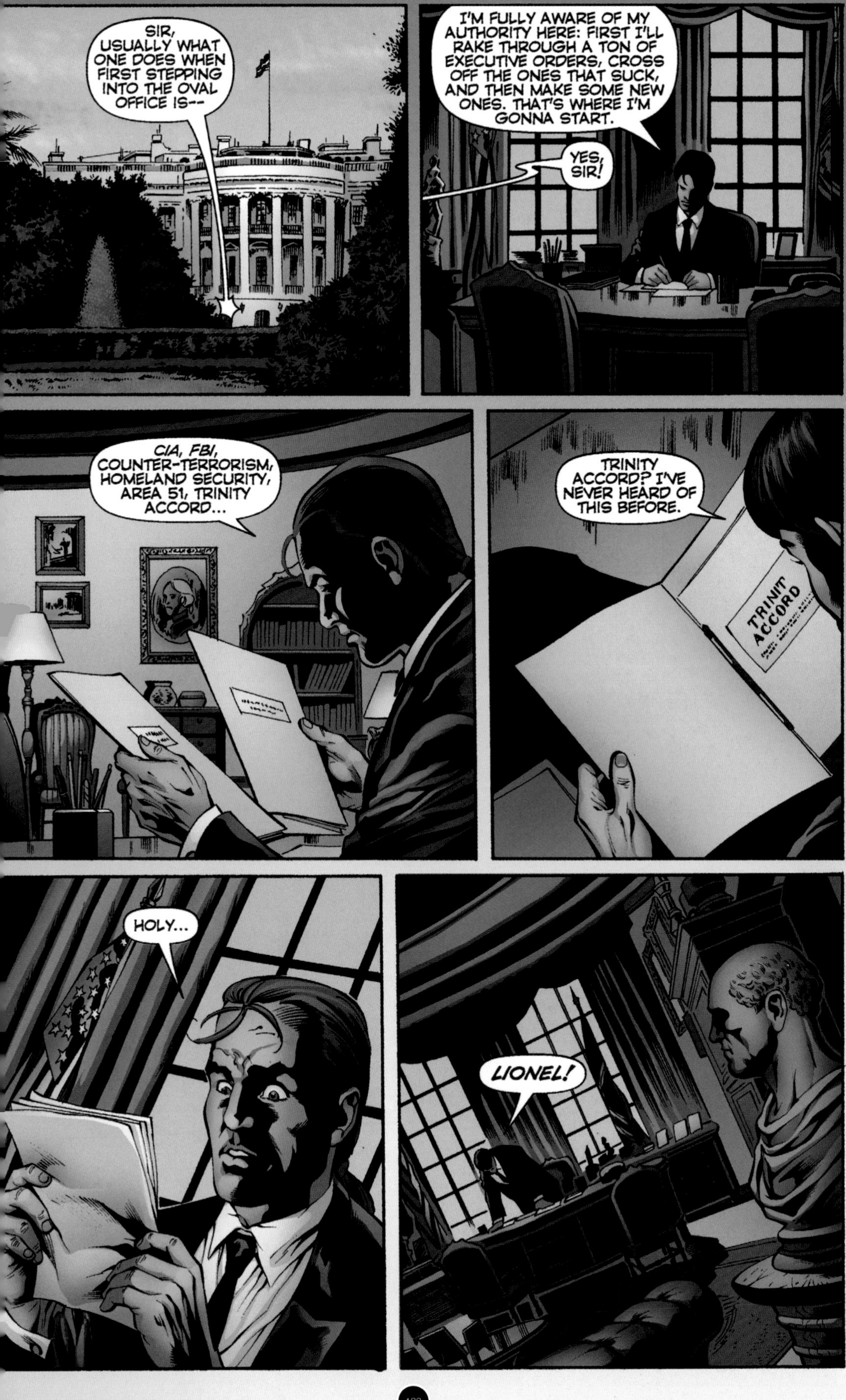
SIR, USUALLY WHAT ONE DOES WHEN FIRST STEPPING INTO THE OVAL OFFICE IS--
I'M FULLY AWARE OF MY AUTHORITY HERE: FIRST I'LL RAKE THROUGH A TON OF EXECUTIVE ORDERS, CROSS OFF THE ONES THAT SUCK, AND THEN MAKE SOME NEW ONES. THAT'S WHERE I'M GONNA START.
YES, SIR!
CIA, FBI, COUNTER-TERRORISM, HOMELAND SECURITY, AREA 51, TRINITY ACCORD...
TRINITY ACCORD? I'VE NEVER HEARD OF THIS BEFORE.
TRINIT ACCORD
HOLY...
LIONEL!

UNBEKNOWNST TO SEVERAL SPECIALS, THE GOVERNMENT WAS MAKING GOOD USE OF ANALYZING THEIR ABILITIES.

THE PSYNET DEVICE, A CONCEPT UNVEILED IN THE SP-7 PAPERS BY J.R. ROWLINGS IN 1972...

...WAS A SYSTEM WHEREBY LIONEL ZERB'S BRAINWAVE FREQUENCIES WERE RECORDED INTO EEG INTERPRETATIONS FOR A DECADE IN ORDER TO BE STUDIED.

WHAT J.R. ROWLINGS ENVISIONED WAS THE RAPID ANALYSIS OF PATTERNS OF THE BRAIN THAT REACTED TO PARANORMAL ACTIVITY.

THESE BRAIN PATTERNS WERE HERETOFORE UNDISCOVERED BY OTHER MEANS OF INVESTIGATION AND ANALYSIS.

FOR THE FIRST TIME, THE GOVERNMENT HAD ACCESS TO VERIFIABLE INFORMATION ON PARANORMALS.

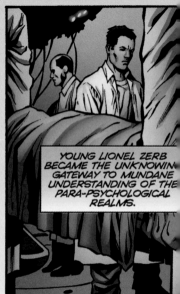

YOUNG LIONEL ZERB BECAME THE UNKNOWIN GATEWAY TO MUNDANE UNDERSTANDING OF THE PARA-PSYCHOLOGICAL REALMS.

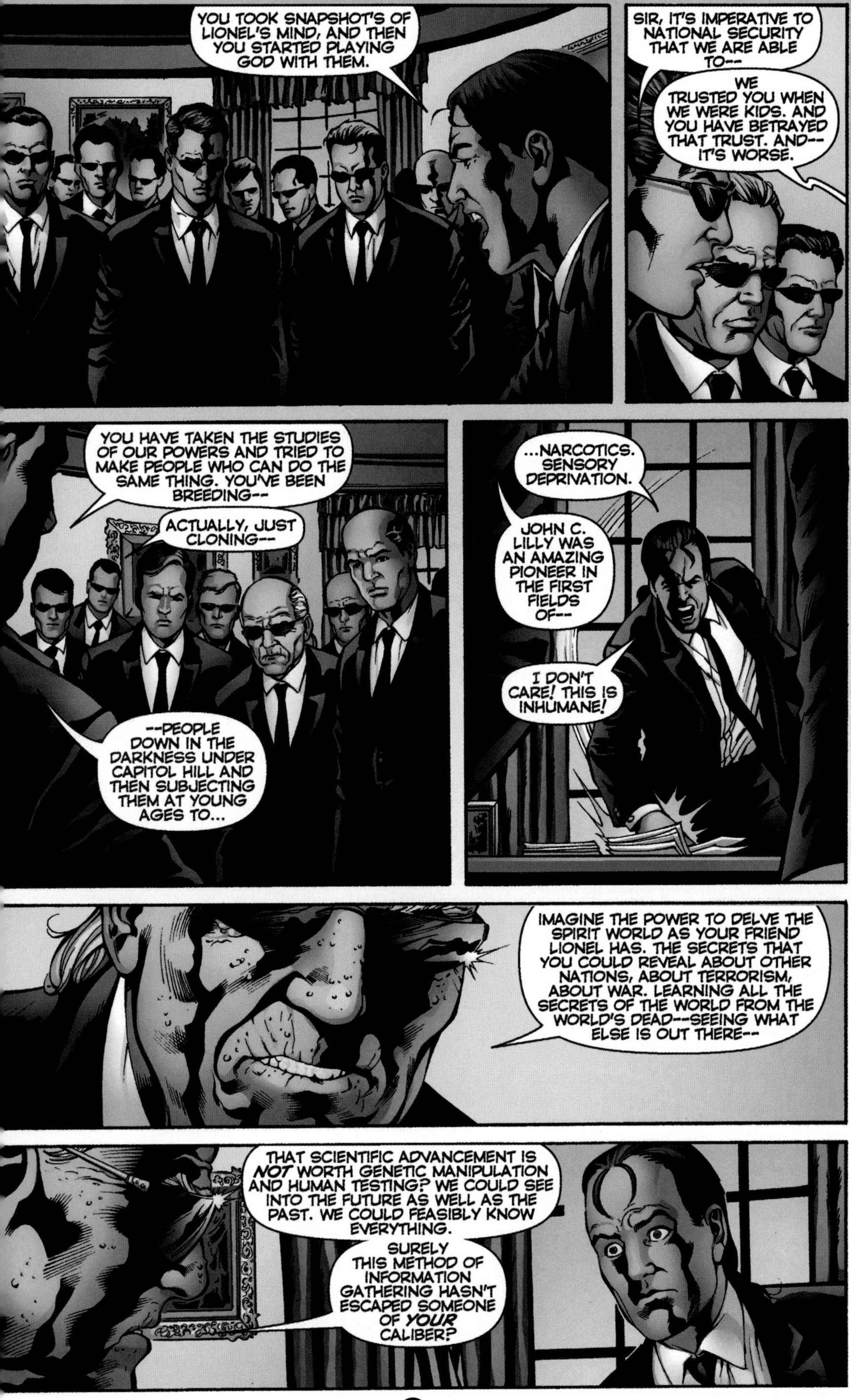

YOU TOOK SNAPSHOT'S OF LIONEL'S MIND, AND THEN YOU STARTED PLAYING GOD WITH THEM.
SIR, IT'S IMPERATIVE TO NATIONAL SECURITY THAT WE ARE ABLE TO--
WE TRUSTED YOU WHEN WE WERE KIDS. AND YOU HAVE BETRAYED THAT TRUST. AND-- IT'S WORSE.
YOU HAVE TAKEN THE STUDIES OF OUR POWERS AND TRIED TO MAKE PEOPLE WHO CAN DO THE SAME THING. YOU'VE BEEN BREEDING--
ACTUALLY, JUST CLONING--
--PEOPLE DOWN IN THE DARKNESS UNDER CAPITOL HILL AND THEN SUBJECTING THEM AT YOUNG AGES TO...
...NARCOTICS. SENSORY DEPRIVATION.
JOHN C. LILLY WAS AN AMAZING PIONEER IN THE FIRST FIELDS OF--
I DON'T CARE! THIS IS INHUMANE!
IMAGINE THE POWER TO DELVE THE SPIRIT WORLD AS YOUR FRIEND LIONEL HAS. THE SECRETS THAT YOU COULD REVEAL ABOUT OTHER NATIONS, ABOUT TERRORISM, ABOUT WAR. LEARNING ALL THE SECRETS OF THE WORLD FROM THE WORLD'S DEAD--SEEING WHAT ELSE IS OUT THERE--
THAT SCIENTIFIC ADVANCEMENT IS *NOT* WORTH GENETIC MANIPULATION AND HUMAN TESTING? WE COULD SEE INTO THE FUTURE AS WELL AS THE PAST. WE COULD FEASIBLY KNOW EVERYTHING.
SURELY THIS METHOD OF INFORMATION GATHERING HASN'T ESCAPED SOMEONE OF *YOUR* CALIBER?

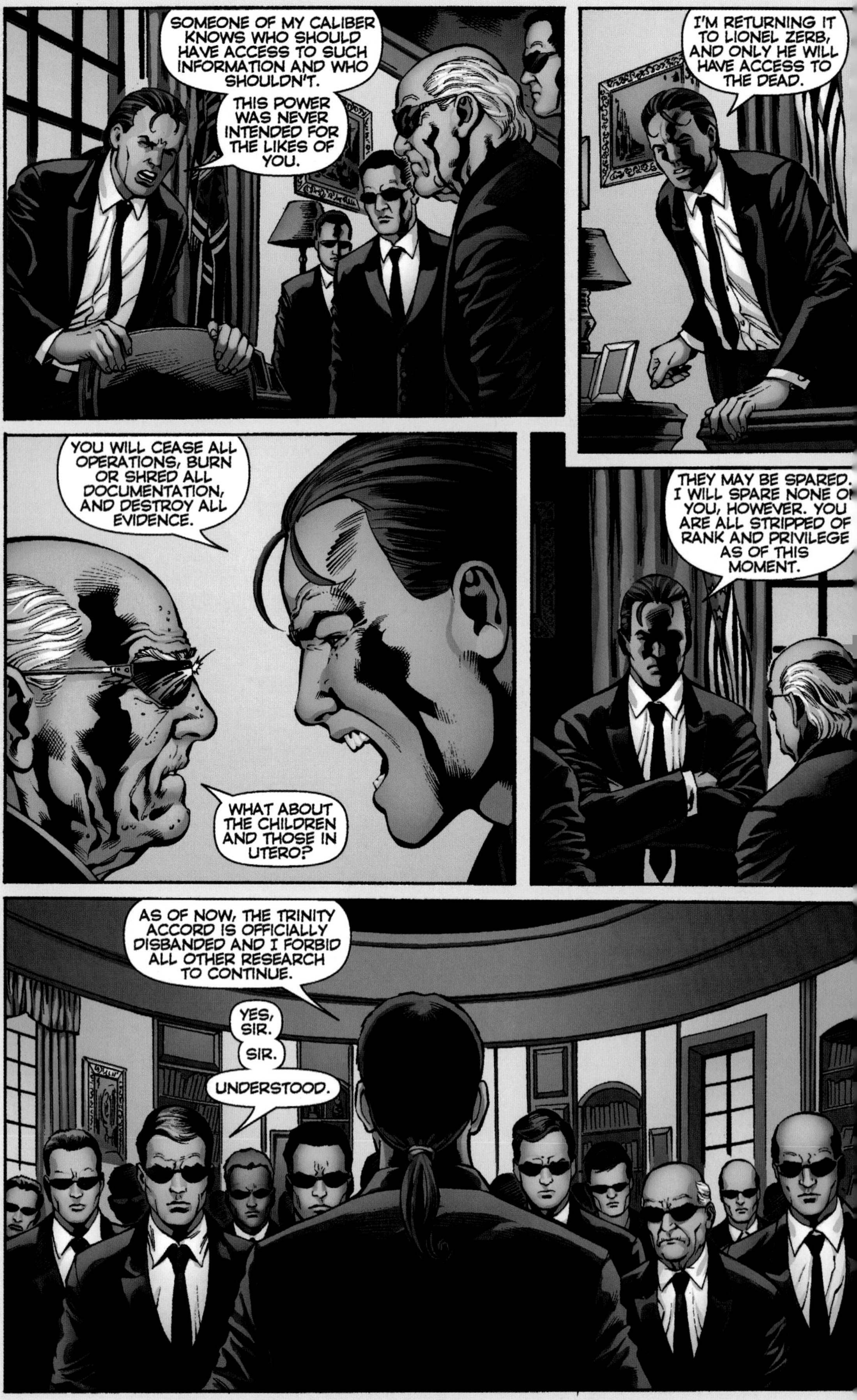
SOMEONE OF MY CALIBER KNOWS WHO SHOULD HAVE ACCESS TO SUCH INFORMATION AND WHO SHOULDN'T.
THIS POWER WAS NEVER INTENDED FOR THE LIKES OF YOU.
I'M RETURNING IT TO LIONEL ZERB, AND ONLY HE WILL HAVE ACCESS TO THE DEAD.
YOU WILL CEASE ALL OPERATIONS, BURN OR SHRED ALL DOCUMENTATION, AND DESTROY ALL EVIDENCE.
WHAT ABOUT THE CHILDREN AND THOSE IN UTERO?
THEY MAY BE SPARED. I WILL SPARE NONE OF YOU, HOWEVER. YOU ARE ALL STRIPPED OF RANK AND PRIVILEGE AS OF THIS MOMENT.
AS OF NOW, THE TRINITY ACCORD IS OFFICIALLY DISBANDED AND I FORBID ALL OTHER RESEARCH TO CONTINUE.
YES, SIR.
SIR.
UNDERSTOOD.

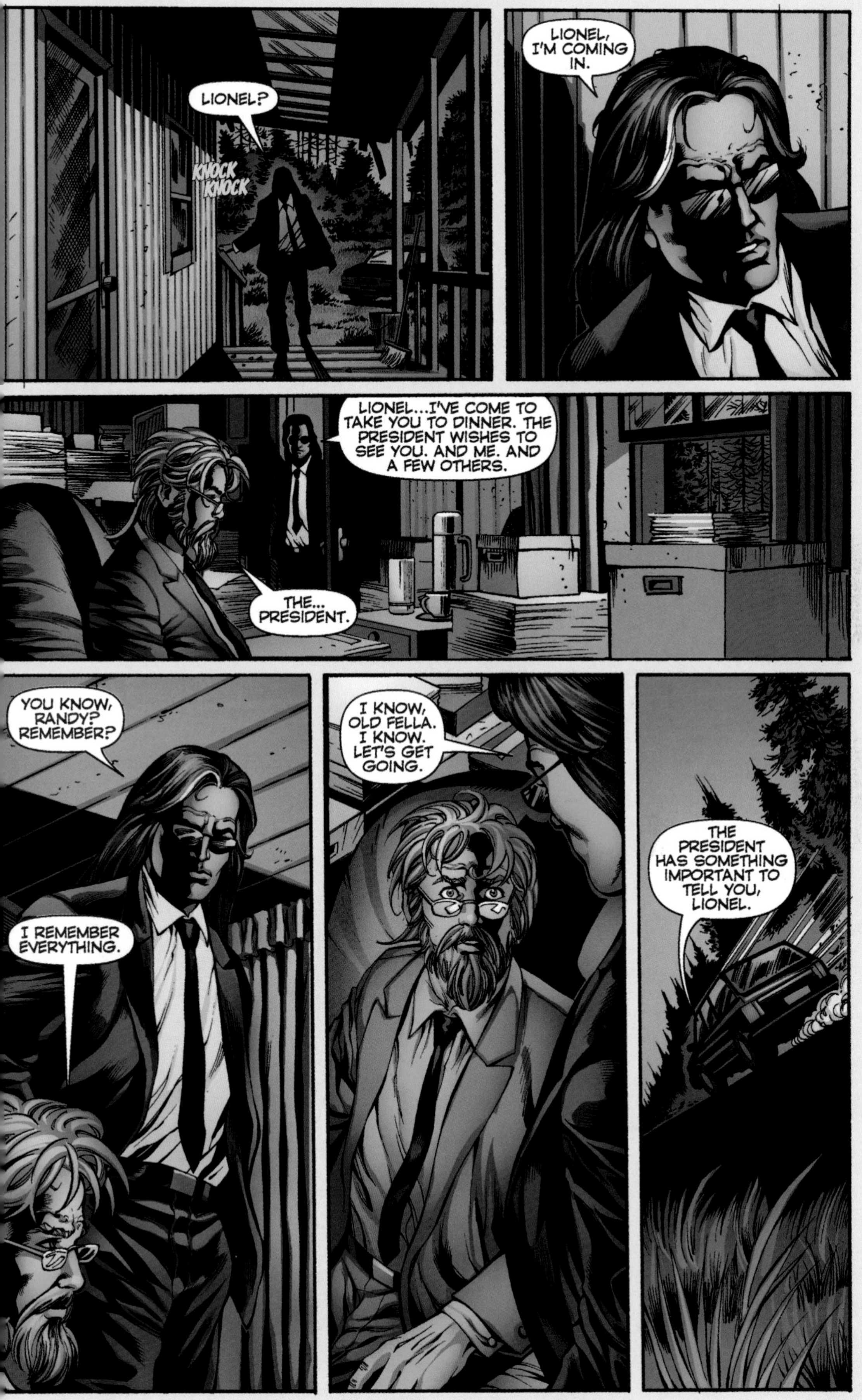
LIONEL?
KNOCK KNOCK
LIONEL, I'M COMING IN.
LIONEL...I'VE COME TO TAKE YOU TO DINNER. THE PRESIDENT WISHES TO SEE YOU. AND ME. AND A FEW OTHERS.
THE... PRESIDENT.
YOU KNOW, RANDY? REMEMBER?
I REMEMBER EVERYTHING.
I KNOW, OLD FELLA. I KNOW. LET'S GET GOING.
THE PRESIDENT HAS SOMETHING IMPORTANT TO TELL YOU, LIONEL.

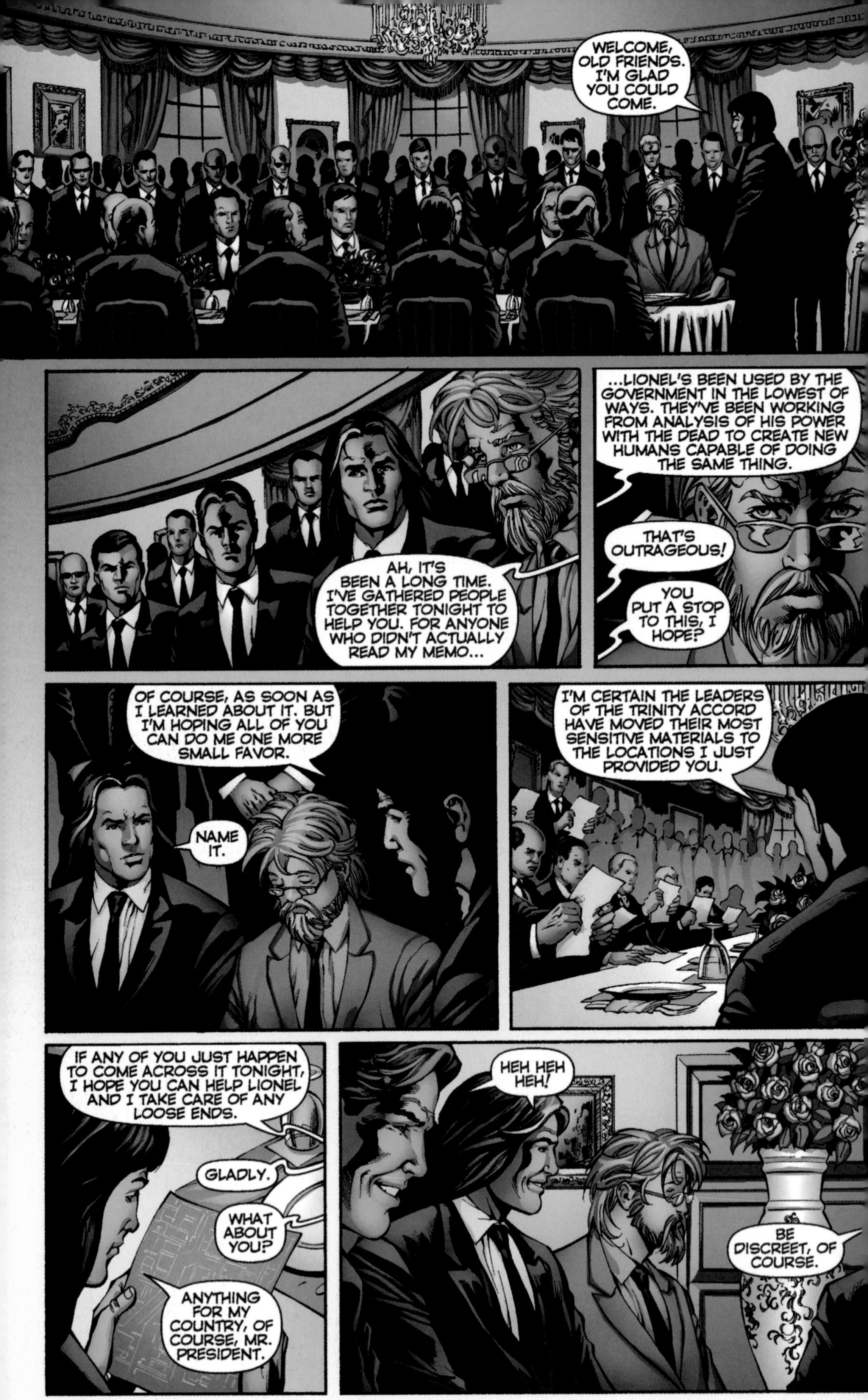
WELCOME, OLD FRIENDS. I'M GLAD YOU COULD COME.
AH, IT'S BEEN A LONG TIME. I'VE GATHERED PEOPLE TOGETHER TONIGHT TO HELP YOU. FOR ANYONE WHO DIDN'T ACTUALLY READ MY MEMO...
...LIONEL'S BEEN USED BY THE GOVERNMENT IN THE LOWEST OF WAYS. THEY'VE BEEN WORKING FROM ANALYSIS OF HIS POWER WITH THE DEAD TO CREATE NEW HUMANS CAPABLE OF DOING THE SAME THING.
THAT'S OUTRAGEOUS!
YOU PUT A STOP TO THIS, I HOPE?
OF COURSE, AS SOON AS I LEARNED ABOUT IT. BUT I'M HOPING ALL OF YOU CAN DO ME ONE MORE SMALL FAVOR.
NAME IT.
I'M CERTAIN THE LEADERS OF THE TRINITY ACCORD HAVE MOVED THEIR MOST SENSITIVE MATERIALS TO THE LOCATIONS I JUST PROVIDED YOU.
IF ANY OF YOU JUST HAPPEN TO COME ACROSS IT TONIGHT, I HOPE YOU CAN HELP LIONEL AND I TAKE CARE OF ANY LOOSE ENDS.
GLADLY.
WHAT ABOUT YOU?
ANYTHING FOR MY COUNTRY, OF COURSE, MR. PRESIDENT.
HEH HEH HEH!
BE DISCREET, OF COURSE.

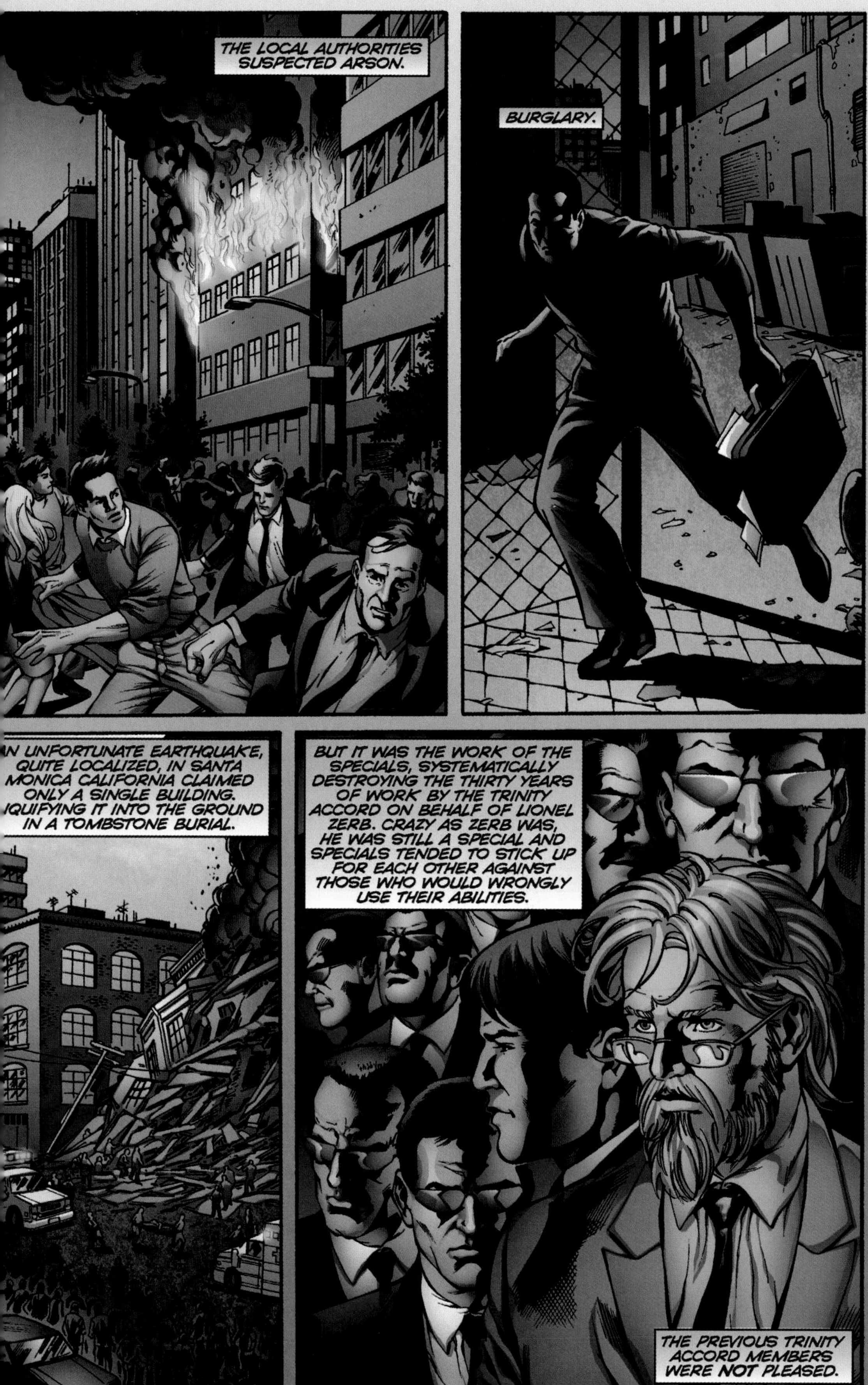
THE LOCAL AUTHORITIES SUSPECTED ARSON.
BURGLARY.
AN UNFORTUNATE EARTHQUAKE, QUITE LOCALIZED, IN SANTA MONICA CALIFORNIA CLAIMED ONLY A SINGLE BUILDING. LIQUIFYING IT INTO THE GROUND IN A TOMBSTONE BURIAL.
BUT IT WAS THE WORK OF THE SPECIALS, SYSTEMATICALLY DESTROYING THE THIRTY YEARS OF WORK BY THE TRINITY ACCORD ON BEHALF OF LIONEL ZERB. CRAZY AS ZERB WAS, HE WAS STILL A SPECIAL AND SPECIALS TENDED TO STICK UP FOR EACH OTHER AGAINST THOSE WHO WOULD WRONGLY USE THEIR ABILITIES.
THE PREVIOUS TRINITY ACCORD MEMBERS WERE NOT PLEASED.

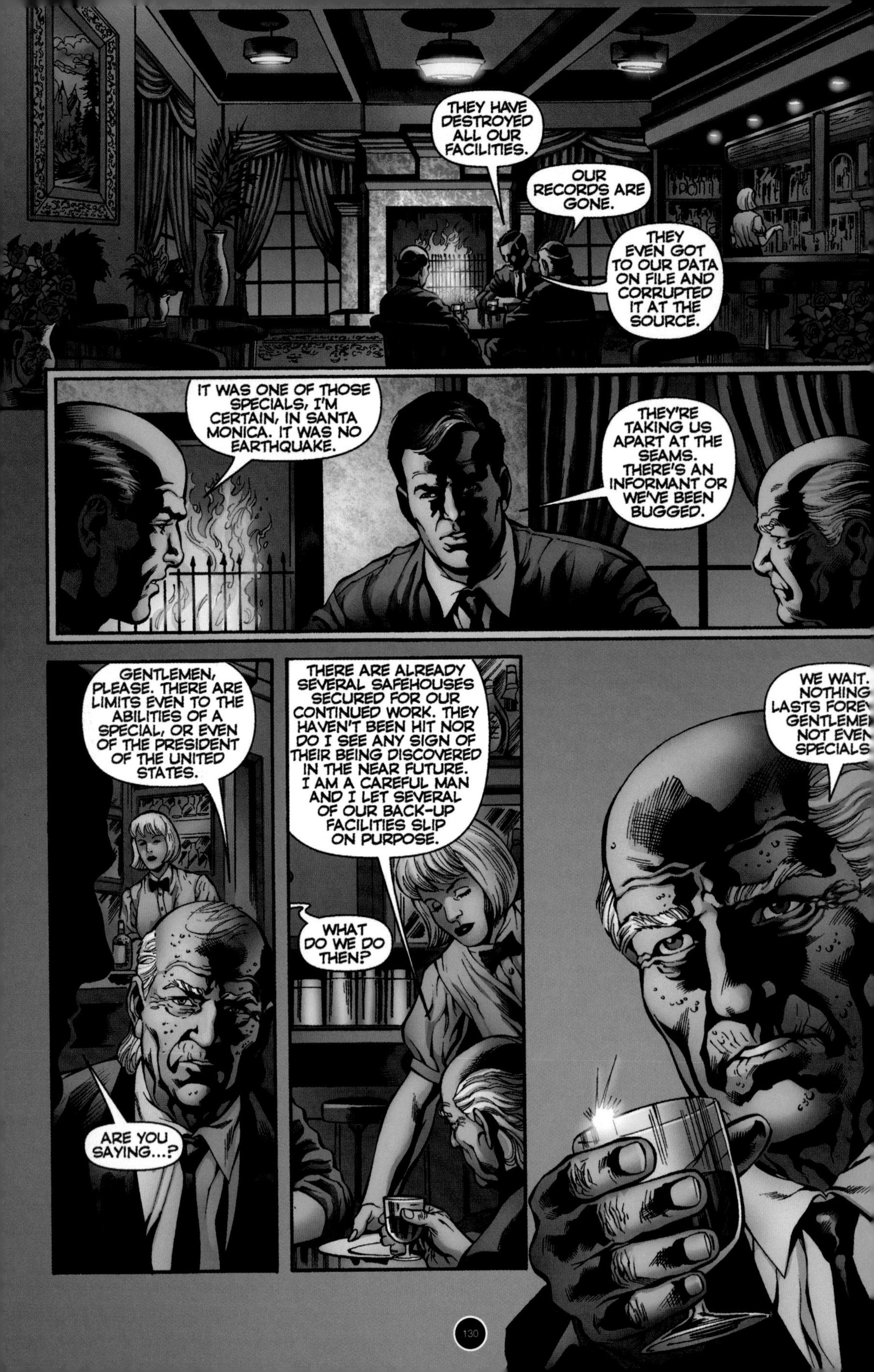

THEY HAVE DESTROYED ALL OUR FACILITIES.
OUR RECORDS ARE GONE.
THEY EVEN GOT TO OUR DATA ON FILE AND CORRUPTED IT AT THE SOURCE.
IT WAS ONE OF THOSE SPECIALS, I'M CERTAIN, IN SANTA MONICA. IT WAS NO EARTHQUAKE.
THEY'RE TAKING US APART AT THE SEAMS. THERE'S AN INFORMANT OR WE'VE BEEN BUGGED.
GENTLEMEN, PLEASE. THERE ARE LIMITS EVEN TO THE ABILITIES OF A SPECIAL, OR EVEN OF THE PRESIDENT OF THE UNITED STATES.
ARE YOU SAYING...?
THERE ARE ALREADY SEVERAL SAFEHOUSES SECURED FOR OUR CONTINUED WORK. THEY HAVEN'T BEEN HIT NOR DO I SEE ANY SIGN OF THEIR BEING DISCOVERED IN THE NEAR FUTURE. I AM A CAREFUL MAN AND I LET SEVERAL OF OUR BACK-UP FACILITIES SLIP ON PURPOSE.
WHAT DO WE DO THEN?
WE WAIT. NOTHING LASTS FOREV GENTLEME NOT EVEN SPECIALS

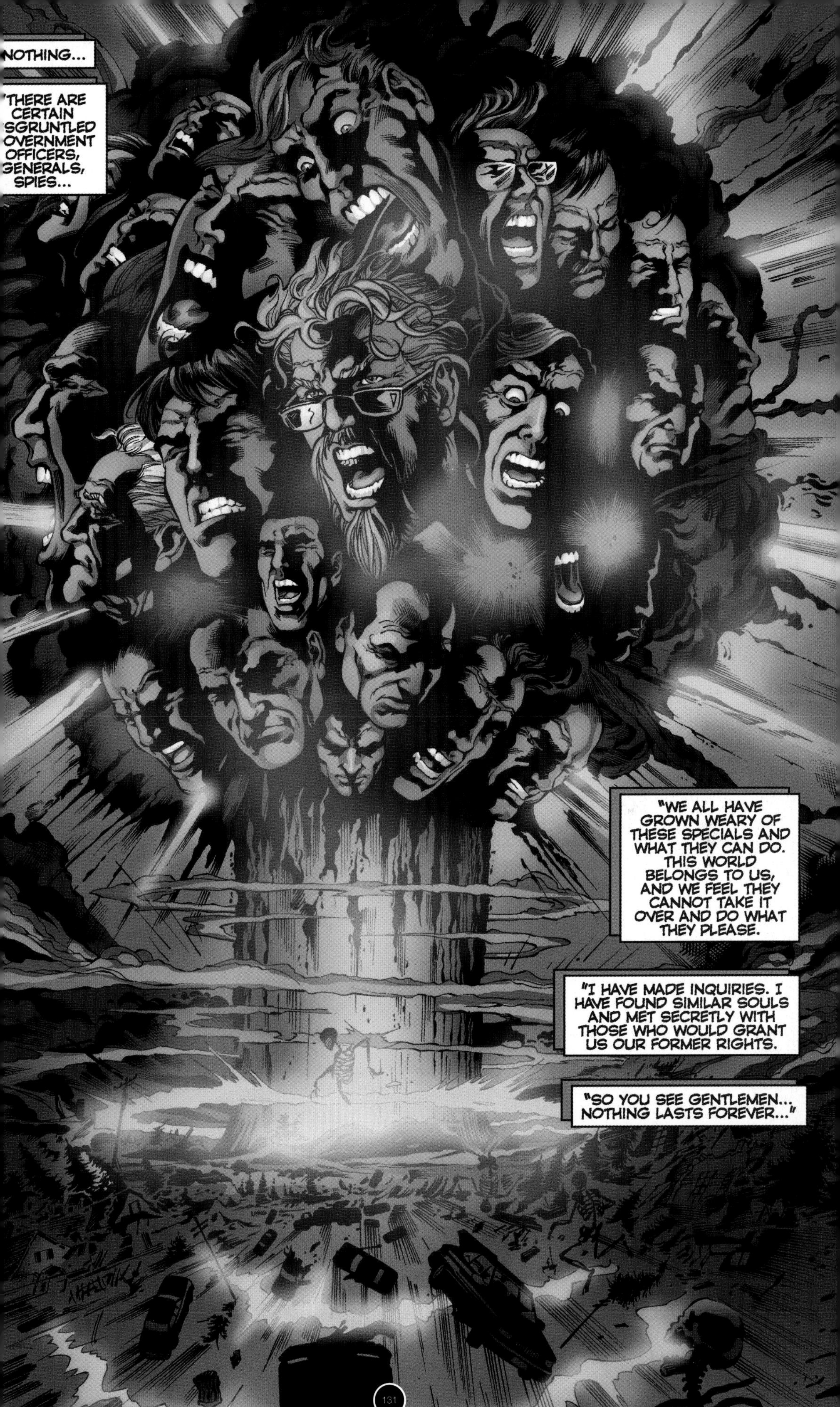
NOTHING...
"THERE ARE CERTAIN SGRUNTLED OVERNMENT OFFICERS, GENERALS, SPIES...
"WE ALL HAVE GROWN WEARY OF THESE SPECIALS AND WHAT THEY CAN DO. THIS WORLD BELONGS TO US, AND WE FEEL THEY CANNOT TAKE IT OVER AND DO WHAT THEY PLEASE.
"I HAVE MADE INQUIRIES. I HAVE FOUND SIMILAR SOULS AND MET SECRETLY WITH THOSE WHO WOULD GRANT US OUR FORMER RIGHTS.
"SO YOU SEE GENTLEMEN... NOTHING LASTS FOREVER..."

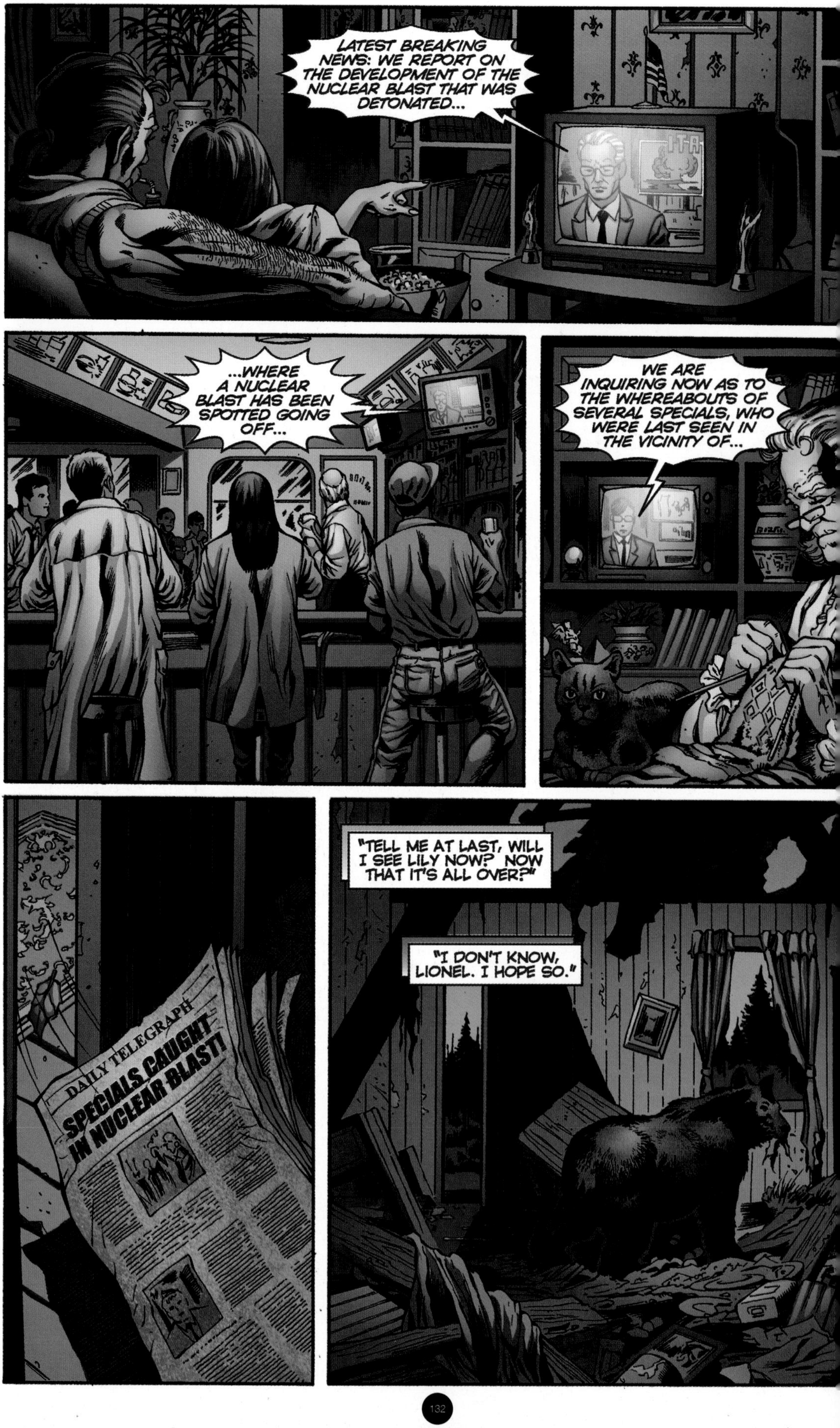
LATEST BREAKING NEWS: WE REPORT ON THE DEVELOPMENT OF THE NUCLEAR BLAST THAT WAS DETONATED...
...WHERE A NUCLEAR BLAST HAS BEEN SPOTTED GOING OFF...
WE ARE INQUIRING NOW AS TO THE WHEREABOUTS OF SEVERAL SPECIALS, WHO WERE LAST SEEN IN THE VICINITY OF...
DAILY TELEGRAPH
SPECIALS CAUGHT IN NUCLEAR BLAST!
"TELL ME AT LAST, WILL I SEE LILY NOW? NOW THAT IT'S ALL OVER?"
"I DON'T KNOW, LIONEL. I HOPE SO."

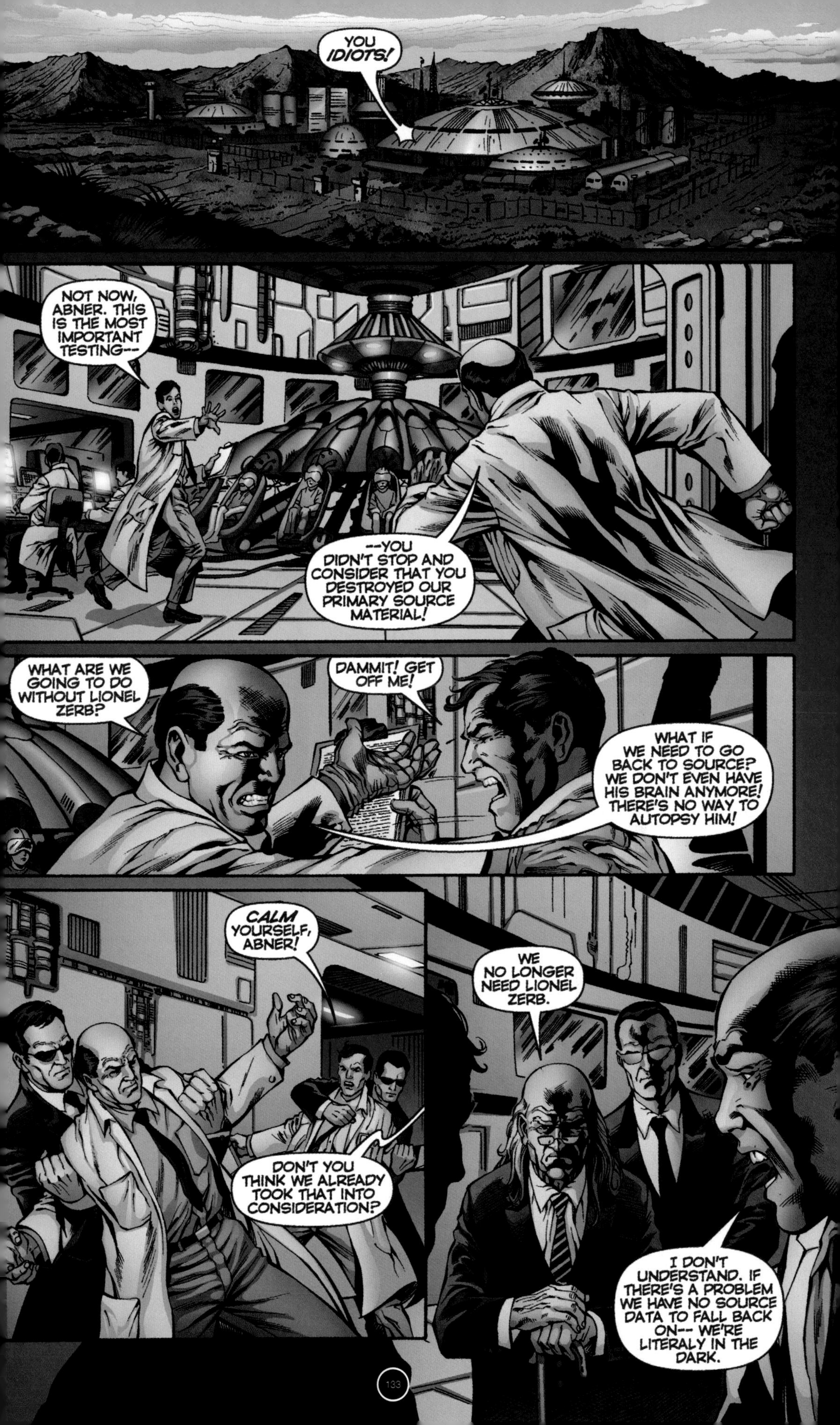
YOU IDIOTS!
NOT NOW, ABNER. THIS IS THE MOST IMPORTANT TESTING--
--YOU DIDN'T STOP AND CONSIDER THAT YOU DESTROYED OUR PRIMARY SOURCE MATERIAL!
WHAT ARE WE GOING TO DO WITHOUT LIONEL ZERB?
DAMMIT! GET OFF ME!
WHAT IF WE NEED TO GO BACK TO SOURCE? WE DON'T EVEN HAVE HIS BRAIN ANYMORE! THERE'S NO WAY TO AUTOPSY HIM!
CALM YOURSELF, ABNER!
DON'T YOU THINK WE ALREADY TOOK THAT INTO CONSIDERATION?
WE NO LONGER NEED LIONEL ZERB.
I DON'T UNDERSTAND. IF THERE'S A PROBLEM WE HAVE NO SOURCE DATA TO FALL BACK ON-- WE'RE LITERALY IN THE DARK.

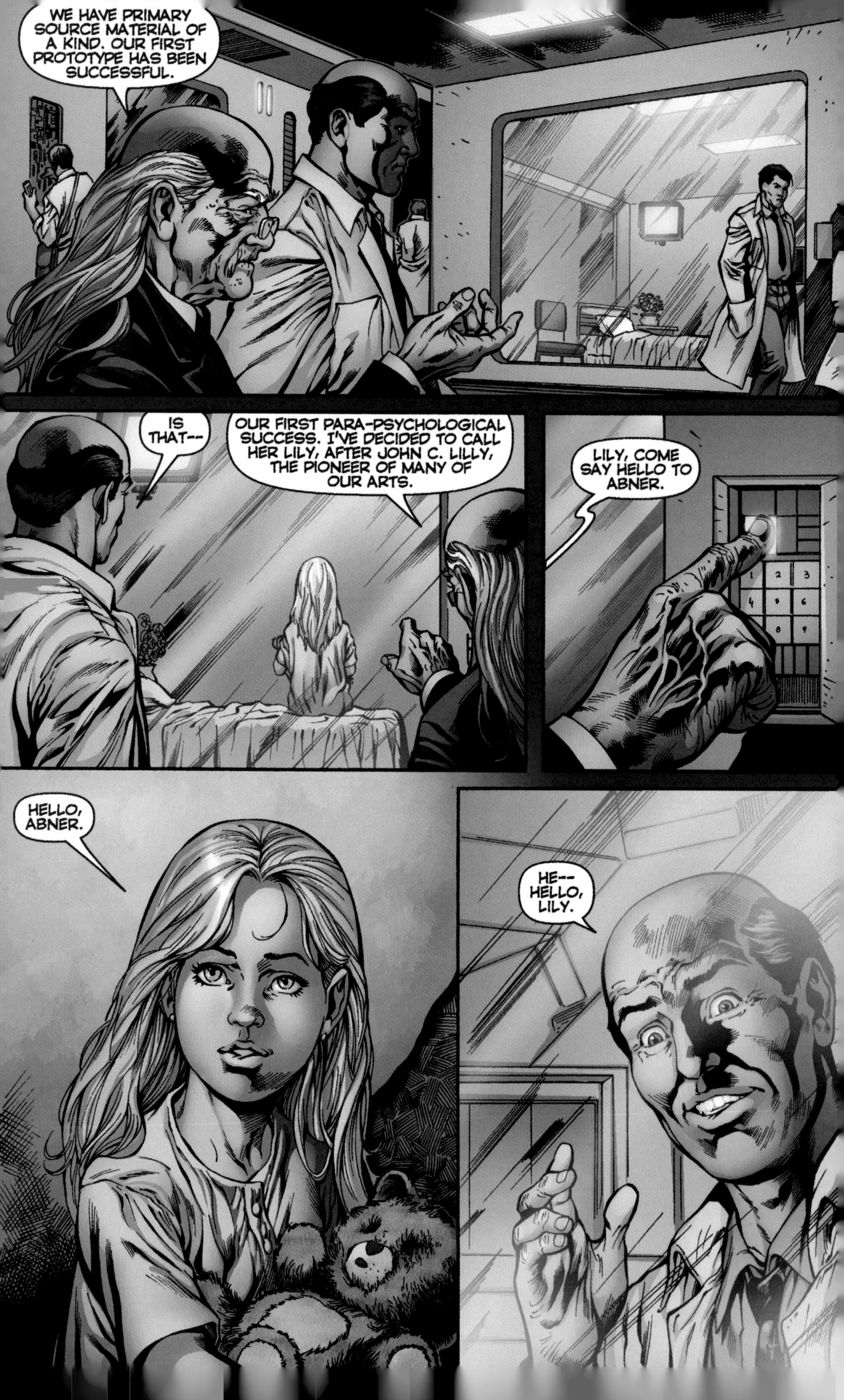
WE HAVE PRIMARY SOURCE MATERIAL OF A KIND. OUR FIRST PROTOTYPE HAS BEEN SUCCESSFUL.
IS THAT--
OUR FIRST PARA-PSYCHOLOGICAL SUCCESS. I'VE DECIDED TO CALL HER LILY, AFTER JOHN C. LILLY, THE PIONEER OF MANY OF OUR ARTS.
LILY, COME SAY HELLO TO ABNER.
HELLO, ABNER.
HE-- HELLO, LILY.

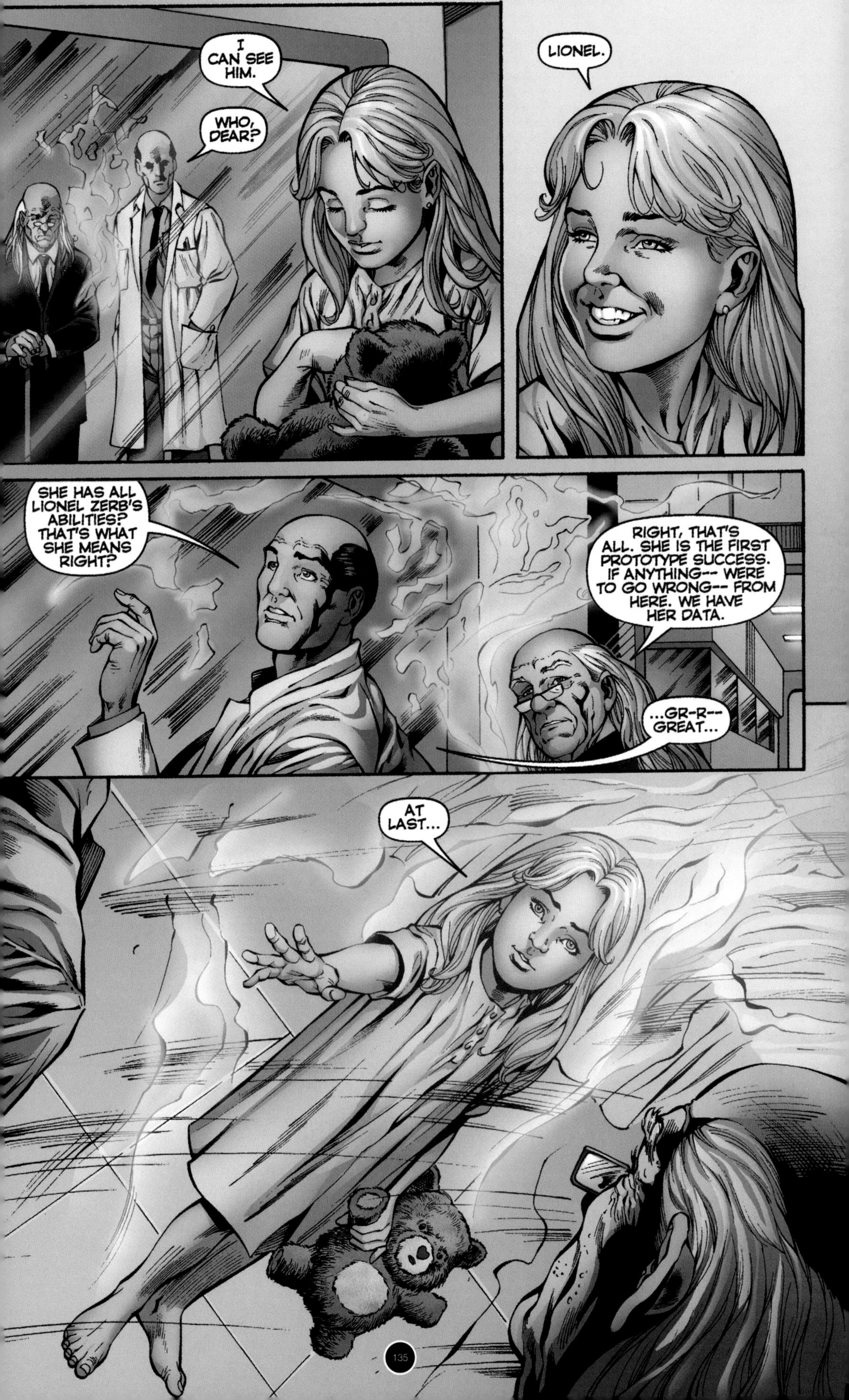
I CAN SEE HIM.
WHO, DEAR?
LIONEL.
SHE HAS ALL LIONEL ZERB'S ABILITIES? THAT'S WHAT SHE MEANS RIGHT?
RIGHT, THAT'S ALL. SHE IS THE FIRST PROTOTYPE SUCCESS. IF ANYTHING-- WERE TO GO WRONG-- FROM HERE. WE HAVE HER DATA.
...GR-R-- GREAT...
AT LAST...

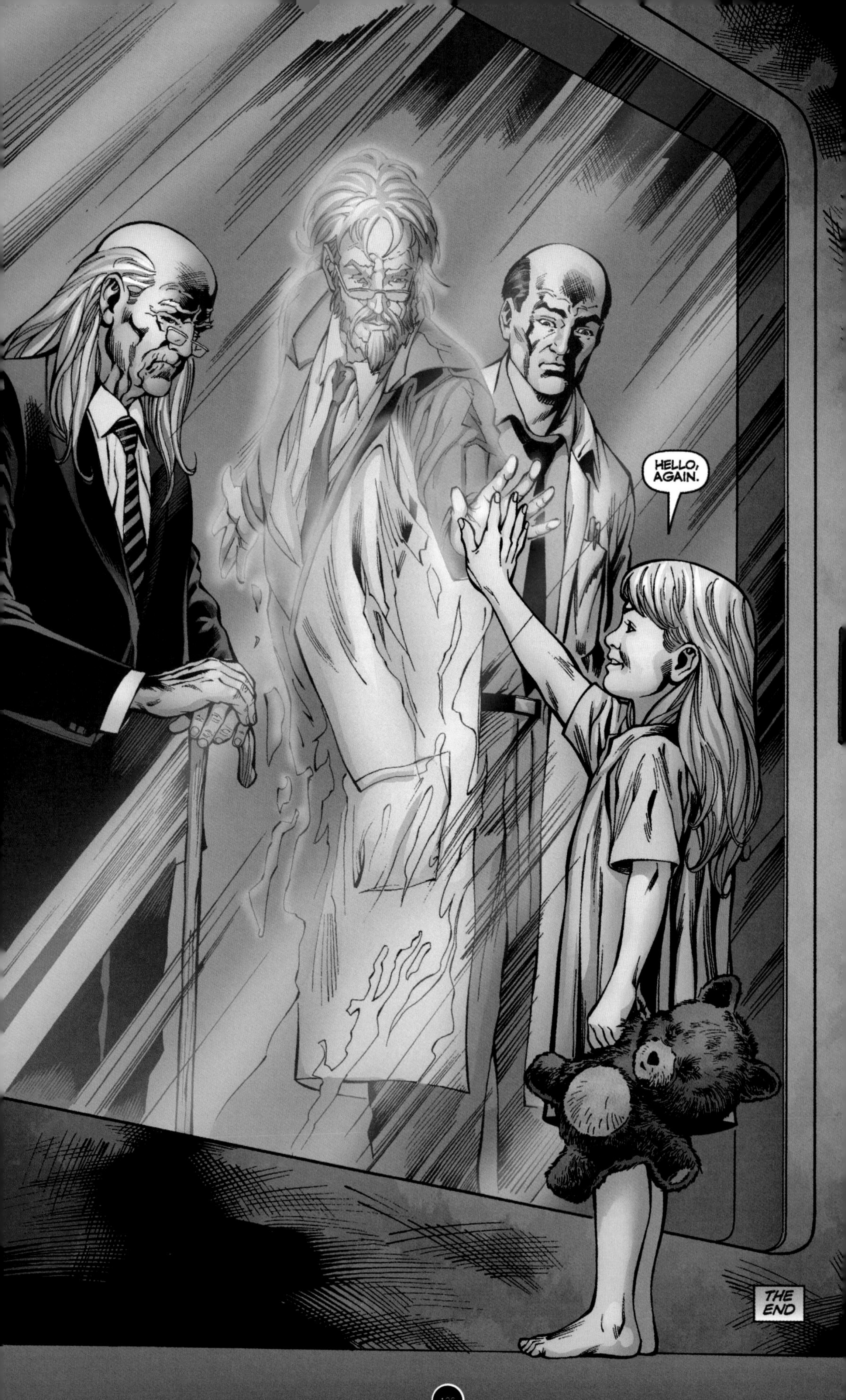
HELLO, AGAIN.
THE END

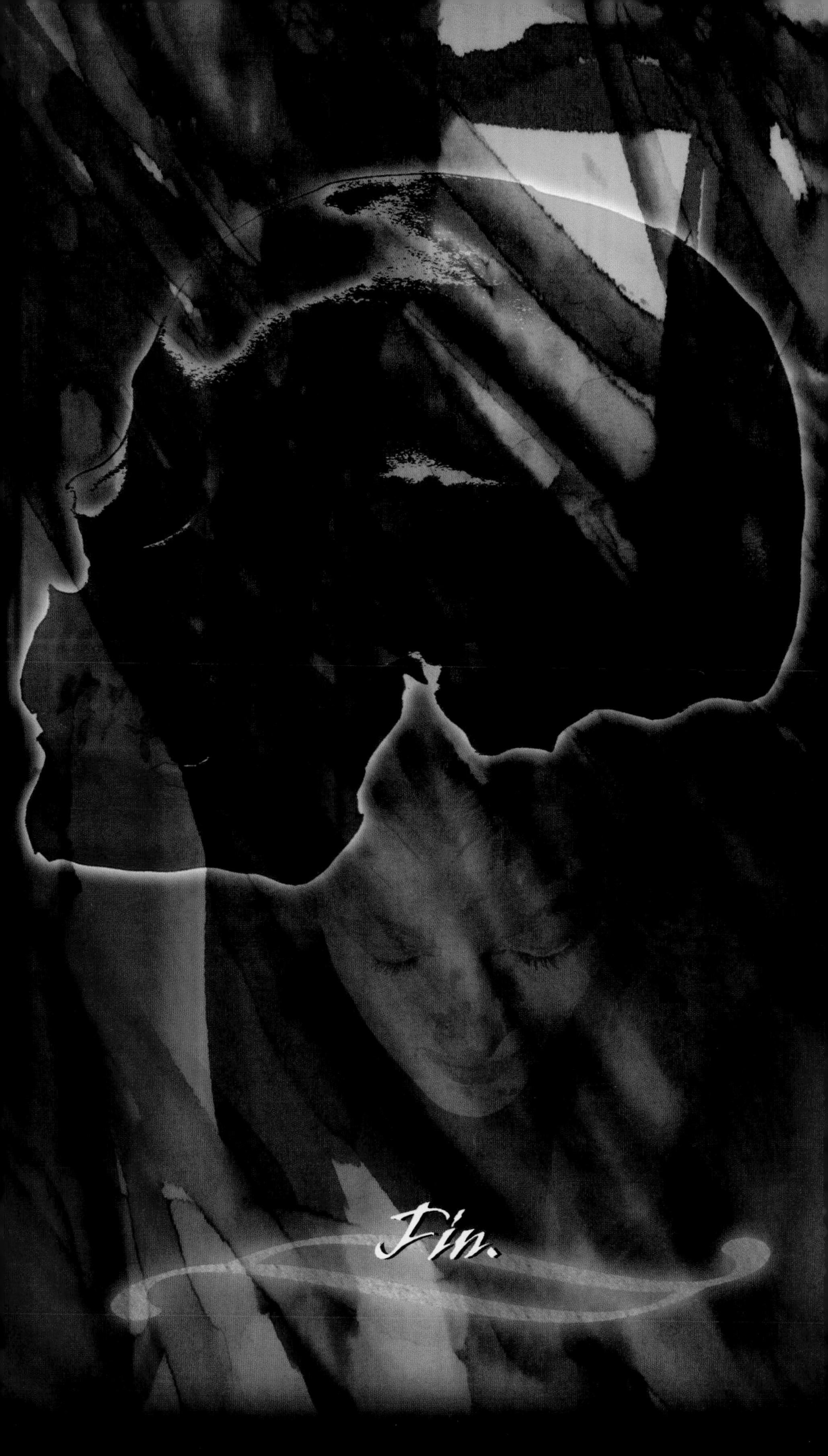
Fin.

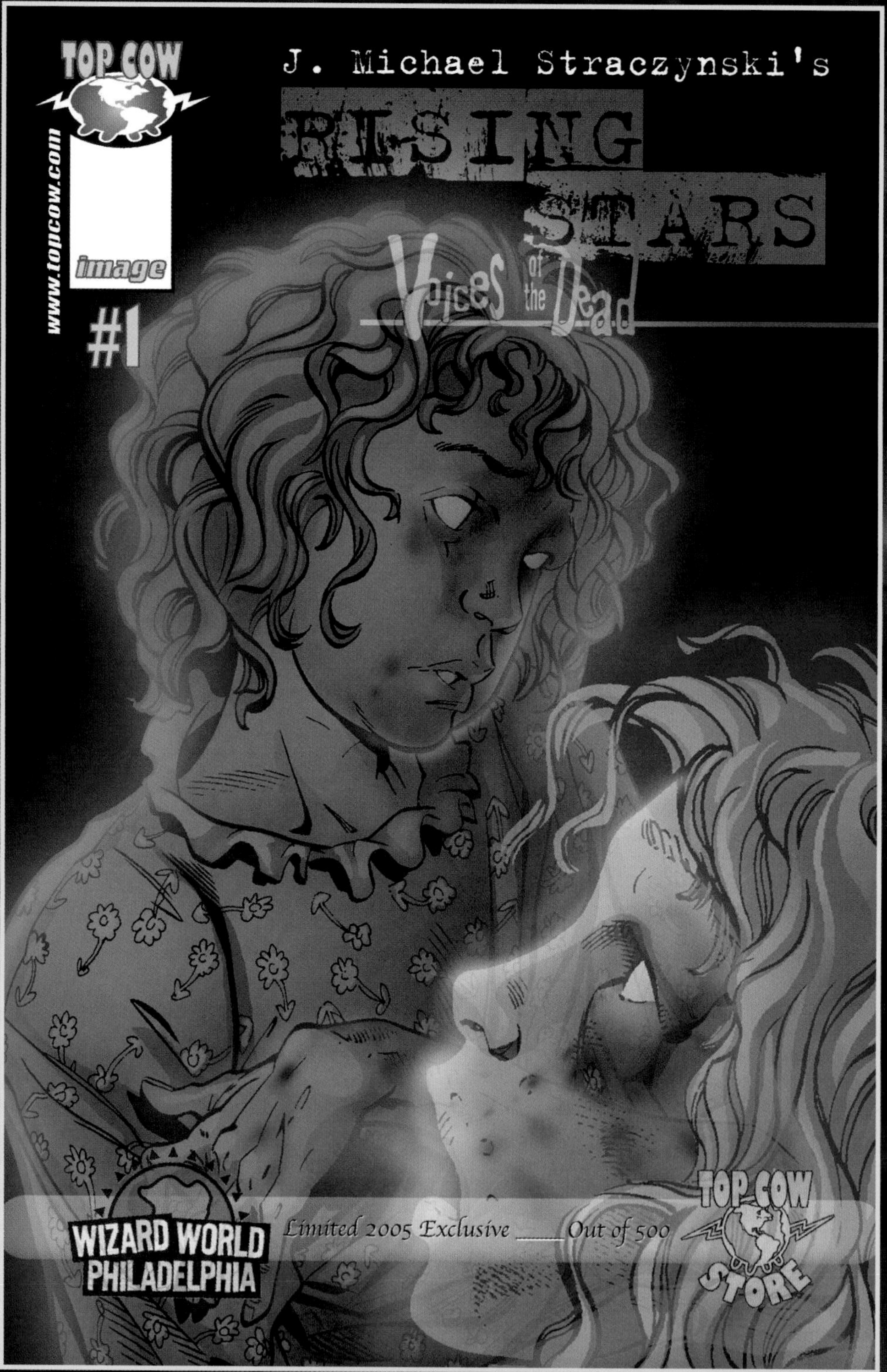
TOP COW
www.topcow.com
image
#1
J. Michael Straczynski's
RISING STARS
Voices of the Dead
WIZARD WORLD PHILADELPHIA
Limited 2005 Exclusive ____ Out of 500
TOP COW STORE

Rising Stars: Voices of the Dead
issue #3
Wizard World Philly variant
Design by:
Chaz Riggs

BRIGHT #1

JURGENS/

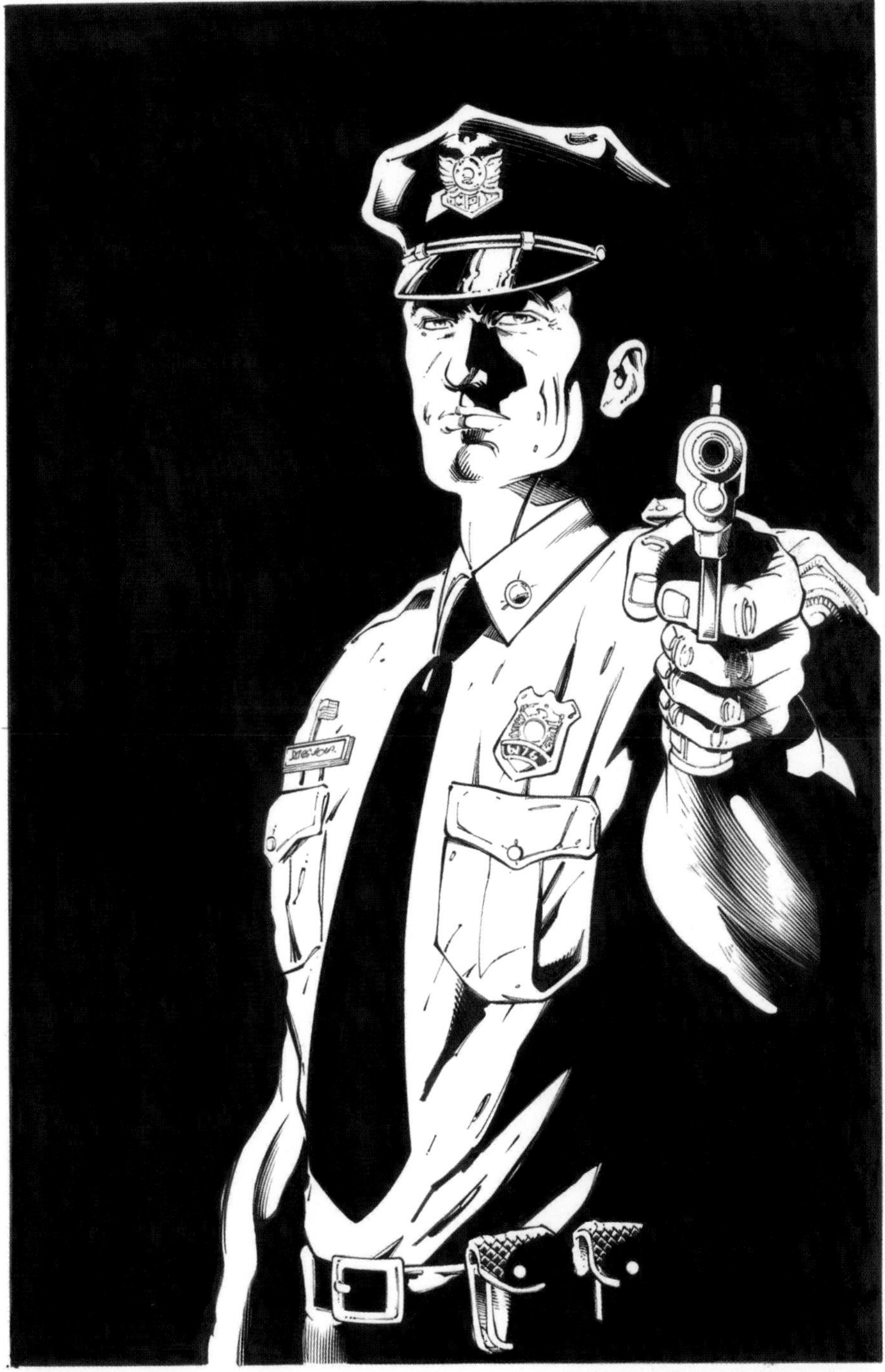

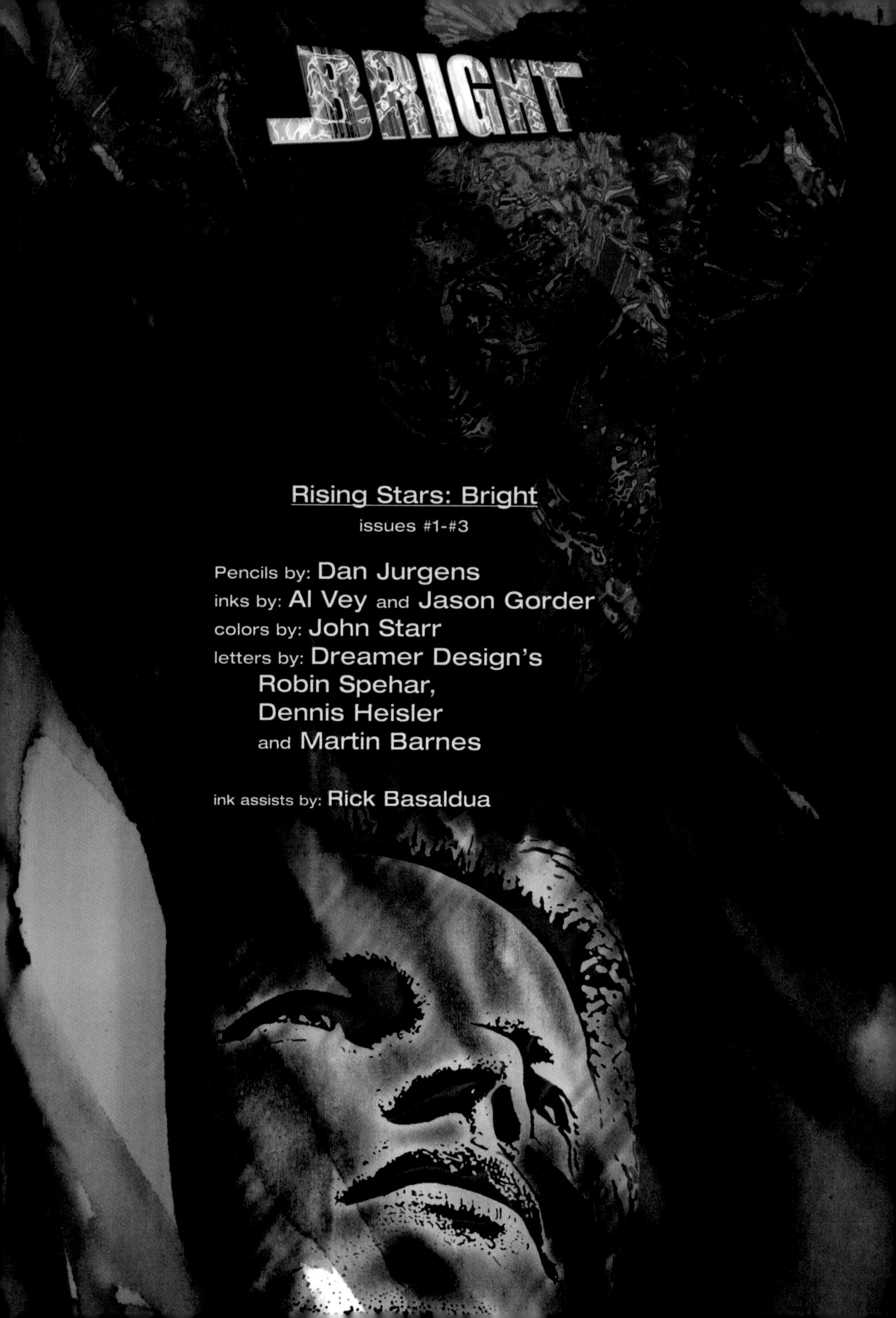
BRIGHT

Rising Stars: Bright

issues #1-#3

Pencils by: Dan Jurgens
inks by: Al Vey and Jason Gorder
colors by: John Starr
letters by: Dreamer Design's
Robin Spehar,
Dennis Heisler
and Martin Barnes

ink assists by: Rick Basaldua

Matt—
You'd better read it over in case
there's something you don't
want broadcast to the
world in here.

FORWARD

by John Simon

Let me tell you something about Matthew Bright.

I could tell you about how many lives he's saved over the years,
both before and after he joined the New York Police Department.
I could tell you about the first time he flew and the disaster
that resulted when gravity, Matthew, and the camp water tower
came into disagreement about the laws of physics. I could tell
you a lot about him.

But I'm going to tell you about the ice cream cone. Because if
you get this, you understand everything you ever need to know
about Matthew Bright.

We were maybe fourteen, fifteen years old and on one of our few
field trips into Pederson, into the territory of normals. It
was a hot day, though we didn't really notice. We were walking
down Fourth Avenue, which is home to lots of little stores, a
couple of restaurants, a clothing store, and Milt's, an old
fashioned ice cream parlor, the kind that makes a proper milk
shake and uses home-made fudge for their sundaes.

Anyway, we were walking past Milt's when this girl came out.
She was probably six or seven, with an ice cream cone as big as
she was. Triple-stacked cone, vanilla, chocolate, strawberry.
Happiest kid you ever saw. But as she came out, she tripped on
the edge of the door, and the cone went flying. She just stared
at it for a moment, as it melted on the hot sidewalk, and she
started crying. Jason, who was with us, said she could get
another one, but she'd apparently spent her whole allowance on
this one cone. She ran off, crying. Devastated.

As Matthew watched her go, I could see his heart break for the
kid. So he went inside, and spent his day's allowance on a new
triple-stacked cone for her. Searched all over the place until
he found her. Gave it to her. Why? Because it made her happy.
And making other people happy makes Matthew happy.

And he never regretted it, not even when one of the older kids
recognized us for what we were, and teased the girl about taking
ice cream from a Special...from a freak...and she tossed the
cone in the garbage.

He did what he had to, he did the right thing, so none of that
bothered him. That's Matthew Bright for you.

Me, I would've decked her.

JOHN—
CAN YOU LOOK THIS OVER?

MATT—
MY CORRECTIONS IN RED

INTRODUCTION

by Matthew A. Bright

When Carlyle House first approached me about writing my autobiography, especially about how I came to join the police academy in New York, the first thing I thought of was that I can't type and my handwriting is about as illegible as a good doctor's.

I called John Simon for some advice. After taking a *(justified)* sound beating in return for asking if he'd type my manuscript for me, he gave me some pointers on how to start. Including how to write an introduction to my own work.

Talking about myself has never come easy. I may have been born with special abilities, but like many in the Police Force or any line of duty, I came to this proffession because it called to me. The side of a squad car reads, "To Serve and Protect." To some people, that's a meaningless pretty phrase. To other people, like my grandfather, his father, my father, and me, that phrase creates a deep and powerful resonance within our spirit. I say those words even now and feel something inside me light up with a proud fire.

My autobiography could really be just a paragraph about my father. He taught me everything I needed to know about how to Protect and to Serve. One: Show mercy to little things. Two: Question authority. Challenge those who hold positions over you while being loyal to your peers. And lastly: Avoid civilian casualties at all costs.

Dad wasn't a special but I feel like he should have been. He was to me. If his words had reached some of us early on the way they reached me, a lot of our history would not have unfolded as it did. I owe him for everything good that I am today.

The tragedies were all our doing.

WHAT DO YOU THINK ABOUT RANDY DOING THE COVER?

You WANT RANDY TO DO THE COVER?

CHANDRA—

HERE'S THE MS. LIKE YOU ASKE[D] COMPLETE WITH JOHN'S FOREWOR[D] I WOULD HAVE BROUGHT IT OVE[R] IN PERSON, BUT YOU KNOW HOW [IT] IS...

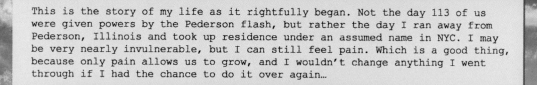

This is the story of my life as it rightfully began. Not the day 113 of us were given powers by the Pederson flash, but rather the day I ran away from Pederson, Illinois and took up residence under an assumed name in NYC. I may be very nearly invulnerable, but I can still feel pain. Which is a good thing, because only pain allows us to grow, and I wouldn't change anything I went through if I had the chance to do it over again...

I went to New York after my first real experience with pain: being denied the opportunity to enroll as a police officer in Pederson. Denied because I was a special. A freak. So I left, determined to prove otherwise.

I'd left Pederson in a fit of rage. Sometimes when you're that angry, you do things that seem like a good idea at the time...

Of course, looking back on it now, I realize that getting a fake identity under the name Brendan Miller was not such a good idea. But you know hindsight-- it's always 20/20.

B.MILLER

MAIL

GET THE STICK! GIMME THE STICK, BOY! HEY! THIS IS FETCH, NOT WWF!

GROWF! GRRRR! WOOF!

YOU *KNOW* WHO'S GONNA WIN A STRENGTH CONTEST, BAX. C'MON NOW...

I've always loved getting the mail. Ever since I was a kid I had this weird fixation on being the first one to the mailbox.

Even if the checks from wherever I was working that week weren't addressed to the real me, they're still good news.

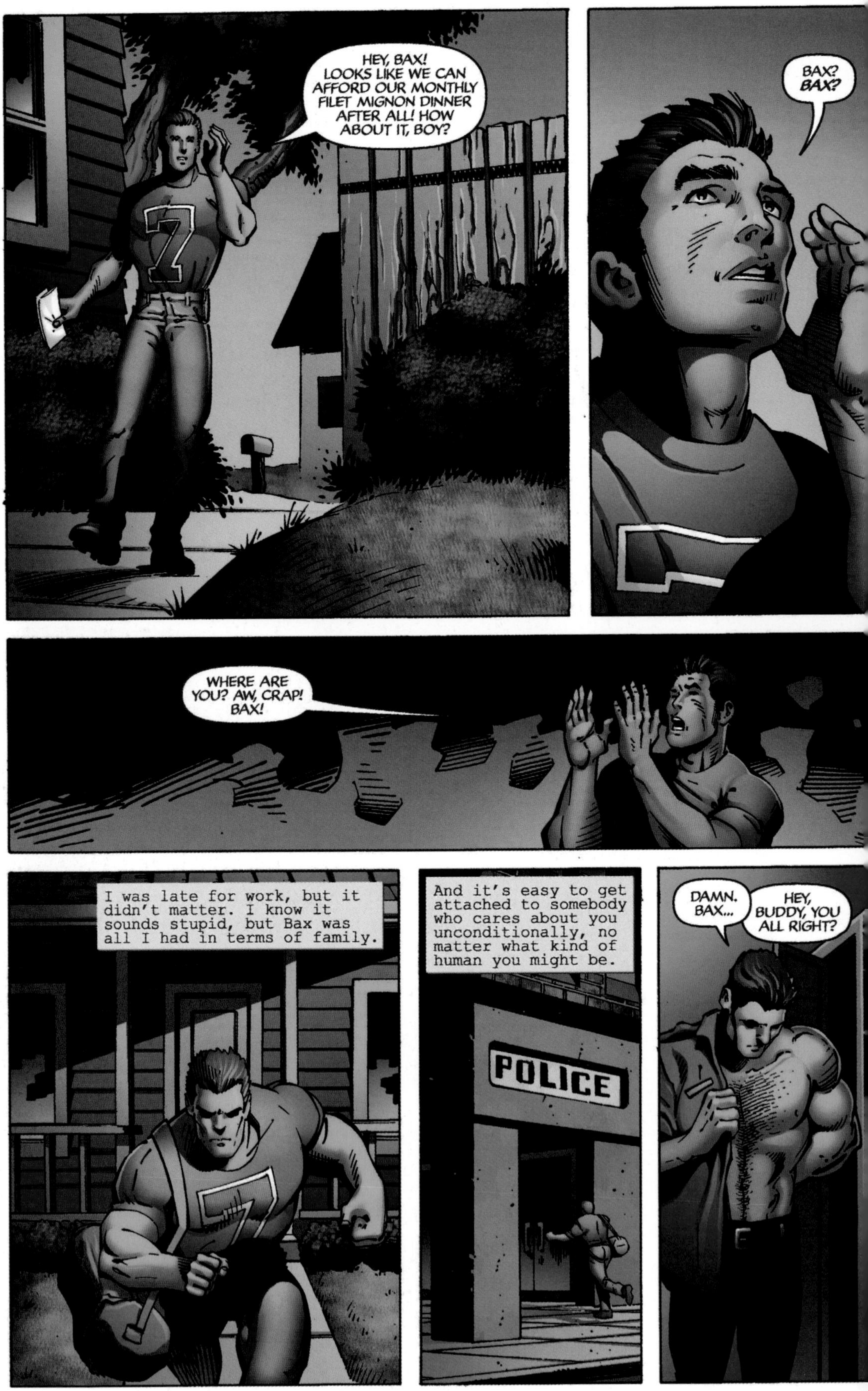

HEY, BAX! LOOKS LIKE WE CAN AFFORD OUR MONTHLY FILET MIGNON DINNER AFTER ALL! HOW ABOUT IT, BOY?
BAX? BAX?
WHERE ARE YOU? AW, CRAP! BAX!
I was late for work, but it didn't matter. I know it sounds stupid, but Bax was all I had in terms of family.
And it's easy to get attached to somebody who cares about you unconditionally, no matter what kind of human you might be.
POLICE
DAMN. BAX...
HEY, BUDDY, YOU ALL RIGHT?

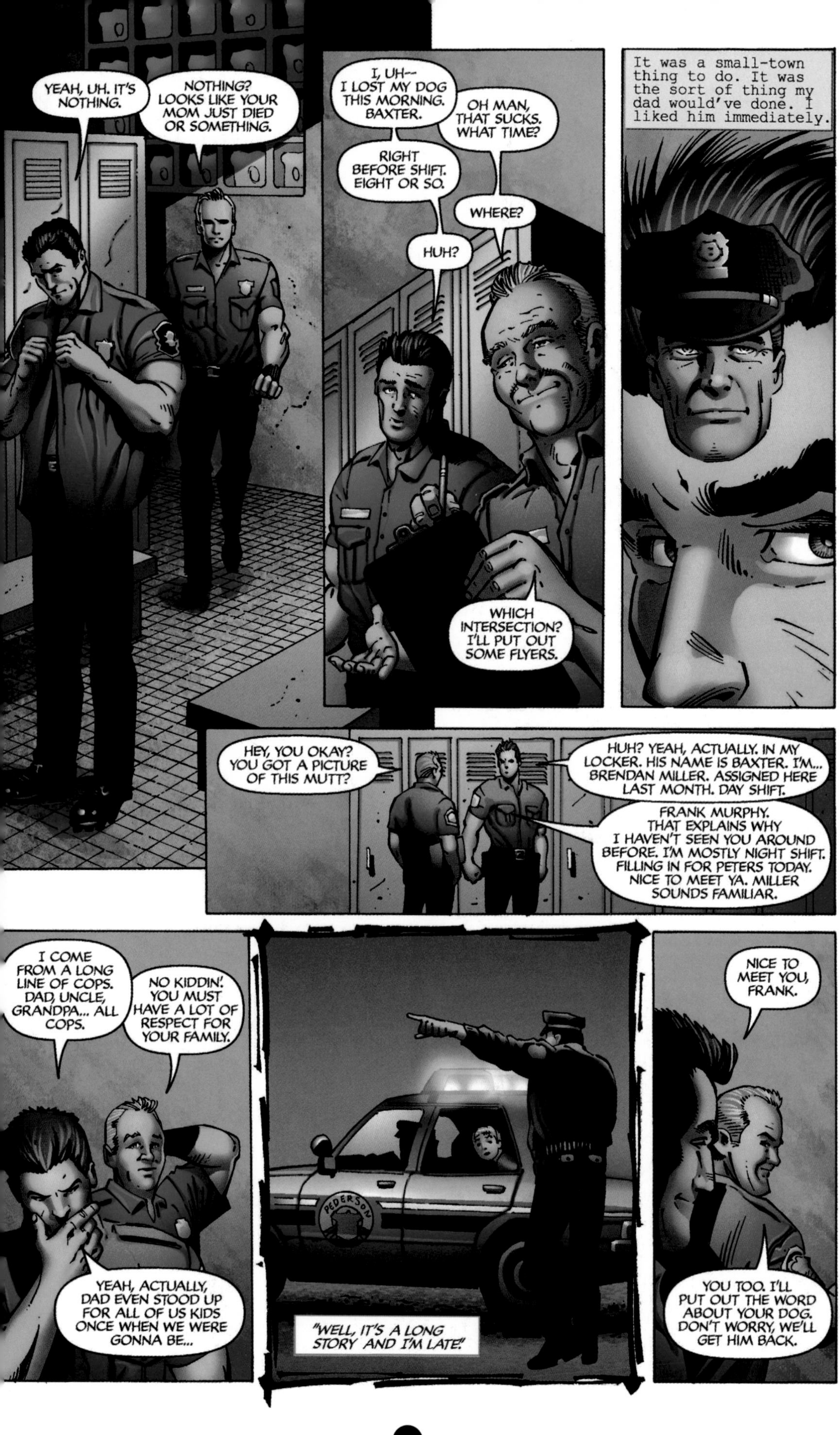
YEAH, UH. IT'S NOTHING.
NOTHING? LOOKS LIKE YOUR MOM JUST DIED OR SOMETHING.
I, UH-- I LOST MY DOG THIS MORNING. BAXTER.
OH MAN, THAT SUCKS. WHAT TIME?
RIGHT BEFORE SHIFT. EIGHT OR SO.
WHERE?
HUH?
WHICH INTERSECTION? I'LL PUT OUT SOME FLYERS.
It was a small-town thing to do. It was the sort of thing my dad would've done. I liked him immediately.
HEY, YOU OKAY? YOU GOT A PICTURE OF THIS MUTT?
HUH? YEAH, ACTUALLY. IN MY LOCKER. HIS NAME IS BAXTER. I'M... BRENDAN MILLER. ASSIGNED HERE LAST MONTH. DAY SHIFT.
FRANK MURPHY. THAT EXPLAINS WHY I HAVEN'T SEEN YOU AROUND BEFORE. I'M MOSTLY NIGHT SHIFT. FILLING IN FOR PETERS TODAY. NICE TO MEET YA. MILLER SOUNDS FAMILIAR.
I COME FROM A LONG LINE OF COPS. DAD, UNCLE, GRANDPA... ALL COPS.
NO KIDDIN'! YOU MUST HAVE A LOT OF RESPECT FOR YOUR FAMILY.
YEAH, ACTUALLY, DAD EVEN STOOD UP FOR ALL OF US KIDS ONCE WHEN WE WERE GONNA BE...
PEDERSON
"WELL, IT'S A LONG STORY AND I'M LATE."
NICE TO MEET YOU, FRANK.
YOU TOO. I'LL PUT OUT THE WORD ABOUT YOUR DOG. DON'T WORRY, WE'LL GET HIM BACK.

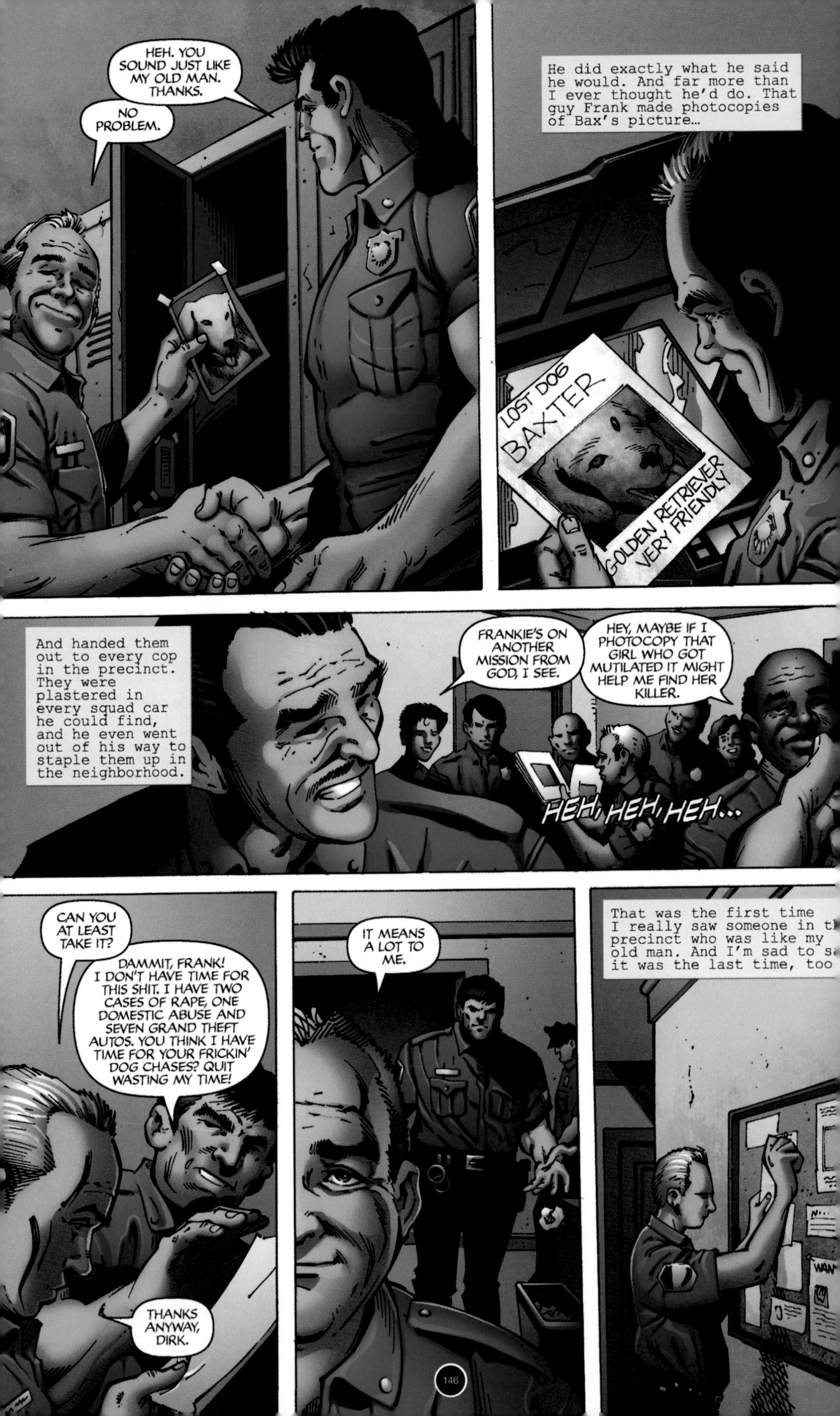
HEH. YOU SOUND JUST LIKE MY OLD MAN. THANKS.
NO PROBLEM.
He did exactly what he said he would. And far more than I ever thought he'd do. That guy Frank made photocopies of Bax's picture...
LOST DOG
BAXTER
GOLDEN RETRIEVER
VERY FRIENDLY
And handed them out to every cop in the precinct. They were plastered in every squad car he could find, and he even went out of his way to staple them up in the neighborhood.
FRANKIE'S ON ANOTHER MISSION FROM GOD, I SEE.
HEY, MAYBE IF I PHOTOCOPY THAT GIRL WHO GOT MUTILATED IT MIGHT HELP ME FIND HER KILLER.
HEH, HEH, HEH...
CAN YOU AT LEAST TAKE IT?
DAMMIT, FRANK! I DON'T HAVE TIME FOR THIS SHIT. I HAVE TWO CASES OF RAPE, ONE DOMESTIC ABUSE AND SEVEN GRAND THEFT AUTOS. YOU THINK I HAVE TIME FOR YOUR FRICKIN' DOG CHASES? QUIT WASTING MY TIME!
THANKS ANYWAY, DIRK.
IT MEANS A LOT TO ME.
That was the first time I really saw someone in t precinct who was like my old man. And I'm sad to s it was the last time, too

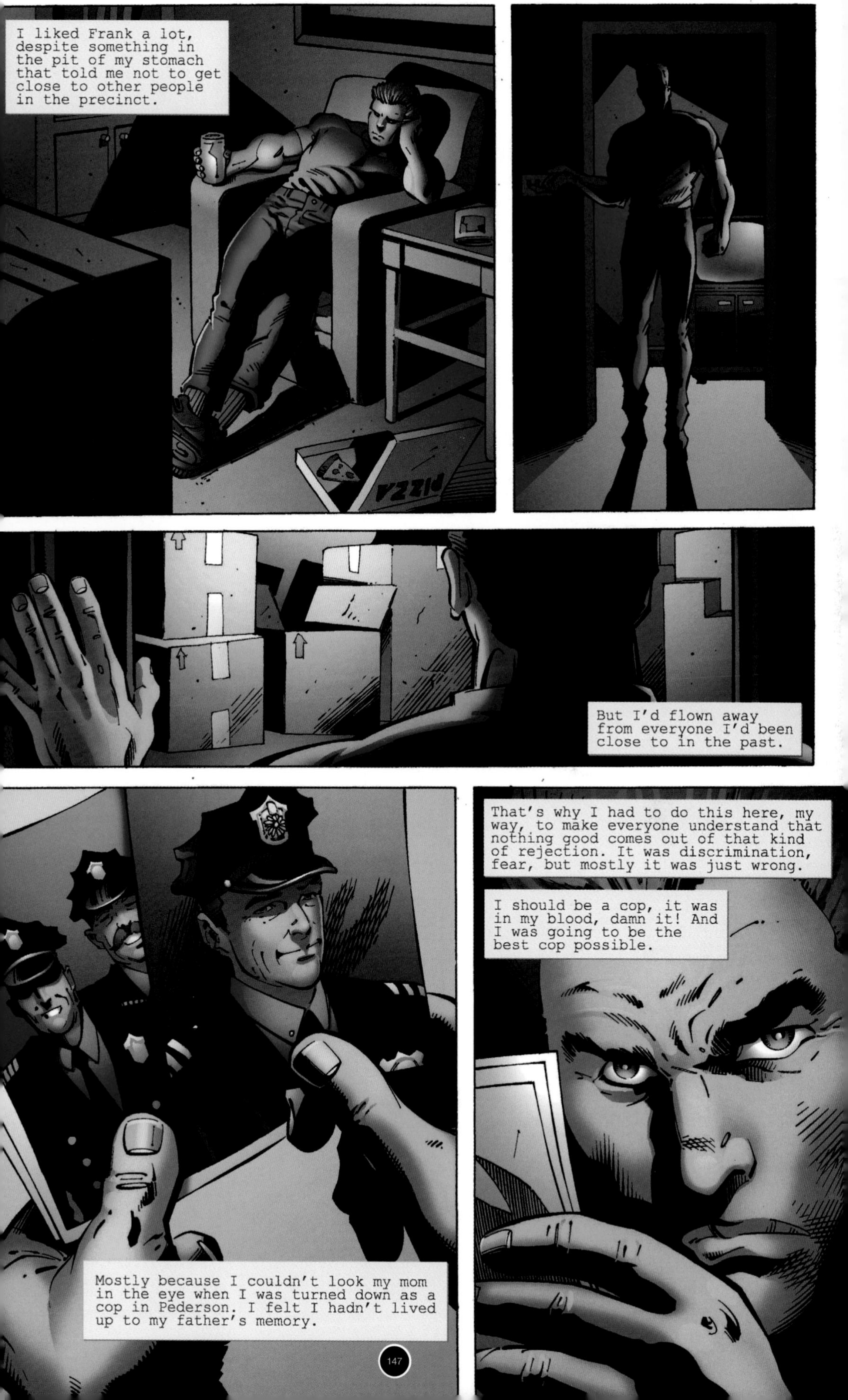
I liked Frank a lot, despite something in the pit of my stomach that told me not to get close to other people in the precinct.
PIZZA
But I'd flown away from everyone I'd been close to in the past.
Mostly because I couldn't look my mom in the eye when I was turned down as a cop in Pederson. I felt I hadn't lived up to my father's memory.
That's why I had to do this here, my way, to make everyone understand that nothing good comes out of that kind of rejection. It was discrimination, fear, but mostly it was just wrong.
I should be a cop, it was in my blood, damn it! And I was going to be the best cop possible.

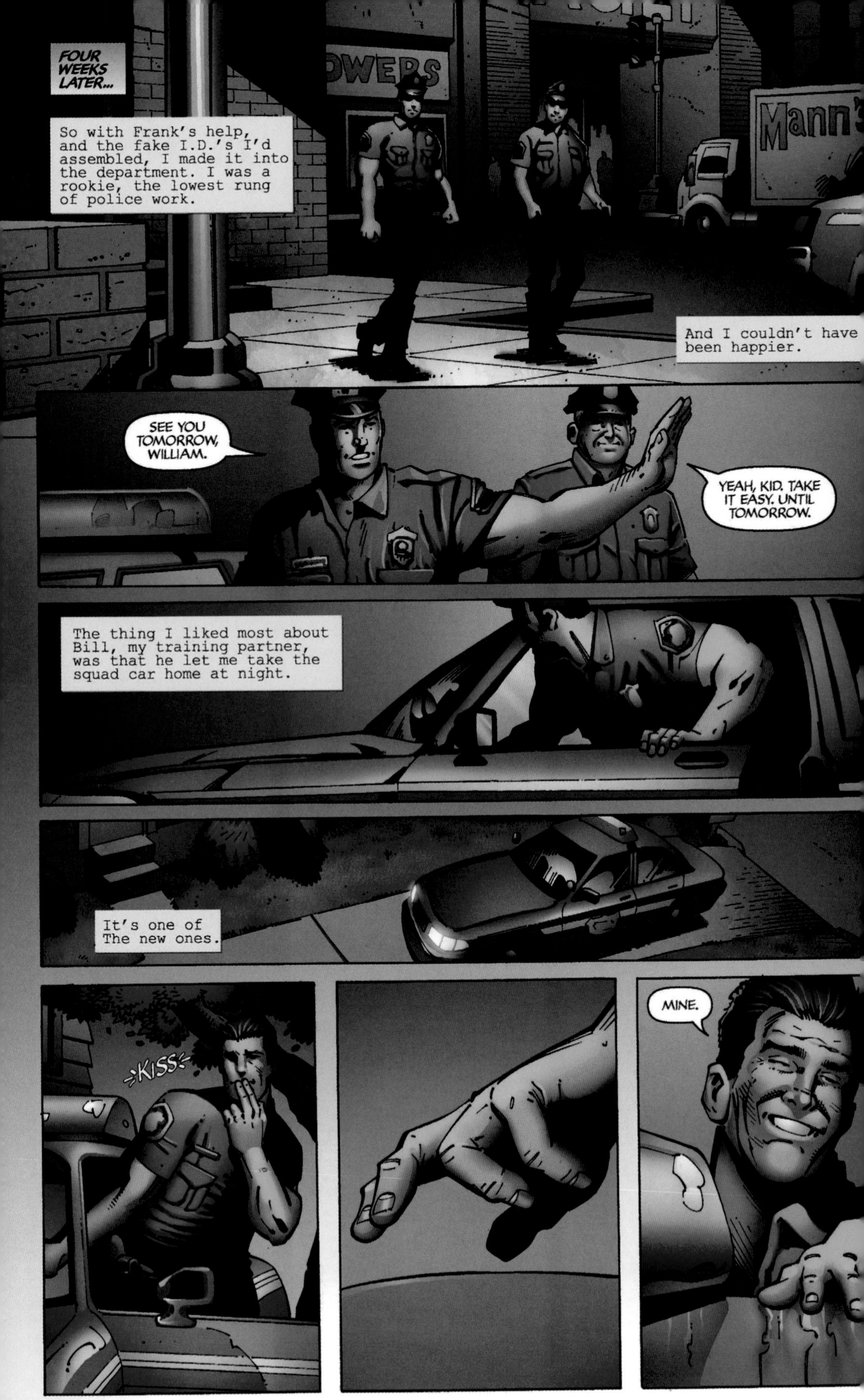
FOUR WEEKS LATER...
So with Frank's help, and the fake I.D.'s I'd assembled, I made it into the department. I was a rookie, the lowest rung of police work.
And I couldn't have been happier.
SEE YOU TOMORROW, WILLIAM.
YEAH, KID. TAKE IT EASY. UNTIL TOMORROW.
The thing I liked most about Bill, my training partner, was that he let me take the squad car home at night.
It's one of The new ones.
KISS
MINE.

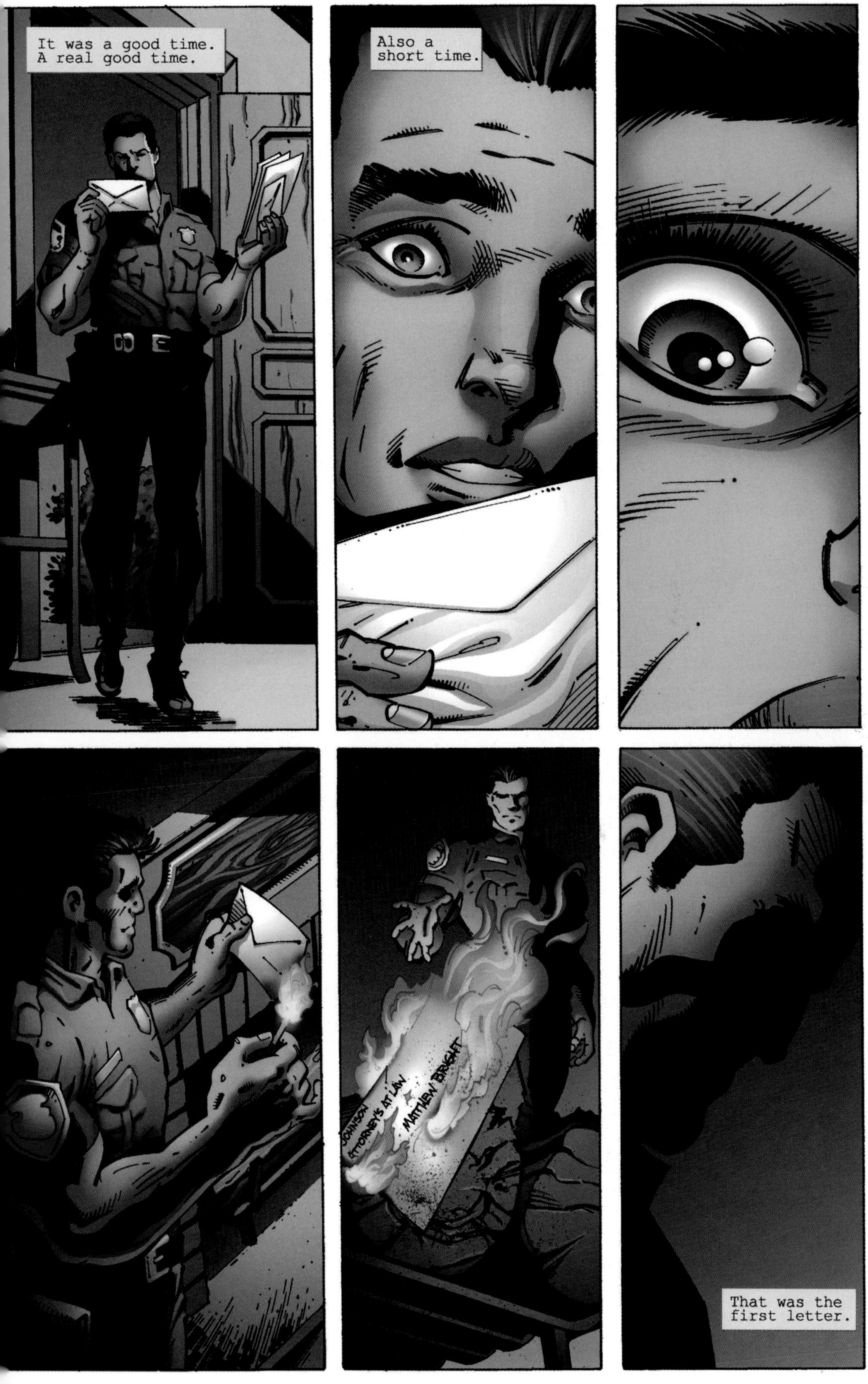
It was a good time. A real good time.
Also a short time.
JOHNSON
ATTORNEYS AT LAW
MATTHEW BRIGHT
That was the first letter.

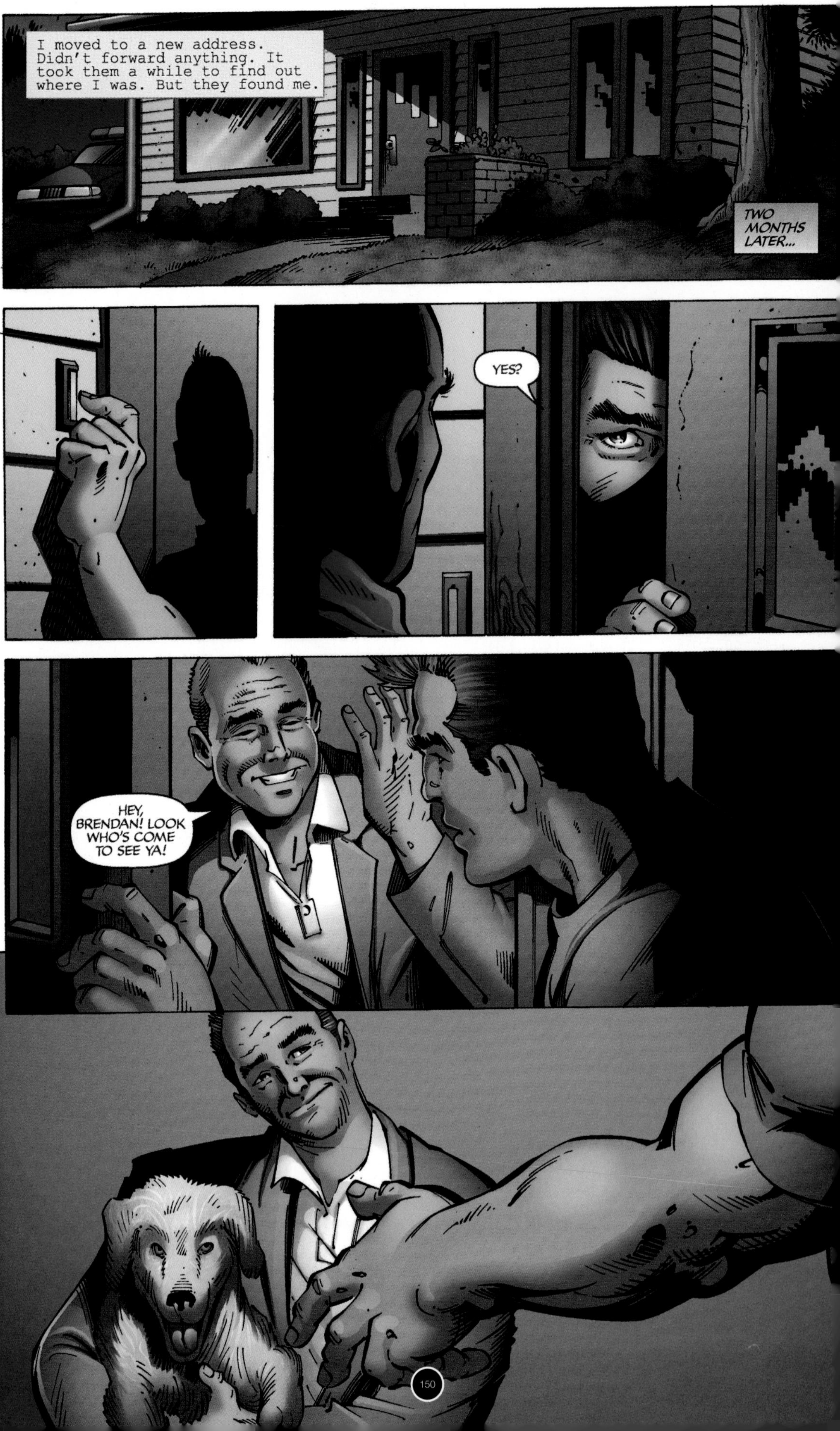
I moved to a new address. Didn't forward anything. It took them a while to find out where I was. But they found me.
TWO MONTHS LATER...
YES?
HEY, BRENDAN! LOOK WHO'S COME TO SEE YA!

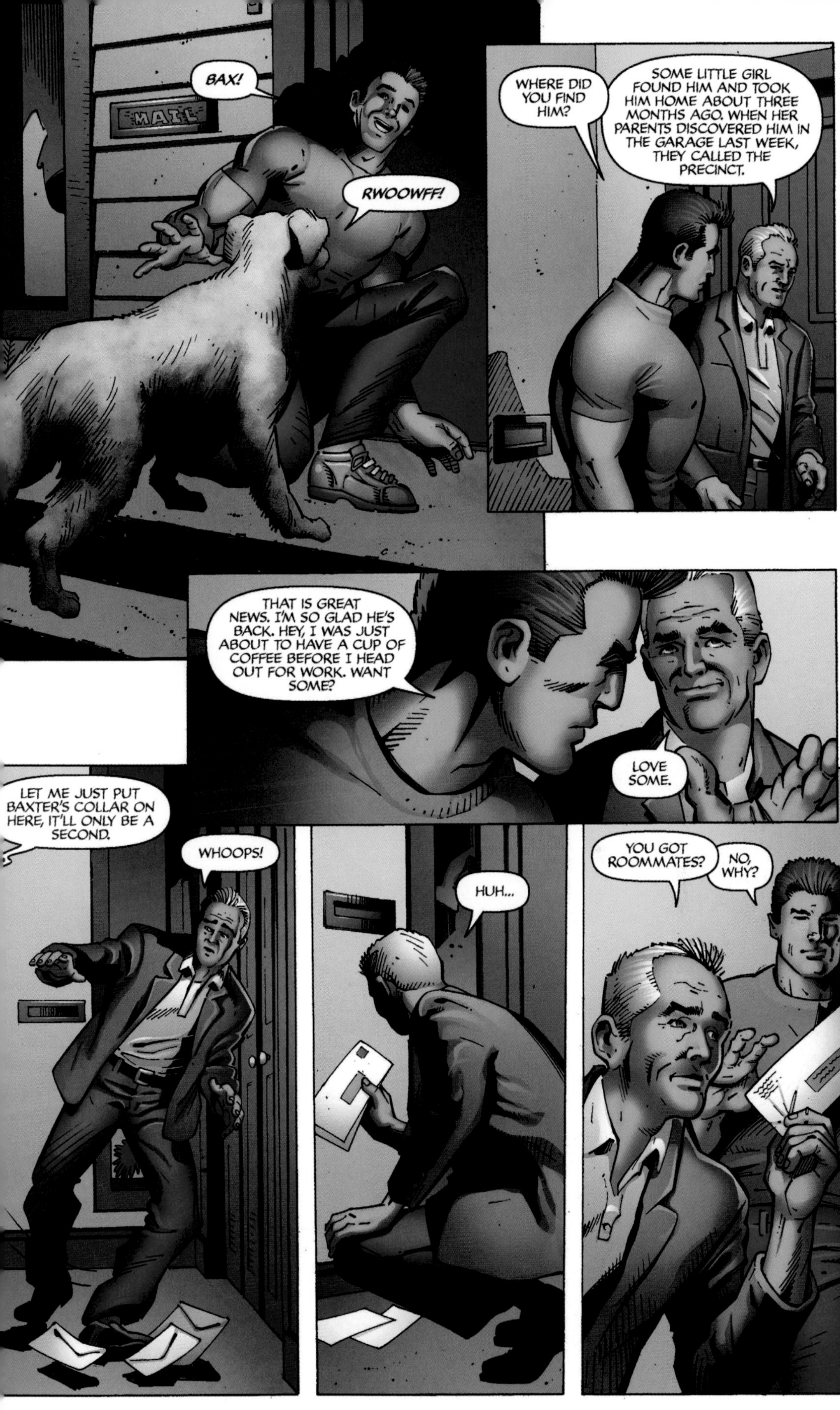
BAX!
RWOOWFF!
WHERE DID YOU FIND HIM?
SOME LITTLE GIRL FOUND HIM AND TOOK HIM HOME ABOUT THREE MONTHS AGO. WHEN HER PARENTS DISCOVERED HIM IN THE GARAGE LAST WEEK, THEY CALLED THE PRECINCT.
THAT IS GREAT NEWS. I'M SO GLAD HE'S BACK. HEY, I WAS JUST ABOUT TO HAVE A CUP OF COFFEE BEFORE I HEAD OUT FOR WORK. WANT SOME?
LOVE SOME.
LET ME JUST PUT BAXTER'S COLLAR ON HERE, IT'LL ONLY BE A SECOND.
WHOOPS!
HUH...
YOU GOT ROOMMATES?
NO, WHY?

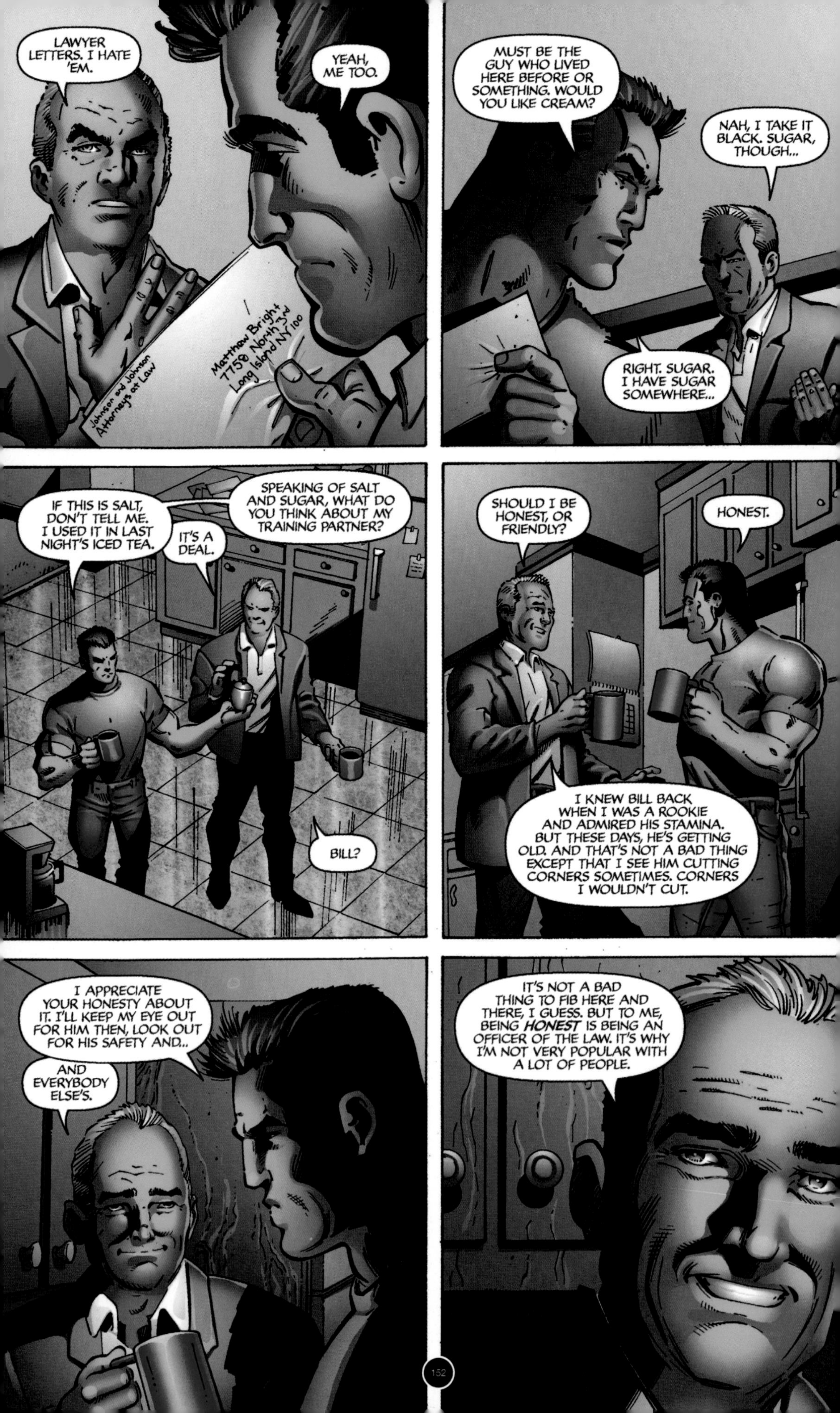
LAWYER LETTERS. I HATE 'EM.
YEAH, ME TOO.
Johnson and Johnson Attorneys at Law
Matthew Bright 7758 North 3rd Long Island NY 100
MUST BE THE GUY WHO LIVED HERE BEFORE OR SOMETHING. WOULD YOU LIKE CREAM?
NAH, I TAKE IT BLACK. SUGAR, THOUGH...
RIGHT. SUGAR. I HAVE SUGAR SOMEWHERE...
IF THIS IS SALT, DON'T TELL ME. I USED IT IN LAST NIGHT'S ICED TEA.
IT'S A DEAL.
SPEAKING OF SALT AND SUGAR, WHAT DO YOU THINK ABOUT MY TRAINING PARTNER?
BILL?
SHOULD I BE HONEST, OR FRIENDLY?
HONEST.
I KNEW BILL BACK WHEN I WAS A ROOKIE AND ADMIRED HIS STAMINA. BUT THESE DAYS, HE'S GETTING OLD. AND THAT'S NOT A BAD THING EXCEPT THAT I SEE HIM CUTTING CORNERS SOMETIMES. CORNERS I WOULDN'T CUT.
I APPRECIATE YOUR HONESTY ABOUT IT. I'LL KEEP MY EYE OUT FOR HIM THEN, LOOK OUT FOR HIS SAFETY AND...
AND EVERYBODY ELSE'S.
IT'S NOT A BAD THING TO FIB HERE AND THERE, I GUESS. BUT TO ME, BEING *HONEST* IS BEING AN OFFICER OF THE LAW. IT'S WHY I'M NOT VERY POPULAR WITH A LOT OF PEOPLE.

~SQUEELLCHH~
ALL-UNITS-NEEDED-
ON-HIT-TO-1414 SEVENTH-
STREET-CONVENIENT-
MART~ ~KSSHHH~
~SQUELCH~ GUNFIRE~
DO YOU COPY?

I'M ON IT!

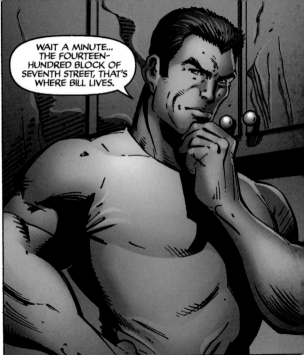

WAIT A MINUTE...
THE FOURTEEN-
HUNDRED BLOCK OF
SEVENTH STREET, THAT'S
WHERE BILL LIVES.

COME ON.

SQUEEEEEAAALLLLLL!

DON'T
SHOOT.

...JUST COME A
LITTLE CLOSER
INSTEAD.

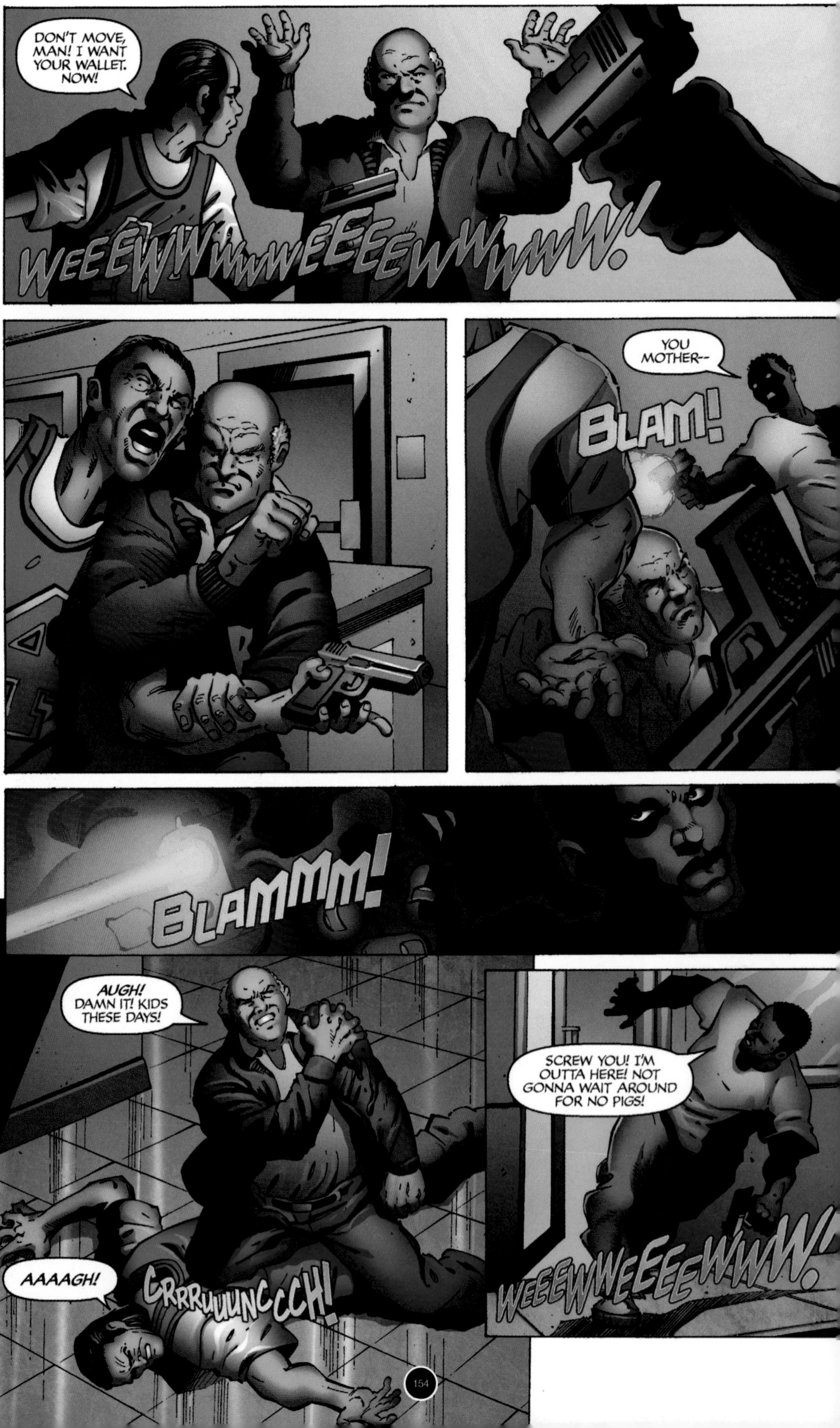

DON'T MOVE, MAN! I WANT YOUR WALLET. NOW!
WEEEWWwwwEEEEwwwwwW!
YOU MOTHER--
BLAM!
BLAMMM!
AUGH! DAMN IT! KIDS THESE DAYS!
AAAAGH!
CRRRUUUNCCCH!
SCREW YOU! I'M OUTTA HERE! NOT GONNA WAIT AROUND FOR NO PIGS!
WEEEWWEEEEWWW!

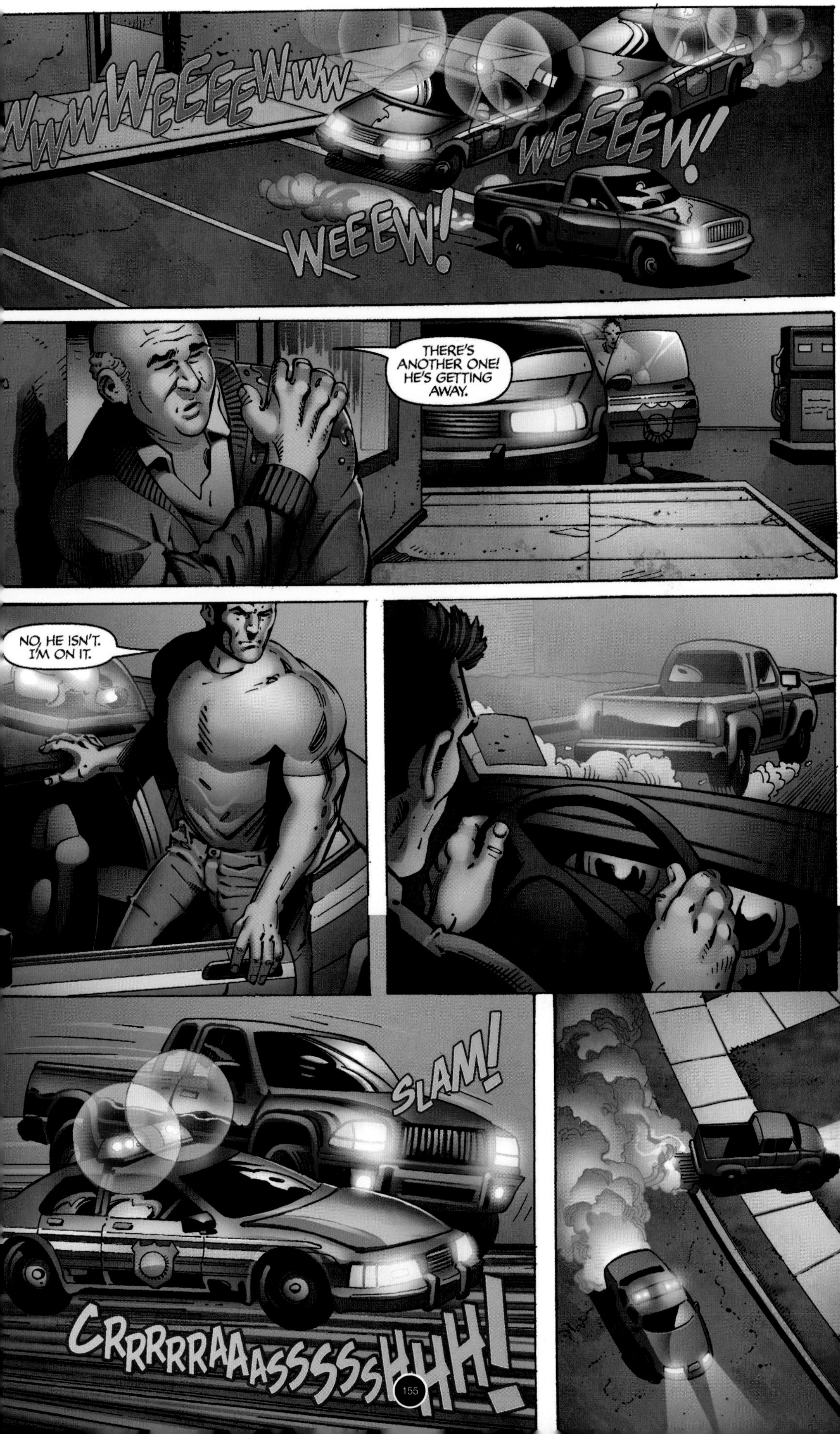
WWWWEEEEWWW
WEEEEW!
WEEEW!
THERE'S ANOTHER ONE! HE'S GETTING AWAY.
NO, HE ISN'T. I'M ON IT.
SLAM!
CRRRRRAAASSSSSHHH!

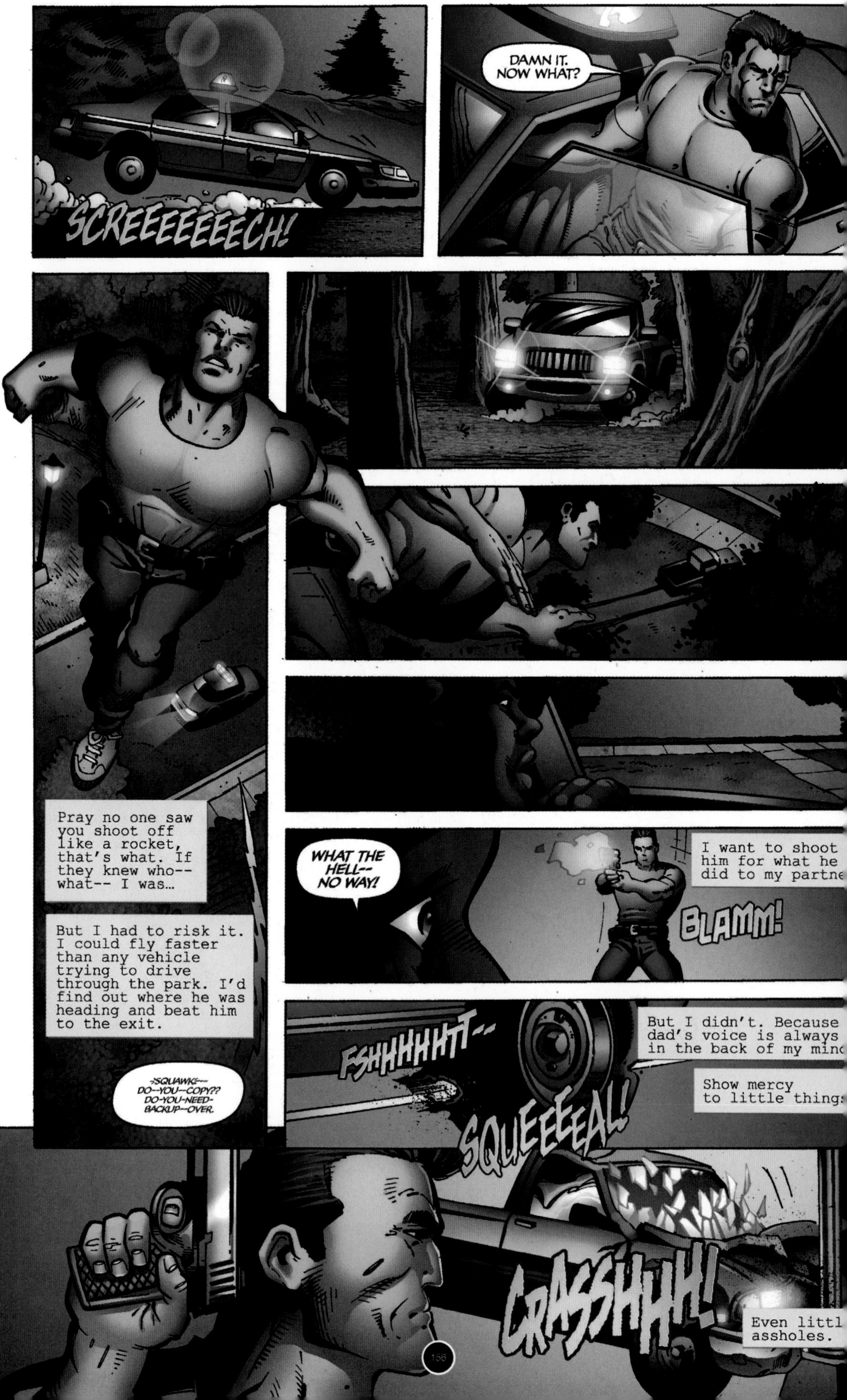
SCREEEEEEECH!
DAMN IT. NOW WHAT?
Pray no one saw you shoot off like a rocket, that's what. If they knew who-- what-- I was...
But I had to risk it. I could fly faster than any vehicle trying to drive through the park. I'd find out where he was heading and beat him to the exit.
SQUAWK-- DO--YOU--COPY?? DO-YOU-NEED-BACKUP--OVER.
WHAT THE HELL-- NO WAY!
I want to shoot him for what he did to my partne
BLAMM!
But I didn't. Because dad's voice is always in the back of my minc
Show mercy to little thing:
FSHHHHHTT--
SQUEEEEAL!
CRASSHHH!
Even littl assholes.

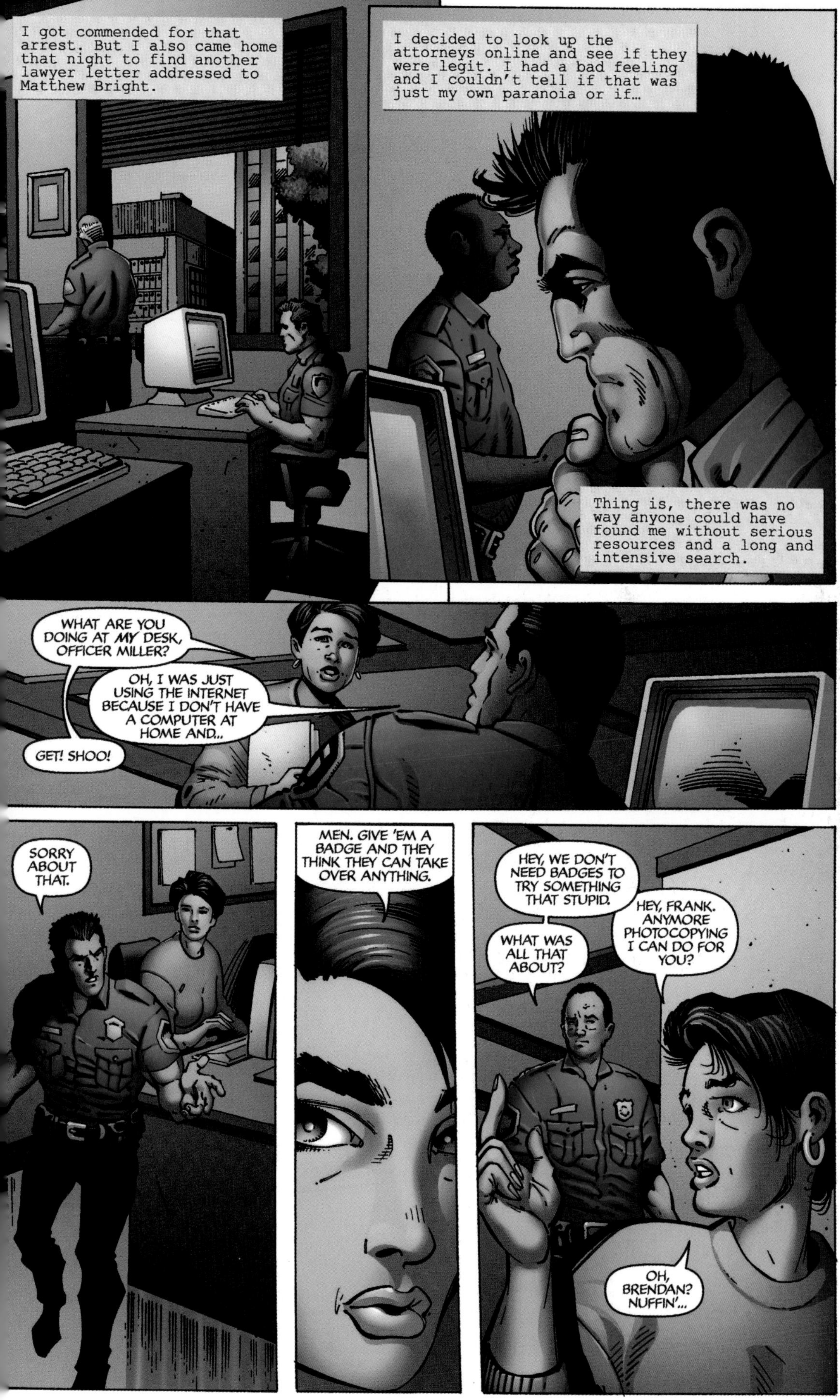
I got commended for that arrest. But I also came home that night to find another lawyer letter addressed to Matthew Bright.
I decided to look up the attorneys online and see if they were legit. I had a bad feeling and I couldn't tell if that was just my own paranoia or if...
Thing is, there was no way anyone could have found me without serious resources and a long and intensive search.
WHAT ARE YOU DOING AT MY DESK, OFFICER MILLER?
OH, I WAS JUST USING THE INTERNET BECAUSE I DON'T HAVE A COMPUTER AT HOME AND...
GET! SHOO!
SORRY ABOUT THAT.
MEN. GIVE 'EM A BADGE AND THEY THINK THEY CAN TAKE OVER ANYTHING.
HEY, WE DON'T NEED BADGES TO TRY SOMETHING THAT STUPID.
HEY, FRANK. ANYMORE PHOTOCOPYING I CAN DO FOR YOU?
WHAT WAS ALL THAT ABOUT?
OH, BRENDAN? NUFFIN'...

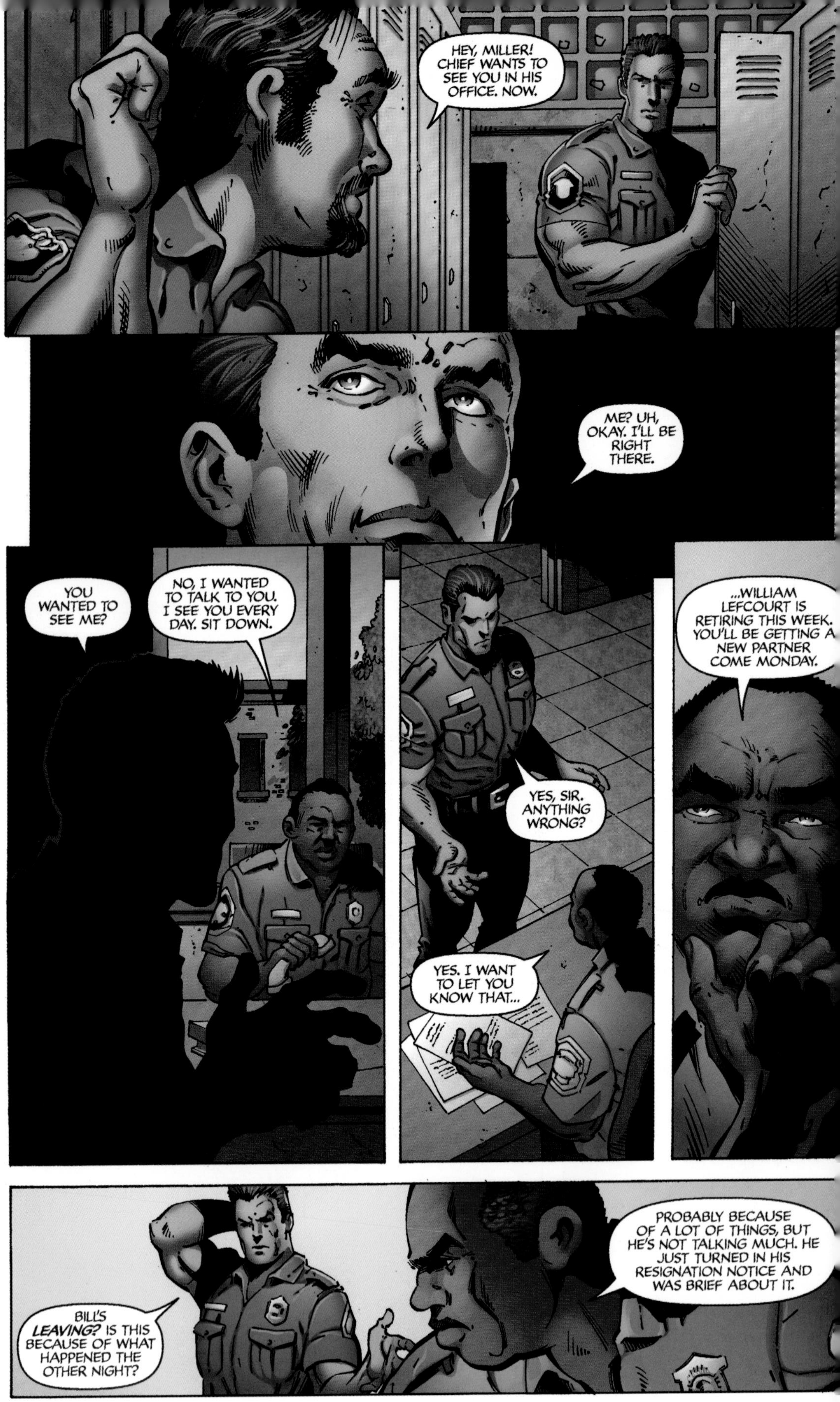
HEY, MILLER! CHIEF WANTS TO SEE YOU IN HIS OFFICE. NOW.
ME? UH, OKAY. I'LL BE RIGHT THERE.
YOU WANTED TO SEE ME?
NO, I WANTED TO TALK TO YOU. I SEE YOU EVERY DAY. SIT DOWN.
YES, SIR. ANYTHING WRONG?
YES. I WANT TO LET YOU KNOW THAT...
...WILLIAM LEFCOURT IS RETIRING THIS WEEK. YOU'LL BE GETTING A NEW PARTNER COME MONDAY.
BILL'S *LEAVING?* IS THIS BECAUSE OF WHAT HAPPENED THE OTHER NIGHT?
PROBABLY BECAUSE OF A LOT OF THINGS, BUT HE'S NOT TALKING MUCH. HE JUST TURNED IN HIS RESIGNATION NOTICE AND WAS BRIEF ABOUT IT.

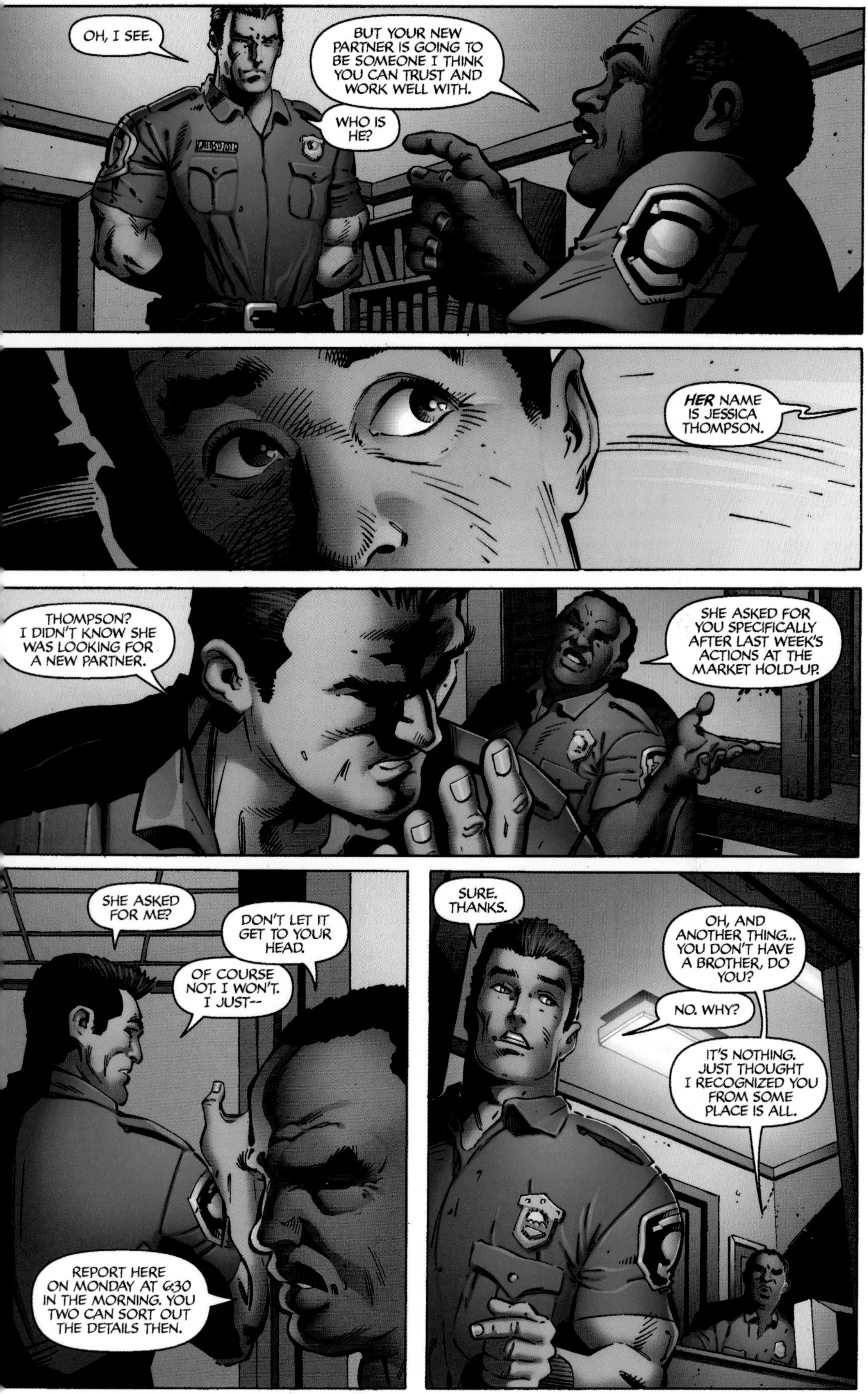
OH, I SEE.
BUT YOUR NEW PARTNER IS GOING TO BE SOMEONE I THINK YOU CAN TRUST AND WORK WELL WITH.
WHO IS HE?
HER NAME IS JESSICA THOMPSON.
THOMPSON? I DIDN'T KNOW SHE WAS LOOKING FOR A NEW PARTNER.
SHE ASKED FOR YOU SPECIFICALLY AFTER LAST WEEK'S ACTIONS AT THE MARKET HOLD-UP.
SHE ASKED FOR ME?
DON'T LET IT GET TO YOUR HEAD.
OF COURSE NOT. I WON'T. I JUST--
REPORT HERE ON MONDAY AT 6:30 IN THE MORNING. YOU TWO CAN SORT OUT THE DETAILS THEN.
SURE. THANKS.
OH, AND ANOTHER THING... YOU DON'T HAVE A BROTHER, DO YOU?
NO. WHY?
IT'S NOTHING. JUST THOUGHT I RECOGNIZED YOU FROM SOME PLACE IS ALL.

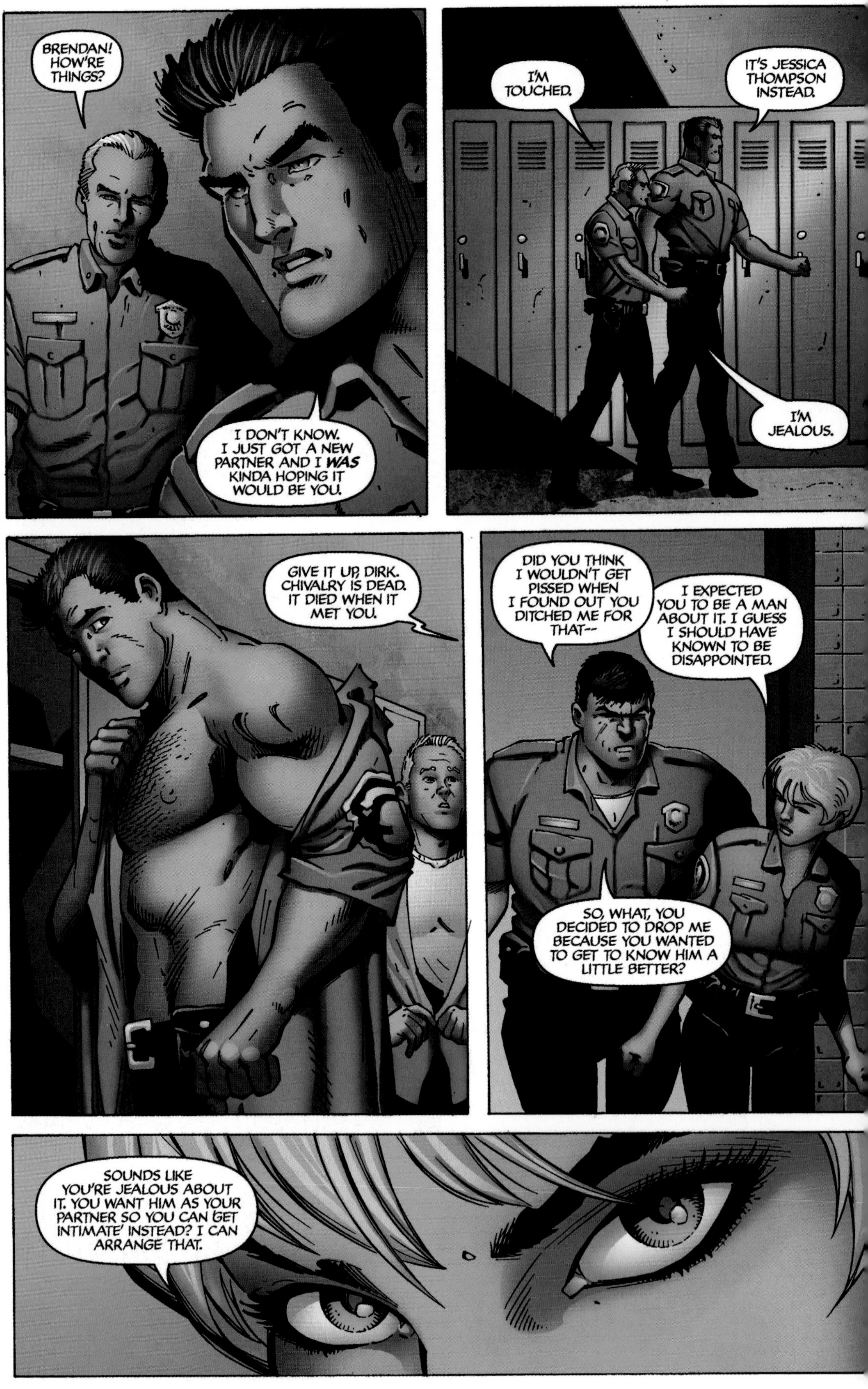
BRENDAN! HOW'RE THINGS?
I DON'T KNOW. I JUST GOT A NEW PARTNER AND I *WAS* KINDA HOPING IT WOULD BE YOU.
I'M TOUCHED.
IT'S JESSICA THOMPSON INSTEAD.
I'M JEALOUS.
GIVE IT UP, DIRK. CHIVALRY IS DEAD. IT DIED WHEN IT MET YOU.
DID YOU THINK I WOULDN'T GET PISSED WHEN I FOUND OUT YOU DITCHED ME FOR THAT--
I EXPECTED YOU TO BE A MAN ABOUT IT. I GUESS I SHOULD HAVE KNOWN TO BE DISAPPOINTED.
SO, WHAT, YOU DECIDED TO DROP ME BECAUSE YOU WANTED TO GET TO KNOW HIM A LITTLE BETTER?
SOUNDS LIKE YOU'RE JEALOUS ABOUT IT. YOU WANT HIM AS YOUR PARTNER SO YOU CAN GET 'INTIMATE' INSTEAD? I CAN ARRANGE THAT.

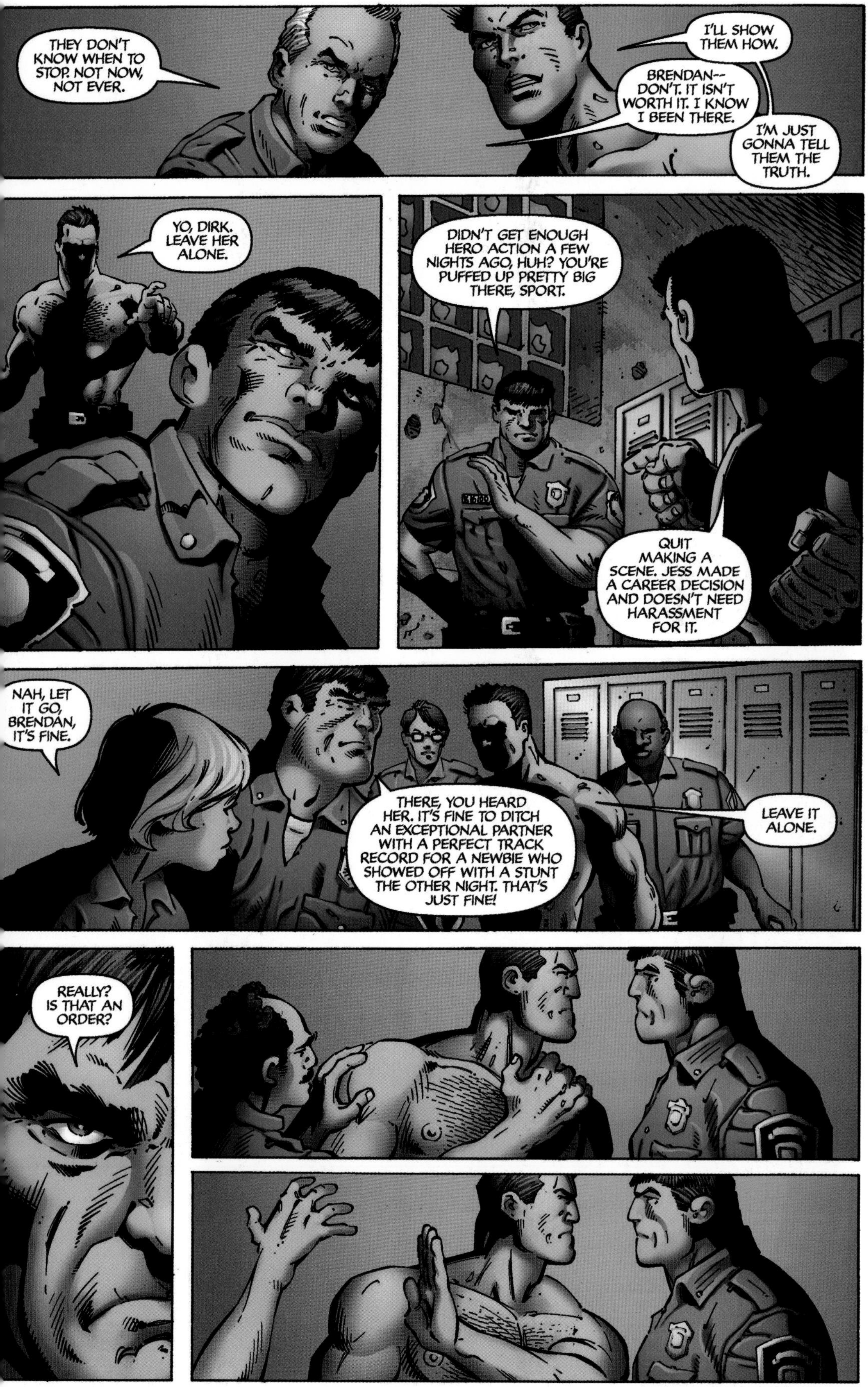
THEY DON'T KNOW WHEN TO STOP. NOT NOW, NOT EVER.
I'LL SHOW THEM HOW.
BRENDAN-- DON'T. IT ISN'T WORTH IT. I KNOW I BEEN THERE.
I'M JUST GONNA TELL THEM THE TRUTH.
YO, DIRK. LEAVE HER ALONE.
DIDN'T GET ENOUGH HERO ACTION A FEW NIGHTS AGO, HUH? YOU'RE PUFFED UP PRETTY BIG THERE, SPORT.
QUIT MAKING A SCENE. JESS MADE A CAREER DECISION AND DOESN'T NEED HARASSMENT FOR IT.
NAH, LET IT GO, BRENDAN, IT'S FINE.
THERE, YOU HEARD HER. IT'S FINE TO DITCH AN EXCEPTIONAL PARTNER WITH A PERFECT TRACK RECORD FOR A NEWBIE WHO SHOWED OFF WITH A STUNT THE OTHER NIGHT. THAT'S JUST FINE!
LEAVE IT ALONE.
REALLY? IS THAT AN ORDER?

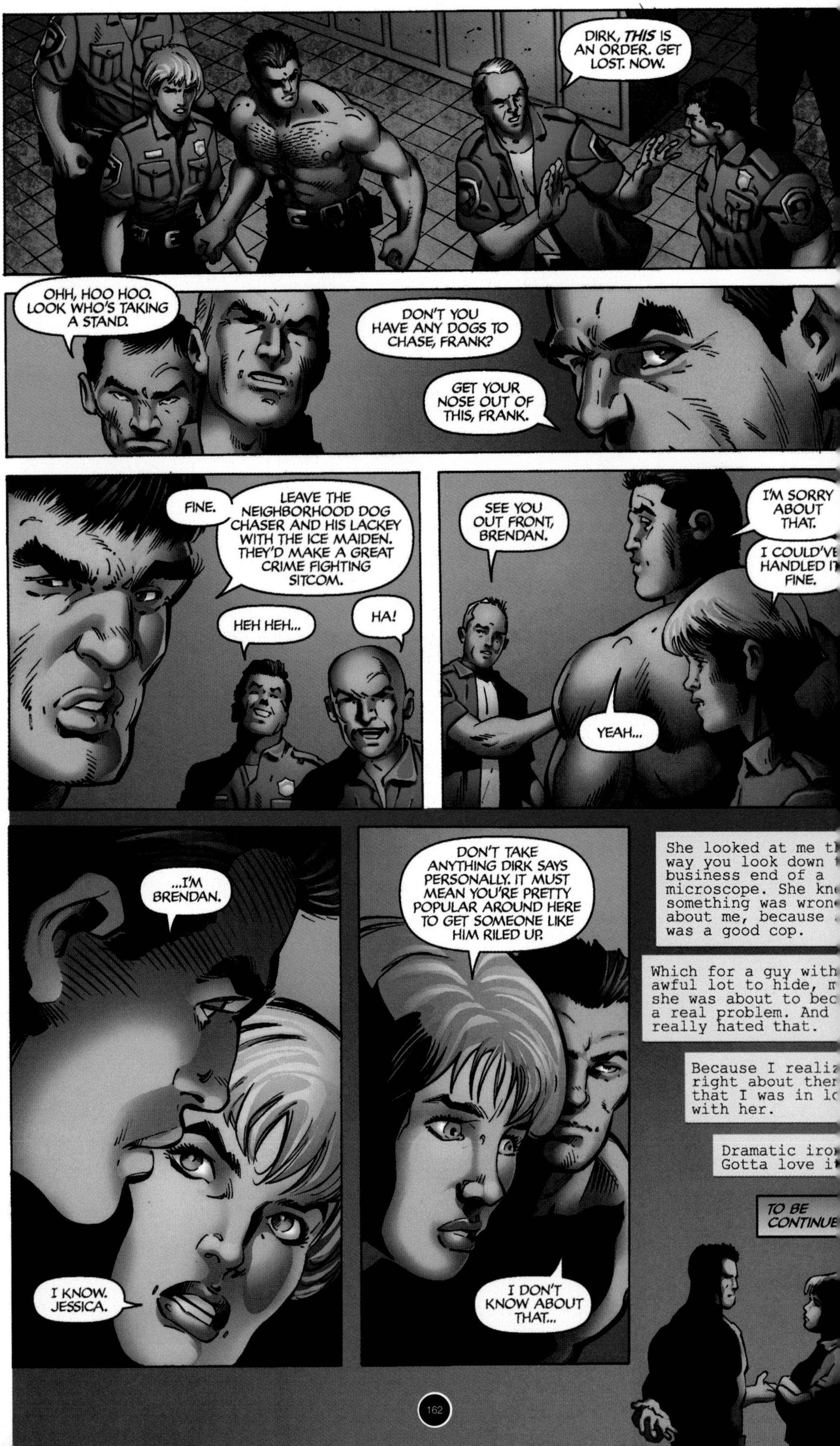
DIRK, THIS IS AN ORDER. GET LOST. NOW.
OHH, HOO HOO. LOOK WHO'S TAKING A STAND.
DON'T YOU HAVE ANY DOGS TO CHASE, FRANK?
GET YOUR NOSE OUT OF THIS, FRANK.
FINE.
LEAVE THE NEIGHBORHOOD DOG CHASER AND HIS LACKEY WITH THE ICE MAIDEN. THEY'D MAKE A GREAT CRIME FIGHTING SITCOM.
HEH HEH...
HA!
SEE YOU OUT FRONT, BRENDAN.
I'M SORRY ABOUT THAT.
I COULD'V HANDLED I FINE.
YEAH...
...I'M BRENDAN.
I KNOW. JESSICA.
DON'T TAKE ANYTHING DIRK SAYS PERSONALLY. IT MUST MEAN YOU'RE PRETTY POPULAR AROUND HERE TO GET SOMEONE LIKE HIM RILED UP.
I DON'T KNOW ABOUT THAT...
She looked at me t way you look down business end of a microscope. She kn something was wron about me, because was a good cop.
Which for a guy with awful lot to hide, she was about to bec a real problem. And really hated that.
Because I realiz right about ther that I was in l with her.
Dramatic iro Gotta love i
TO BE CONTINUE

It was
the best
of times…

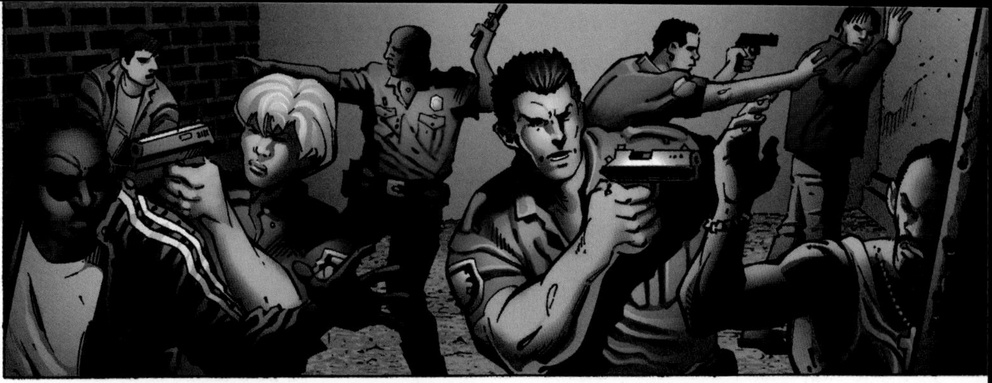

It was
The worst
of times.

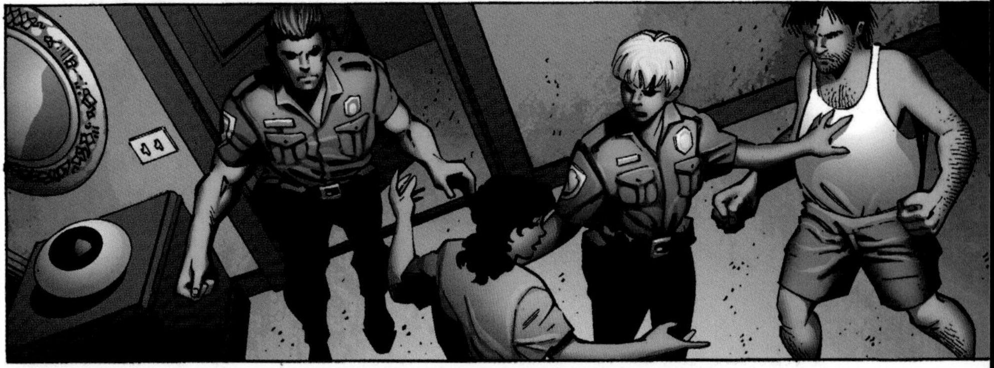

But it was
my first
time outside
in the real
world doing
things that
meant
something.

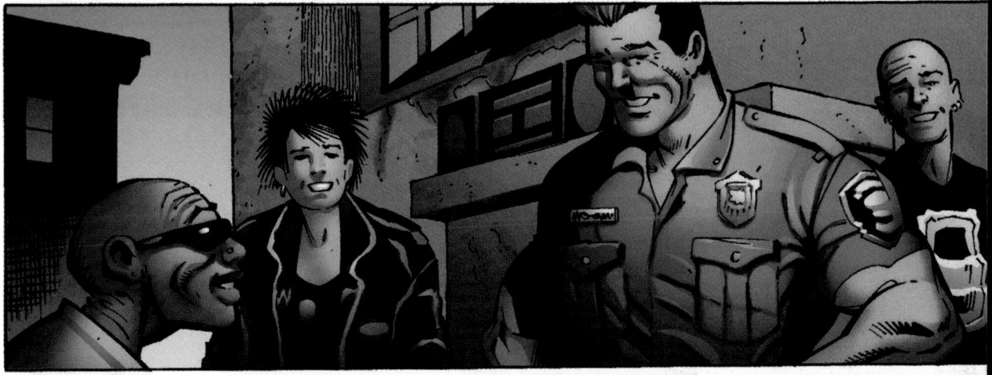

And
stopping
crimes. It
would have
made dad
proud.

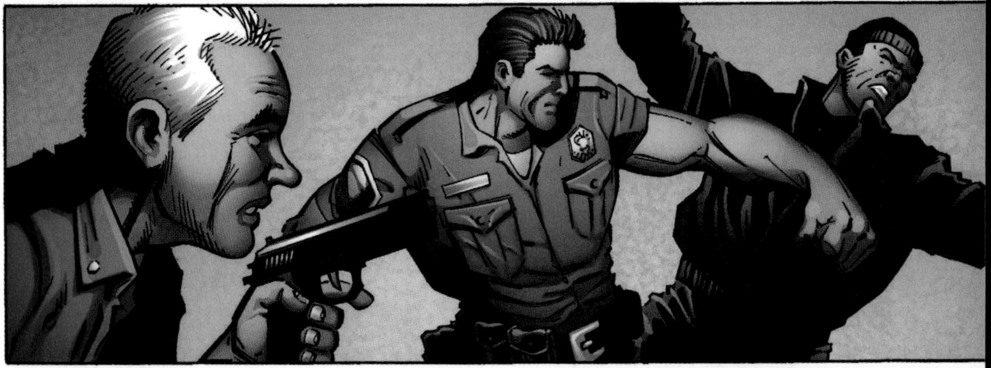

Mom would
have been
proud too. If
I'd ever been
able to call
or write and
tell her.

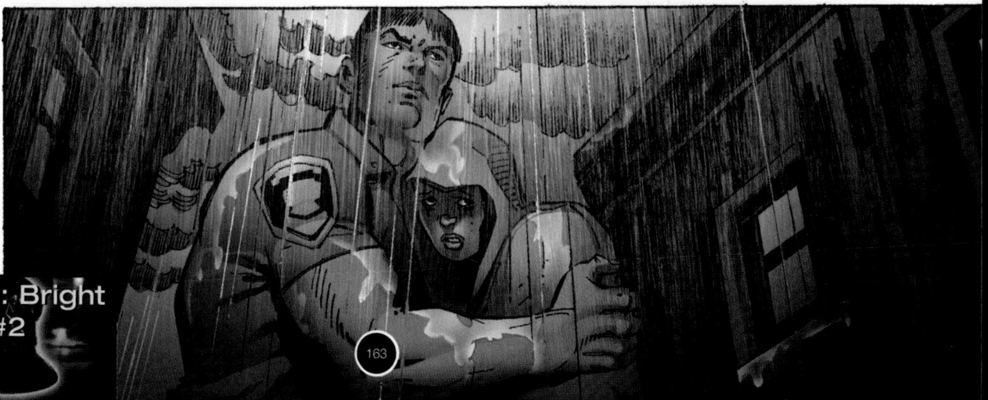

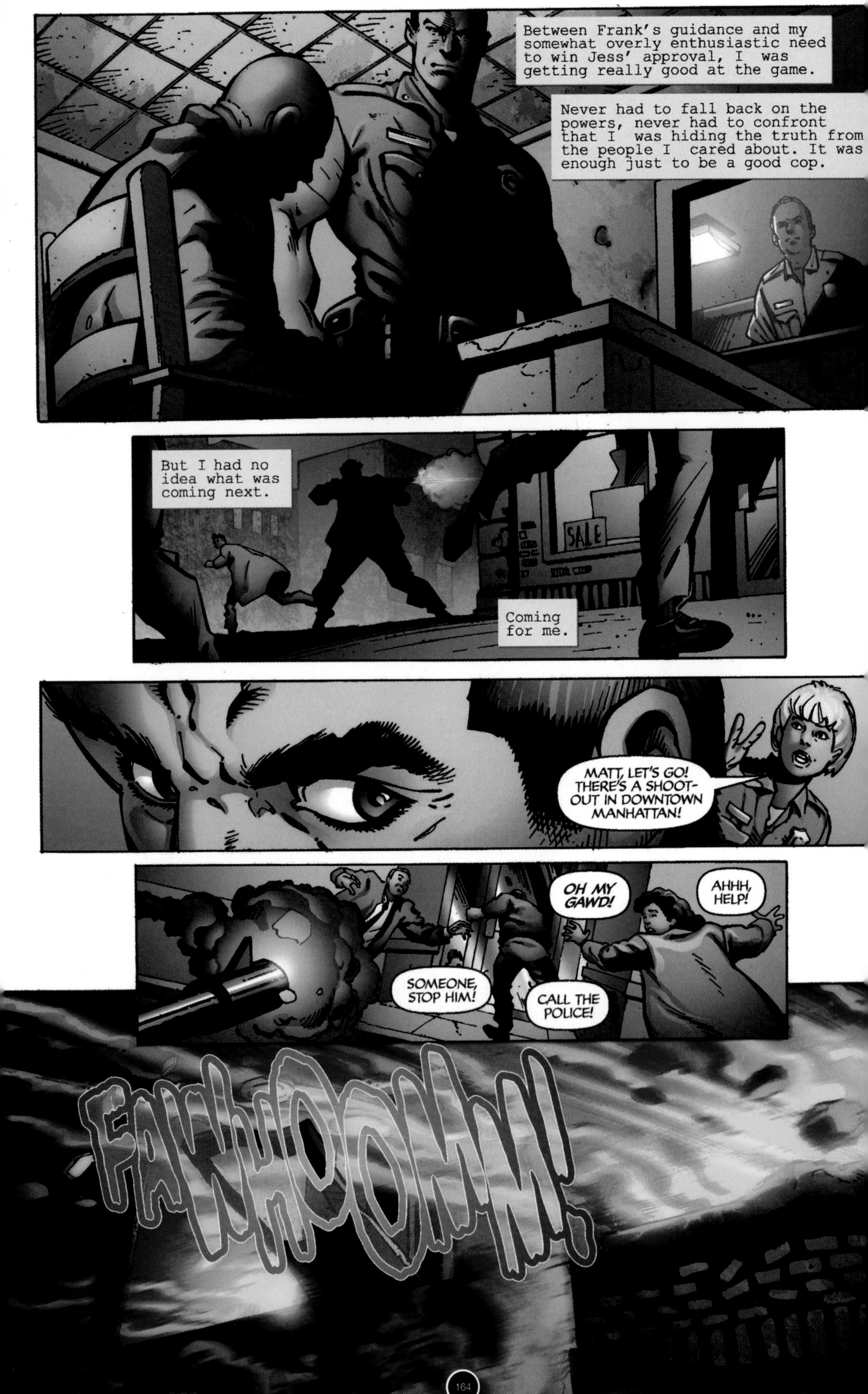
Between Frank's guidance and my somewhat overly enthusiastic need to win Jess' approval, I was getting really good at the game.
Never had to fall back on the powers, never had to confront that I was hiding the truth from the people I cared about. It was enough just to be a good cop.
But I had no idea what was coming next.
SALE
Coming for me.
MATT, LET'S GO! THERE'S A SHOOT-OUT IN DOWNTOWN MANHATTAN!
OH MY GAWD!
AHHH, HELP!
SOMEONE, STOP HIM!
CALL THE POLICE!
FAWHOOOMM!

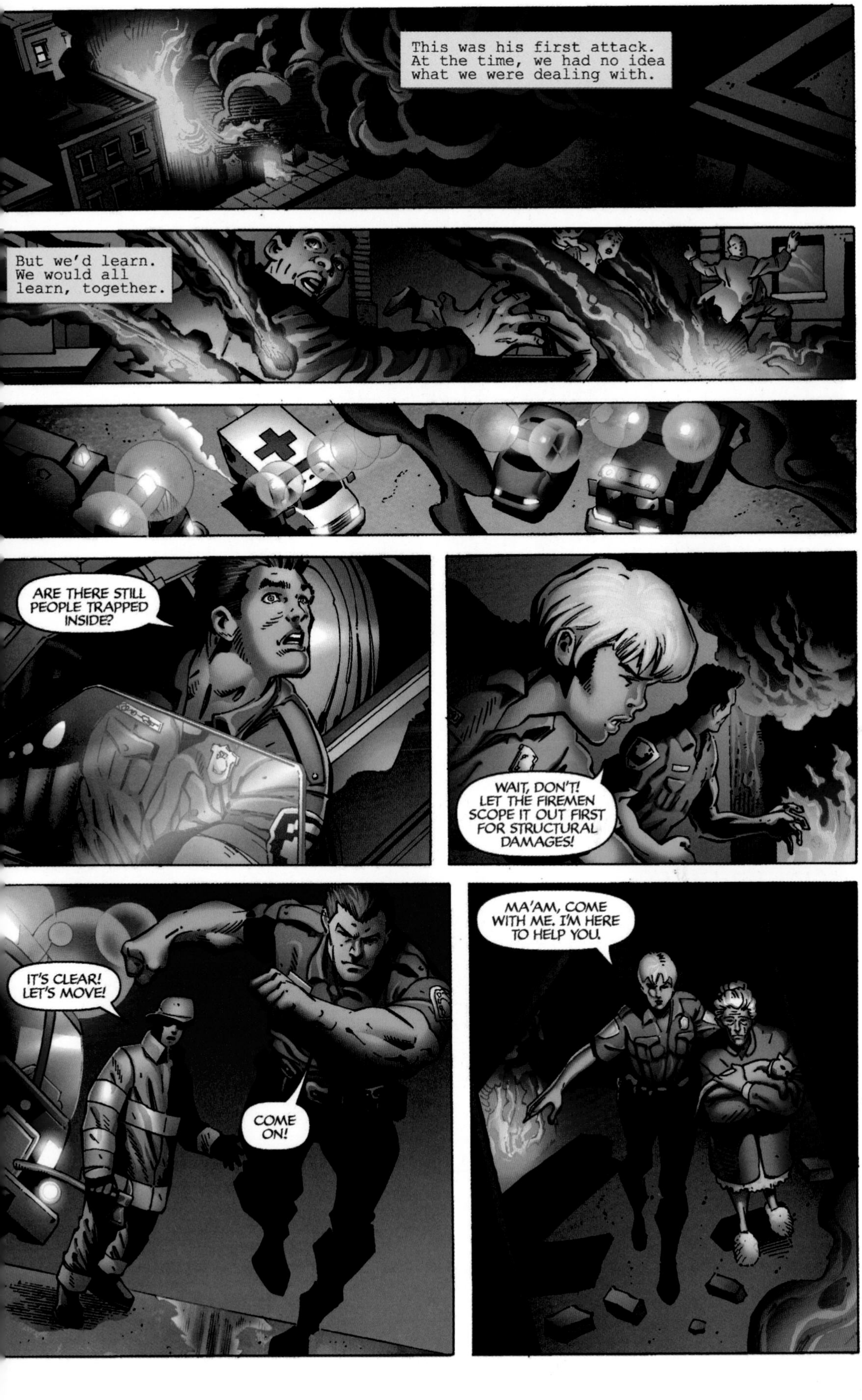
This was his first attack. At the time, we had no idea what we were dealing with.
But we'd learn. We would all learn, together.
ARE THERE STILL PEOPLE TRAPPED INSIDE?
WAIT, DON'T! LET THE FIREMEN SCOPE IT OUT FIRST FOR STRUCTURAL DAMAGES!
IT'S CLEAR! LET'S MOVE!
COME ON!
MA'AM, COME WITH ME. I'M HERE TO HELP YOU.

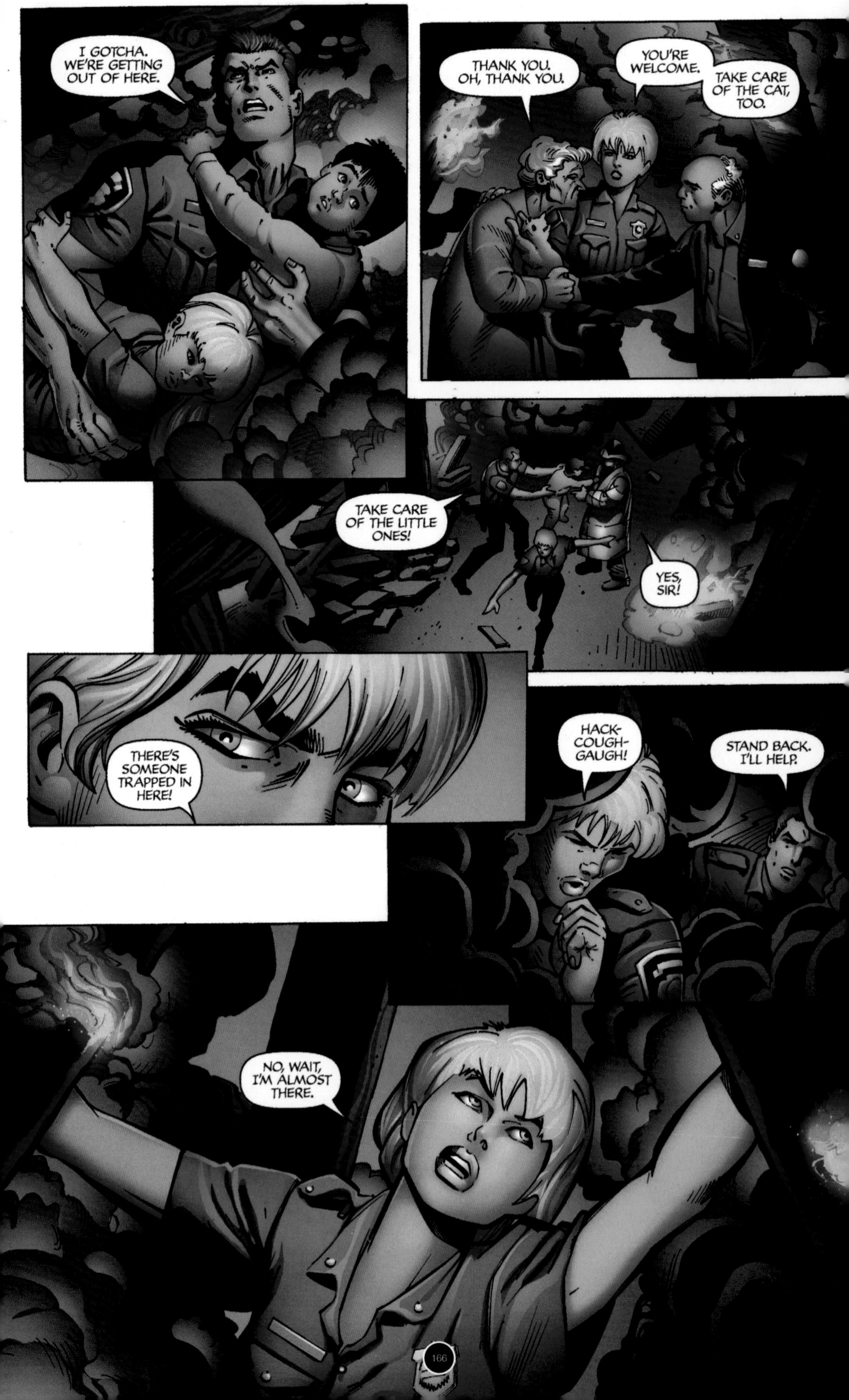
I GOTCHA. WE'RE GETTING OUT OF HERE.
THANK YOU. OH, THANK YOU.
YOU'RE WELCOME.
TAKE CARE OF THE CAT, TOO.
TAKE CARE OF THE LITTLE ONES!
YES, SIR!
THERE'S SOMEONE TRAPPED IN HERE!
HACK-COUGH-GAUGH!
STAND BACK. I'LL HELP.
NO, WAIT, I'M ALMOST THERE.

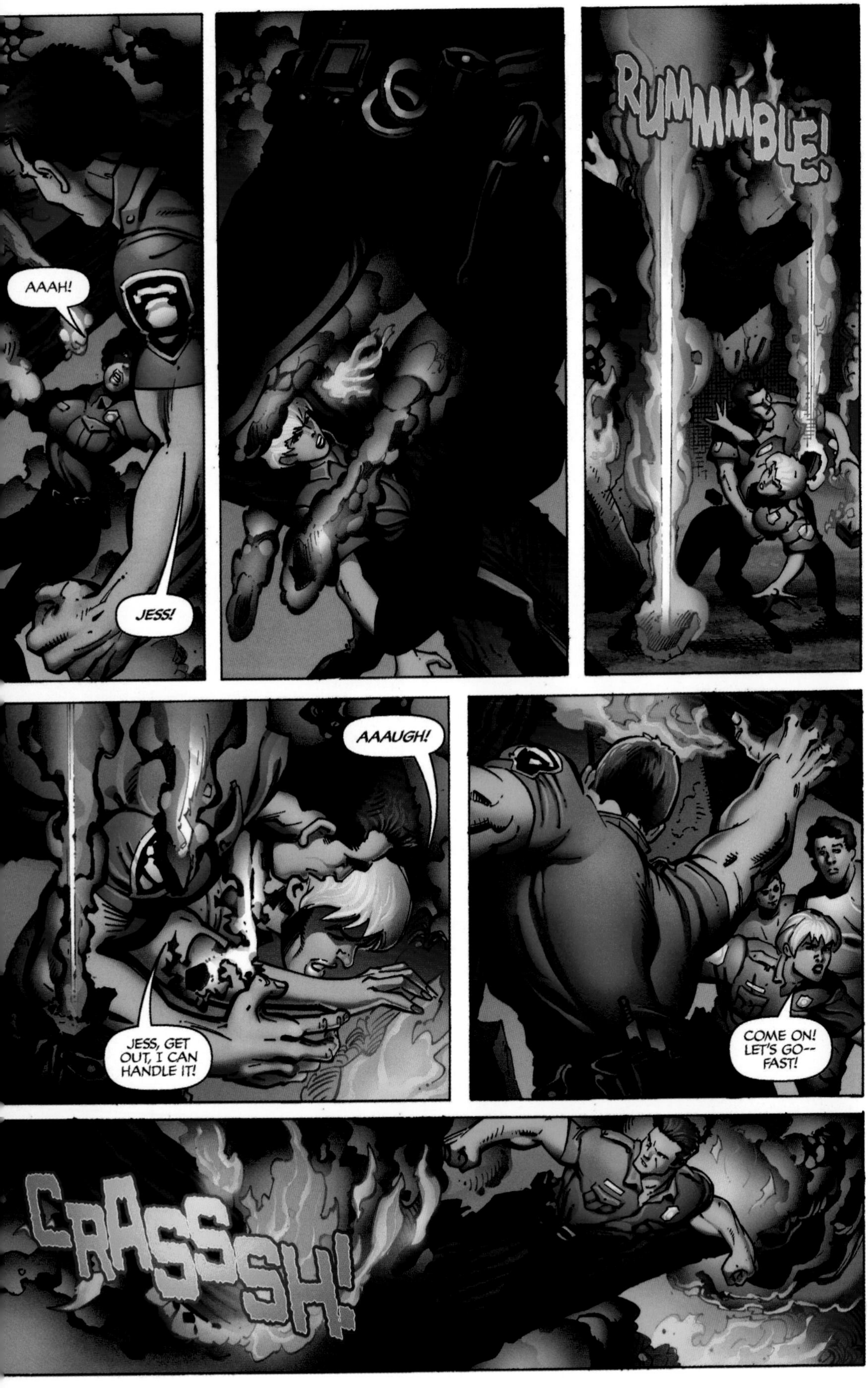
AAAH!
JESS!
RUMMMBLE!
AAAUGH!
JESS, GET OUT, I CAN HANDLE IT!
COME ON! LET'S GO-- FAST!
CRASSSH!

NEW YORK HERALD

BOMBER STRIKES AGAIN

I read up on every attack after that. But I never discussed what happened that day.

FEAR GRIPS CITY

And Jess never asked me about it, even though no man should ever have been able to hold up that much of a collapsing wall.

HEY, MILLER!

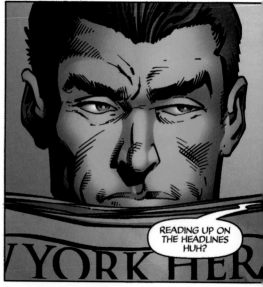

READING UP ON THE HEADLINES HUH?

YEP.

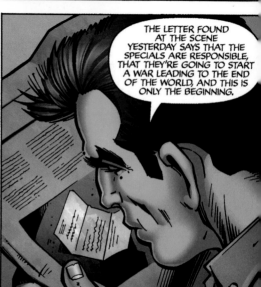

THE LETTER FOUND AT THE SCENE YESTERDAY SAYS THAT THE SPECIALS ARE RESPONSIBLE, THAT THEY'RE GOING TO START A WAR LEADING TO THE END OF THE WORLD, AND THIS IS ONLY THE BEGINNING.

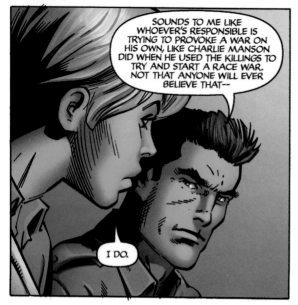

SOUNDS TO ME LIKE WHOEVER'S RESPONSIBLE IS TRYING TO PROVOKE A WAR ON HIS OWN, LIKE CHARLIE MANSON DID WHEN HE USED THE KILLINGS TO TRY AND START A RACE WAR. NOT THAT ANYONE WILL EVER BELIEVE THAT—

I DO.

I DON'T BELIEVE THE SPECIALS HAD ANYTHING TO DO WITH THIS KILLING SPREE. THEY'RE JUST AN EXCUSE FOR SOMEBODY WHO WANTS TO KILL PEOPLE. AND WE'VE ALWAYS HAD THOSE.

ALWAYS.

THE SHEPHERD OF DEATH BOMBER LEFT TAUNTING NOTE, POLICE SAY

The bomber stalking New York city, called "The Shepherd of Death" for his sprays of gunshots before the bombing, and linked to two Manhattan mass bombings left a taunting message for authorities outside the community college last night, police sources confirmed.

"Dear Normals, the end is near," the message said. Police said it was found scrawled inside a Holy Bible one that could easily found in any hotel drawer across the country. It was spotted in a wooden storage entrance.

The message, first reported last

night on WNT-TV (Channel 6) reporter, that the leak about the was the first known Holy Bible of Death. tion from the Shepherd of Death had severely impaired the NYPD.

Despite devoting an increasing NYPD Police Captain Jessica level of resources to the investiga- Thompson, speaking at an early tion authorities have few clues. morning news briefing, said it is few authorities on finding the serial inappropriate to comment on bomber or even compiling a pro- evidence involving the Bible.

"It is inappropriate to comment Contacted last night after the about this piece of evidence," television report aired, NYPD Thompson said. "We don't Police Chief Wallace Madison, try to do anything to hinder our declined to comment. "Madison ability to bring this person or into our said of the TV report, "There's custody." I can't confirm that Madison said, "There's nothing to say regarding that."

An officer close to the case told a

The killings continued and our ability to catch him created a growing sense of impotence in the NYPD for weeks.

THE SHEPHERD OF DEATH STILL FACELESS

New York-- Witnesses saw a man with a gun at the scene of the latest bombing, but couldn't provide enough information to create a composite drawing, police said yesterday.

Last night's slaying outside a National Princelet Bank was the first time anyone caught a glimpse of the bomber who uses gunfire to force victims into buildings rigged with explosives, maximizing the death and destruction when the bombs are detonated.

More than one bystander told New York Police they saw the Shepherd of Death fire a rifle into crowded streets of evening shoppers and movie-goers. But NYPD police Capt. Jessica Thompson said the details were too inconsistent to produce a

[see SHEPHERD Page A11]

EXPERT: SHEPHERD OF DEATH DRAWN TO AREA

Two of the serial killer's mass bombings have occurred in the Manhattan area for a reason, according to a geographical profiler.

Something here--either home or work--draws the killer to the region.

"My research over the last sixteen years tells me that there is something going on in the Manhattan area," said Marline Sexton, assistant professor of criminal justice studies at SUNY Stonybrook, New York.

Sexton and other geographical profilers say they believe that serial criminals tend to travel and commit their crimes within a "comfort zone," the area they are familiar with because of their home or work.

They are residents that live within geographic areas, she said. People work and shop according to well-developed patterns.

"The way in which criminals travel when committing crimes reflects the way they travel when they're not," she said.

Sexton bases this observation on her study of 100 convicted serial killers and 1024 murder victims.

The Daily Reporter

25¢ Designated Areas Higher

FORMER CIA SPY: SNIPER HAS MILITARY TRAINING

THE QUESTION REMAINS: WHO IS THE SHEPHERD OF DEATH?

Experts say that the serial bomber, who has committed two attacks in New York's Manhattan Island since May 5, is intelligent, methodical, and has special training to know how to disappear. Or, as some have suggested, a special ability to disappear, fueling speculation that there may be Specials involvement.

Many experts have also speculated that this could be some kind of terrorist plot, but a former CIA spy told the New York Times that he's convinced that is not the case.

"He's a pro. This man is an assassin and we don't know how extensively those Specials were training under the eye of the government and for what reasons," Thomas Klimt said.

In his decades of service as a spy, Klimt learned about how terrorists operate. Based on that experience, he believes this secretive bomber doesn't operate the same way as large terror groups.

Based on the fact that this Shepherd of Death, as he prefers to be known, fires into a crowd of people, drawing them into the building set to detonate in a false illusion of protection, Klimt feels this killer has military training, and if not a Special, then it's likely he was a previous CIA or commando operative.

"I worked with people designated to use such tactical attempts in foreign countries." Klimt refused to comment on specifics or name names as such programs, often known as Wet Works, are supposedly illegal under the Constitution.

"He's a pro in the sense that he's comfortable handling a military-type weapon, marching through the woods in the middle of the night if necessary. He knows what he's doing," Klimt said.

"And he's able to escape better than any normal person I've ever seen. That's the part that still gives me trouble and where I waver on whether or not he's a Special."

MESSAGE AT SCENE COULD BE SNIPER'S

The serial bomber, The Shepherd of Death, who has killed nine people since May 5, may have left a message for police at the scene of the latest bombing, sources say.

NYPD Police Chief Wallace Madison referred cryptically to a message found after the latest bombing. To the person who wrote us a message at the Trinity Church, we will be speaking news in NYPD Headquarters, Madison said Sunday. Street want to speak with you...

Chief Madison did not discuss the wording of the dis- near night in upper Manhattan col- at the scene Saturday a bomb was detonated on May 7.

night in New York's upper class Manhattan. He also did not say whether investigators could identify the serial bomber from the message. Police sources said they might be from the man whose dialogue between police and bomber. In the only other case police sources said they found a Holy Bible with the message scrawled inside. Policeman, I am The Shepherd of Death. The bible was a high-school Junior college.

Local and federal investigators have struggled to nail down a profile of the killer or killers. The bombing on Saturday, if linked to the serial bomber, would mark the serial bomber's first attack on a bombing appear to have noth-

---

DRAGNET COMES UP EMPTY AGAIN

Search Hindered by Availability of Detours, Lack of Witness Accounts

Saturday night's dragnet was the most aggressive yet in the Shepherd of Death investigation, with the first police cars taking only several minutes to seal off interstate ramps in a highway shutdown that soon stretched 10 miles along the interstate, authorities said.

But despite the speed of the response, police are now 0 for 4 with dragnets, pointing to the problems inherent in such tactics even when hundreds of law enforcement officers are available. "It's like the guy's invisible, or really fast," one officer stated.

Other sources suggest that the bomber could have taken a prearranged route on secondary roads, then listened to radio reports to learn when it was safe to return to major highways, law enforcement experts said.

"I think they're doing it out of desperation as much as anything else," said F.M. McClintock, a former NYPD homicide detective who investigated the shotgun stalker who terrorized neighborhoods in Northwest Washington for two months during 1993.

"It's better than nothing," McClintock said of the dragnets. "You'd really be screwed if you had the resources and you didn't do it."

After Saturday's mass bombing, police pulled over white vans as far north as Maine but they said they lacked a credible description.

Meanwhile, protest marches have begun in Washington, DC and New York demanding a full investigation of any possible connections between the bombings and the Pederson Specials. "If the guy's saying he's one of them, why isn't that being investigated?" said one source involved with the protests. "If they hate us as much as some of us hate them, I'd say that qualified as motivation, wouldn't you?"

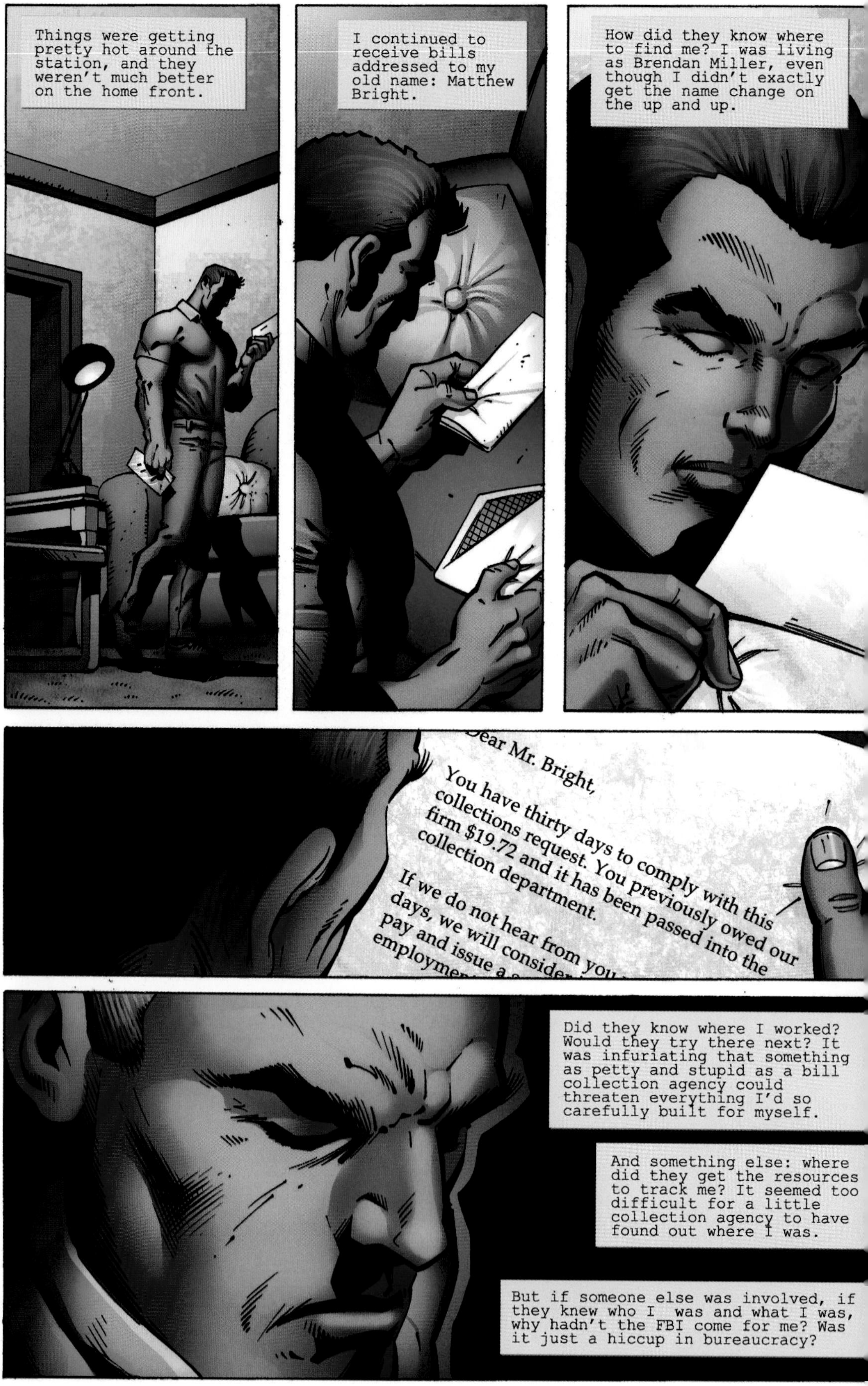
Things were getting pretty hot around the station, and they weren't much better on the home front.
I continued to receive bills addressed to my old name: Matthew Bright.
How did they know where to find me? I was living as Brendan Miller, even though I didn't exactly get the name change on the up and up.
Dear Mr. Bright,
You have thirty days to comply with this collections request. You previously owed our firm $19.72 and it has been passed into the collection department.
If we do not hear from you
days, we will consider
pay and issue a
Did they know where I worked? Would they try there next? It was infuriating that something as petty and stupid as a bill collection agency could threaten everything I'd so carefully built for myself.
And something else: where did they get the resources to track me? It seemed too difficult for a little collection agency to have found out where I was.
But if someone else was involved, if they knew who I was and what I was, why hadn't the FBI come for me? Was it just a hiccup in bureaucracy?

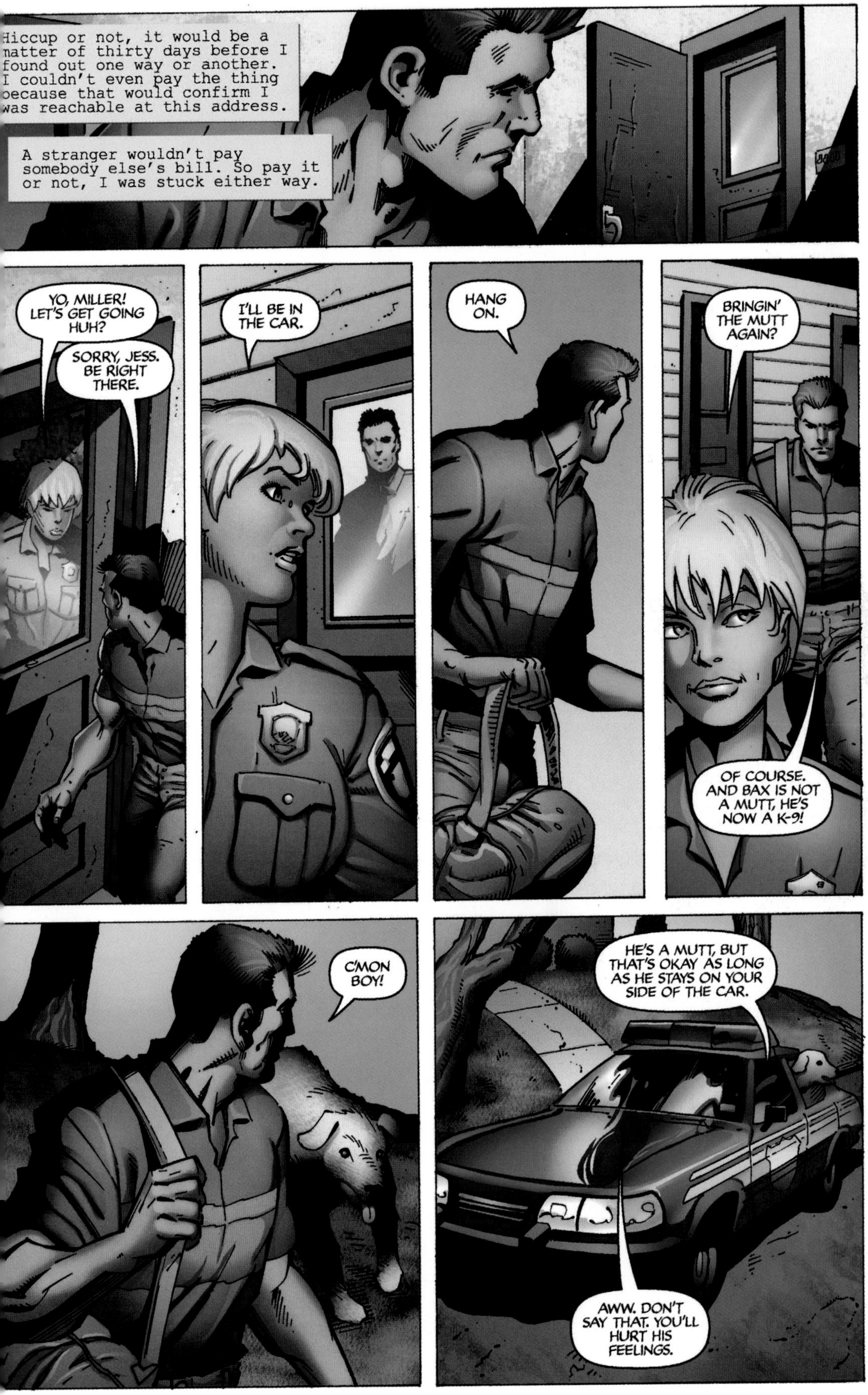

Hiccup or not, it would be a matter of thirty days before I found out one way or another. I couldn't even pay the thing because that would confirm I was reachable at this address.
A stranger wouldn't pay somebody else's bill. So pay it or not, I was stuck either way.
YO, MILLER! LET'S GET GOING HUH?
SORRY, JESS. BE RIGHT THERE.
I'LL BE IN THE CAR.
HANG ON.
BRINGIN' THE MUTT AGAIN?
OF COURSE. AND BAX IS NOT A MUTT, HE'S NOW A K-9!
C'MON BOY!
HE'S A MUTT, BUT THAT'S OKAY AS LONG AS HE STAYS ON YOUR SIDE OF THE CAR.
AWW. DON'T SAY THAT. YOU'LL HURT HIS FEELINGS.

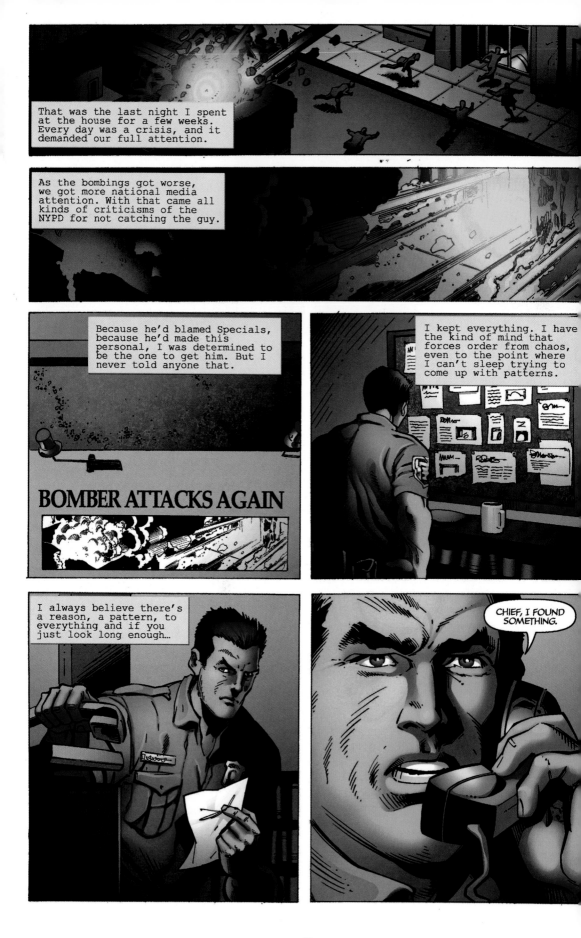

That was the last night I spent at the house for a few weeks. Every day was a crisis, and it demanded our full attention.

As the bombings got worse, we got more national media attention. With that came all kinds of criticisms of the NYPD for not catching the guy.

Because he'd blamed Specials, because he'd made this personal, I was determined to be the one to get him. But I never told anyone that.

BOMBER ATTACKS AGAIN

I kept everything. I have the kind of mind that forces order from chaos, even to the point where I can't sleep trying to come up with patterns.

I always believe there's a reason, a pattern, to everything and if you just look long enough...

CHIEF, I FOUND SOMETHING.

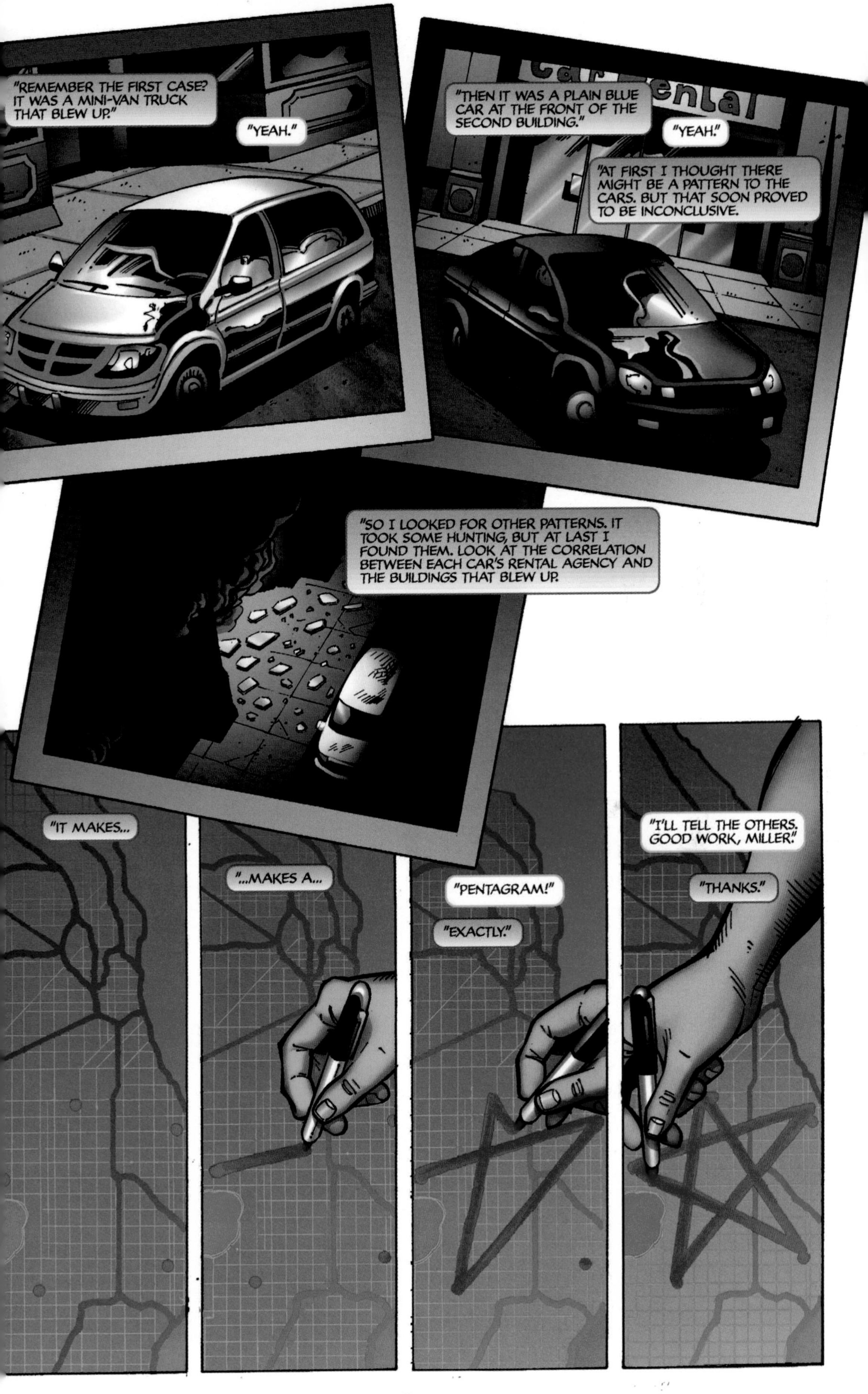
"REMEMBER THE FIRST CASE? IT WAS A MINI-VAN TRUCK THAT BLEW UP."
"YEAH."
"THEN IT WAS A PLAIN BLUE CAR AT THE FRONT OF THE SECOND BUILDING."
"YEAH."
"AT FIRST I THOUGHT THERE MIGHT BE A PATTERN TO THE CARS. BUT THAT SOON PROVED TO BE INCONCLUSIVE.
"SO I LOOKED FOR OTHER PATTERNS. IT TOOK SOME HUNTING, BUT AT LAST I FOUND THEM. LOOK AT THE CORRELATION BETWEEN EACH CAR'S RENTAL AGENCY AND THE BUILDINGS THAT BLEW UP.
"IT MAKES...
"...MAKES A...
"PENTAGRAM!"
"EXACTLY."
"I'LL TELL THE OTHERS. GOOD WORK, MILLER."
"THANKS."

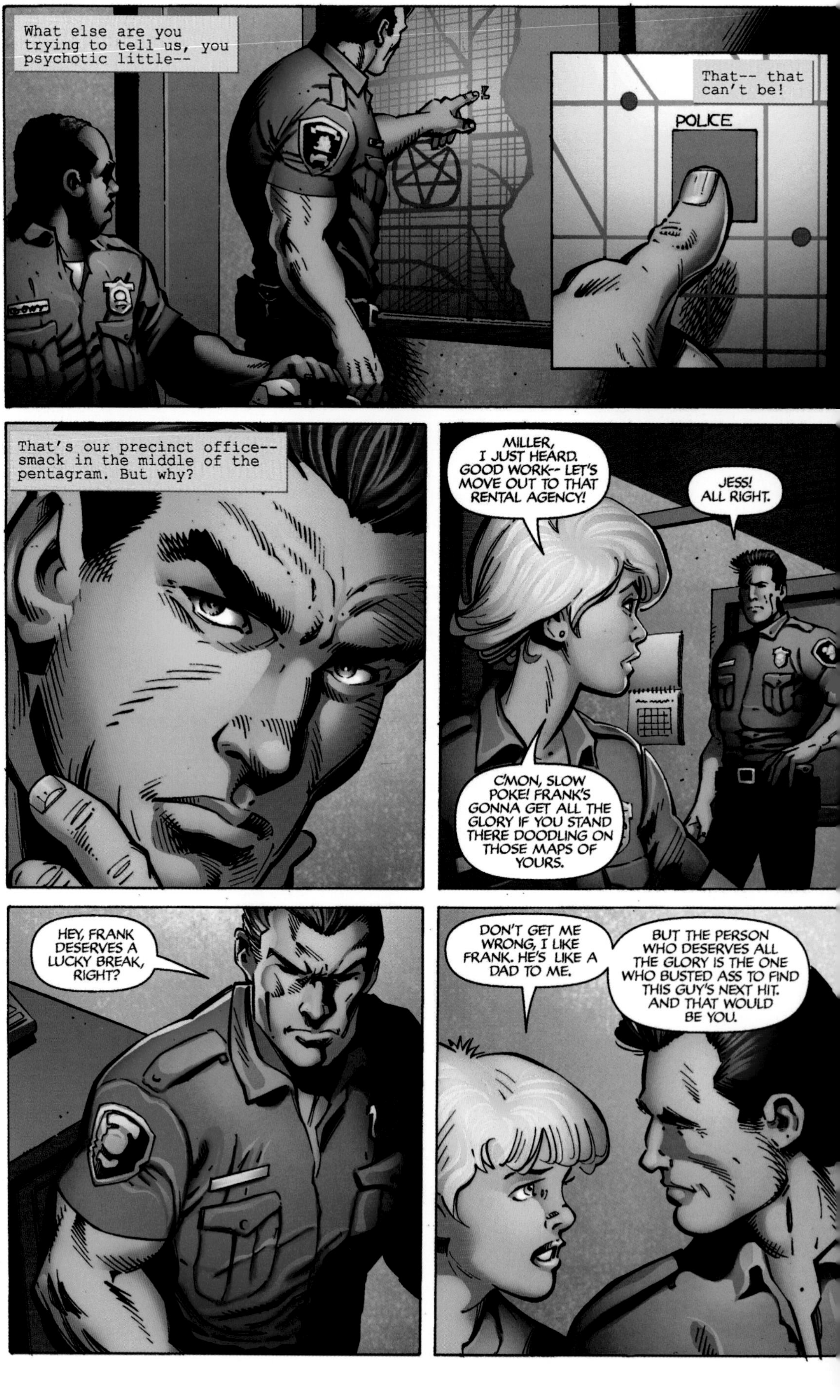

What else are you trying to tell us, you psychotic little--
That-- that can't be!
POLICE
That's our precinct office-- smack in the middle of the pentagram. But why?
MILLER, I JUST HEARD. GOOD WORK-- LET'S MOVE OUT TO THAT RENTAL AGENCY!
JESS! ALL RIGHT.
C'MON, SLOW POKE! FRANK'S GONNA GET ALL THE GLORY IF YOU STAND THERE DOODLING ON THOSE MAPS OF YOURS.
HEY, FRANK DESERVES A LUCKY BREAK, RIGHT?
DON'T GET ME WRONG, I LIKE FRANK. HE'S LIKE A DAD TO ME.
BUT THE PERSON WHO DESERVES ALL THE GLORY IS THE ONE WHO BUSTED ASS TO FIND THIS GUY'S NEXT HIT. AND THAT WOULD BE YOU.

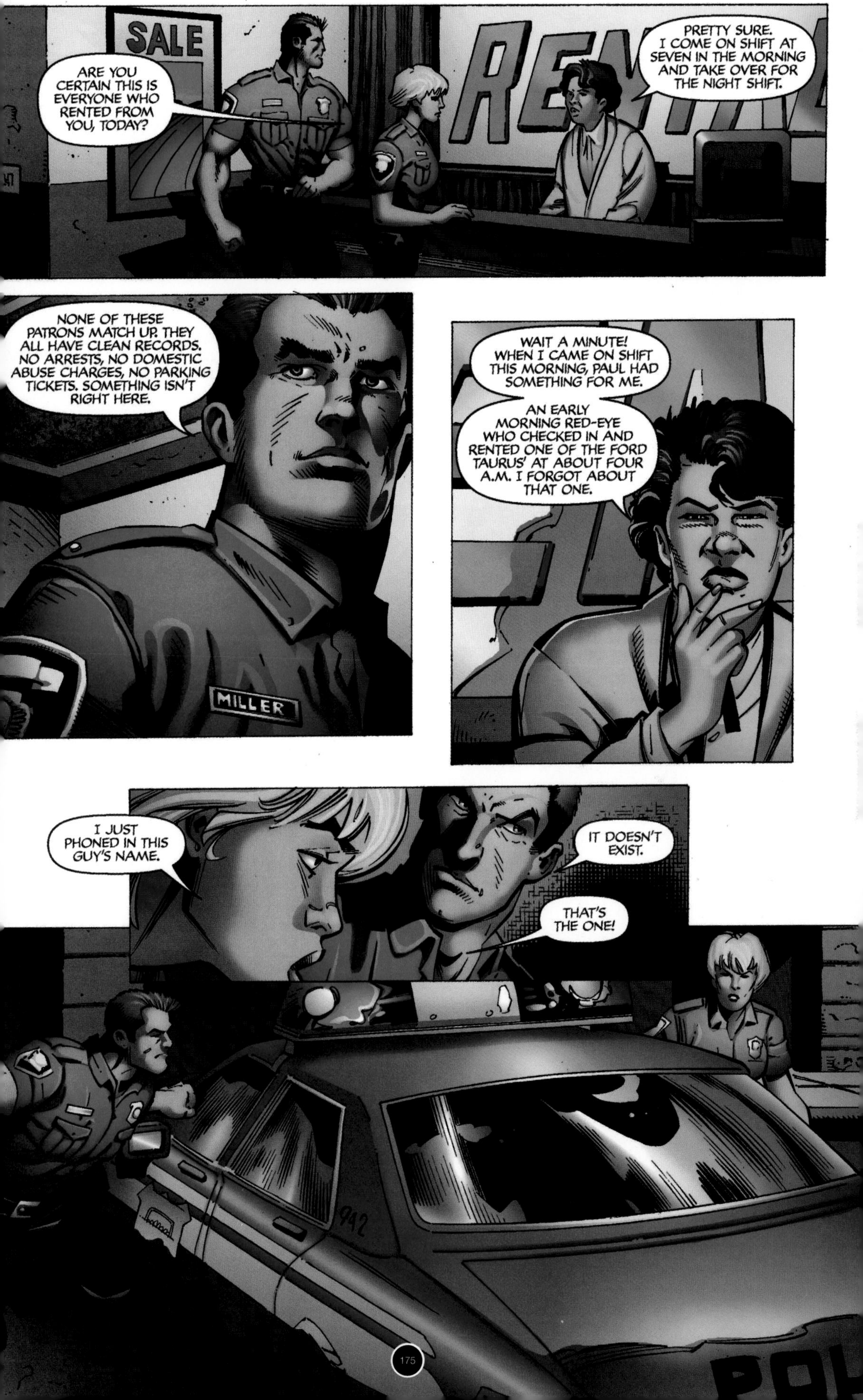
SALE
ARE YOU CERTAIN THIS IS EVERYONE WHO RENTED FROM YOU, TODAY?
PRETTY SURE. I COME ON SHIFT AT SEVEN IN THE MORNING AND TAKE OVER FOR THE NIGHT SHIFT.
NONE OF THESE PATRONS MATCH UP. THEY ALL HAVE CLEAN RECORDS. NO ARRESTS, NO DOMESTIC ABUSE CHARGES, NO PARKING TICKETS. SOMETHING ISN'T RIGHT HERE.
MILLER
WAIT A MINUTE! WHEN I CAME ON SHIFT THIS MORNING, PAUL HAD SOMETHING FOR ME.
AN EARLY MORNING RED-EYE WHO CHECKED IN AND RENTED ONE OF THE FORD TAURUS' AT ABOUT FOUR A.M. I FORGOT ABOUT THAT ONE.
I JUST PHONED IN THIS GUY'S NAME.
IT DOESN'T EXIST.
THAT'S THE ONE!

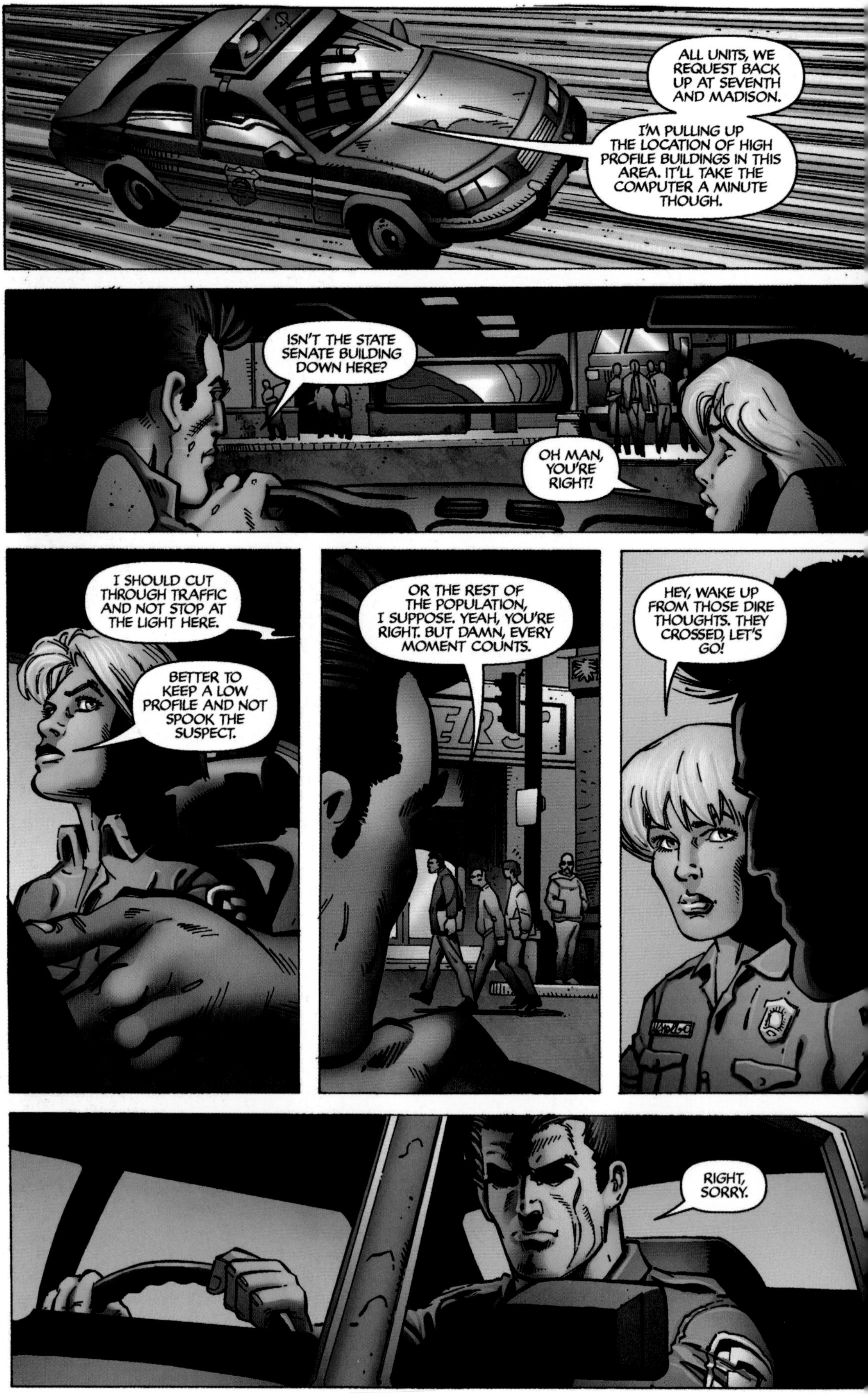
ALL UNITS, WE REQUEST BACK UP AT SEVENTH AND MADISON.
I'M PULLING UP THE LOCATION OF HIGH PROFILE BUILDINGS IN THIS AREA. IT'LL TAKE THE COMPUTER A MINUTE THOUGH.
ISN'T THE STATE SENATE BUILDING DOWN HERE?
OH MAN, YOU'RE RIGHT!
I SHOULD CUT THROUGH TRAFFIC AND NOT STOP AT THE LIGHT HERE.
BETTER TO KEEP A LOW PROFILE AND NOT SPOOK THE SUSPECT.
OR THE REST OF THE POPULATION, I SUPPOSE. YEAH, YOU'RE RIGHT. BUT DAMN, EVERY MOMENT COUNTS.
HEY, WAKE UP FROM THOSE DIRE THOUGHTS. THEY CROSSED, LET'S GO!
RIGHT, SORRY.

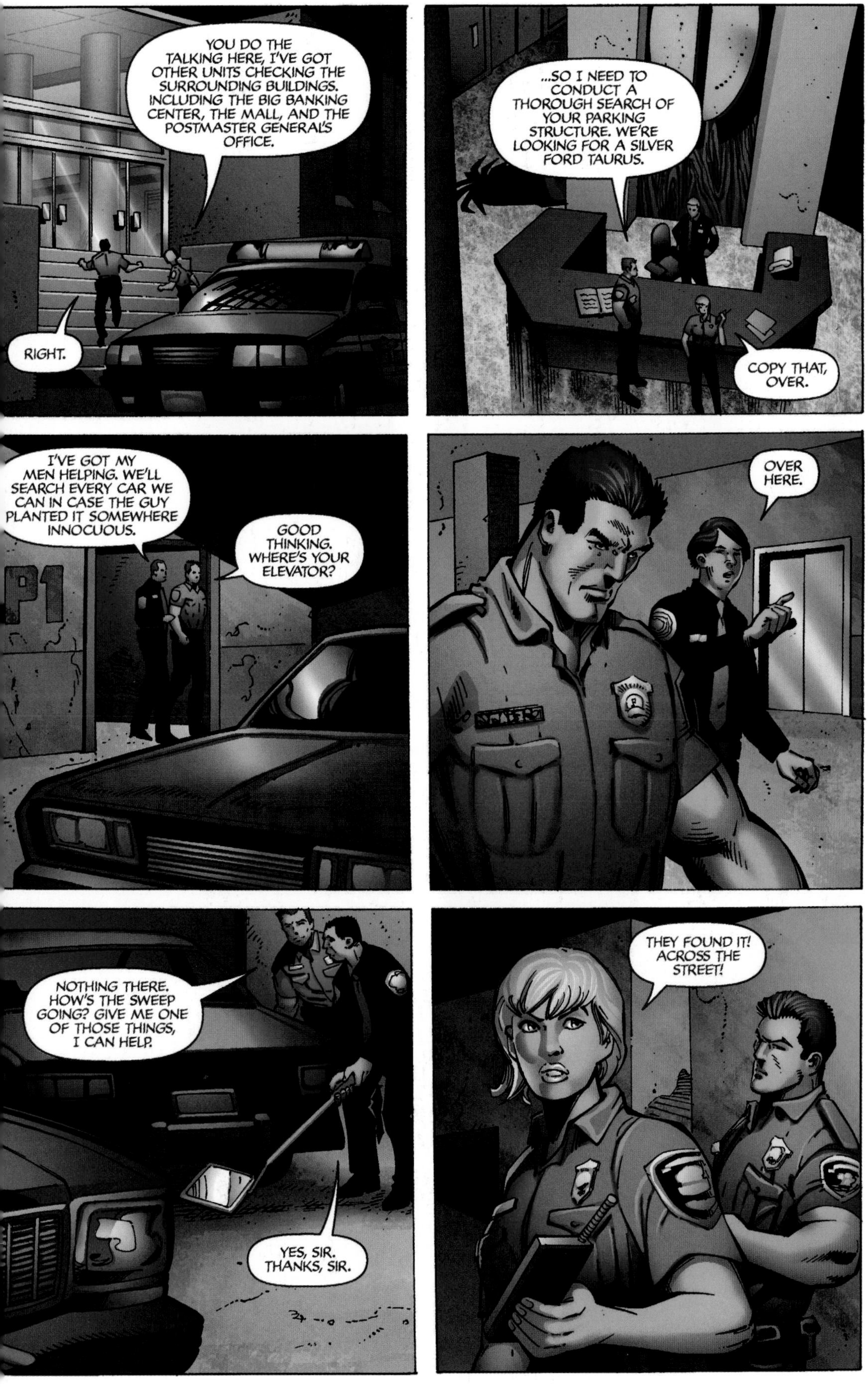
YOU DO THE TALKING HERE, I'VE GOT OTHER UNITS CHECKING THE SURROUNDING BUILDINGS. INCLUDING THE BIG BANKING CENTER, THE MALL, AND THE POSTMASTER GENERAL'S OFFICE.
RIGHT.
...SO I NEED TO CONDUCT A THOROUGH SEARCH OF YOUR PARKING STRUCTURE. WE'RE LOOKING FOR A SILVER FORD TAURUS.
COPY THAT, OVER.
I'VE GOT MY MEN HELPING. WE'LL SEARCH EVERY CAR WE CAN IN CASE THE GUY PLANTED IT SOMEWHERE INNOCUOUS.
GOOD THINKING. WHERE'S YOUR ELEVATOR?
P1
OVER HERE.
NOTHING THERE. HOW'S THE SWEEP GOING? GIVE ME ONE OF THOSE THINGS, I CAN HELP.
YES, SIR. THANKS, SIR.
THEY FOUND IT! ACROSS THE STREET!

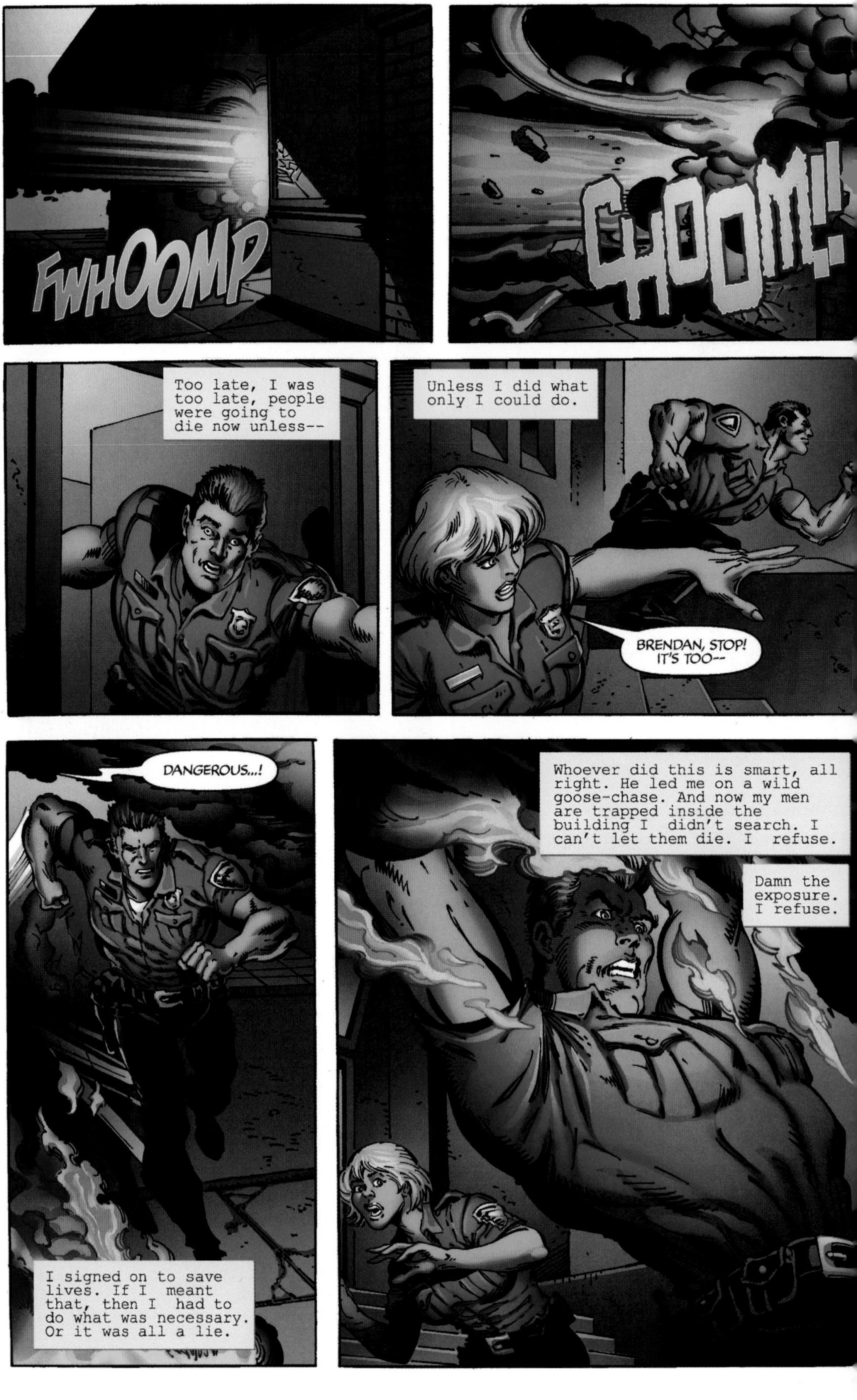
FWHOOMP
CHOOM!!
Too late, I was too late, people were going to die now unless--
Unless I did what only I could do.
BRENDAN, STOP! IT'S TOO--
DANGEROUS...!
I signed on to save lives. If I meant that, then I had to do what was necessary. Or it was all a lie.
Whoever did this is smart, all right. He led me on a wild goose-chase. And now my men are trapped inside the building I didn't search. I can't let them die. I refuse.
Damn the exposure. I refuse.

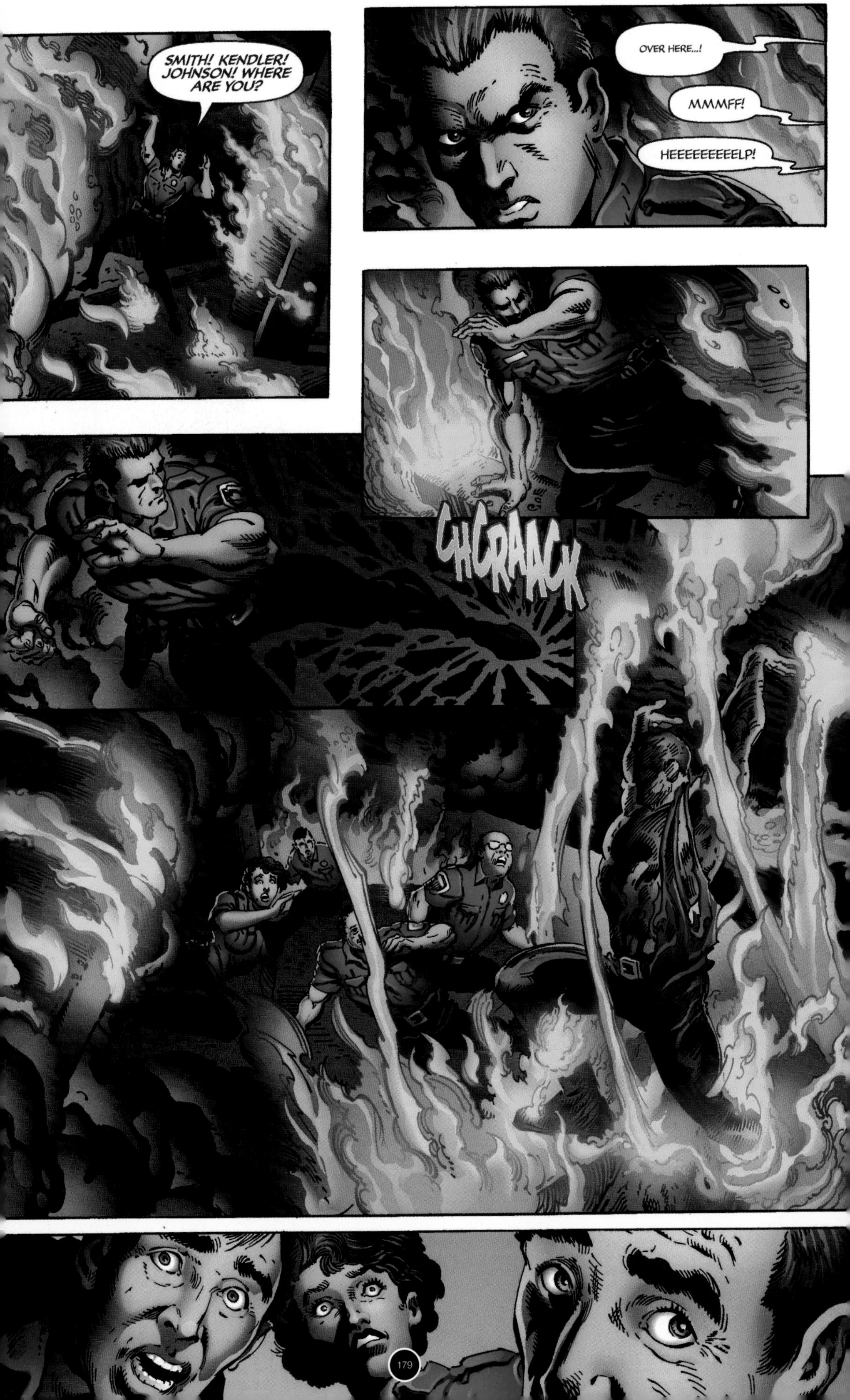
SMITH! KENDLER! JOHNSON! WHERE ARE YOU?
OVER HERE...!
MMMFF!
HEEEEEEEEELP!
CHCRAACK

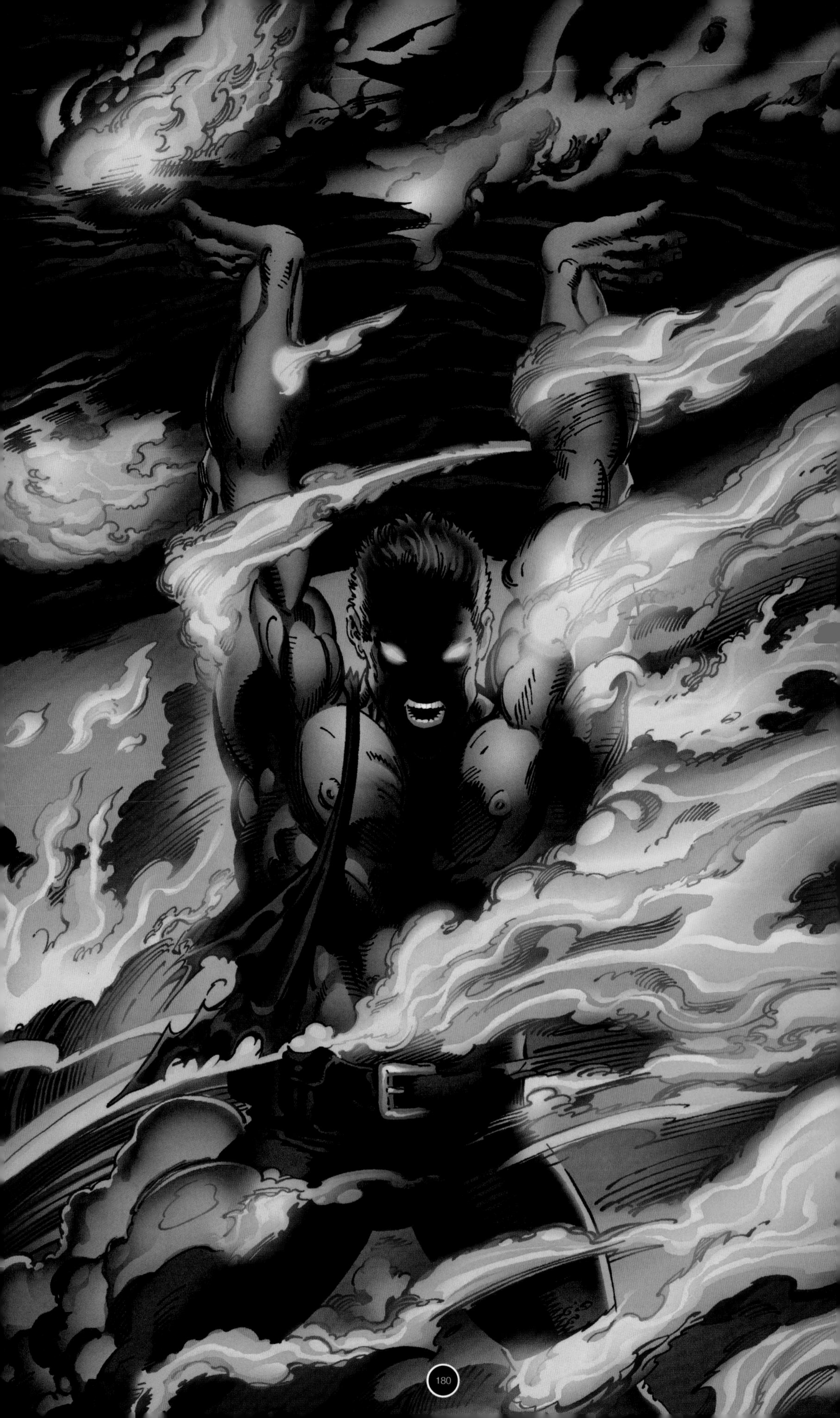

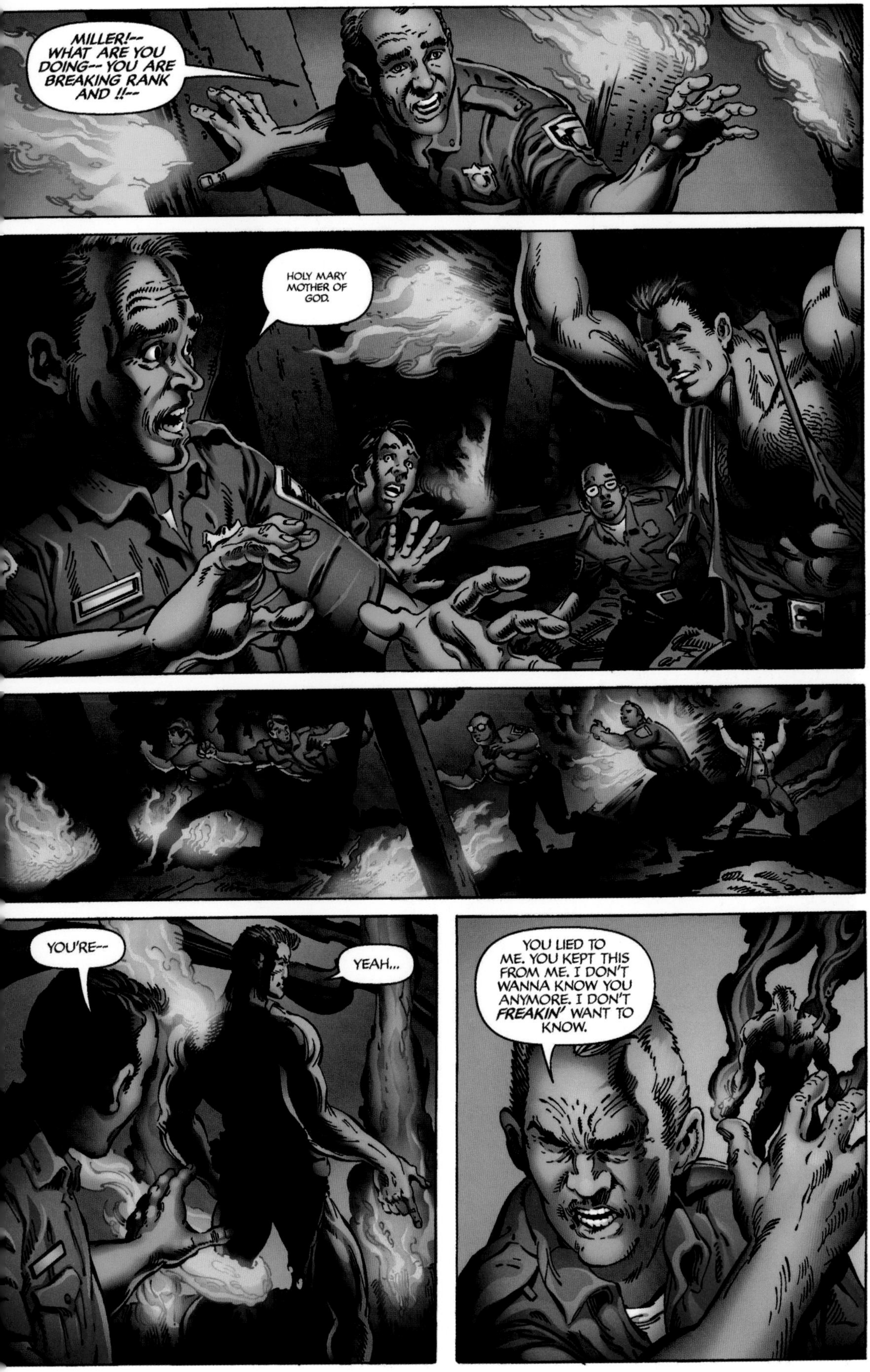
MILLER!-- WHAT ARE YOU DOING-- YOU ARE BREAKING RANK AND !!--
HOLY MARY MOTHER OF GOD.
YOU'RE--
YEAH...
YOU LIED TO ME. YOU KEPT THIS FROM ME. I DON'T WANNA KNOW YOU ANYMORE. I DON'T FREAKIN' WANT TO KNOW.

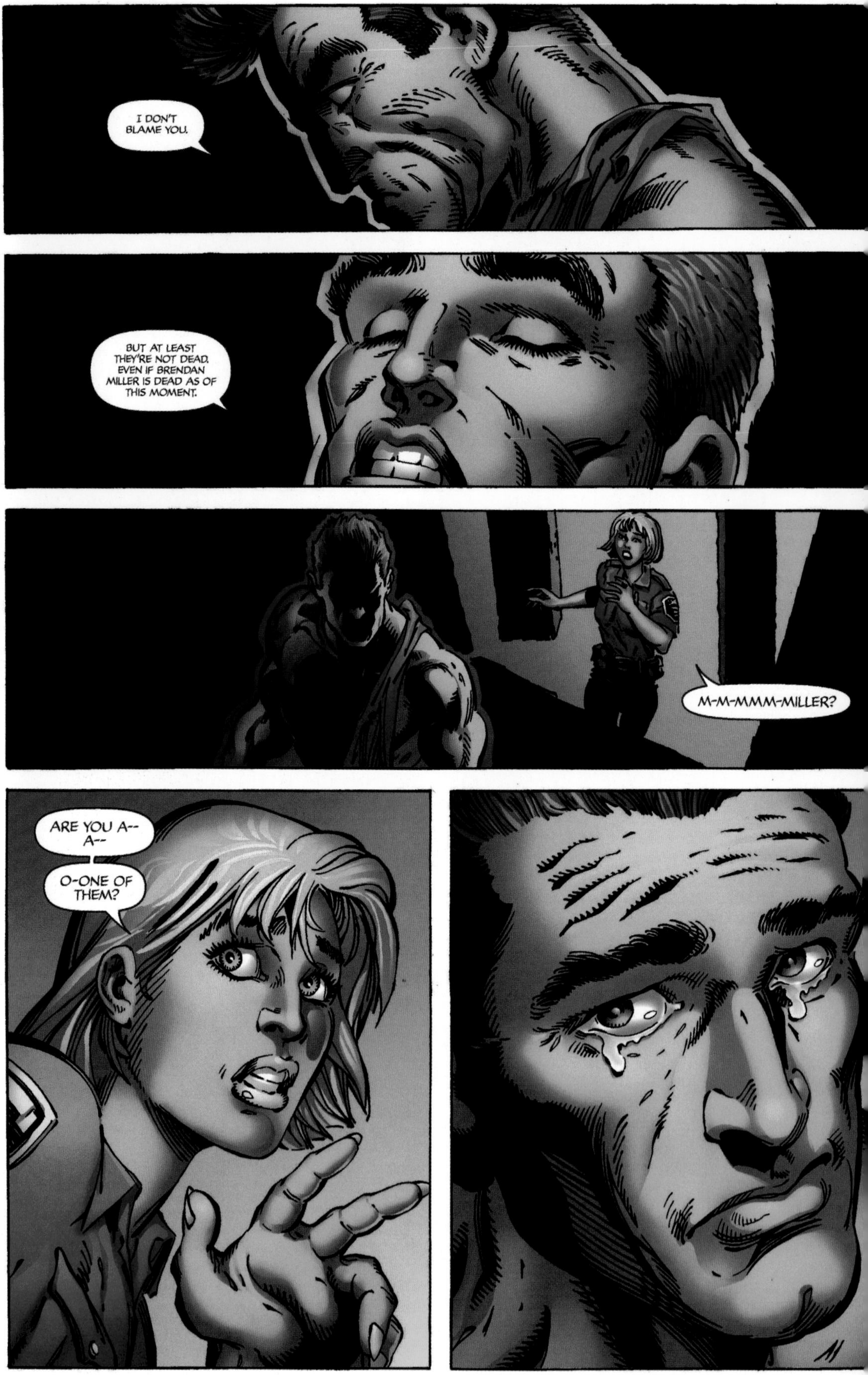

I DON'T BLAME YOU.
BUT AT LEAST THEY'RE NOT DEAD. EVEN IF BRENDAN MILLER IS DEAD AS OF THIS MOMENT.
M-M-MMM-MILLER?
ARE YOU A-- A--
O-ONE OF THEM?

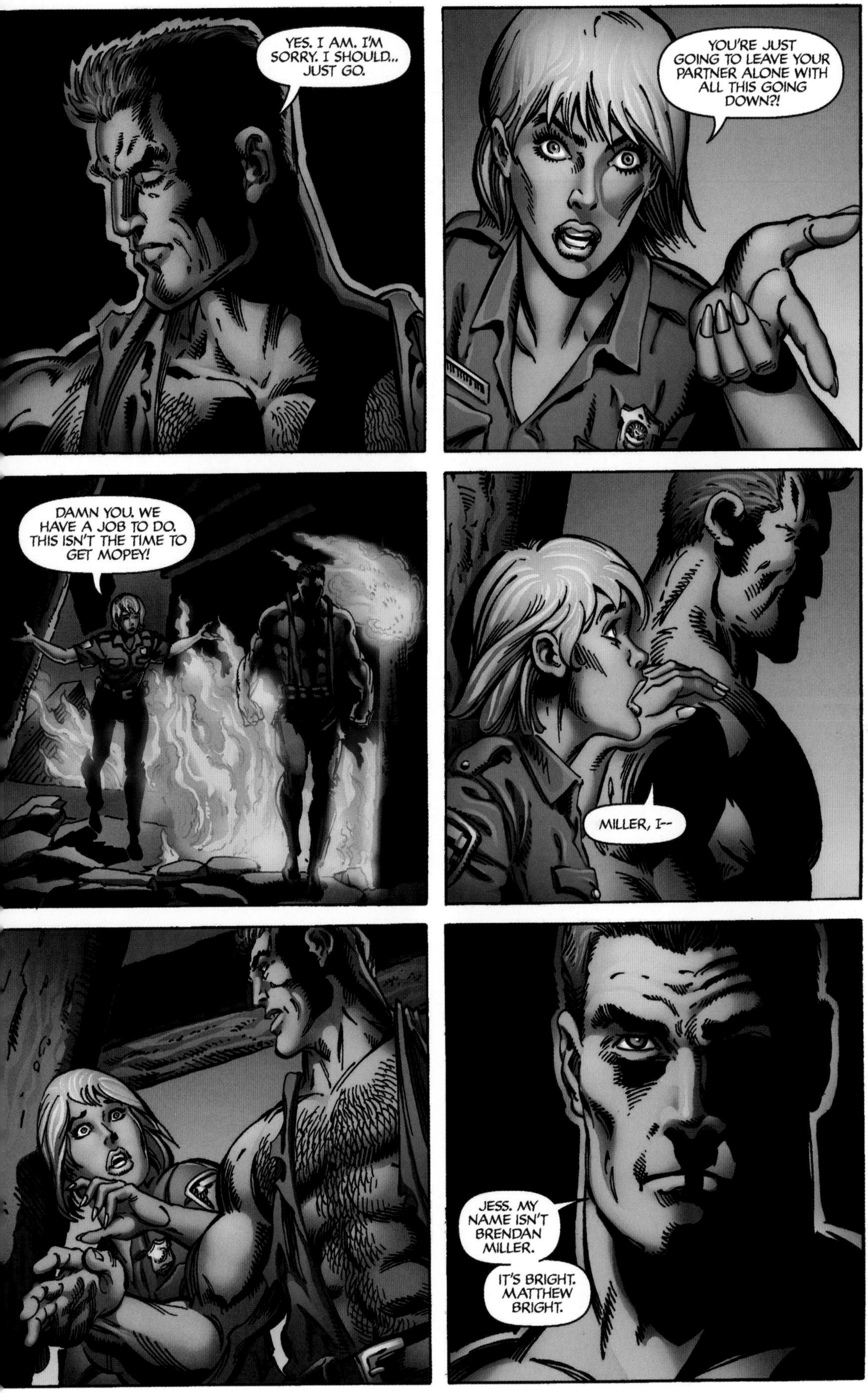
YES. I AM. I'M SORRY. I SHOULD... JUST GO.
YOU'RE JUST GOING TO LEAVE YOUR PARTNER ALONE WITH ALL THIS GOING DOWN?!
DAMN YOU. WE HAVE A JOB TO DO. THIS ISN'T THE TIME TO GET MOPEY!
MILLER, I--
JESS. MY NAME ISN'T BRENDAN MILLER.
IT'S BRIGHT. MATTHEW BRIGHT.

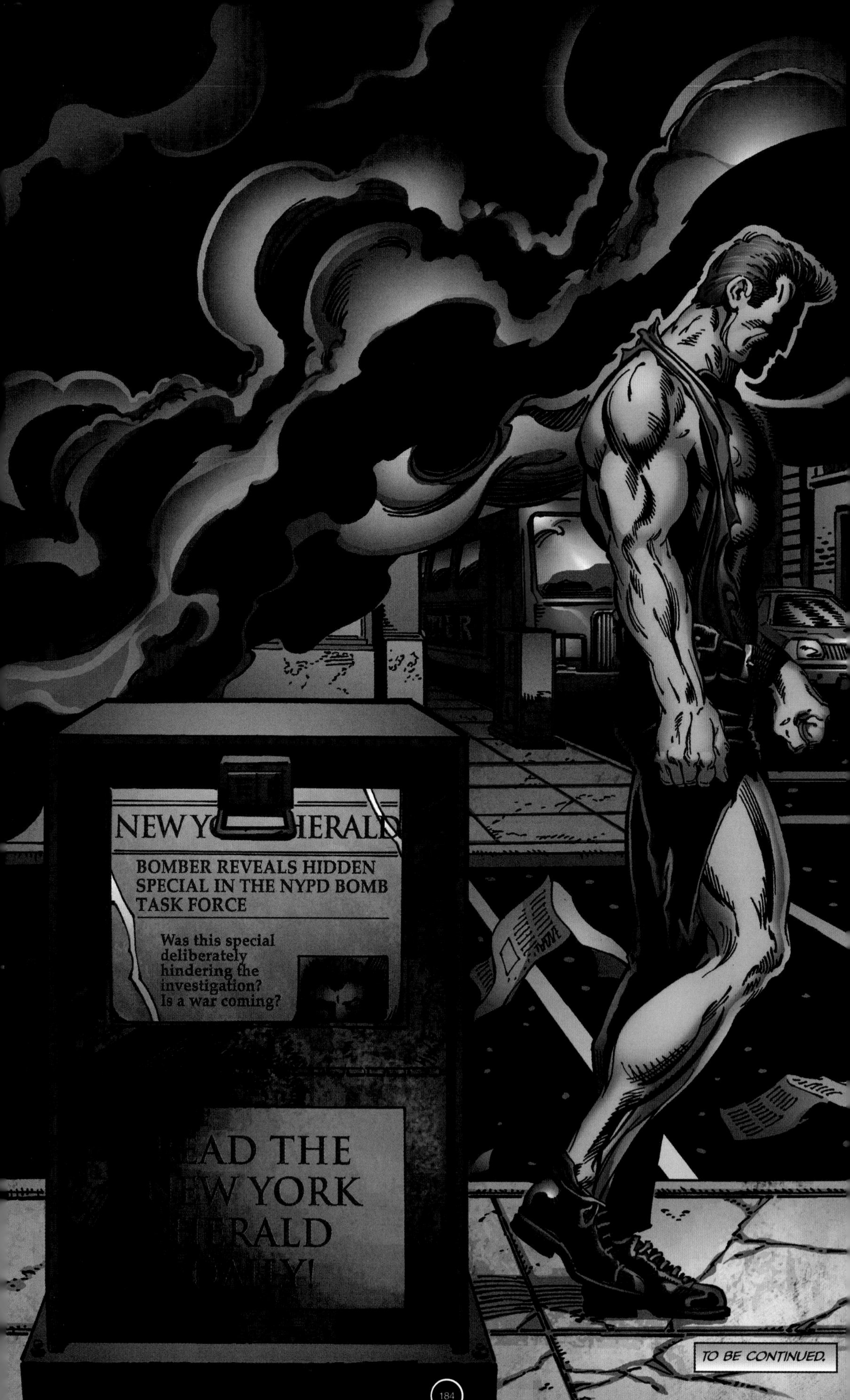
NEW Y HERALD
BOMBER REVEALS HIDDEN SPECIAL IN THE NYPD BOMB TASK FORCE
Was this special deliberately hindering the investigation? Is a war coming?
EAD THE EW YORK ERALD
TO BE CONTINUED.

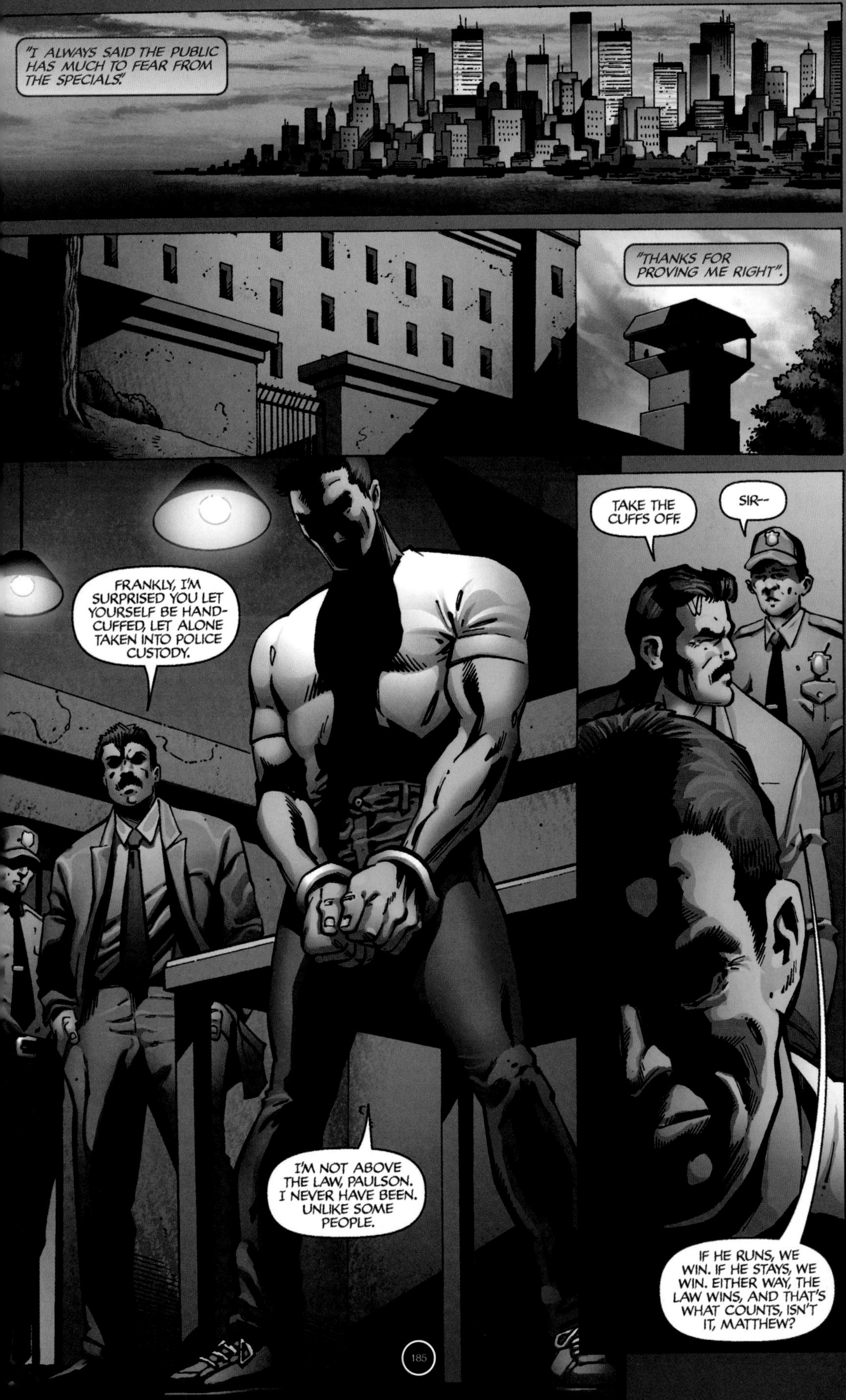
"I ALWAYS SAID THE PUBLIC HAS MUCH TO FEAR FROM THE SPECIALS."
"THANKS FOR PROVING ME RIGHT".
FRANKLY, I'M SURPRISED YOU LET YOURSELF BE HAND-CUFFED, LET ALONE TAKEN INTO POLICE CUSTODY.
I'M NOT ABOVE THE LAW, PAULSON. I NEVER HAVE BEEN. UNLIKE SOME PEOPLE.
TAKE THE CUFFS OFF.
SIR--
IF HE RUNS, WE WIN. IF HE STAYS, WE WIN. EITHER WAY, THE LAW WINS, AND THAT'S WHAT COUNTS, ISN'T IT, MATTHEW?

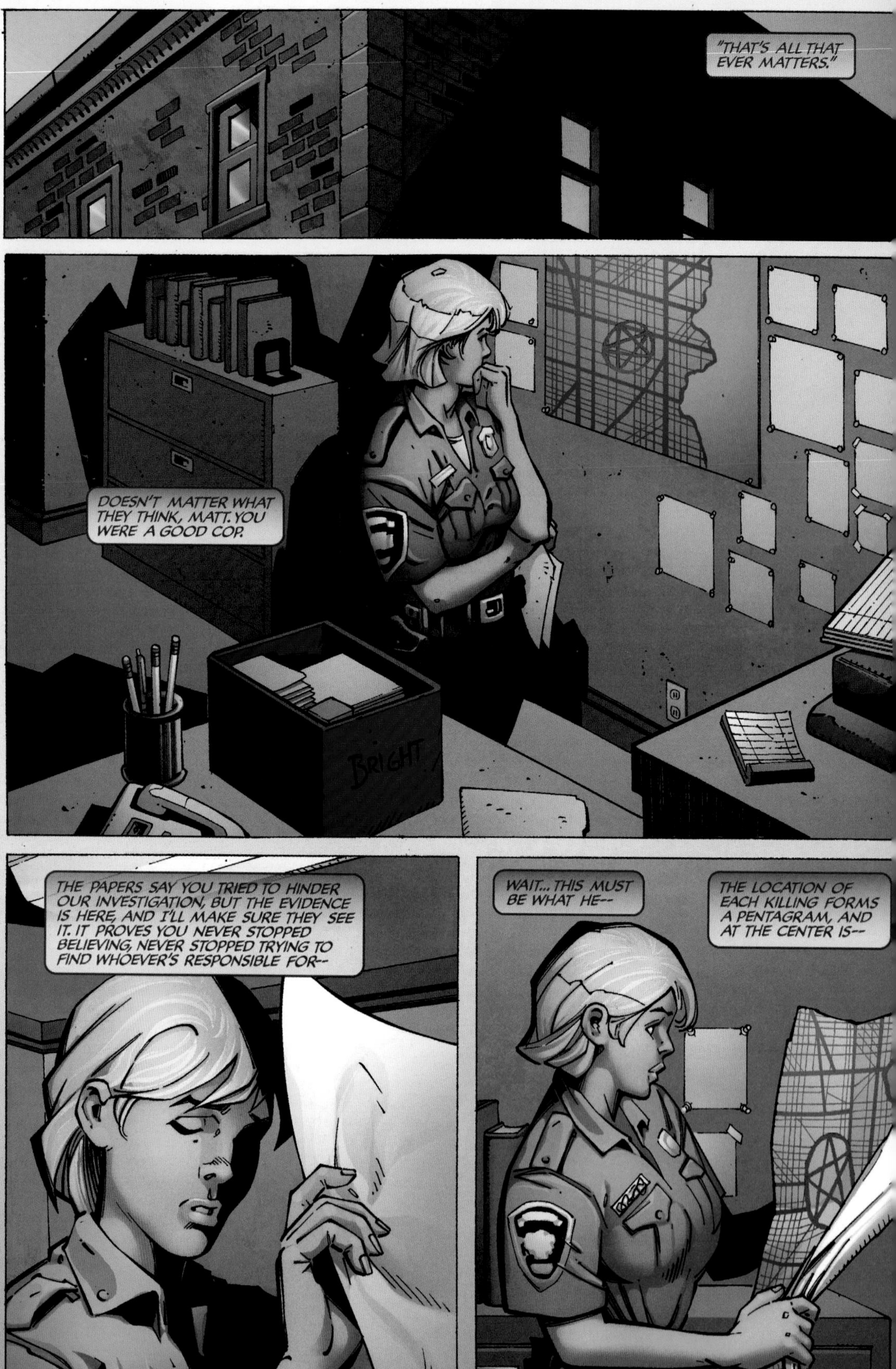
"THAT'S ALL THAT EVER MATTERS."
DOESN'T MATTER WHAT THEY THINK, MATT. YOU WERE A GOOD COP.
BRIGHT
THE PAPERS SAY YOU TRIED TO HINDER OUR INVESTIGATION, BUT THE EVIDENCE IS HERE, AND I'LL MAKE SURE THEY SEE IT. IT PROVES YOU NEVER STOPPED BELIEVING, NEVER STOPPED TRYING TO FIND WHOEVER'S RESPONSIBLE FOR--
WAIT... THIS MUST BE WHAT HE--
THE LOCATION OF EACH KILLING FORMS A PENTAGRAM, AND AT THE CENTER IS--
--RIGHT HERE.

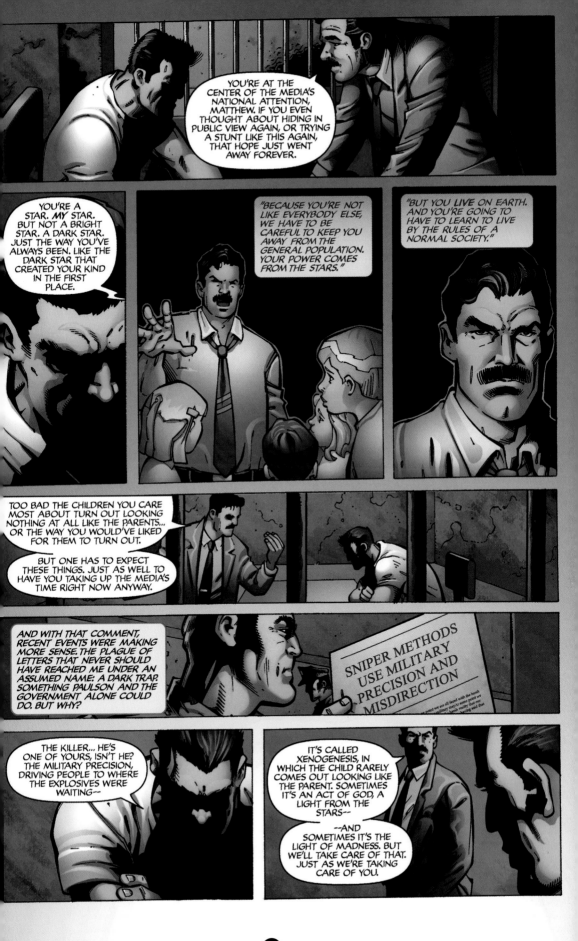

YOU'RE AT THE CENTER OF THE MEDIA'S NATIONAL ATTENTION, MATTHEW. IF YOU EVEN THOUGHT ABOUT HIDING IN PUBLIC VIEW AGAIN, OR TRYING A STUNT LIKE THIS AGAIN, THAT HOPE JUST WENT AWAY FOREVER.

YOU'RE A STAR. MY STAR. BUT NOT A BRIGHT STAR. A DARK STAR. JUST THE WAY YOU'VE ALWAYS BEEN. LIKE THE DARK STAR THAT CREATED YOUR KIND IN THE FIRST PLACE.

"BECAUSE YOU'RE NOT LIKE EVERYBODY ELSE, WE HAVE TO BE CAREFUL TO KEEP YOU AWAY FROM THE GENERAL POPULATION. YOUR POWER COMES FROM THE STARS."

"BUT YOU LIVE ON EARTH. AND YOU'RE GOING TO HAVE TO LEARN TO LIVE BY THE RULES OF A NORMAL SOCIETY."

TOO BAD THE CHILDREN YOU CARE MOST ABOUT TURN OUT LOOKING NOTHING AT ALL LIKE THE PARENTS... OR THE WAY YOU WOULD'VE LIKED FOR THEM TO TURN OUT.

BUT ONE HAS TO EXPECT THESE THINGS. JUST AS WELL TO HAVE YOU TAKING UP THE MEDIA'S TIME RIGHT NOW ANYWAY.

AND WITH THAT COMMENT, RECENT EVENTS WERE MAKING MORE SENSE. THE PLAGUE OF LETTERS THAT NEVER SHOULD HAVE REACHED ME UNDER AN ASSUMED NAME: A DARK TRAP. SOMETHING PAULSON AND THE GOVERNMENT ALONE COULD DO. BUT WHY?

SNIPER METHODS USE MILITARY PRECISION AND MISDIRECTION

THE KILLER... HE'S ONE OF YOURS, ISN'T HE? THE MILITARY PRECISION, DRIVING PEOPLE TO WHERE THE EXPLOSIVES WERE WAITING--

IT'S CALLED XENOGENESIS, IN WHICH THE CHILD RARELY COMES OUT LOOKING LIKE THE PARENT. SOMETIMES IT'S AN ACT OF GOD, A LIGHT FROM THE STARS--

--AND SOMETIMES IT'S THE LIGHT OF MADNESS. BUT WE'LL TAKE CARE OF THAT. JUST AS WE'RE TAKING CARE OF YOU.

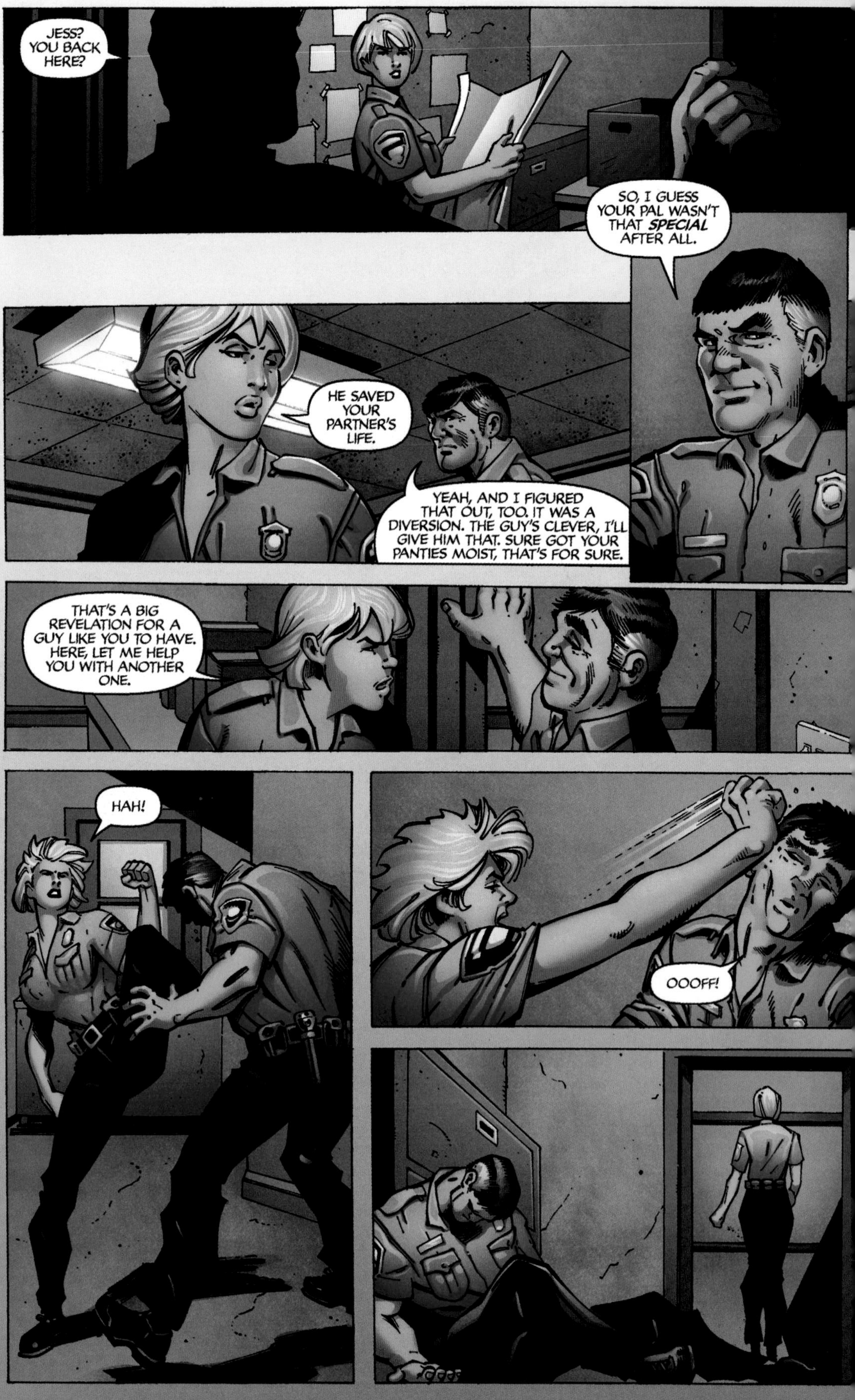

JESS? YOU BACK HERE?
SO, I GUESS YOUR PAL WASN'T THAT *SPECIAL* AFTER ALL.
HE SAVED YOUR PARTNER'S LIFE.
YEAH, AND I FIGURED THAT OUT, TOO. IT WAS A DIVERSION. THE GUY'S CLEVER, I'LL GIVE HIM THAT. SURE GOT YOUR PANTIES MOIST, THAT'S FOR SURE.
THAT'S A BIG REVELATION FOR A GUY LIKE YOU TO HAVE. HERE, LET ME HELP YOU WITH ANOTHER ONE.
HAH!
OOOFF!

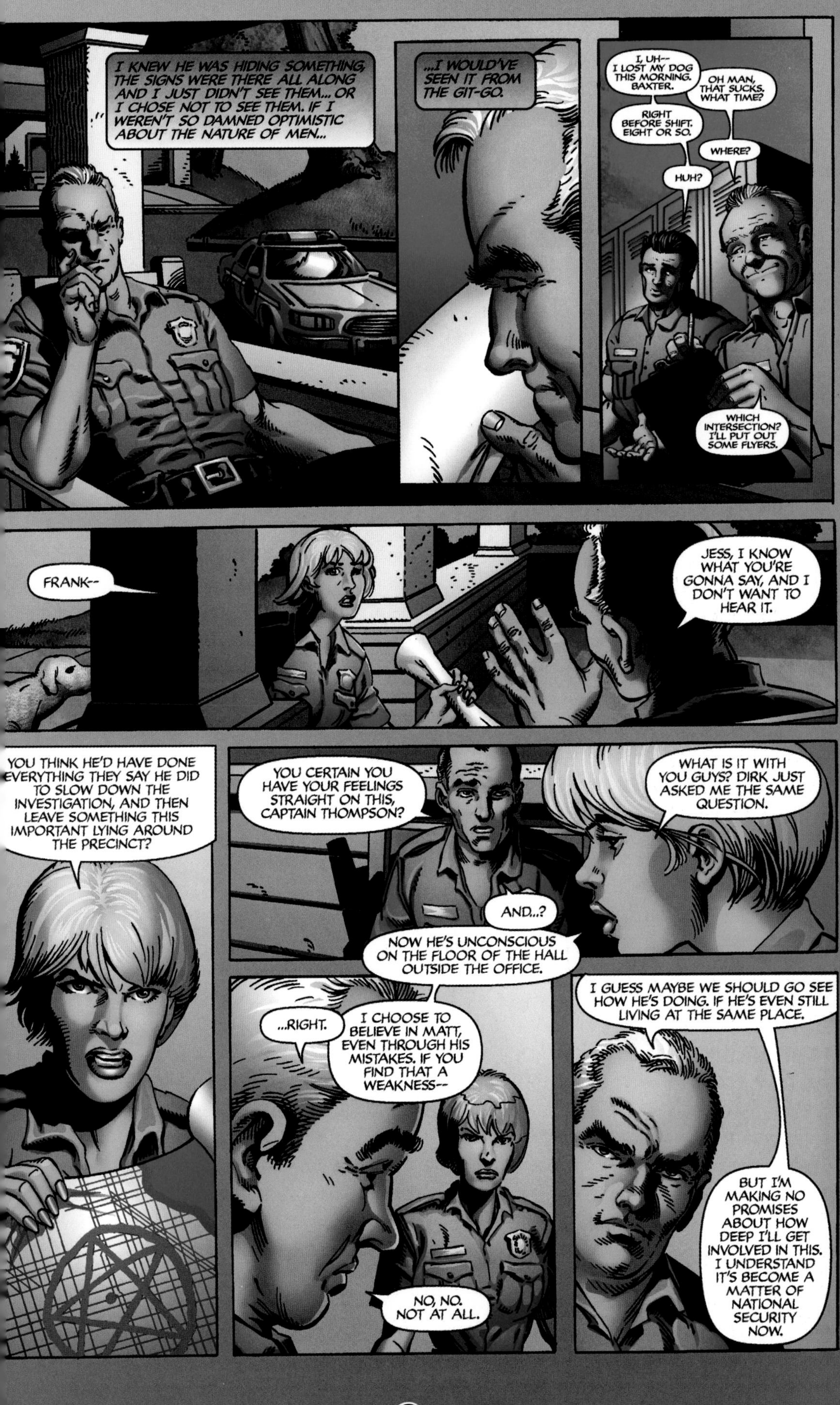
I KNEW HE WAS HIDING SOMETHING. THE SIGNS WERE THERE ALL ALONG AND I JUST DIDN'T SEE THEM... OR I CHOSE NOT TO SEE THEM. IF I WEREN'T SO DAMNED OPTIMISTIC ABOUT THE NATURE OF MEN...
...I WOULD'VE SEEN IT FROM THE GIT-GO.
I, UH-- I LOST MY DOG THIS MORNING. BAXTER.
OH MAN, THAT SUCKS. WHAT TIME?
RIGHT BEFORE SHIFT. EIGHT OR SO.
WHERE?
HUH?
WHICH INTERSECTION? I'LL PUT OUT SOME FLYERS.
FRANK--
JESS, I KNOW WHAT YOU'RE GONNA SAY, AND I DON'T WANT TO HEAR IT.
YOU THINK HE'D HAVE DONE EVERYTHING THEY SAY HE DID TO SLOW DOWN THE INVESTIGATION, AND THEN LEAVE SOMETHING THIS IMPORTANT LYING AROUND THE PRECINCT?
YOU CERTAIN YOU HAVE YOUR FEELINGS STRAIGHT ON THIS, CAPTAIN THOMPSON?
WHAT IS IT WITH YOU GUYS? DIRK JUST ASKED ME THE SAME QUESTION.
AND...?
NOW HE'S UNCONSCIOUS ON THE FLOOR OF THE HALL OUTSIDE THE OFFICE.
...RIGHT.
I CHOOSE TO BELIEVE IN MATT, EVEN THROUGH HIS MISTAKES. IF YOU FIND THAT A WEAKNESS--
NO, NO. NOT AT ALL.
I GUESS MAYBE WE SHOULD GO SEE HOW HE'S DOING. IF HE'S EVEN STILL LIVING AT THE SAME PLACE.
BUT I'M MAKING NO PROMISES ABOUT HOW DEEP I'LL GET INVOLVED IN THIS. I UNDERSTAND IT'S BECOME A MATTER OF NATIONAL SECURITY NOW.

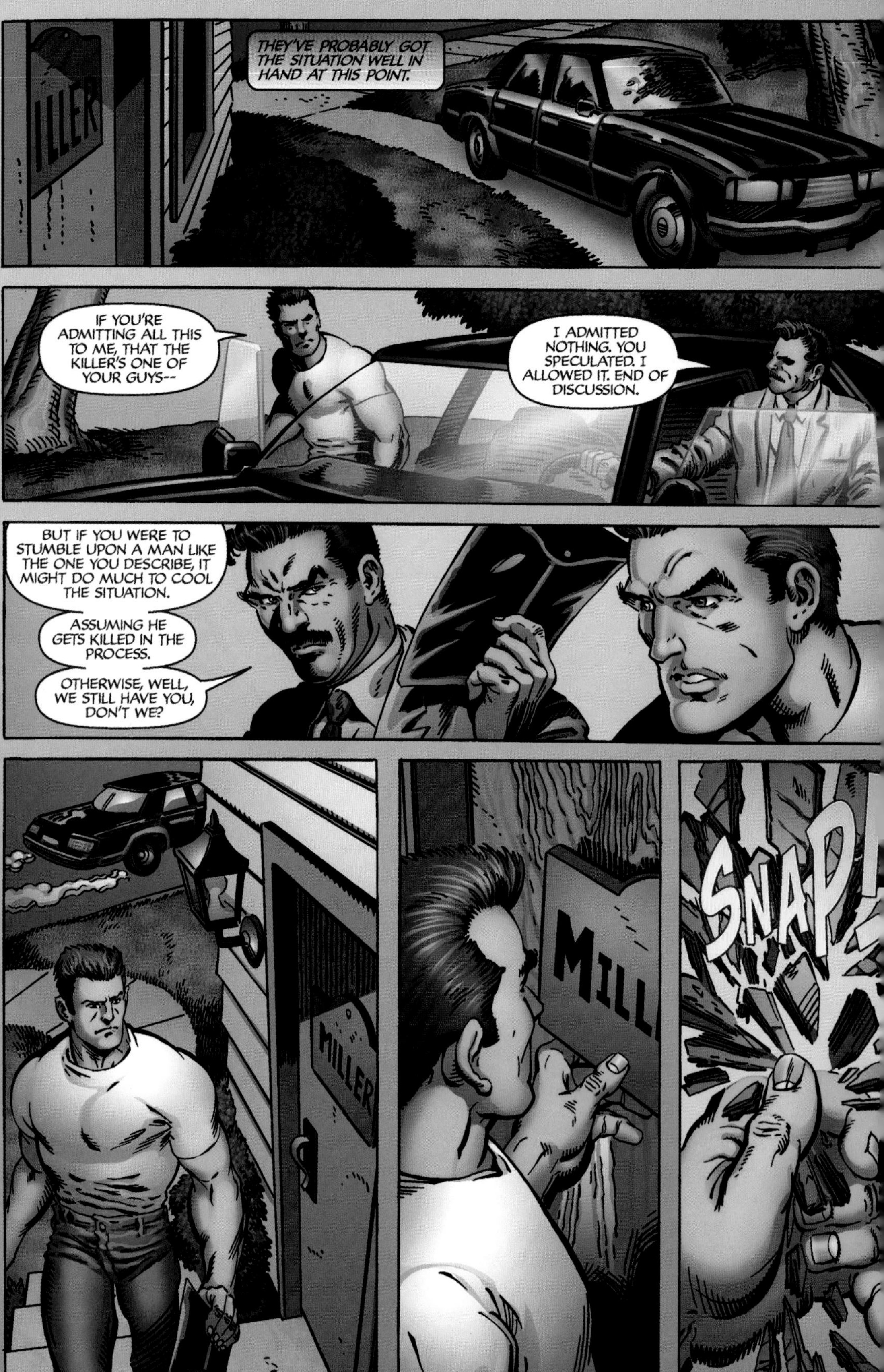

THEY'VE PROBABLY GOT THE SITUATION WELL IN HAND AT THIS POINT.
ILLER
IF YOU'RE ADMITTING ALL THIS TO ME, THAT THE KILLER'S ONE OF YOUR GUYS--
I ADMITTED NOTHING. YOU SPECULATED. I ALLOWED IT. END OF DISCUSSION.
BUT IF YOU WERE TO STUMBLE UPON A MAN LIKE THE ONE YOU DESCRIBE, IT MIGHT DO MUCH TO COOL THE SITUATION.
ASSUMING HE GETS KILLED IN THE PROCESS.
OTHERWISE, WELL, WE STILL HAVE YOU, DON'T WE?
MILLER
MILL
SNAP!

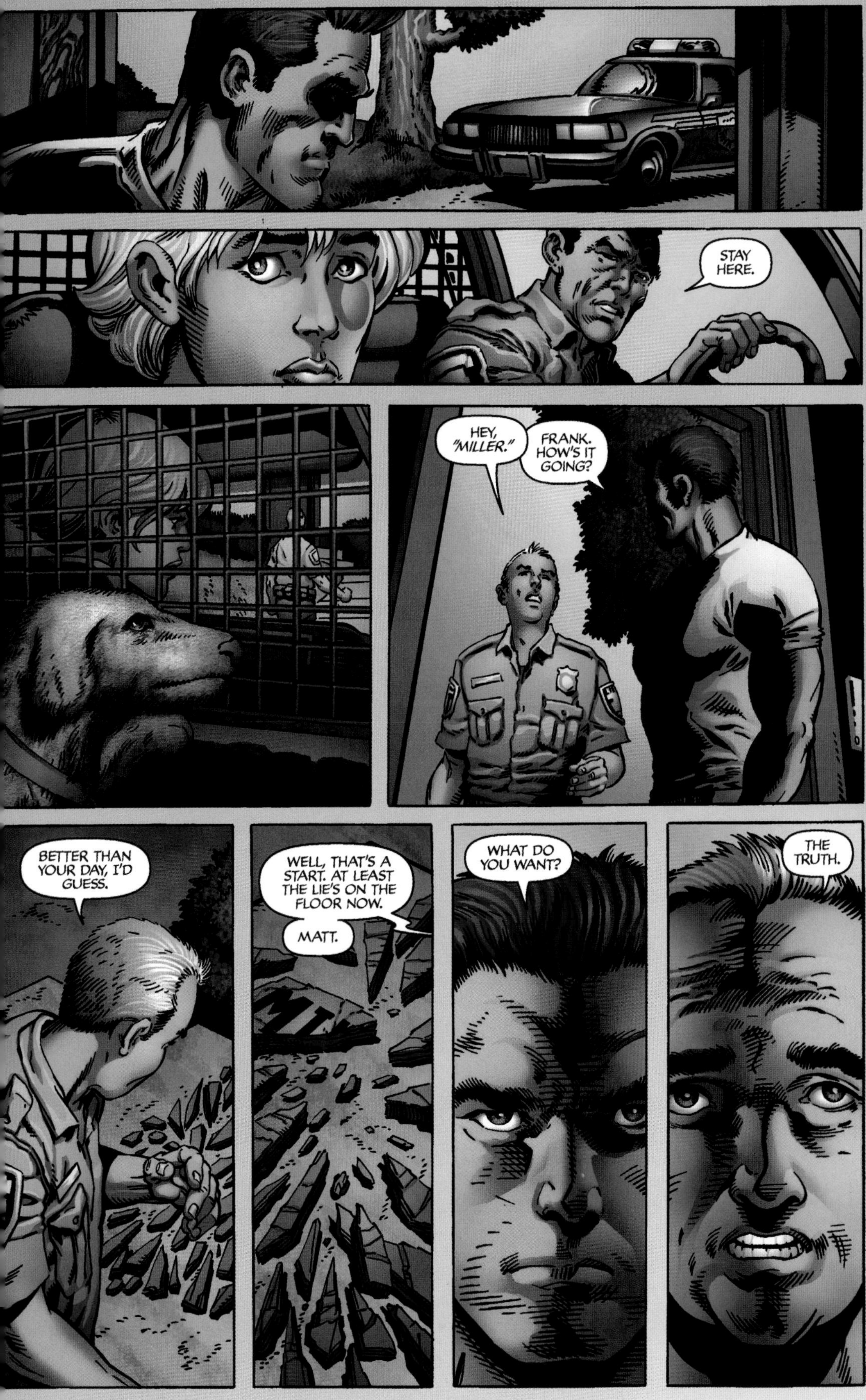
STAY HERE.
HEY, "MILLER."
FRANK. HOW'S IT GOING?
BETTER THAN YOUR DAY, I'D GUESS.
WELL, THAT'S A START. AT LEAST THE LIE'S ON THE FLOOR NOW.
MATT.
WHAT DO YOU WANT?
THE TRUTH.

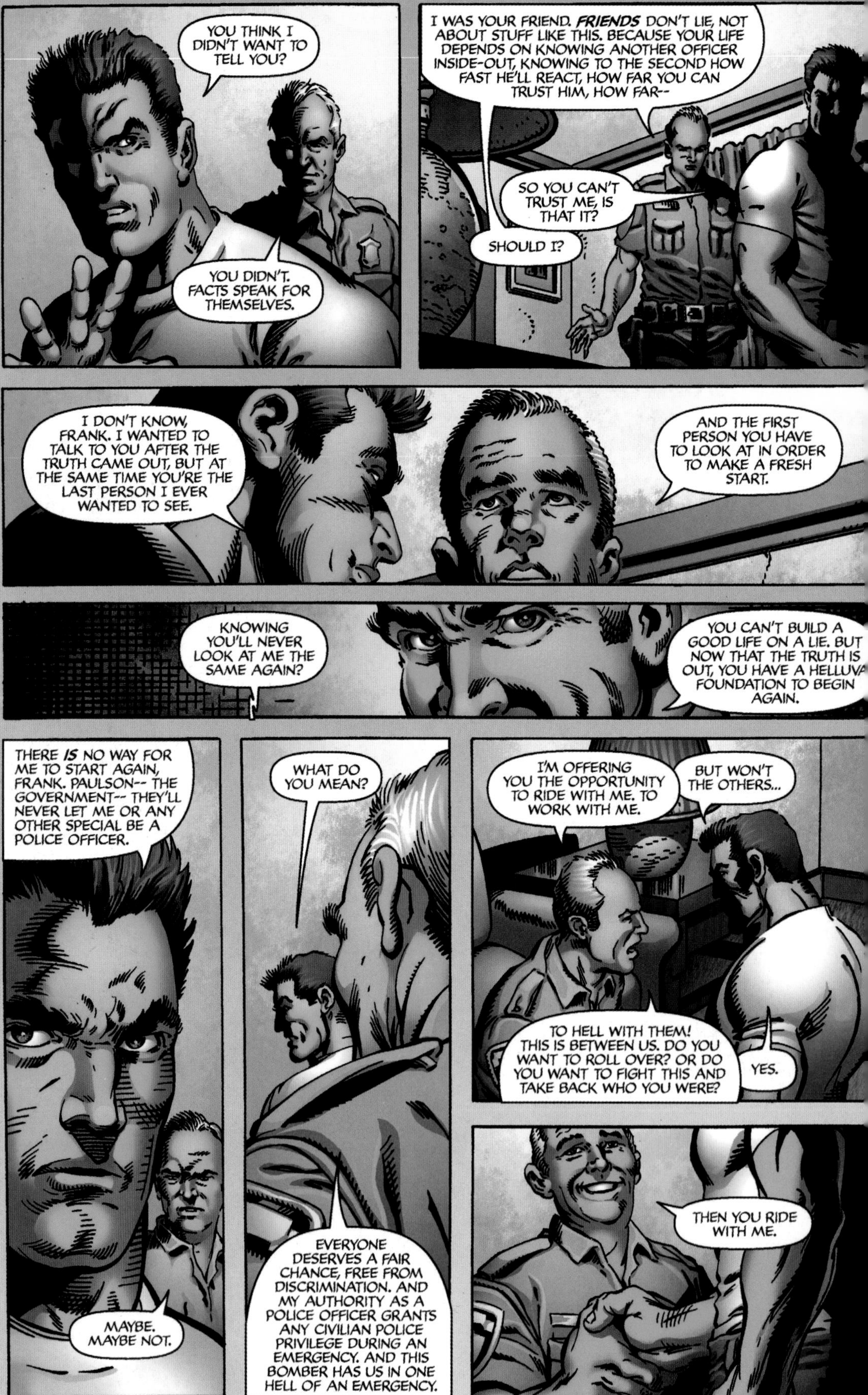
YOU THINK I DIDN'T WANT TO TELL YOU?
YOU DIDN'T. FACTS SPEAK FOR THEMSELVES.
I WAS YOUR FRIEND. FRIENDS DON'T LIE, NOT ABOUT STUFF LIKE THIS. BECAUSE YOUR LIFE DEPENDS ON KNOWING ANOTHER OFFICER INSIDE-OUT, KNOWING TO THE SECOND HOW FAST HE'LL REACT, HOW FAR YOU CAN TRUST HIM, HOW FAR--
SO YOU CAN'T TRUST ME, IS THAT IT?
SHOULD I?
I DON'T KNOW, FRANK. I WANTED TO TALK TO YOU AFTER THE TRUTH CAME OUT, BUT AT THE SAME TIME YOU'RE THE LAST PERSON I EVER WANTED TO SEE.
AND THE FIRST PERSON YOU HAVE TO LOOK AT IN ORDER TO MAKE A FRESH START.
KNOWING YOU'LL NEVER LOOK AT ME THE SAME AGAIN?
YOU CAN'T BUILD A GOOD LIFE ON A LIE. BUT NOW THAT THE TRUTH IS OUT, YOU HAVE A HELLUVA FOUNDATION TO BEGIN AGAIN.
THERE IS NO WAY FOR ME TO START AGAIN, FRANK. PAULSON-- THE GOVERNMENT-- THEY'LL NEVER LET ME OR ANY OTHER SPECIAL BE A POLICE OFFICER.
MAYBE. MAYBE NOT.
WHAT DO YOU MEAN?
EVERYONE DESERVES A FAIR CHANCE, FREE FROM DISCRIMINATION. AND MY AUTHORITY AS A POLICE OFFICER GRANTS ANY CIVILIAN POLICE PRIVILEGE DURING AN EMERGENCY. AND THIS BOMBER HAS US IN ONE HELL OF AN EMERGENCY.
I'M OFFERING YOU THE OPPORTUNITY TO RIDE WITH ME. TO WORK WITH ME.
BUT WON'T THE OTHERS...
TO HELL WITH THEM! THIS IS BETWEEN US. DO YOU WANT TO ROLL OVER? OR DO YOU WANT TO FIGHT THIS AND TAKE BACK WHO YOU WERE?
YES.
THEN YOU RIDE WITH ME.

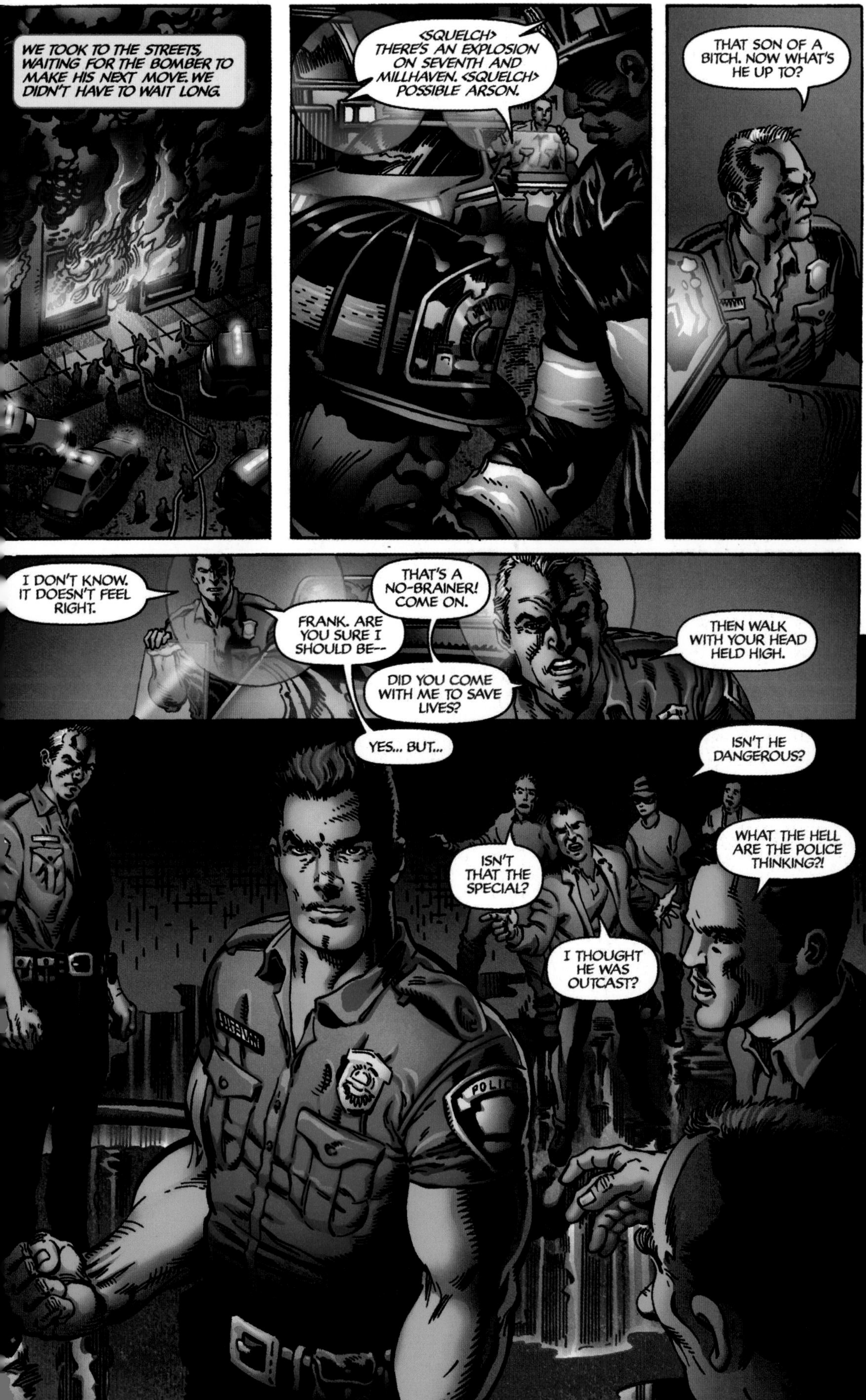

WE TOOK TO THE STREETS, WAITING FOR THE BOMBER TO MAKE HIS NEXT MOVE. WE DIDN'T HAVE TO WAIT LONG.
<SQUELCH> THERE'S AN EXPLOSION ON SEVENTH AND MILLHAVEN. <SQUELCH> POSSIBLE ARSON.
THAT SON OF A BITCH. NOW WHAT'S HE UP TO?
I DON'T KNOW. IT DOESN'T FEEL RIGHT.
THAT'S A NO-BRAINER! COME ON.
FRANK. ARE YOU SURE I SHOULD BE--
DID YOU COME WITH ME TO SAVE LIVES?
YES... BUT...
THEN WALK WITH YOUR HEAD HELD HIGH.
ISN'T HE DANGEROUS?
WHAT THE HELL ARE THE POLICE THINKING?!
ISN'T THAT THE SPECIAL?
I THOUGHT HE WAS OUTCAST?
POLICE

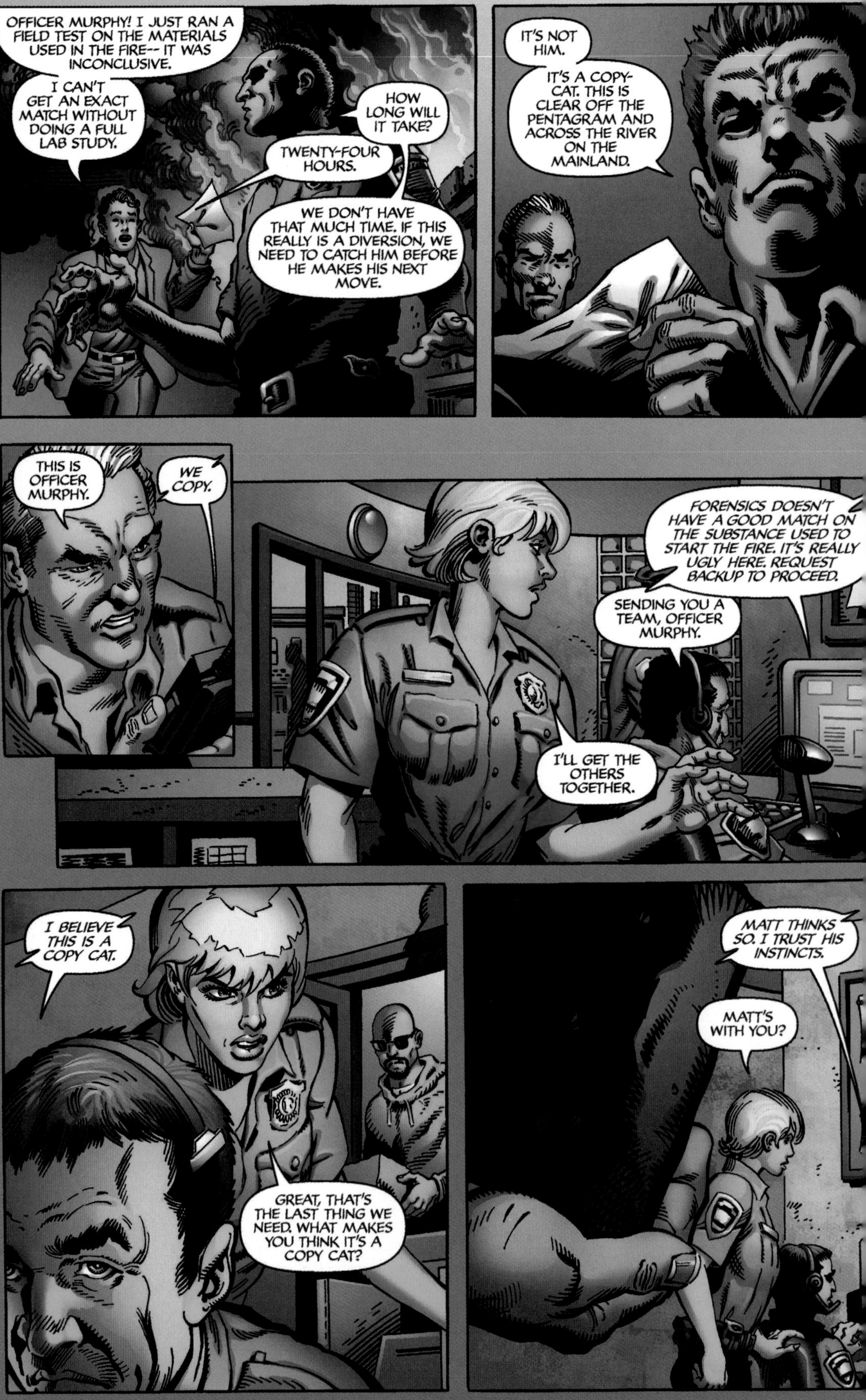
OFFICER MURPHY! I JUST RAN A FIELD TEST ON THE MATERIALS USED IN THE FIRE-- IT WAS INCONCLUSIVE.
I CAN'T GET AN EXACT MATCH WITHOUT DOING A FULL LAB STUDY.
HOW LONG WILL IT TAKE?
TWENTY-FOUR HOURS.
WE DON'T HAVE THAT MUCH TIME. IF THIS REALLY IS A DIVERSION, WE NEED TO CATCH HIM BEFORE HE MAKES HIS NEXT MOVE.
IT'S NOT HIM.
IT'S A COPY-CAT. THIS IS CLEAR OFF THE PENTAGRAM AND ACROSS THE RIVER ON THE MAINLAND.
THIS IS OFFICER MURPHY.
WE COPY.
FORENSICS DOESN'T HAVE A GOOD MATCH ON THE SUBSTANCE USED TO START THE FIRE. IT'S REALLY UGLY HERE. REQUEST BACKUP TO PROCEED.
SENDING YOU A TEAM, OFFICER MURPHY.
I'LL GET THE OTHERS TOGETHER.
I BELIEVE THIS IS A COPY CAT.
GREAT, THAT'S THE LAST THING WE NEED. WHAT MAKES YOU THINK IT'S A COPY CAT?
MATT THINKS SO. I TRUST HIS INSTINCTS.
MATT'S WITH YOU?

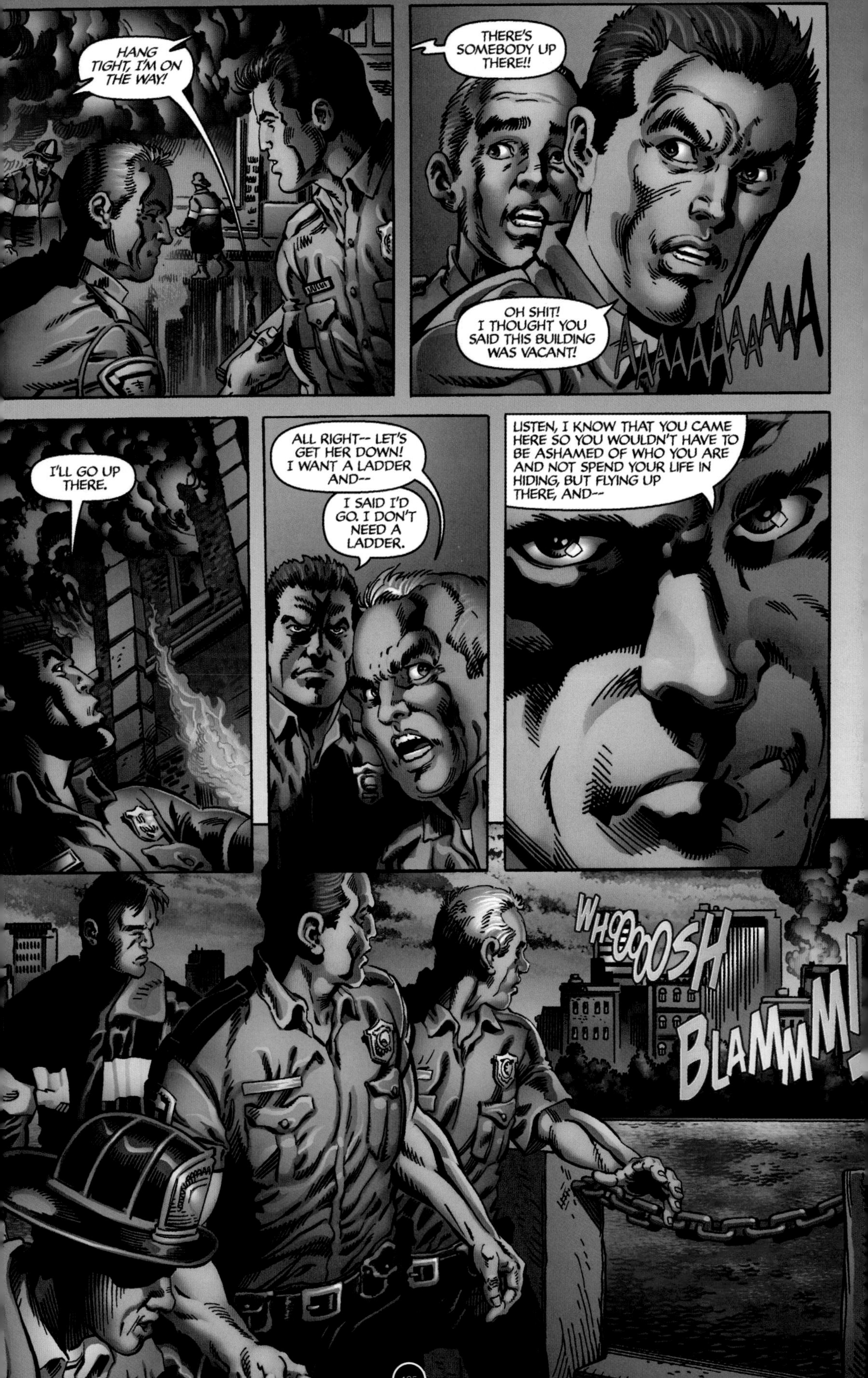

HANG TIGHT, I'M ON THE WAY!
THERE'S SOMEBODY UP THERE!!
OH SHIT! I THOUGHT YOU SAID THIS BUILDING WAS VACANT!
AAAAAAAAAAA
I'LL GO UP THERE.
ALL RIGHT-- LET'S GET HER DOWN! I WANT A LADDER AND--
I SAID I'D GO. I DON'T NEED A LADDER.
LISTEN, I KNOW THAT YOU CAME HERE SO YOU WOULDN'T HAVE TO BE ASHAMED OF WHO YOU ARE AND NOT SPEND YOUR LIFE IN HIDING, BUT FLYING UP THERE, AND--
WHOOOOOSH
BLAMMM!

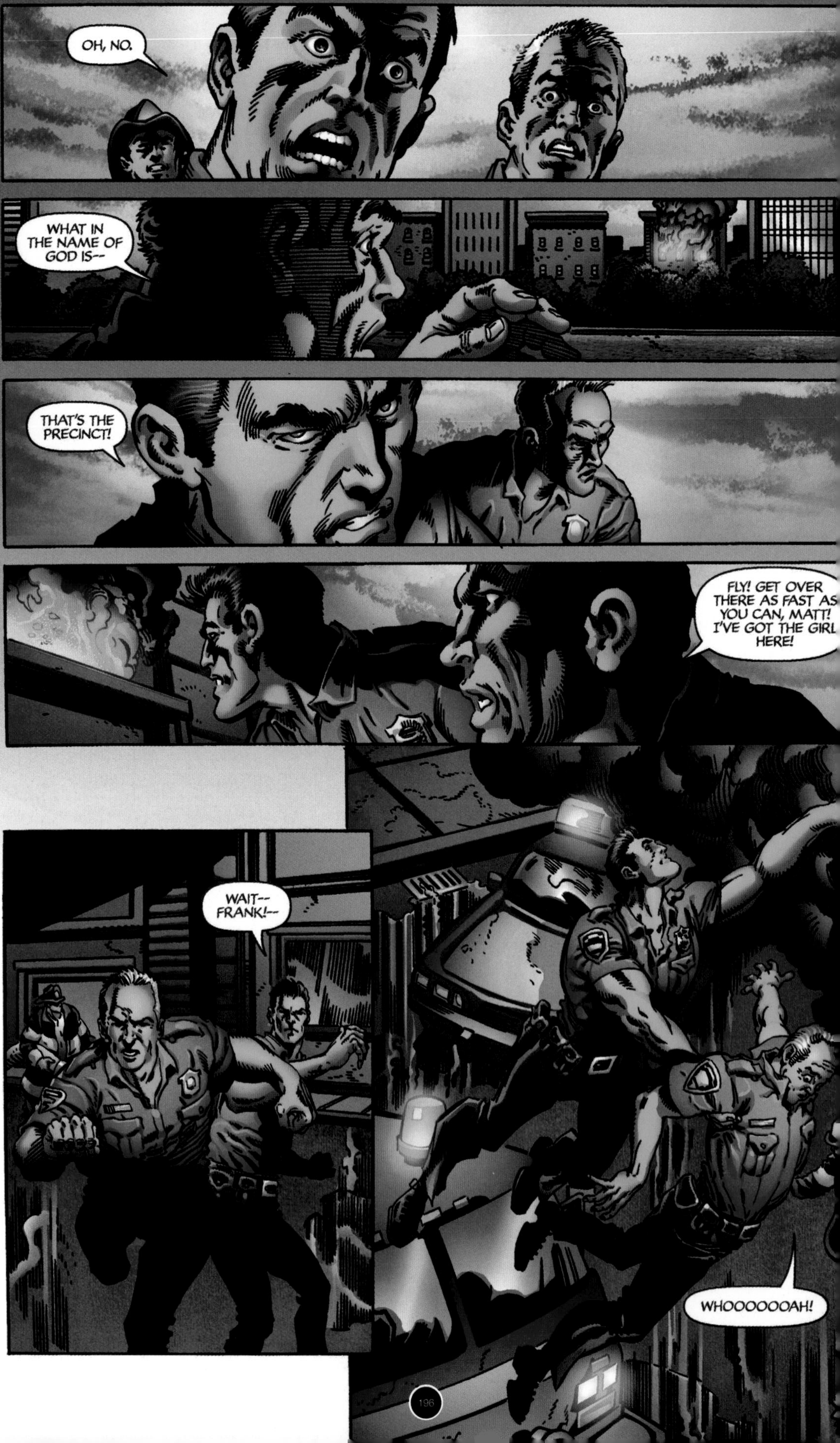
OH, NO.
WHAT IN THE NAME OF GOD IS--
THAT'S THE PRECINCT!
FLY! GET OVER THERE AS FAST AS YOU CAN, MATT! I'VE GOT THE GIRL HERE!
WAIT-- FRANK!--
WHOOOOOOAH!

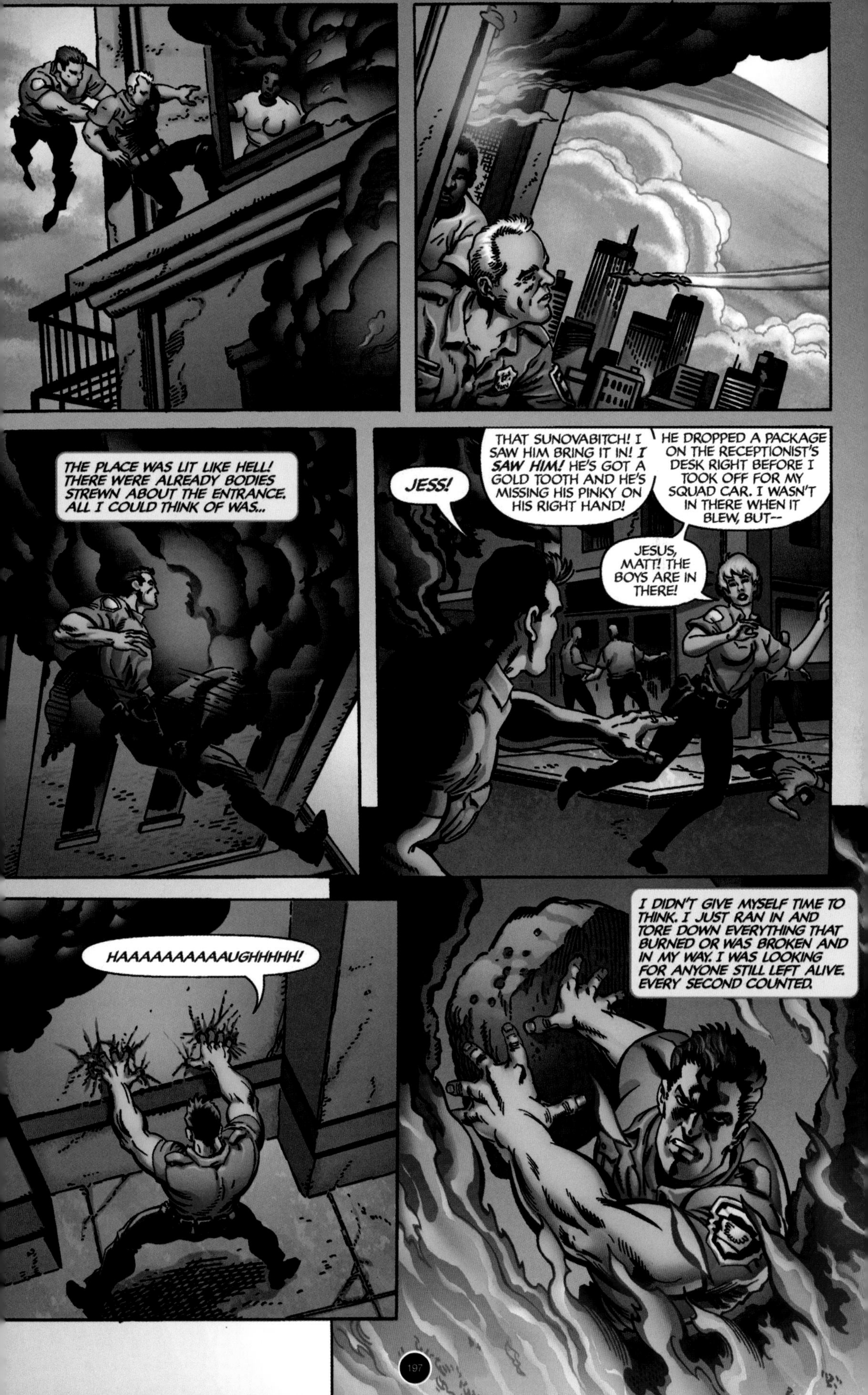

THE PLACE WAS LIT LIKE HELL! THERE WERE ALREADY BODIES STREWN ABOUT THE ENTRANCE. ALL I COULD THINK OF WAS...
JESS!
THAT SUNOVABITCH! I SAW HIM BRING IT IN! I SAW HIM! HE'S GOT A GOLD TOOTH AND HE'S MISSING HIS PINKY ON HIS RIGHT HAND!
HE DROPPED A PACKAGE ON THE RECEPTIONIST'S DESK RIGHT BEFORE I TOOK OFF FOR MY SQUAD CAR. I WASN'T IN THERE WHEN IT BLEW, BUT--
JESUS, MATT! THE BOYS ARE IN THERE!
HAAAAAAAAAAUGHHHHH!
I DIDN'T GIVE MYSELF TIME TO THINK. I JUST RAN IN AND TORE DOWN EVERYTHING THAT BURNED OR WAS BROKEN AND IN MY WAY. I WAS LOOKING FOR ANYONE STILL LEFT ALIVE. EVERY SECOND COUNTED.

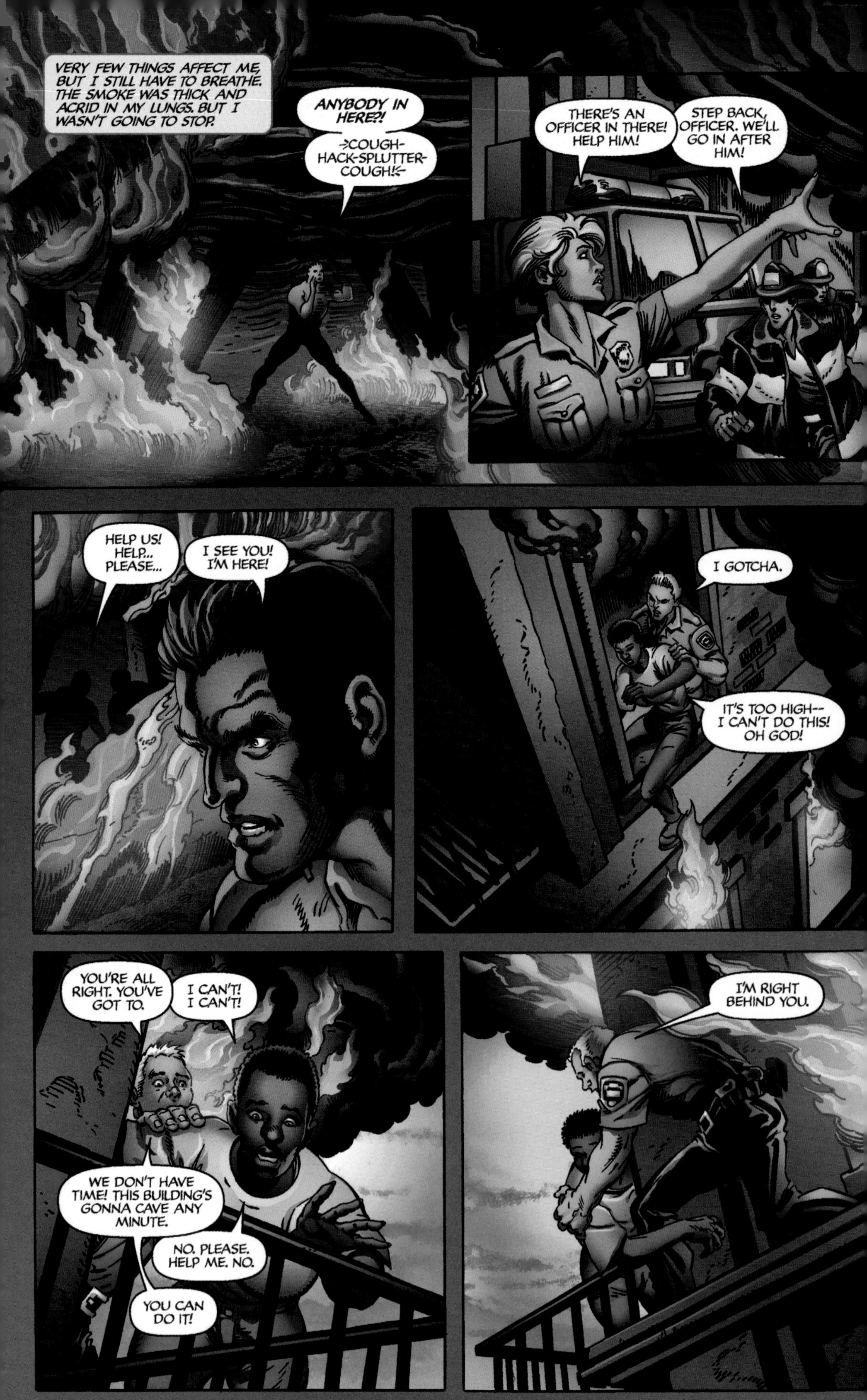
VERY FEW THINGS AFFECT ME, BUT I STILL HAVE TO BREATHE. THE SMOKE WAS THICK AND ACRID IN MY LUNGS. BUT I WASN'T GOING TO STOP.
ANYBODY IN HERE?!
-COUGH-HACK-SPLUTTER-COUGH!-
THERE'S AN OFFICER IN THERE! HELP HIM!
STEP BACK, OFFICER. WE'LL GO IN AFTER HIM!
HELP US! HELP... PLEASE...
I SEE YOU! I'M HERE!
I GOTCHA.
IT'S TOO HIGH-- I CAN'T DO THIS! OH GOD!
YOU'RE ALL RIGHT. YOU'VE GOT TO.
I CAN'T! I CAN'T!
WE DON'T HAVE TIME! THIS BUILDING'S GONNA CAVE ANY MINUTE.
NO. PLEASE. HELP ME. NO.
YOU CAN DO IT!
I'M RIGHT BEHIND YOU.

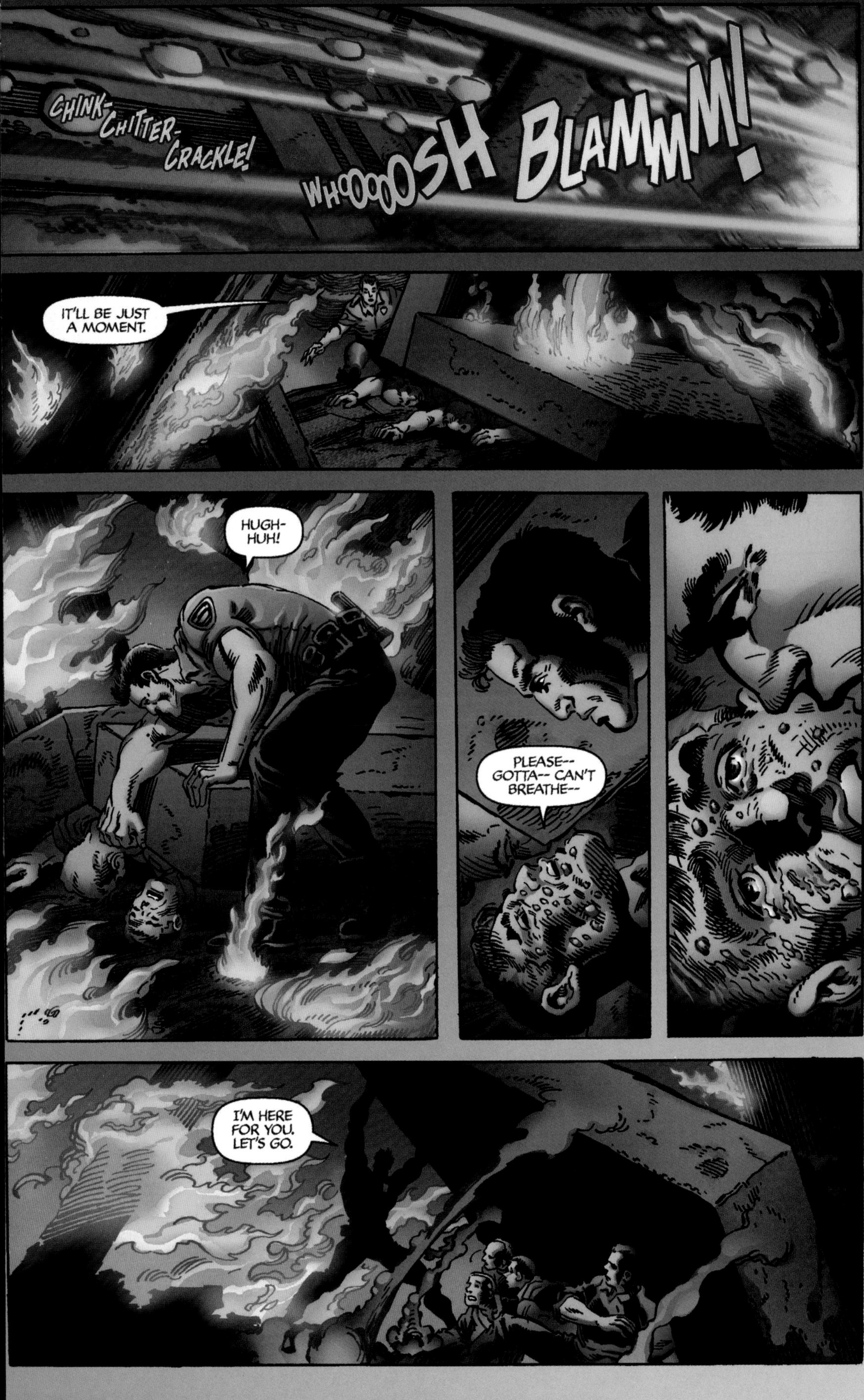
CHINK-CHITTER-CRACKLE!
WHOOOOOSH
BLAMMM!
IT'LL BE JUST A MOMENT.
HUGH-HUH!
PLEASE-- GOTTA-- CAN'T BREATHE--
I'M HERE FOR YOU. LET'S GO.

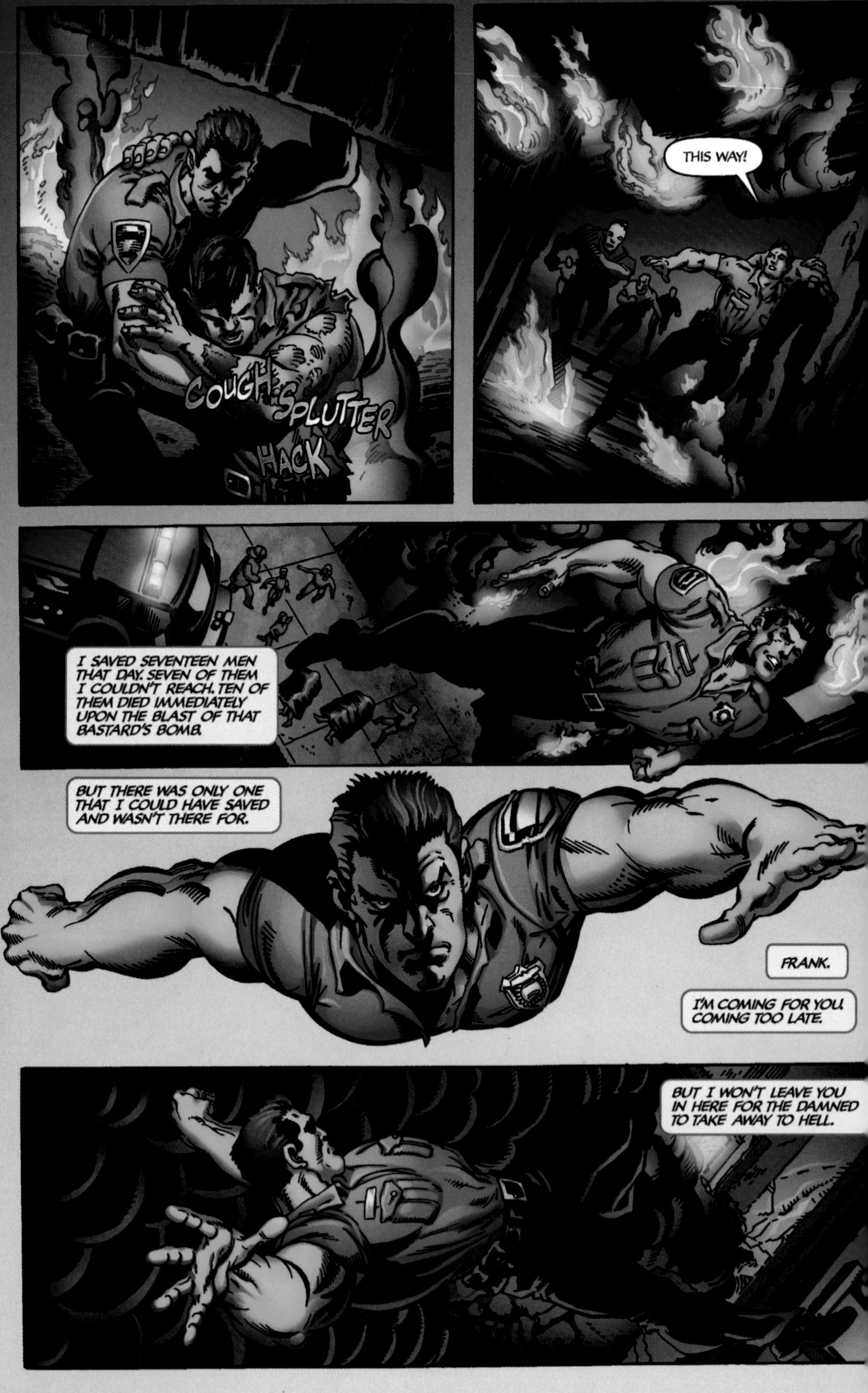
COUGH SPLUTTER
HACK
THIS WAY!
I SAVED SEVENTEEN MEN THAT DAY. SEVEN OF THEM I COULDN'T REACH. TEN OF THEM DIED IMMEDIATELY UPON THE BLAST OF THAT BASTARD'S BOMB.
BUT THERE WAS ONLY ONE THAT I COULD HAVE SAVED AND WASN'T THERE FOR.
FRANK.
I'M COMING FOR YOU. COMING TOO LATE.
BUT I WON'T LEAVE YOU IN HERE FOR THE DAMNED TO TAKE AWAY TO HELL.

I WON'T LEAVE YOU BECAUSE EVEN THOUGH YOU HAD EVERY REASON TO, YOU NEVER LEFT ME.

I COULDN'T FIX THINGS THIS TIME. COULDN'T FIND THE ANSWER BEFORE THE COST WAS TOO GREAT.

"THAT SUNOVABITCH! I SAW HIM BRING IT IN! I SAW HIM!"

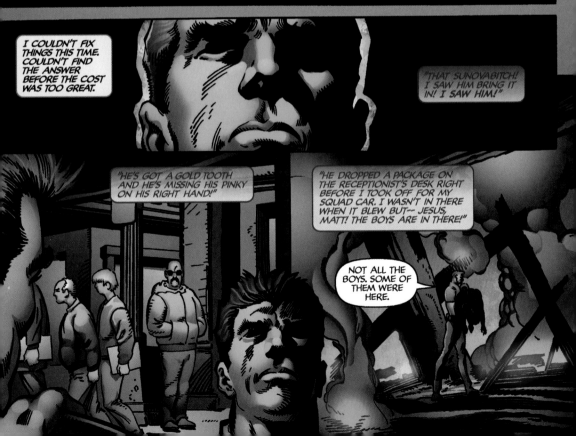

"HE'S GOT A GOLD TOOTH AND HE'S MISSING HIS PINKY ON HIS RIGHT HAND!"

"HE DROPPED A PACKAGE ON THE RECEPTIONIST'S DESK RIGHT BEFORE I TOOK OFF FOR MY SQUAD CAR. I WASN'T IN THERE WHEN IT BLEW BUT-- JESUS, MATT! THE BOYS ARE IN THERE!"

NOT ALL THE BOYS. SOME OF THEM WERE HERE.

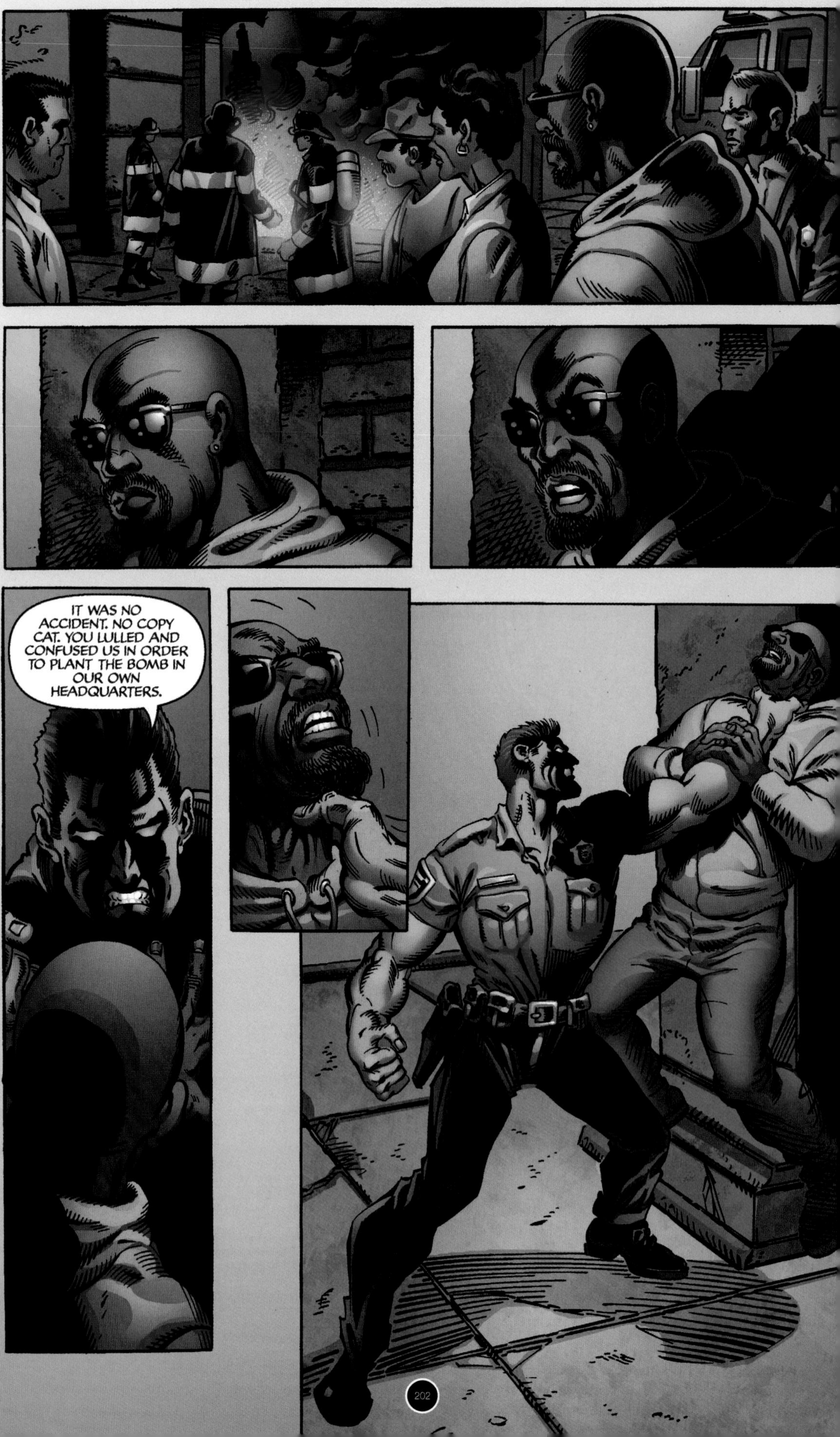
IT WAS NO ACCIDENT. NO COPY CAT. YOU LULLED AND CONFUSED US IN ORDER TO PLANT THE BOMB IN OUR OWN HEADQUARTERS.

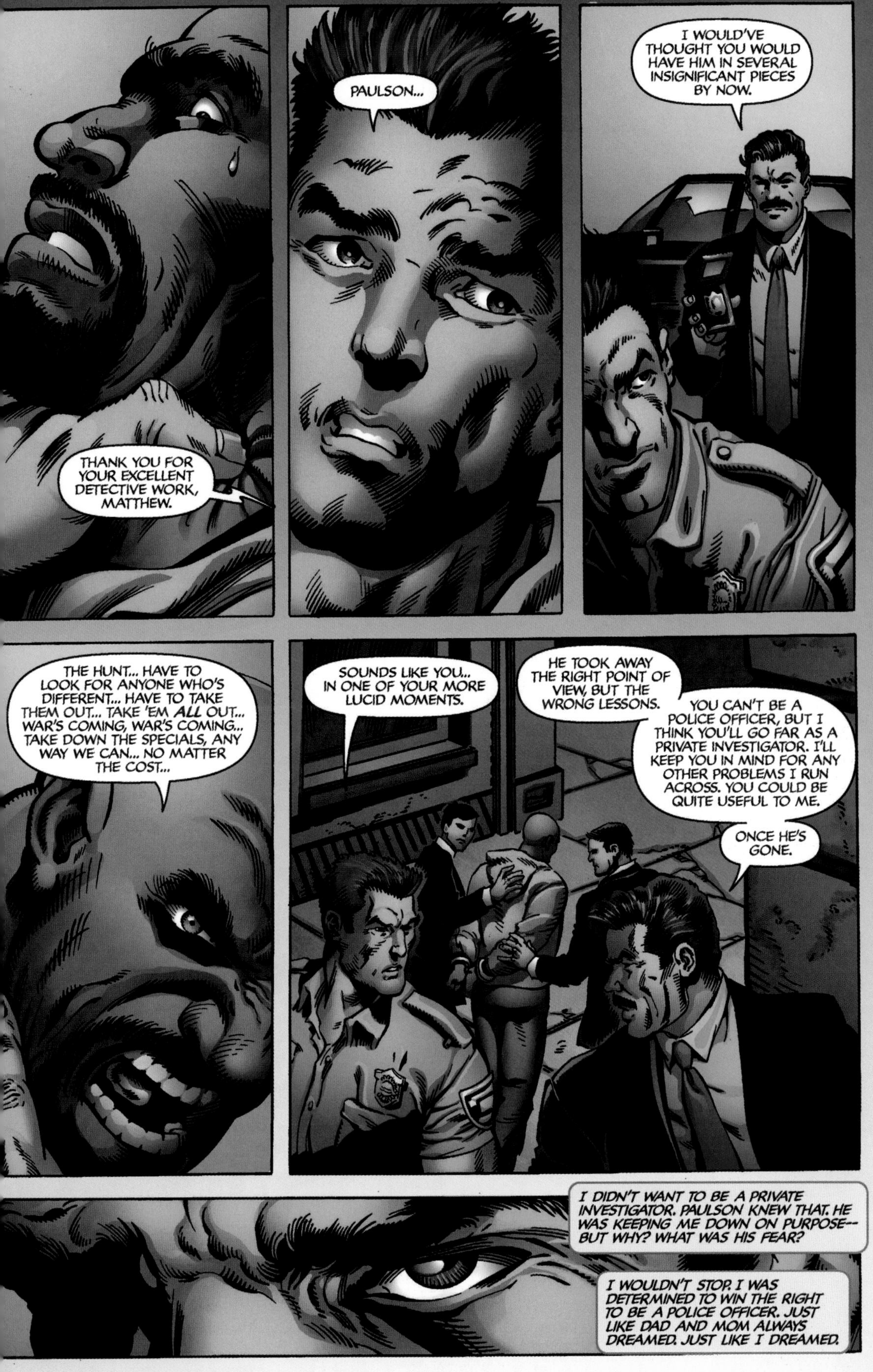
PAULSON...
I WOULD'VE THOUGHT YOU WOULD HAVE HIM IN SEVERAL INSIGNIFICANT PIECES BY NOW.
THANK YOU FOR YOUR EXCELLENT DETECTIVE WORK, MATTHEW.
THE HUNT... HAVE TO LOOK FOR ANYONE WHO'S DIFFERENT... HAVE TO TAKE THEM OUT... TAKE 'EM ALL OUT... WAR'S COMING, WAR'S COMING... TAKE DOWN THE SPECIALS, ANY WAY WE CAN... NO MATTER THE COST...
SOUNDS LIKE YOU... IN ONE OF YOUR MORE LUCID MOMENTS.
HE TOOK AWAY THE RIGHT POINT OF VIEW, BUT THE WRONG LESSONS.
YOU CAN'T BE A POLICE OFFICER, BUT I THINK YOU'LL GO FAR AS A PRIVATE INVESTIGATOR. I'LL KEEP YOU IN MIND FOR ANY OTHER PROBLEMS I RUN ACROSS. YOU COULD BE QUITE USEFUL TO ME.
ONCE HE'S GONE.
I DIDN'T WANT TO BE A PRIVATE INVESTIGATOR. PAULSON KNEW THAT. HE WAS KEEPING ME DOWN ON PURPOSE-- BUT WHY? WHAT WAS HIS FEAR?
I WOULDN'T STOP. I WAS DETERMINED TO WIN THE RIGHT TO BE A POLICE OFFICER. JUST LIKE DAD AND MOM ALWAYS DREAMED. JUST LIKE I DREAMED.

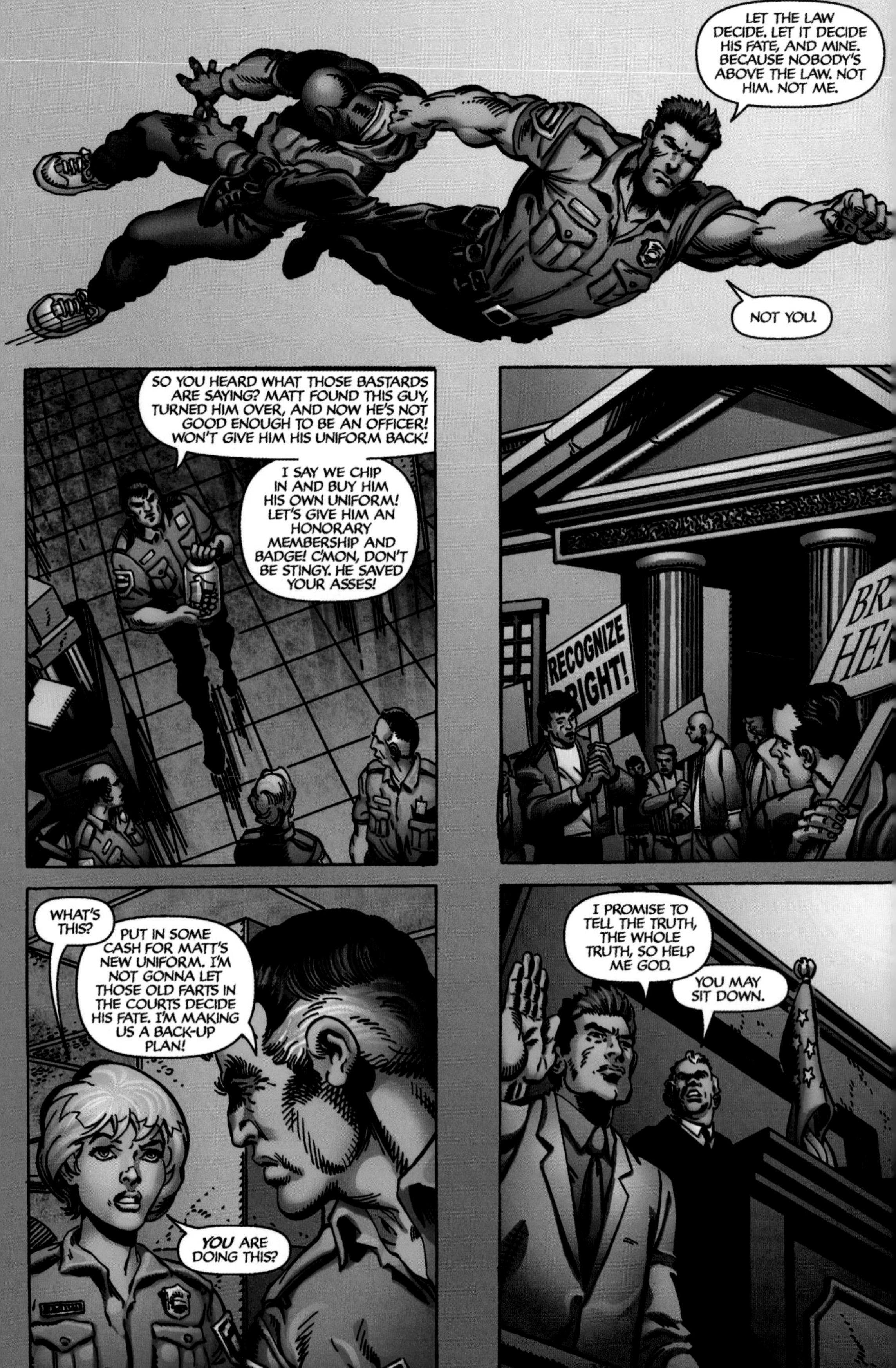
LET THE LAW DECIDE. LET IT DECIDE HIS FATE, AND MINE. BECAUSE NOBODY'S ABOVE THE LAW. NOT HIM. NOT ME.
NOT YOU.
SO YOU HEARD WHAT THOSE BASTARDS ARE SAYING? MATT FOUND THIS GUY, TURNED HIM OVER, AND NOW HE'S NOT GOOD ENOUGH TO BE AN OFFICER! WON'T GIVE HIM HIS UNIFORM BACK!
I SAY WE CHIP IN AND BUY HIM HIS OWN UNIFORM! LET'S GIVE HIM AN HONORARY MEMBERSHIP AND BADGE! C'MON, DON'T BE STINGY. HE SAVED YOUR ASSES!
RECOGNIZE RIGHT!
WHAT'S THIS?
PUT IN SOME CASH FOR MATT'S NEW UNIFORM. I'M NOT GONNA LET THOSE OLD FARTS IN THE COURTS DECIDE HIS FATE. I'M MAKING US A BACK-UP PLAN!
YOU ARE DOING THIS?
I PROMISE TO TELL THE TRUTH, THE WHOLE TRUTH, SO HELP ME GOD.
YOU MAY SIT DOWN.

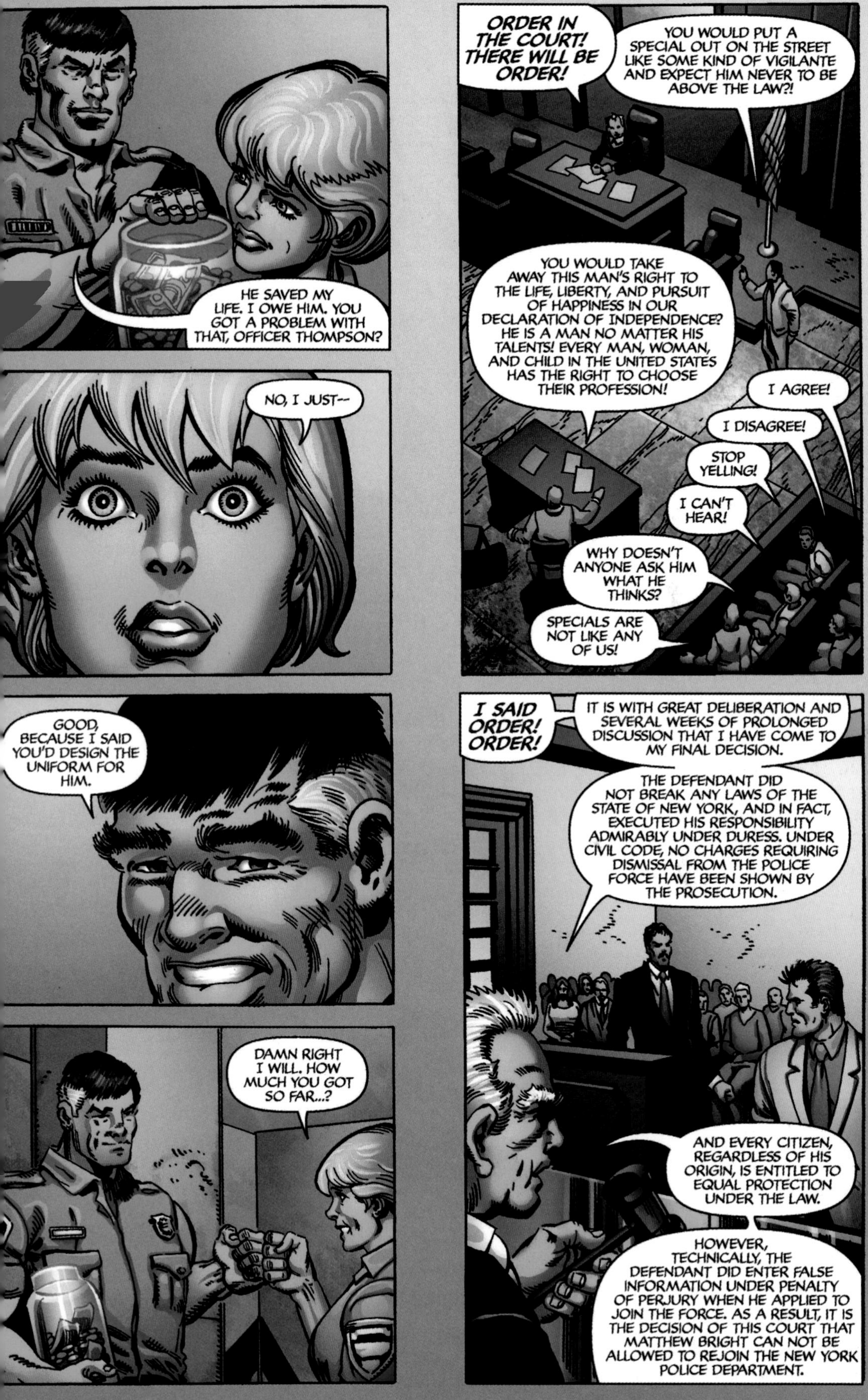
HE SAVED MY LIFE. I OWE HIM. YOU GOT A PROBLEM WITH THAT, OFFICER THOMPSON?
NO, I JUST--
GOOD, BECAUSE I SAID YOU'D DESIGN THE UNIFORM FOR HIM.
DAMN RIGHT I WILL. HOW MUCH YOU GOT SO FAR...?
ORDER IN THE COURT! THERE WILL BE ORDER!
YOU WOULD PUT A SPECIAL OUT ON THE STREET LIKE SOME KIND OF VIGILANTE AND EXPECT HIM NEVER TO BE ABOVE THE LAW?!
YOU WOULD TAKE AWAY THIS MAN'S RIGHT TO THE LIFE, LIBERTY, AND PURSUIT OF HAPPINESS IN OUR DECLARATION OF INDEPENDENCE? HE IS A MAN NO MATTER HIS TALENTS! EVERY MAN, WOMAN, AND CHILD IN THE UNITED STATES HAS THE RIGHT TO CHOOSE THEIR PROFESSION!
I AGREE!
I DISAGREE!
STOP YELLING!
I CAN'T HEAR!
WHY DOESN'T ANYONE ASK HIM WHAT HE THINKS?
SPECIALS ARE NOT LIKE ANY OF US!
I SAID ORDER! ORDER!
IT IS WITH GREAT DELIBERATION AND SEVERAL WEEKS OF PROLONGED DISCUSSION THAT I HAVE COME TO MY FINAL DECISION.
THE DEFENDANT DID NOT BREAK ANY LAWS OF THE STATE OF NEW YORK, AND IN FACT, EXECUTED HIS RESPONSIBILITY ADMIRABLY UNDER DURESS. UNDER CIVIL CODE, NO CHARGES REQUIRING DISMISSAL FROM THE POLICE FORCE HAVE BEEN SHOWN BY THE PROSECUTION.
AND EVERY CITIZEN, REGARDLESS OF HIS ORIGIN, IS ENTITLED TO EQUAL PROTECTION UNDER THE LAW.
HOWEVER, TECHNICALLY, THE DEFENDANT DID ENTER FALSE INFORMATION UNDER PENALTY OF PERJURY WHEN HE APPLIED TO JOIN THE FORCE. AS A RESULT, IT IS THE DECISION OF THIS COURT THAT MATTHEW BRIGHT CAN NOT BE ALLOWED TO REJOIN THE NEW YORK POLICE DEPARTMENT.

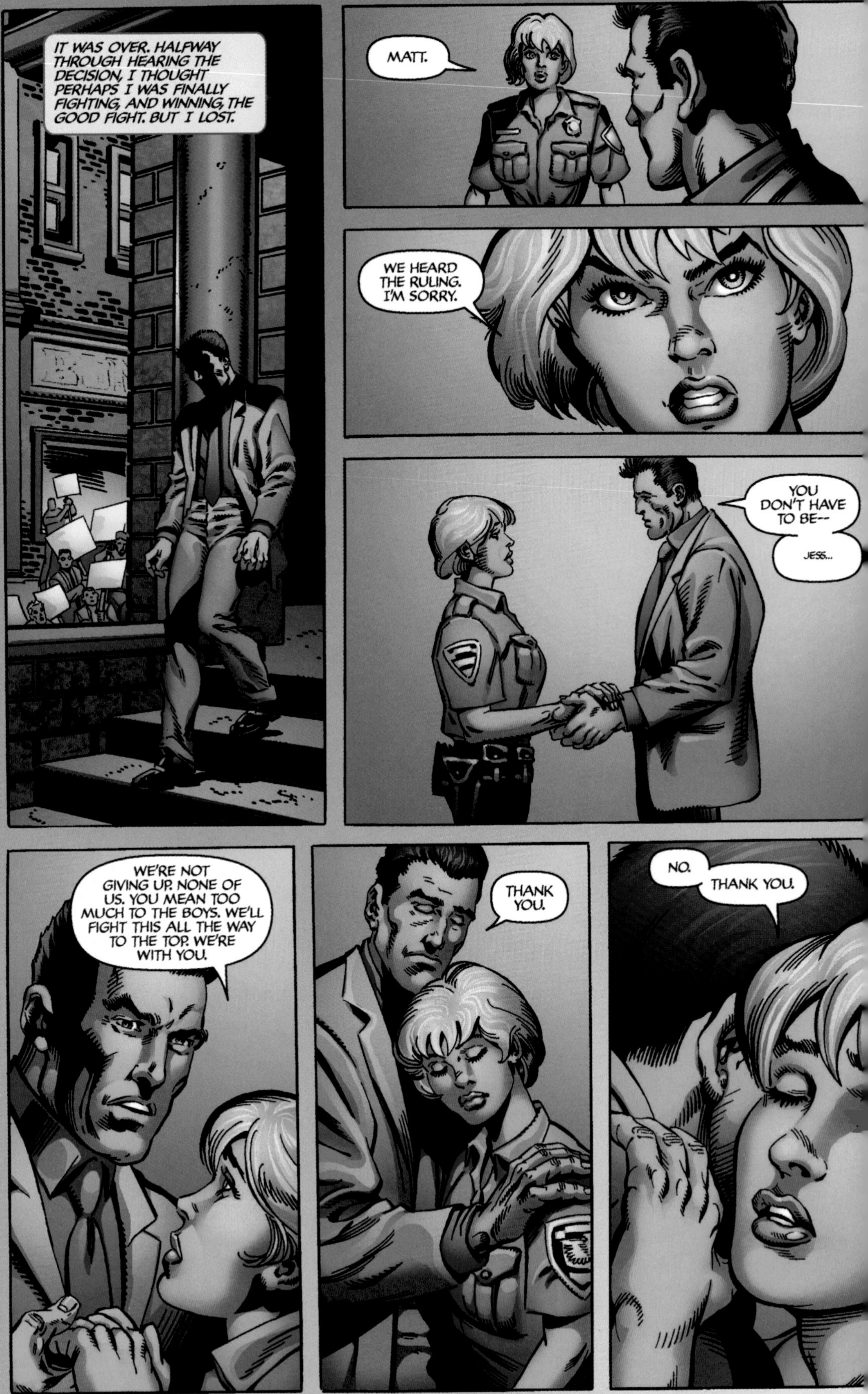
IT WAS OVER. HALFWAY THROUGH HEARING THE DECISION, I THOUGHT PERHAPS I WAS FINALLY FIGHTING, AND WINNING, THE GOOD FIGHT. BUT I LOST.
MATT.
WE HEARD THE RULING. I'M SORRY.
YOU DON'T HAVE TO BE--
JESS...
WE'RE NOT GIVING UP. NONE OF US. YOU MEAN TOO MUCH TO THE BOYS. WE'LL FIGHT THIS ALL THE WAY TO THE TOP. WE'RE WITH YOU.
THANK YOU.
NO.
THANK YOU.

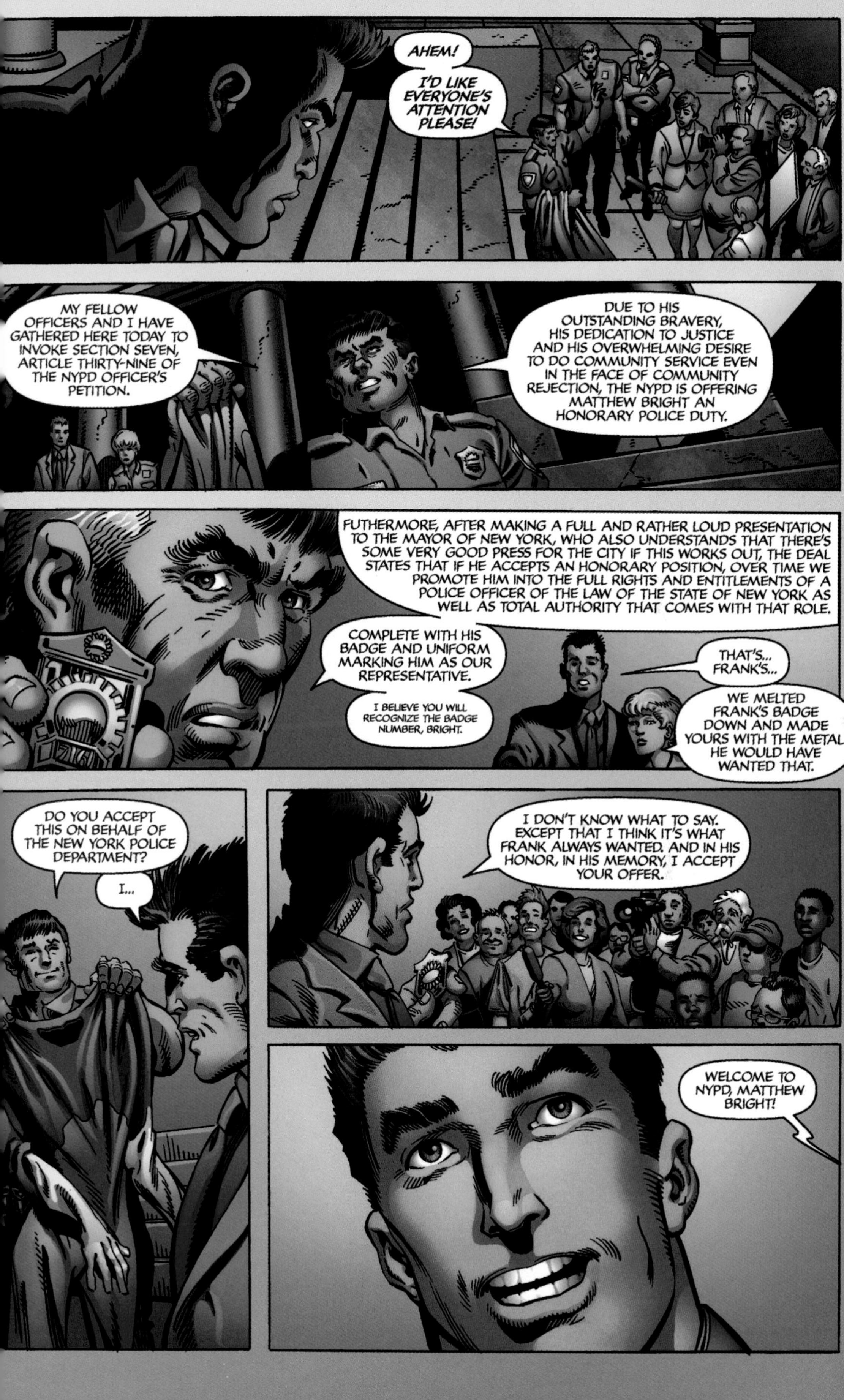
AHEM!
I'D LIKE EVERYONE'S ATTENTION PLEASE!
MY FELLOW OFFICERS AND I HAVE GATHERED HERE TODAY TO INVOKE SECTION SEVEN, ARTICLE THIRTY-NINE OF THE NYPD OFFICER'S PETITION.
DUE TO HIS OUTSTANDING BRAVERY, HIS DEDICATION TO JUSTICE AND HIS OVERWHELMING DESIRE TO DO COMMUNITY SERVICE EVEN IN THE FACE OF COMMUNITY REJECTION, THE NYPD IS OFFERING MATTHEW BRIGHT AN HONORARY POLICE DUTY.
FUTHERMORE, AFTER MAKING A FULL AND RATHER LOUD PRESENTATION TO THE MAYOR OF NEW YORK, WHO ALSO UNDERSTANDS THAT THERE'S SOME VERY GOOD PRESS FOR THE CITY IF THIS WORKS OUT, THE DEAL STATES THAT IF HE ACCEPTS AN HONORARY POSITION, OVER TIME WE PROMOTE HIM INTO THE FULL RIGHTS AND ENTITLEMENTS OF A POLICE OFFICER OF THE LAW OF THE STATE OF NEW YORK AS WELL AS TOTAL AUTHORITY THAT COMES WITH THAT ROLE.
COMPLETE WITH HIS BADGE AND UNIFORM MARKING HIM AS OUR REPRESENTATIVE.
I BELIEVE YOU WILL RECOGNIZE THE BADGE NUMBER, BRIGHT.
THAT'S... FRANK'S...
WE MELTED FRANK'S BADGE DOWN AND MADE YOURS WITH THE METAL. HE WOULD HAVE WANTED THAT.
DO YOU ACCEPT THIS ON BEHALF OF THE NEW YORK POLICE DEPARTMENT?
I...
I DON'T KNOW WHAT TO SAY. EXCEPT THAT I THINK IT'S WHAT FRANK ALWAYS WANTED. AND IN HIS HONOR, IN HIS MEMORY, I ACCEPT YOUR OFFER.
WELCOME TO NYPD, MATTHEW BRIGHT!

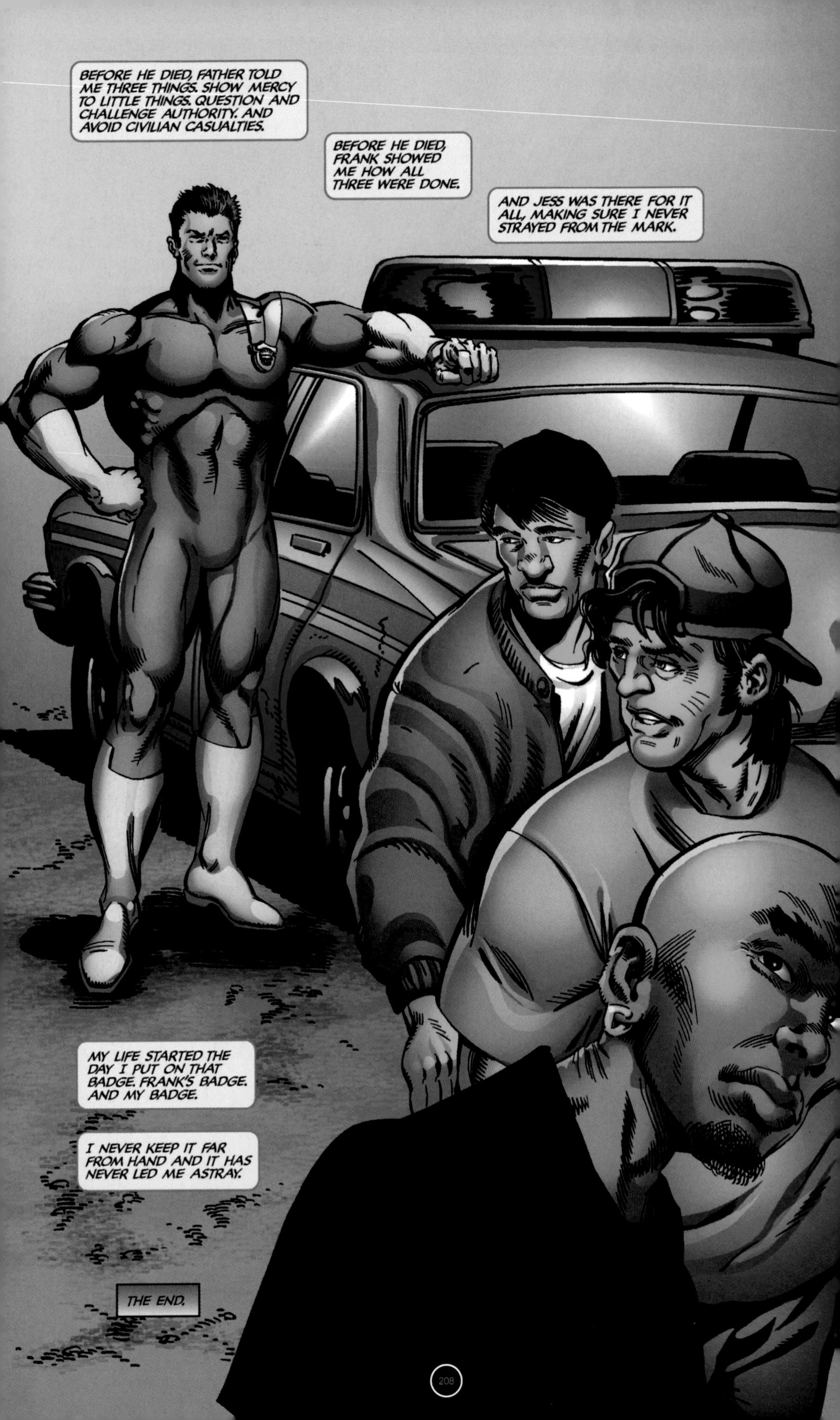
BEFORE HE DIED, FATHER TOLD ME THREE THINGS. SHOW MERCY TO LITTLE THINGS. QUESTION AND CHALLENGE AUTHORITY. AND AVOID CIVILIAN CASUALTIES.
BEFORE HE DIED, FRANK SHOWED ME HOW ALL THREE WERE DONE.
AND JESS WAS THERE FOR IT ALL, MAKING SURE I NEVER STRAYED FROM THE MARK.
MY LIFE STARTED THE DAY I PUT ON THAT BADGE. FRANK'S BADGE. AND MY BADGE.
I NEVER KEEP IT FAR FROM HAND AND IT HAS NEVER LED ME ASTRAY.
THE END.

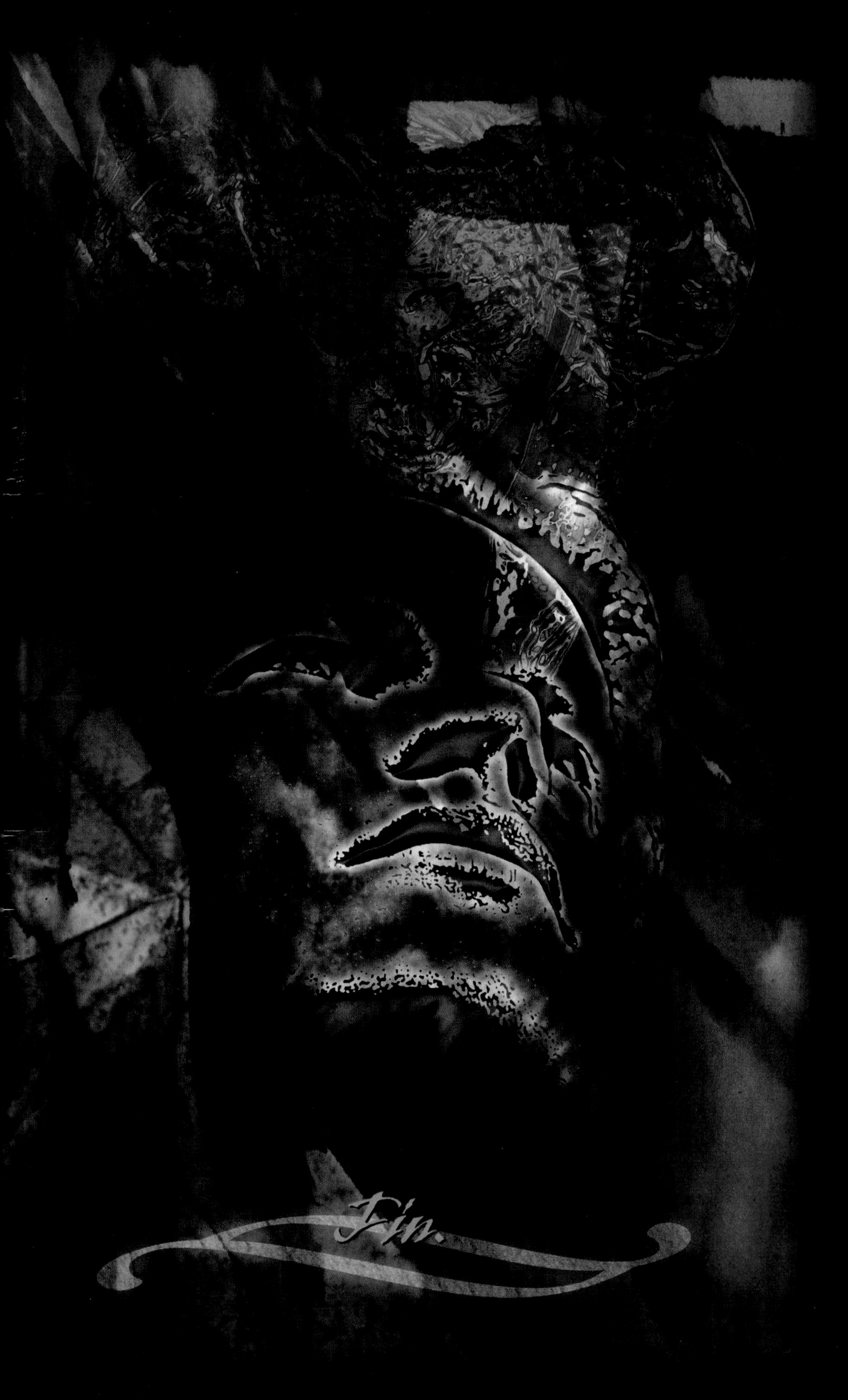
Fin.

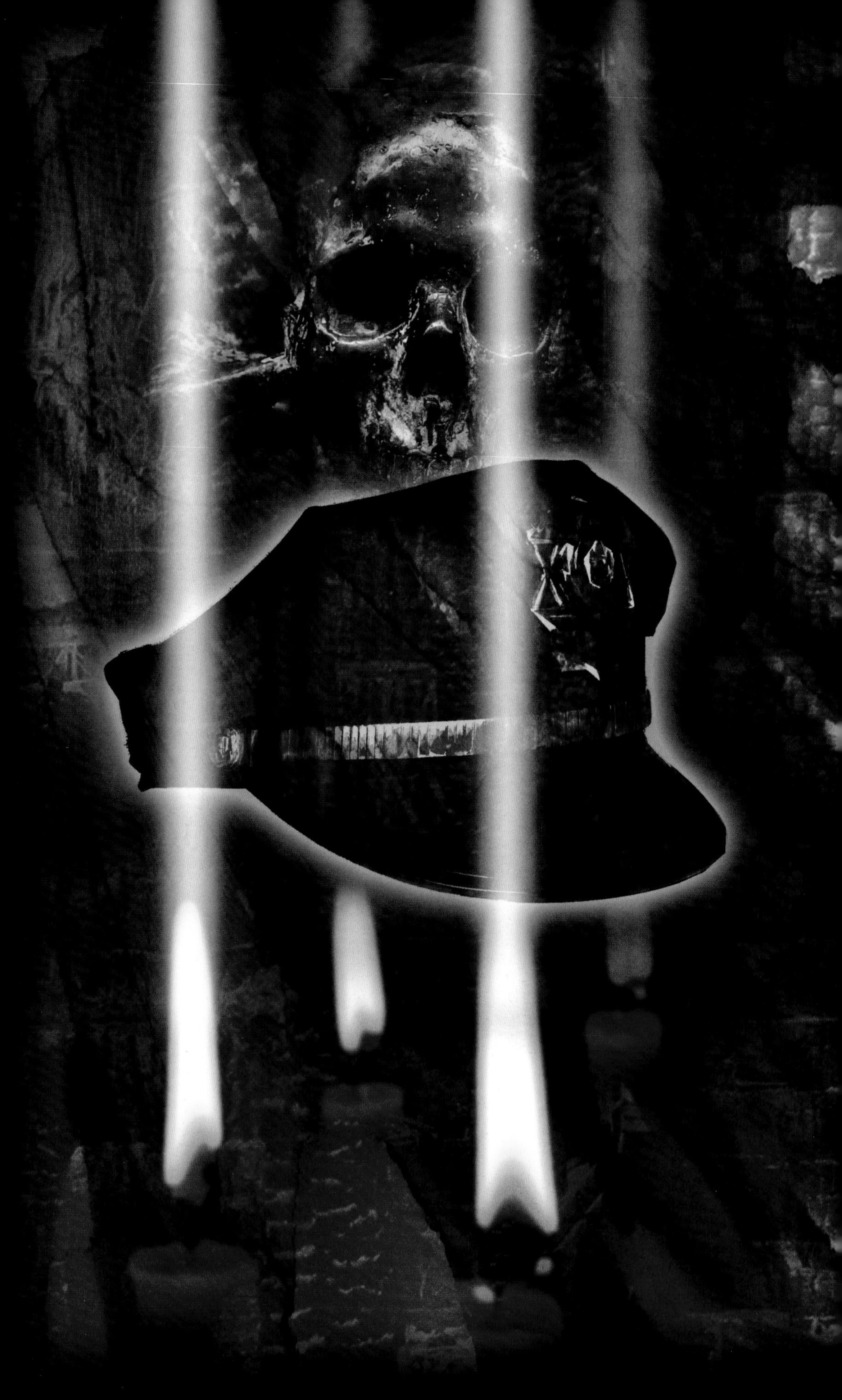

Cover Gallery

Rising Stars:
Voices of the Dead

Rising Stars:
Bright

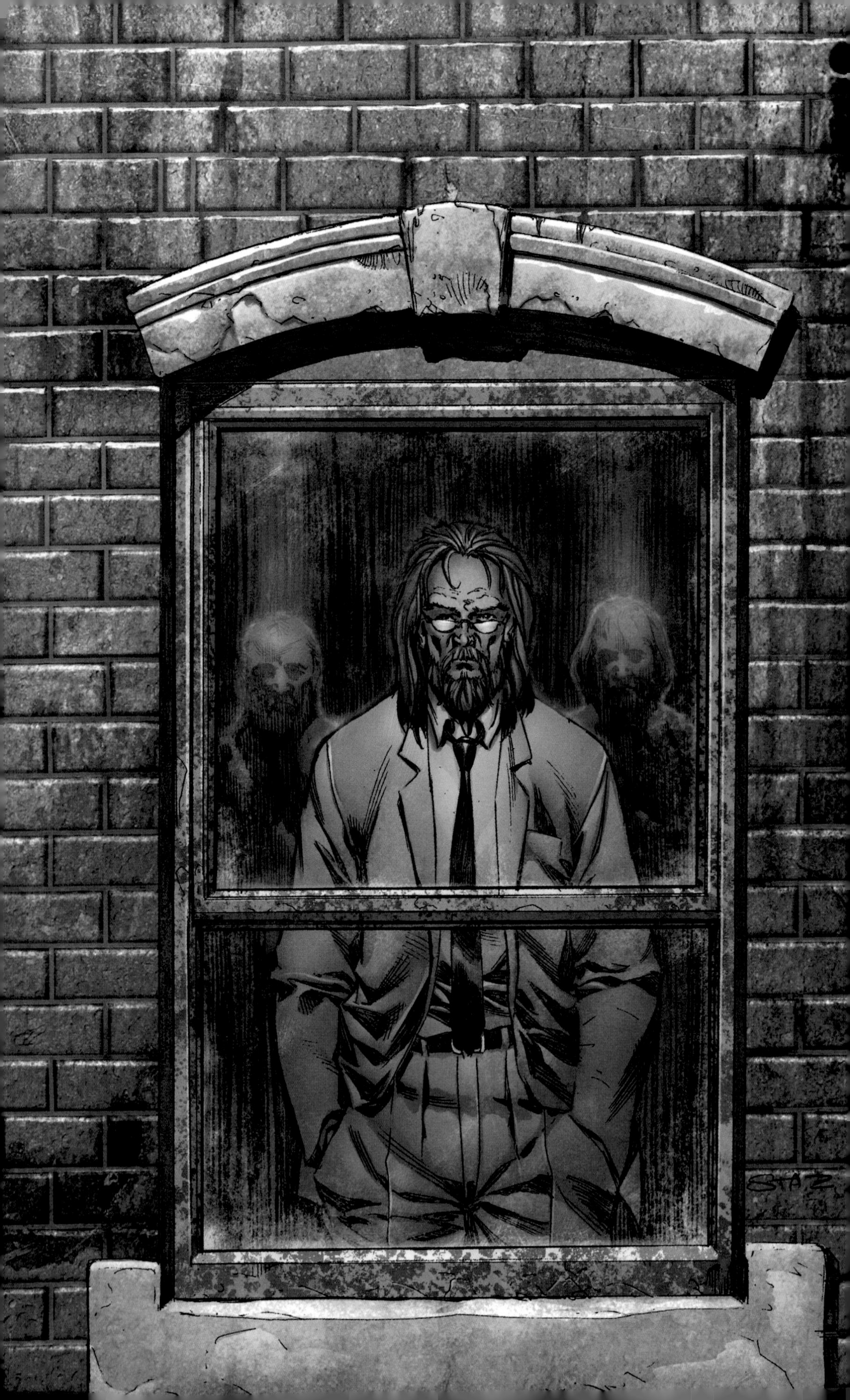

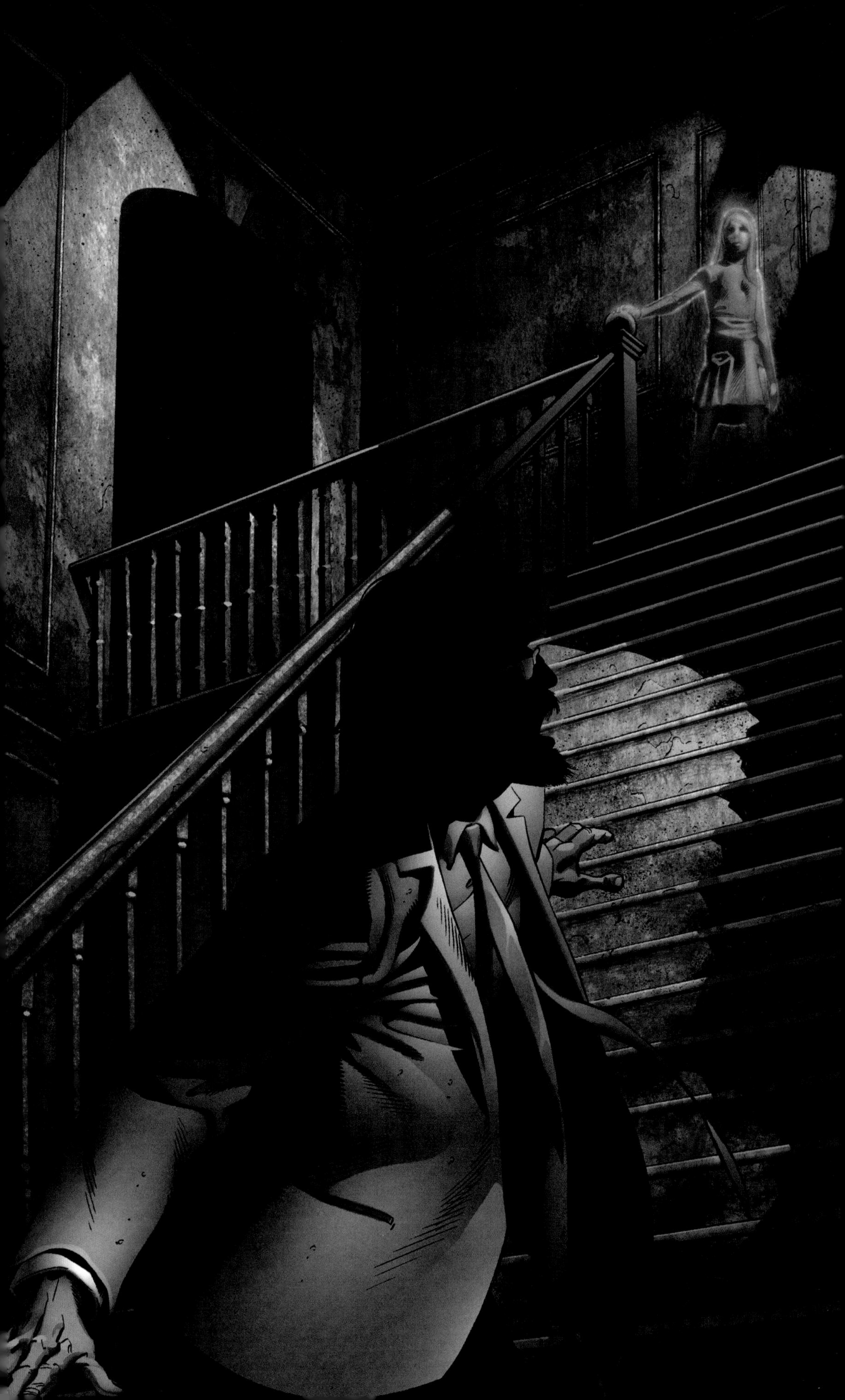

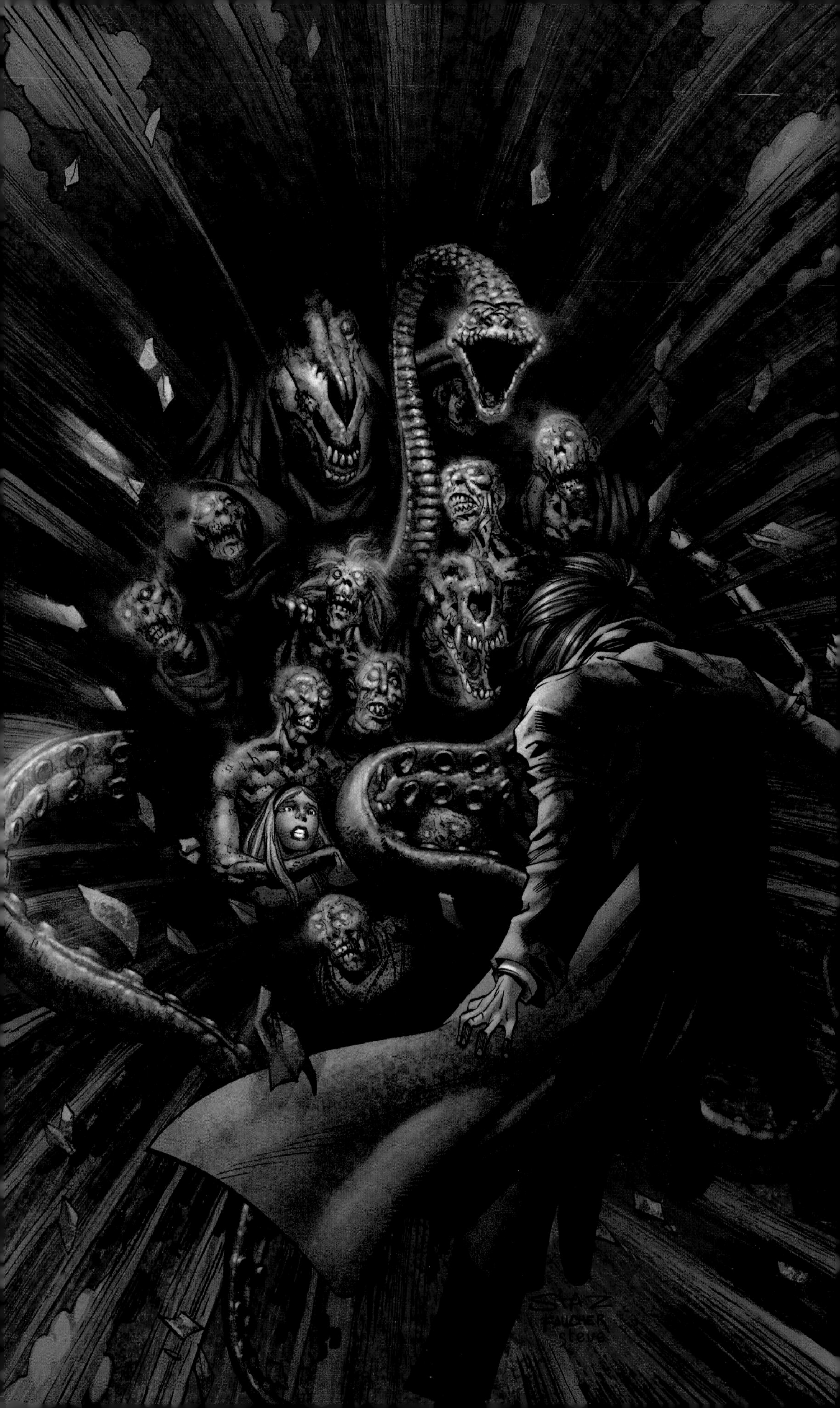

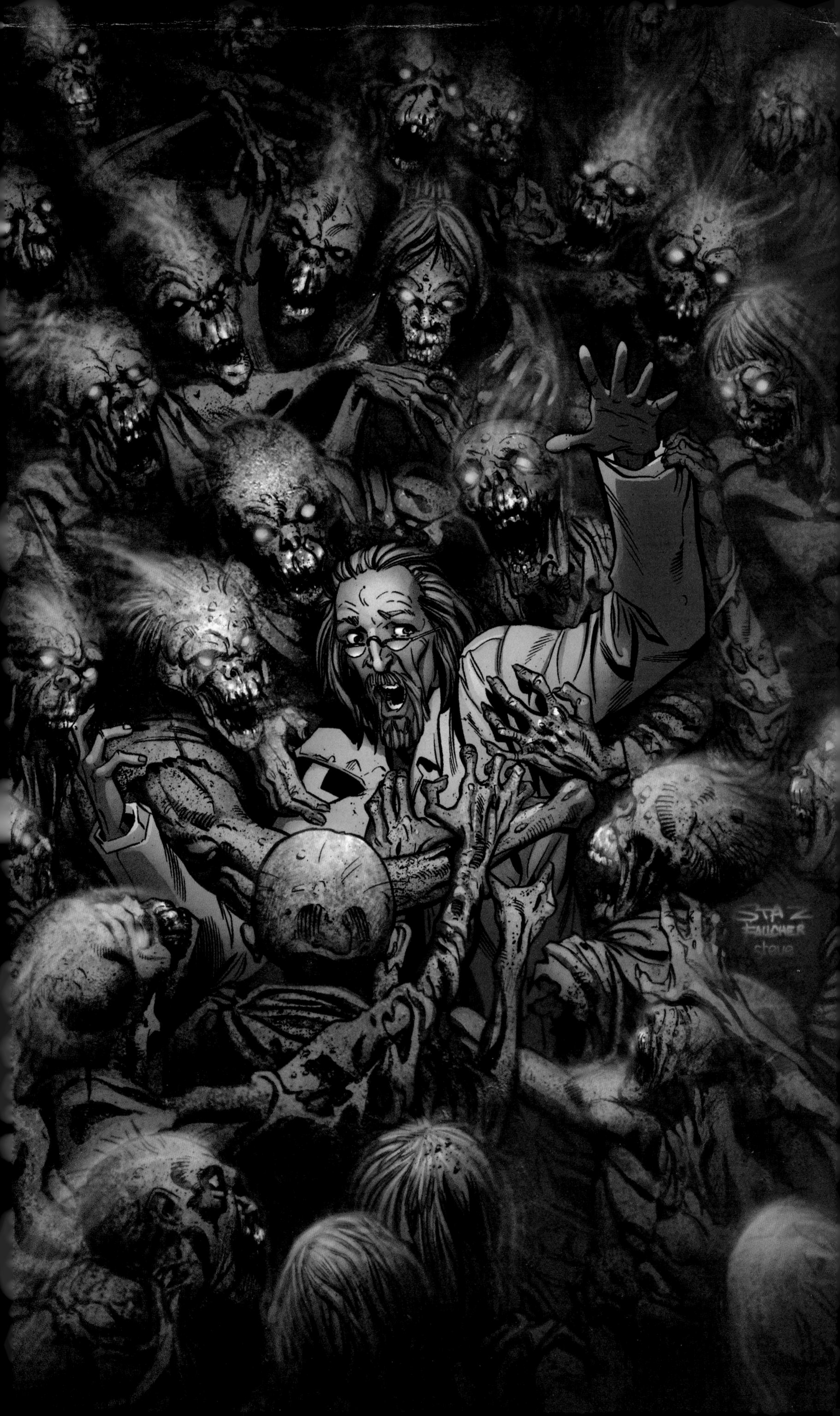
STAZ
FAUCHER
steve

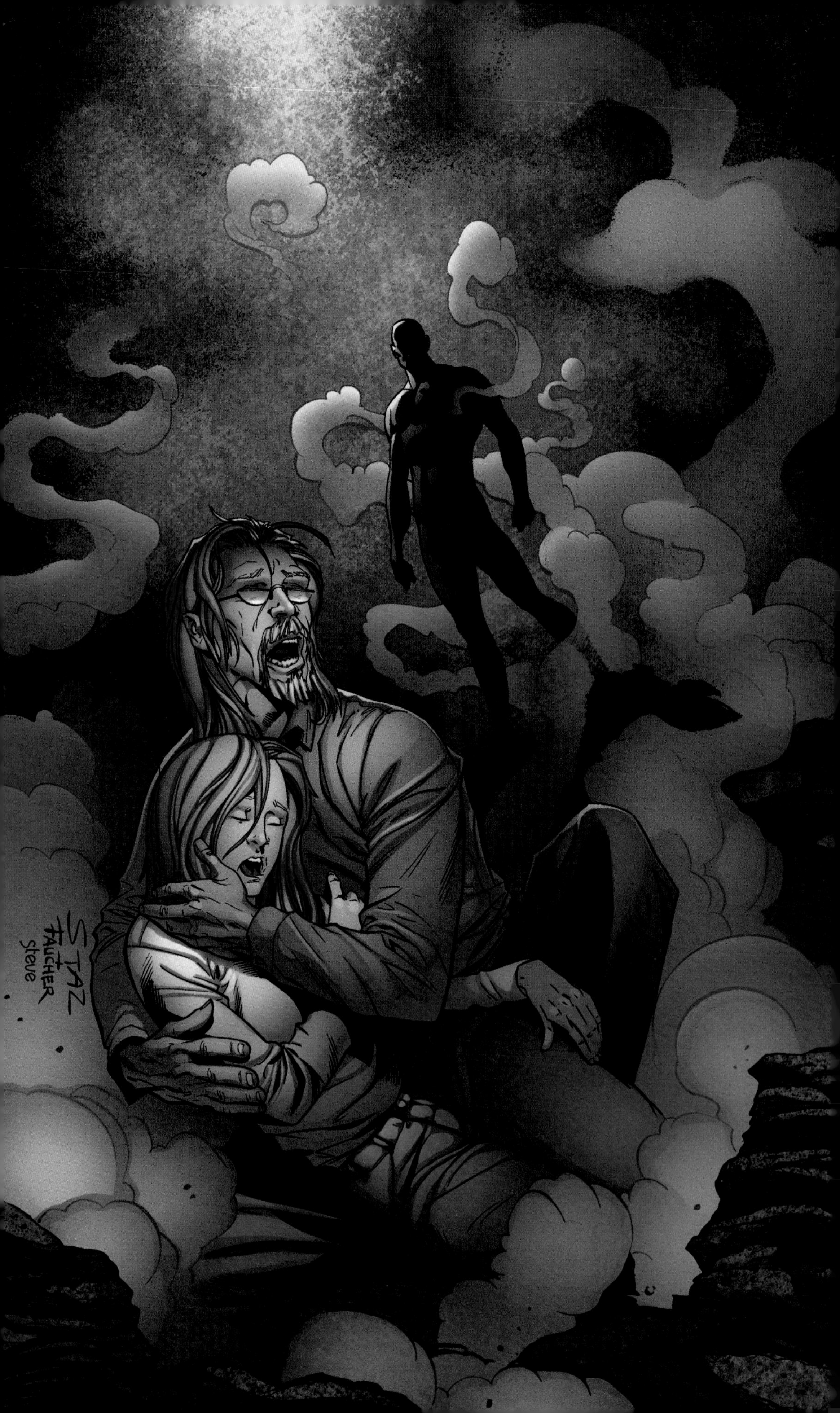
STAZ
+FAUCHER
steve

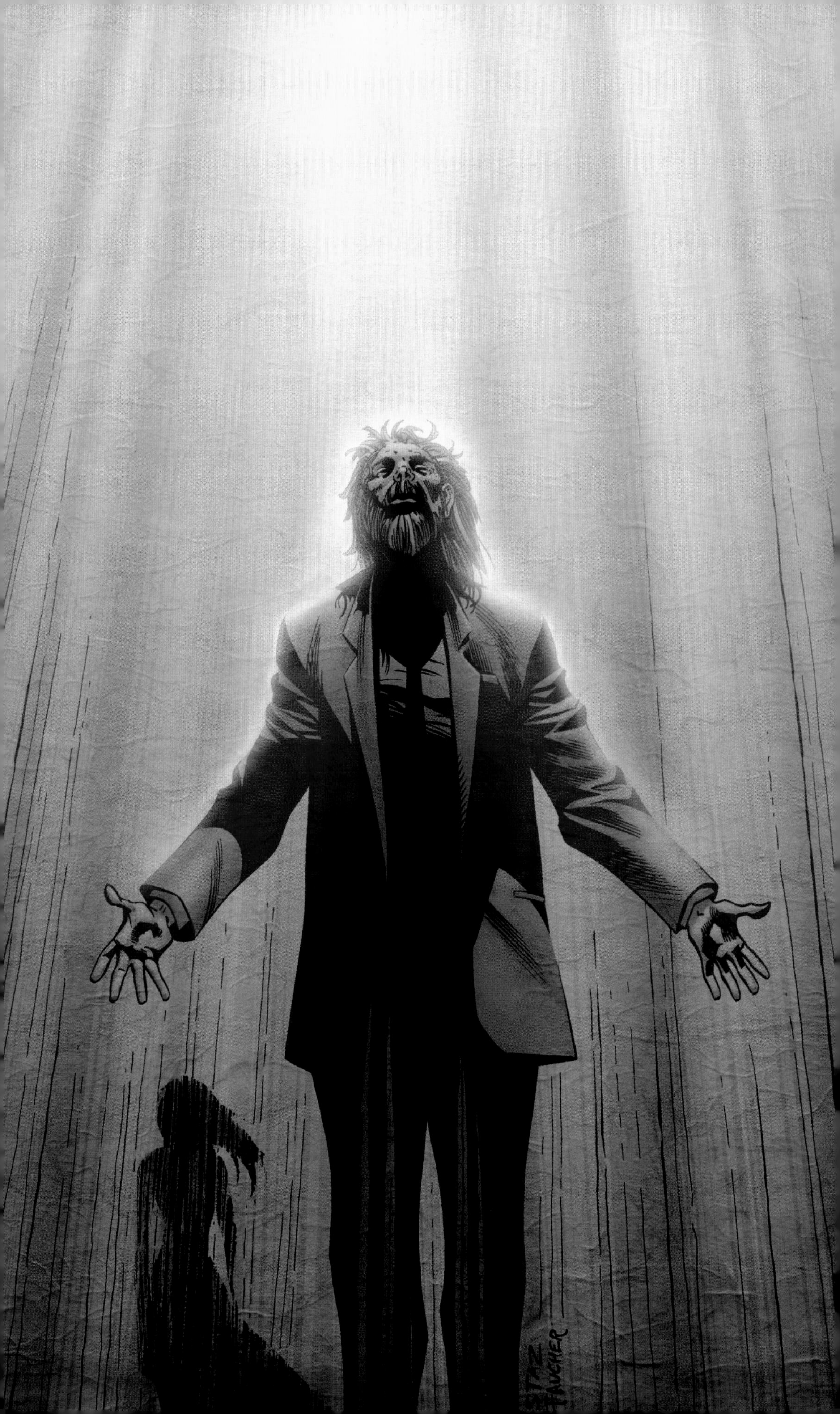

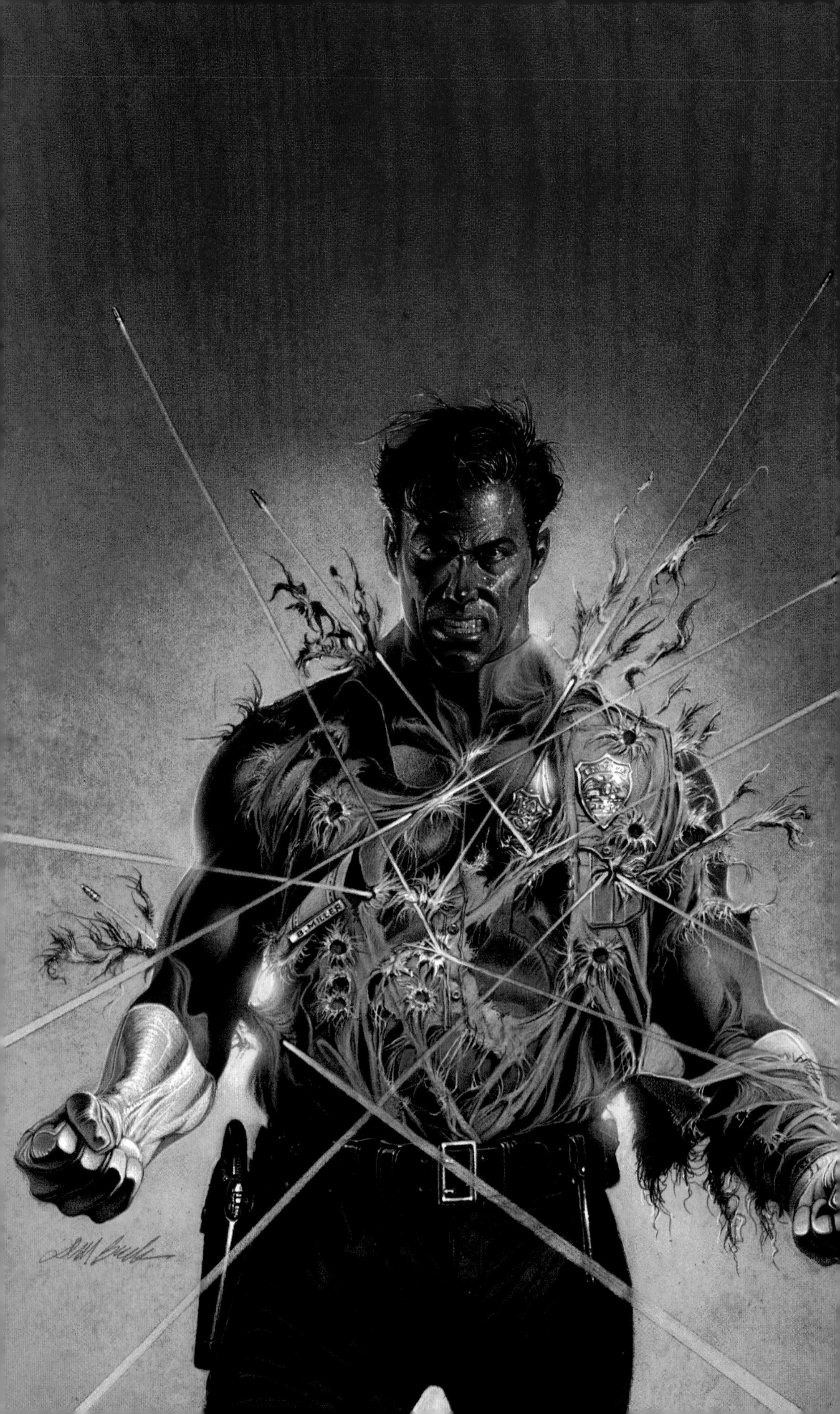
B. MILLER

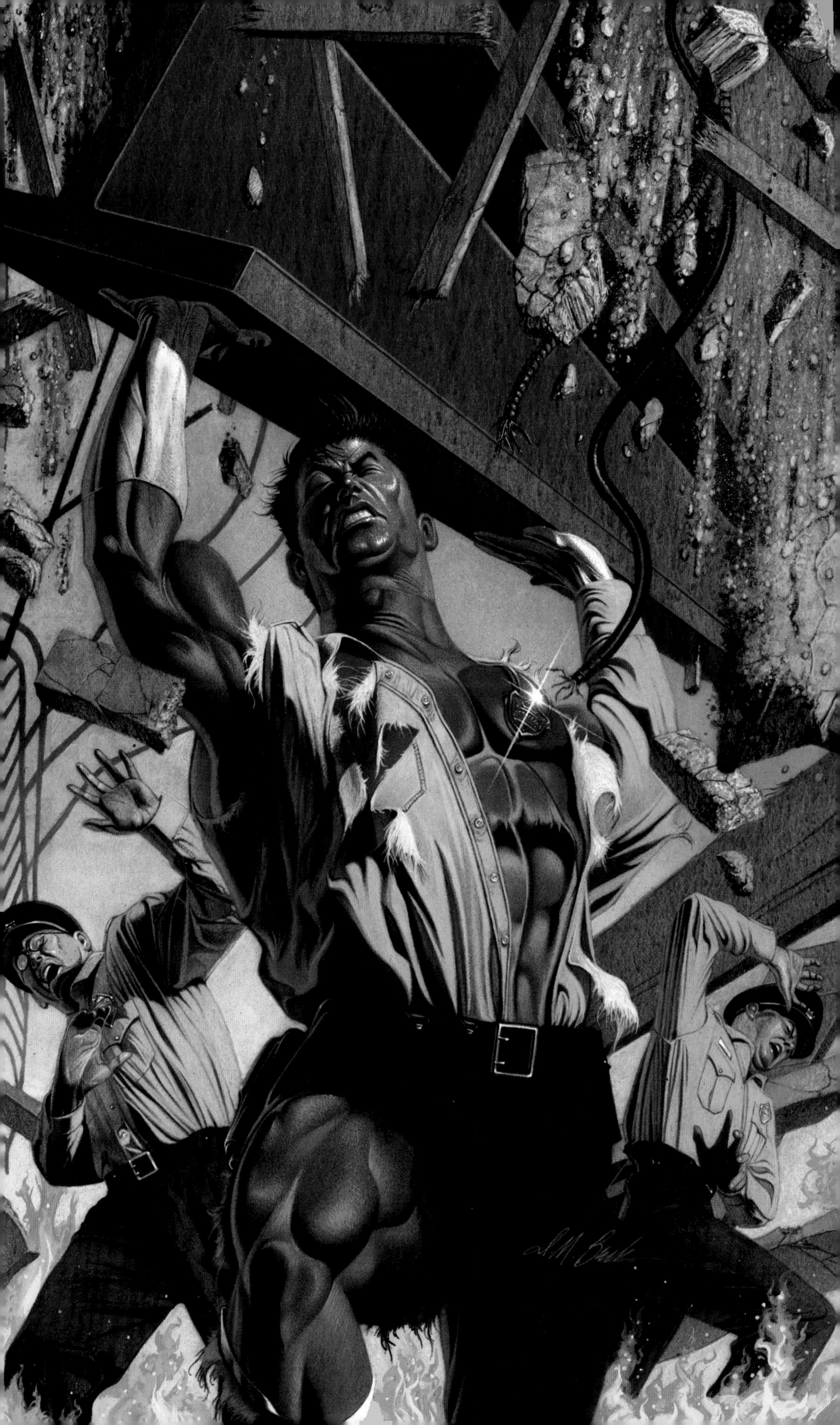

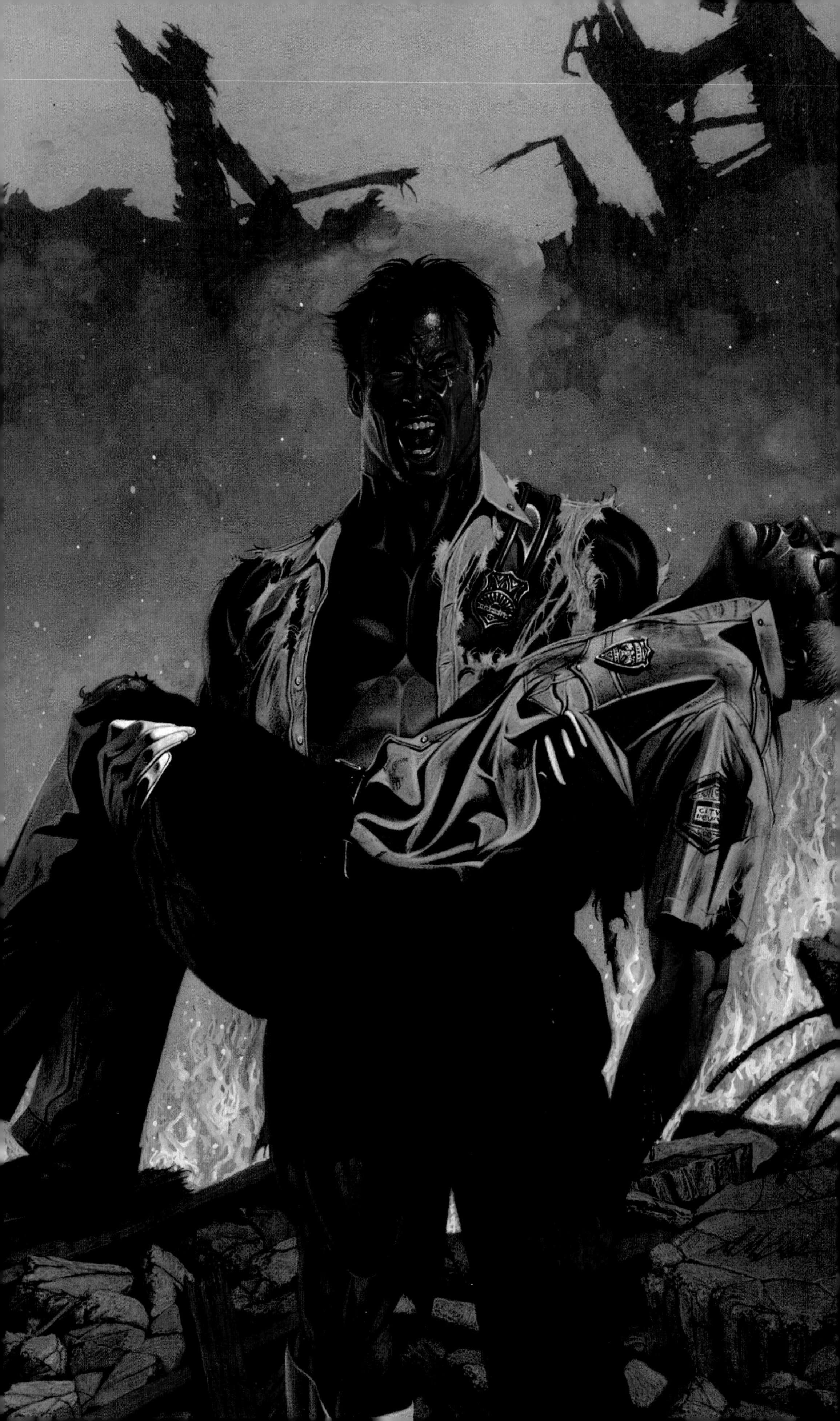

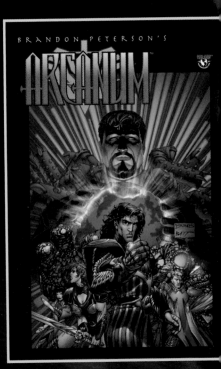